POSSIBLE WORLDS

BIBLIOTHECA HISTORICA 75

Riikka Forsström

Possible Worlds

The Idea of Happiness in the Utopian
Vision of Louis-Sébastien Mercier

Suomalaisen Kirjallisuuden Seura ▪ Helsinki 2002

Cover Picture: The time traveler in L´An 2440 has just arrived in Paris in the twenty- fifth century and discovers to his surprise that he has slept through many centuries and is almost seven hundred years old. Illustration of L´An deux mille quatre cent quarante. Rêve s´il en fut jamais, engraving by E. Bovinet.

ISSN 1238-3503

ISBN 951-746-355-3

www.finlit.fi

Hakapaino Oy

Helsinki 2002

Dedicated to my mother

with gratitude.

Le plaisir sans égal seroit de fonder la félicité publique.

Louis-Sébastien Mercier, *L´An deux mille quatre cent quarante*

Quel est l´objet général du desir de tous le peuples qui couvrent
la face de la terre, le bonheur? Le bonheur!

Louis-Sébastien Mercier, *De Jean-Jacques Rousseau, considéré
comme l´un des premiers auteurs de la Révolution*

Contents

Acknowledgements

It was not a difficult decision to choose Mercier's utopian thought as the topic for my thesis. As an ardent reader, I have been fascinated by utopias and fantasies for as long as I can remember. The academic study of utopias is not widely established in Finland as an acknowledged field of scientific research, and this was one of the reasons why I seized an opportunity to do my share in filling the gap.

Over the years, many people have shown sympathy and understanding towards my research. The first initiative for this project was inspired by one of my teachers, lecturer Matti Männikkö, from the Department of General History in the University of Turku. He played a major role in my initial discovery of utopian and future-oriented thinking in the eighteenth-century French Enlightenment. Despite my far-reaching interest in French culture and history, this was unknown territory for me, which I wanted to explore more deeply. Once the seeds of interest in Mercier's utopian world were thus sown, I gradually proceeded in my academic endeavors to encompass wider and deeper stages of knowledge. Where I now stand, I have to admit that when I first started working on my project, I had no idea how time-consuming and often a lonely pursuit the writing of a thesis can be. I am, however, equally sure that it was worth all the time spent and all the hard work needed - especially in view of the fact that no comprehensive survey of Mercier's utopian thought has, to my knowledge, previously been published.

In the subsequent phases of my study I have been graciously encouraged by Professor Keijo Virtanen, now Rector of the University of Turku, who regardless of his many responsibilities also found time to read and comment on my work. I have also been supervised by Professor Kari Immonen and Professor Hannu Salmi, and am indebted to them for valuable scholarly advice. Professor Salmi has also generously offered his time to assist me in many practical questions related to my thesis, which has very much facilitated the final stages of my endeavour. For the revision of my English language I thank Dr. Keith Battarbee, who has shown great patience in correcting my work. I am also most grateful to Mr. Mika Aarnio, who has spent numerous hours in stylizing the external appearance of the text.

This research has been backed by several foundations and other sources. I owe a major debt of gratitude to the TOP-Foundation, the Turku University Foundation, the Faculty of Humanities at the University of Turku, the Finnish Cultural Foundation, the Regional Fund of Varsinais-Suomi, the Niilo Helander Foundation and to the Ella and Georg Ehrnrooth´s Foundation.Without their contributions I would never have been able to complete my study. Financial support has also made possible my visits to Paris, where I have had the pleasure of doing research in the Bibliothèque Nationale, in the Bibliothèque de la

Sorbonne and in the Bibliothèque Historique de la Ville de Paris. Their collections, which I was permitted to consult without any difficulties, opened totally new vistas into Mercier's visionary imagination and into eighteenth-century French utopianism more generally.

I wish to express my deepest gratitude to my mother, to whom I dedicate my book. Her unfailing emotional support has been of immeasurable value in carrying through this project.

Turku, March 2002

Riikka Forsström

I Introduction

A Preliminary View of the Research Problem

In all epochs and cultures, despite their differences, men have always been united by one common denominator: they have wanted to be happy. Happiness has been called the *summum bonum*, i.e., the ultimate goal of all human thoughts and actions.[1] This important argument was already advanced by Aristotle, who postulates in his *Nicomachean Ethics* that happiness is "the end of human things", and belongs to the class of activities which are "desirable in themselves".[2]

It is no exaggeration to argue that the desire for happiness forms such a constituent element in man that if he ceases to hope for this, he has lost his very essence as a sentient creature. Yet, in a world torn apart by miseries from devastating natural disasters to social, political and economic inequalities, happiness often turns out to be a mere illusion. It is like a mirage which escapes man in the wilderness at the moment when he imagines he has reached it.

In the course of the centuries the desire to find happiness has assumed many different forms. Since the existing conditions rarely provide the optimal ground for the realization of happiness, men have turned to creating in their imagination images of some ideal condition either in this life or beyond the grave. As Karl Mannheim has pointed out, the fantasizing faculty has throughout the ages formed an constitutive element in human life: "Myths, fairy tales, other-worldly promises of religion, humanistic fantasies, travel romances, have been continually changing expressions of that which was lacking in actual life."[3]

Utopian visions represent one branch of wishful thinking. Most scholars of utopianism share the view that utopia means a portrayal of a good, and radically different ideal society, and is the expression of the desire for a better way of being which would diminish human misery.[4] Following Mannheim's argumentation, "a state of mind is utopian when it is incongruous with the state of reality within which it occurs", and it is expressly this incongruence which drives mankind to dream of a condition beyond the existent social order, which would transcend the actual situation.[5] As Ernst Bloch, one of the most prominent specialists of utopian thinking, has put it, "the criticism of imperfection presupposes the conception of, and a longing for, a possible perfection".[6]

. . . .

1   Telfer 1980, 1.
2   Aristotle, *The Nicomachean Ethics* 1897, 332.
3   Mannheim 1972, 184.
4   Polak 1961, 437; Ruyer 1988, 53; Levitas 1990, 4, 8; Baczko 1997, 172.
5   Mannheim 1972, 173.
6   Bloch 1989, 16.

The French writer Louis-Sébastien Mercier (1740–1814) was one of those dreamers blessed with the talent of giving birth to fantastic worlds of dreams, where man could live happily, free from oppression and distress. He has left his mark in the history of utopian literature above all as the creator of the first utopian novel situated into a remote future: *L'An deux mille quatre cent quarante. Rêve s'il en fut jamais* (1770 or 1771; expanded edition, in three volumes, 1786) opens a vision of Paris in the imaginary year 2440, when the world is supposed to have changed into a place of general happiness, prosperity and well-being.[7] The publication of Mercier's utopia meant a decisive turn in the tradition of modern utopias, for before Mercier the creators of utopian societies had usually situated their descriptions of ideal states in some far and exotic place, most often on an island. The dominant mode of modern utopias was set by Thomas More in his famous treatise *Utopia* (1516).[8]

In his *L'An 2440* Mercier sets out an ideal of happiness or the "good life" on earth which is contrasted with the conditions prevailing in the author's contemporary society. Starting from the realization of the imperfections in the present state of society, the novel breaks the limits imposed by the existing social order in order to embrace a brave new world freed from sorrow and pain. The dramatic tension of Mercier's utopia is based on a strictly polarized juxtaposition between the categories of "spleen" and "ideal", or "is" and "ought". It is expressly the dualism between those two contradictory modes of existence, i.e., the way things are and how they should be if everything were well, which forms an important starting point for my study.

The aim of my examination is to explore the utopian novel as a representation of happiness through the vision conveyed by Mercier's *L'An 2440*. Despite the complexity of the issue, the major problems can be stated simply as follows: What is Mercier's image of an ideal society, and what are the components which he views as contributing to the increase of human happiness or tending to diminish it? How does Mercier explain the process of transformation from the society of the eighteenth century to the ideal state of 2440? Does he envisage a real possibility that the gulf separating the miseries of the contemporary world from utopian perfection could ever be annihilated? If the answer is affirmative, how could this be accomplished in practise?

When one aims at providing an overall analysis of the theme of happiness in the writings of a single author, one could scarcely find a more appropriate object of study than Mercier, since the theme of happiness is a focal theme to which he incessantly returns in his diverse writings, including those not classifiable as utopias. In a brief, charming essay of only a little over 100 pages, entitled *Le Bonheur des gens de lettres* (1763), as the title of the work suggests, Mercier approaches the idea of happiness from the viewpoint of a man of letters.

. . . .

7   Cioranescu 1972, 193–196; Trousson 1975, 175; Clarke 1979, 26; Alkon 1987, 4, 43; Alkon 1994, 21; Ruyer 1988, 205; Delumeau 1995, 307, 310; Jean 1997, 68. For the sake of convenience, in this study the title of Mercier's utopia is abbreviated in the form *L'An 2440*.
8   See for example Minois 1996, 293.

Mercier's other writings which are of major concern here are *L'Homme sauvage* (1767), *Songes philosophiques* (1768, republished as an extended edition in 1788 under the title *Songes et visions philosophiques*), *Mon Bonnet de nuit* (1784–1786), *Tableau de Paris* (1781–1788) and *Notions claires sur les gouvernemens* (1787).

These works encompass the most important part of Mercier's literary production. Even in the measure of eighteenth-century France, notorious for its lengthy novels and philosophical treatises, often filling several volumes, he stands out as a prolific journalist and "polygraph"[9] whose creative imagination knew no limits. Mercier's literary production – over a hundred volumes in its entirety – consists of novels, dramas, poetry, pamphlets, moral allegories, utopian fantasies and reports on contemporary items. Alexandre Cioranescu's bibliography of French literature gives some idea of the extent of Mercier's production.[10] Moreover, Mercier had a habit of constantly repairing and modifying his earlier writings, thus even further expanding the total volume of his production. For example, the collection *Mon bonnet de nuit* contains many of the same texts which had been published earlier in *Songes philosophiques*.[11]

The period that concerns this study covers the three decades stretching from the early 1760s until the outbreak of the French Revolution. This is a natural choice, taking into consideration that Mercier's most important works were created during this pre-Revolutionary period. With a few rare exceptions (i.e. when the analysis is focused on changes in Mercier's opinions as a consequence of the Terror), post-1789 events are referred to only in passing.

For the purposes of any study in cultural history, the decades immediately preceding the French Revolution provide insights of immense richness. The period was characterized by a profound tension between tradition and innovation. In the eighteenth century France was still ruled by an absolute monarch, the sole source of legitimate power. The society was divided in orders, and the center of the courtly society was Versailles, the perfect symbol of the *ancien*

. . . .

9   Bollème 1978, 7–83, passim.
10   Cioranescu 1969, 1234–1239.
11   Mercier also left to posterity a vast number of unpublished texts, containing diverse matter such as unfinished projects and letters, which have since 1967 been preserved in the Bibliothèque de l'Arsenal in Paris. A selection of this immense material, including all the texts focused on Paris which had not been published before in any other context, is included in the re-edition of Mercier's *Le Nouveau Paris*. See "Paris dans le "fonds Mercier" de l'Arsenal", Ms. 15079 (1), ff. 7–8 – Ms. 15079 (2), ff. 302–305. Mercier, *Le Nouveau Paris* 1994b, 1049–1361. One of Mercier's manuscripts has been transcribed under the title *Parallèle de Paris et de Londres* (Ms. 15079(3)). For a closer survey, see Gilles 1973, 311–334. With few exceptions, Mercier's unpublished writings fall beyond the scope of the present investigation, since the main focus here is on a comprehensive analysis of *L'An 2440* as an authentic document of its time. Considering that the novel itself contains an enormous amount of subject matter about eighteenth-century French society, this restriction was a necessity. It should not be inferred, however that the value of Mercier's unpublished writings should be ignored. A large selection of them has already been published, which testifies to their relevance and to the rising interest in Mercier and his work in recent years. Especially for studies focused on Mercier's post-Revolutionary years, they may provide many valuable insights.

régime[12]. Moreover, the revocation of the Edict of Nantes (1685) had consecrated the king as the protector of the powerful Catholic church, the ally of
absolutist monarchy. King Louis XVI, who had mounted the throne in 1774,
and Queen Marie-Antoinette, were however far from being an ideal royal
couple, which led to the erosion of the power of the monarchy towards the end
of the century. In addition to this, the century was marked by other elements of
crisis: military defeats such as the Seven Years War (1756–63) and the crystal-
lization of anti-aristocratic feeling. As a consequence, although French civilization had never been as "aristocratic" as in this epoch, the nobility were entering
a situation of crisis, and the society of orders was falling apart under the
pressure of economic improvement as money replaced "birth". The century
ended with the violent abolition of hereditary privilege and the adoption of the
Declaration of the Rights of Man in 1789 and with the execution of the King in
1793.[13]

The dramatic overthrow of the political *status quo* in a brief time span
testifies that under the veil of society of orders the seeds of change were already
sown; the tension between "is" and "ought" had escalated to the point of
explosion. In the gradual formation of a more secular outlook in the course of
the eighteenth century the new philosophical thinking was of decisive
importance. The great philosophers, from Voltaire (1694–1778), Rousseau
(1712–1778), Diderot (1713–84) to Montesquieu (1689–1755), considered it
their sacred duty to liberate man from his self-imposed state of enslavement.
The absolute monarchy, reinforced by the intolerant Catholic Church with its
dogma of Original Sin, served as natural targets for the philosophers' attack.[14]
The most visible landmark of this new philosophical attitude was *Encyclopédie,
ou Dictionnaire raisonné des sciences, des arts et des métiers* (1751–1772), an
anthology of Enlightenment opinions on a wide range of topics.[15]

Despite their mutual disagreements, all the leading philosophers were united
by the same intention to liberate men from fear and establish their sovereignty.
As Adorno and Horkheimer write, "the program of the Enlightenment was the
disenchantment of the world; the dissolution of myths and the substitution of
knowledge for fancy".[16] This was a secular movement which aimed at the
demystification of knowledge and social organization.[17] The novelty of the
eighteenth century derived, precisely, from the shift away from a religious
frame of reference. This displacement of human ends, brought from heaven
down to earth, secularized thinking, art, and everyday life. This was the first

. . . .

12   The name *ancien régime* was given later as a pejorative label by the French Revolutionaries
     to all that they had abolished, expressing their wish to create a complete break with the past,
     to cast it into the shadows of barbarism. Furet 1988, 21; Bluche 1993, 7–8.
13   Furet 1988, 21–29, passim., 39, 42–43, 88–89, 130.
14   See for example Rudé 1985, 155; Furet 1988, 28.
15   See for example Duby & Mandrou 1958, 120–122; Hampson 1981, 86; Rudé 1985, 154;
     Delon, Mauzi & Menant 1998, 268–279.
16   Adorno & Horkheimer 1979, 3.
17   Harvey 1990, 12–13.

epoch in the history of western civilization that dared to define its ideals without consulting the gods.[18]

To label the eighteenth century as an epoch characterized by unprecedented optimism has become a cliché. The standard account of the Enlightenment is founded on the argument that philosophers were no longer willing to accept older assumptions that the earth is a vale of tears and that all human effort should be directed toward the avoidance of sin; the new credo was that life could be good already on earth, if it was rationally managed.[19] The eighteenth century was permeated by a faith in the unity and immutability of Reason, thought of as identical for every thinking subject, nation, epoch and culture.[20]

This new, dignified image of man, liberated from the blight of Original Sin, represented the culmination of an extended and gradual process of secularization and modernization, the starting point of which can be traced at least as far back as to the beginning of the Renaissance, the Protestant Reformation and the Scientific Revolution.[21] In the consolidation of the ideology of the Enlightenment, the abandonment of persecution for witchcraft and the spread of the philosophy of Spinoza and Bayle (around 1680) related to the appearance of Newton's *Principia Mathematica* (1687) and Locke's *Essay concerning Human Understanding* (1690) signified important watersheds.[22] Despite the fact that the philosophical empire constituted an international phenomenon,[23] in this study the emphasis is on the French Enlightenment.

The increase of general optimism gave rise to a feeling that everything was possible, and it laid the ground for a new gospel of terrestrial happiness. Robert Mauzi, the scholar best acquainted with the theme of happiness in eighteenth-century French literature, argues in his study *L'idée du bonheur dans la littérature et la pensée françaises au XVIIIe siècle* (1961) that in that epoch happiness constituted one of the *idea-forces* which animated the whole century, extending in all directions. In his view this theme often assumed obsessive dimensions, and the purpose of every human action was the desire to be happy.[24]

The centrality of the theme of happiness can be seen both in the novels and in the philosophical treatises produced in pre-Revolutionary France, where the concepts *"bonheur"* and *"félicité"*[25] are incessantly repeated. A sudden prolif-

. . . .

18   Pomeau 1991, 54–55.
19   Mornet 1969, 42.
20   Cassirer 1966, 44. See also Koivisto, Mäki & Uusitupa 1995, xii–xiii; Delon, Mauzi & Menant 1998, 118.
21   Coates, White & Schapiro 1966, 177–178. See also Gagliardo 1968, 1.
22   Kennedy 1989, 55–56.
23   See for example Becker 1965, 33–34.
24   Mauzi 1994, 13, 80. For example the words of the materialist philosopher d'Holbach in his treatise *Système de la nature* (1770) provide a good image of the "obsessional" attitude assumed by eighteenth-century French writers towards this theme: "Toutes nos institutions, nos réflexions, nos connoissances n'ont pour objet que de nous procurer un bonheur vers lequel notre propre nature nous force de tendre sans cesse."[d'Holbach], *Système de la nature I* 1771, 3.
25   The *Encyclopédie* tries to clarify the possible confusion between these two concepts by explaining that while *"bonheur"* is something that comes from outside, *"félicité"* is a state of the soul possessed by a content person. The latter is a state of mind in the same way as wisdom, tranquility or rest. *Encyclopédie XIII* 1778, 919.

eration of various utopian images, projects of reform and models of ideal cities constituted one of the most visible manifestations of this concern with happiness on the eve of the French Revolution. Mercier's *L'An 2440* provides one example of the utopian fascination in that epoch.

The preachers of happiness tended to stress that Nature had given mankind life to profit from: Man was now seen as enjoying a special "vocation" of happiness.[26] Henceforward, happiness was considered as man's natural state, a common possession uniting the entire humankind, and if he did not yet possess it, at least he had every right to hope for it. The writers of *Encyclopédie* express this new article of faith concisely: "Tous les hommes se réunissent dans de desir d'être heureux. La nature nous a fait à tous une loi de notre propre bonheur."[27]

As stated at the outset, however, a yearning for happiness in eighteenth-century intellectual debate was not as such a new motif. What was new compared with the previous epochs, dominated by predictions of a Day of Judgement and the end of the world, was a shift of emphasis from expectations of salvation in celestial beatitude to more earth-bound considerations, and man's terrestrial happiness preferred to some state beyond the grave.[28] It is manifestly this secular ideal of happiness which is at the focus of this study: apart from the chapters on Mercier's visions of death and spirituality, the emphasis is on the terrestrial aspects of happiness.

In eighteenth-century French philosophical discourse this new idea of terrestrial happiness assumed two principal forms. The first of these new philosophies of happiness was founded on the dignity of instinctual life. According to this individualist theory of happiness, which pulsated with Rabelaisian energy, the arch-enemy of happiness was the denial of earthly pleasures: from now on, happiness was redefined as a natural, instinctual pursuit of pleasure. This also implied that durable happiness was an impossibility. Secondly, there emerged a new form of collective happiness, which was based on the philosophy of progress and on the pursuit of a perfect social order.[29]

Together with the term "utopia", the idea of "progress" forms a focal concept in this investigation. As has been suggested by Robert Nisbet, one of the most

. . . .

26 Cioranescu 1995, 26.
27 *Encyclopédie V* 1778, 260.
28 Hazard 1961, 87–102; Charlton 1984, 3; Ehrard 1994, 543–544; D'Hont 1995, 270–271. See also Roche 1998, 596–599. In his *Le Bonheur* (1795) Claude Adrien Helvétius gives visible form to this new ideal of terrestrial happiness by attacking the moralists of his age on the grounds that "ils exilent le bonheur dans le ciel, et ne supposent pas qu'il habite la terre". Helvétius, *Oeuvres complètes XIII* 1967, 9.
29 Cioranescu 1995, 26. The division between individual and collective happiness corresponds in its main points to the distinction between the terms hedonistic happiness and *eudaemonia*. One criterion of differentiation between these two is that whereas hedonistic happiness is defined merely in terms of the kind of life the possessor wants for himself (subjective valuation), *eudaemonia* has only one ingredient, morality, which is argued to be "good in itself" (objectibe valuation). Whilst the former is defined in terms of pleasure in the sense of what man himself finds as pleasant, *eudaemonia* disregards the wishes of the individual, its emphasis being placed on what is "intrisically good in itself". Telfer 1980, 37, 39, 42–43, 52–53.

prominent specialists in this field, the idea of progress dominated the ideology of Western societies from the mid-eighteenth century till the beginning of the twentieth,[30] and it is often alleged that in that epoch a belief in terrestrial progress gained the status of a kind of substitute or secular religion.[31]

Nisbet defines the idea of progress as a theory according to which "mankind has advanced in the past – from some aboriginal condition of primitiveness, barbarism, or even nullity – is now advancing, and will continue to advance through the foreseeable future".[32] In other words, the idea of progress is "a theory which involves a synthesis of the past and a prophecy of the future", as J.B. Bury argued in his classical study on this theme. As this reveals, embedded in the modern notion of progress is the idea of a goal or a specific destination. For most people this destination is a condition of society which could offer the maximum amount of happiness for everyone already this side of the grave.[33]

The theory of collective happiness thus attempts to provide an answer for the problem of happiness on the level of the whole of humankind. Conversely, if one wishes to survey the experience of happiness on a personalized level, as an inner sentiment, it is necessary to focus attention on individual desires and on the role that passions perform for the experience of happiness. The dualism between individual and collective happiness constitutes one of the major themes of this study.

Mauzi suggests that although the symbolic dualism that divides man between the "temptation of vertigo" and the "dream of repose" is doubtlessly eternal, in the eighteenth century it was stressed even more vigorously than before. In his view the whole problem of happiness in that epoch can be reduced to the attempt to achieve a reconciliation between *movement* and *repose*, and he argues that there have been few epochs which have simultaneously dreamed with equal fervor of both "solid wisdom" and "unexpexted sensations" and "ecstasies".[34] The same dualism forms the starting point in Jean Deprun's study *La philosophie de l'inquiétude en France au XVIIIe siècle* (1979), where he distinguishes two alternative conceptualizations of happiness: either it was understood as repose or equilibrium, or, by contrast, following Locke and Leibniz, it was argued that "restlessness is essential for the felicity of men".[35] To solve the relation between these two states of existence forms one of the major challenges in this study: Does Mercier represent perpetual change as an optimal condition for happiness, or does he envisage absolute rest as the state better responding to the ideal of a "good life"?

· · · · · · · · ·

30   Nisbet 1980, 171; Viikari 1995, 359–360.
31   Polak 1971, 87–88; Cioranescu 1972, 192; Keohane 1982, 25; Delumeau 1995, 311. Cf. Bury 1920, 6–7, 20–22; Iggers 1982, 45–46.
32   Nisbet 1980, 4–5. See also Keohane 1982, 22–23.
33   Bury 1920, 2, 5.
34   Mauzi 1994, 127.
35   Deprun 1979, 9–10.

This two-dimensional attitude testifies to the fact that the eighteenth-century thinkers themselves were far from blind to the complexities of existence, but rather acutely aware of the shadows lurking amidst the bright light of reason. I am here suggesting that it would be oversimplified to label the eighteenth century one-sidedly as an optimistic age. Contrary to what has been sometimes argued, the thought of the Enlightenment did not ignore dissatisfaction and restlessness, the sense of void, an aspiration towards an "unknown good".[36] By the 1750's the belief in the omnipotence of reason was in fact already beginning to fade, and there were signs of a return to a more sentimental attitude to life. The rise of empiricism, which emerged to challenge Cartesian rationalism, emphasized the role of the passions and "sensibility".[37] The intermediary phase between the Classical age, dominated by reason, and the Romantic age, dominated by the heart, has sometimes been labeled "pre-Romanticism",[38] and Mercier has quite often been labeled a "pre-Romantic".[39] It is expressly in this double position of Mercier, on the watershed between tradition and innovation, where his originality lies.

As Mauzi has observed, however, a strict chronological division between the "philosophy of the Enlightenment" and "sensible souls" cannot be maintained; the argument that the first part of the century was "philosophical", whilst the second half was Romantic, is untenable. The truth is more complex: philosophical thinking did not attain its peak until the materialist systems of d'Holbach and Helvétius in the second half of the century, whereas the great novels of abbé Antoine Prévost, where all the "pre-Romantic" themes are already present, were published between 1730 and 1740.[40]

It is precisely in order to avoid too monolithic and homogeneous an image of the eighteenth century that in this study the use of the term "Enlightenment" is largely replaced by more neutral attributes such as "eighteenth-century France". This preference is also justified in view of the fact that the term "Enlightenment" is itself problematic, for it can be applied in multiple frames of reference. It can be used to describe a particular historical epoch (the "Age of Enlightenment"); secondly, it can refer to a particular group of eighteenth-century philosophical thinkers (the "*philosophes*"); thirdly, it can refer to a particular set of ideas, which are not bound to this particular time.[41] There have been "enlightened" individuals in all historical periods; the eighteenth century did not possess a monopoly in this respect.

Following these preliminary observations, a brief overview will now be offered of the topics to be explored in this study. Chapter II begins with a biographical

. . . .

36   Ibid., 11.
37   Mortier 1969, 115–117.
38   Gaillard 1975, 62–63.
39   Henry F. Majewski uses this attribute in the title of his work *The Preromantic Imagination of L.- S. Mercier* (1971).
40   Mauzi 1994, 12. See also Mortier 1969, 114–124; Fabre 1980, ix–xix; Asplund 1981, 135–137.
41   Nyman 1994, 11–12. See also Adorno & Horkheimer 1979, especially 43–80.

portrait of Mercier and a summary of his major works. Mercier's utopian thinking is then situated in the tradition of modern utopianism. A general overview is provided of the main lines of the earlier utopian tradition and of the utopian literature produced in eighteenth-century France, with special emphasis on the invention in the second half of the century of the modern future-oriented utopia. The chapter ends in a brief analysis of the significance of dreams in Mercier's visionary thinking.

The following section comprises Chapters III–VII, which explore the focal themes of Mercier's *L'An 2440* from various angles. These approaches share the same concern to shed light on the nature of Mercier's vision of an ideal society, where man could maximize the amount of his personal happiness without offending the sentiments of his fellow creatures or the general well-being of the community of which he or she forms a part. This focal issue is examined in the context of the relation between individual happiness and collective well-being, and of the quest for a functional reconciliation between these seemingly conflicting forms of existence.

Chapter III introduces the urban landscape of Mercier's Paris of 2440, providing an analysis of the image conveyed by *L'An 2440* of the ideal city as a public space and as a lived environment. The focus then shifts from everyday realities towards more solemn spheres in Chapter IV, which deals with the religious practises and the meaning of spirituality in the lives of Mercier's utopians.

Chapter V is an exploration of the political and social aspects of Mercier's utopian vision. The chapter starts with a presentation of the governmental organization in Mercier's imaginary future France. Central questions relate to what kind of political system could, in Mercier's view, provide the best nurturing ground for the general well-being, and what purposes the social contract is intended to fulfill. The chapter ends with a consideration of gender and the ways in which gender expectations determine the prospects of happiness in Mercier's utopia.

Chapter VI approaches Mercier's ideal of happiness from the viewpoint of material prosperity, raising the question of the desirability of luxury and consumption in general. The issue is explored whether men should work in order to earn their living, or would it be more profitable to spend one's days in total idleness, amidst abundance. What was Mercier's view of "noble savages"? Where they happier than "civilized" men?

Chapter VII explores the manifestations of evil in Mercier's ideal society. Is there evil in the "best of possible worlds", and if so, what guises does it assume? Is it possible to find a satisfactory explanation for the persistence of evil? In order to solve these questions, it is necessary to decipher the content of such fundamental concepts as sin, criminality, deviance, normality and abnormality as they are dealt with in *L'An 2440*. The goal is to provide a picture of the mechanisms through which Mercier aims at eliminating from his utopia the potential obstacles to happiness. At the same time, however, the entire idea of happiness is reversed, and the status of *L'An 2440* as a representation of a happier society is subjected to critical re-examination.

The second main part of the study (Chapters VIII and IX) deals with the significance of time and temporal change in Mercier's utopian vision. The main focus in Chapter VIII is on a survey of the mechanisms used by Mercier to explain the process of transformation from eighteenth-century France to the remote year 2440. Central questions are related to the issues of the linearity of time manifested in Mercier's utopia and who or what is suggested to be responsible for the shift towards an ameliorated world. What does it tell about the mental structures of late eighteenth-century French society itself that Mercier's vision of an ideal city is, for the first time in the history of modern utopianism, situated in a remote future instead of on some contemporary but exotic island or in a mythical past?

In order to avoid a one-sided image of Mercier as merely a cold rational thinker, with no awareness of the tragic aspects of life, Chapter IX opens a new vista on his visionary imagination by evaluating it in terms of optimism vs. pessimism. A more complex image of Mercier's personality and his production is offered in pp. 253–265, by also examining his more pessimistic visions of disasters and doomsday prophesies. Should these be interpreted merely as expressions of pessimism and despair, or do they perhaps also contain latent potentiality for a new and more dignified order of things? How are the cyclical and linear conceptions of time intertwined in Mercier's utopian thinking? Does a progressive vision of the future necessarily mean a rush forward, toward the totally new and unprecedented?

The final chapter (X) is on the theme of death and its function in relation to the idea of happiness in Mercier's utopian vision. The aim is to seek a solution to the following question: Does Mercier view death as the most serious threat to man's terrestrial happiness, or is there also something positive in his understanding of the experience of death? Is it possible to find peace of mind in the world, where man is doomed to live under the oppressive shadow of inevitable death?

Methods, Sources and Research Situation

Despite his extraordinarily prolific creativity, Mercier has typically been considered merely as a second-class writer, both by his contemporaries and among later scholars and historians of literature. It is characteristic that in Charles Monselet's work *Les Oubliés et les Dédaignés. Figures littéraires de la fin du 18 siècle* (1857) he is classified in the same category with other "forgotten" and "despised" French eighteenth-century writers who scarcely deserve a footnote in the histories of literature.

As the American scholar Robert Darnton has pointed out, this dismissive attitude has also, until fairly recently, set the dominant tone in the majority of studies of the French eighteenth-century Enlightenment; scholarly interest has almost exclusively been focused on the texts of the generally acknowledged philosophers. This exclusive concern with the cultural products of the elite culture (the approach chosen for example by Ernst Cassirer and Peter Gay) has resulted in a very one-sided picture of the Enlightenment as a monolithic movement or distinct phase in western civilization. It therefore is high time to approach the Enlightenment from a new "bottom-up" perspective, i.e., to write history "from below", which means a shift of interest from the great writers to the marginal literary figures.[42]

The present inquiry is an attempt to reanimate one of those voices on the margins of the cultural elites – a voice which in its own age was so often silenced by ridicule, scorn and neglect. No voice can reverberate in a vacuum, however, detached and abstracted from the surrounding society. In order to obtain a complete image of Mercier's utopian ideal of happiness, the only possible method has been to survey it in the larger framework of its age. Therefore, it is necessary to have a knowledge of the social, political, economic and cultural conditions for which Mercier wanted to offer a critical counterpoint in his utopia. Due to the fact that in this study the image of the ideal state in the pages of Mercier's novel is explored as a vision of an "other" better and preferable compared with the existing, i.e., late eighteeth-century French society, the goal is to find out how his image of an ameliorated world is intertwined with the writer's contemporary society. What does Mercier's vision of the future tell about prevailing conditions in the second half of the eighteenth century itself, how does it reflect the fears and hopes of men then living? What was that social reality from which it drew its inspiration? To put it briefly: How does Mercier's utopia of the year 2440 function as a mirror image of the society where it was produced?

Contextualization and the quest for a holistic understanding are key issues in cultural history,[43] and the methodological stance adopted in this study converges approximately with what Darnton has termed the "social history of ideas", by which he refers to the importance of situating the Enlightenment firmly in its social context in order to avoid ending up in mere generalizations and abstractions.[44] Considering that the principal function of utopias is to serve as tools of social criticism, any relevant inquiry of utopian thinking would be inadequate if the ideas represented in a utopian work were treated as mere abstractions, stripped from the context of the actual milieu in which they were produced.

In this study Mercier's utopian vision is taken as serious documentary evidence of the society in which it was produced, which means rejection of all pejorative labels occasionally attached to utopian longing as "pure fantasizing". Utopian planning forms a constructive part of the history of ideas, and all the great ideologies, from liberalism to romanticism and Marxism, which have

. . . .

42 Darnton 1982, viii; Darnton 1990, 191–252. See also Outram 1995, 1–13, passim. This re-calls the assertion by Arlette Farge that the eighteenth century was full of (often punishable) words which did not make history, and the "topicality" of that century consists precisely of those words "spoken by people of no, or little, importance in the heated environment of the public sphere". Farge 1994, vii–ix
43 Virtanen 1987, 85, 90.
44 Darnton 1990, 193, 219.

shaped the history of Western civilization in past centuries, first took shape in an utopian format. On the other hand, the utopian images have been influenced by the prevailing conceptions of society. As F.L. Polak puts it: "If the history of this age (the Age of Enlightenment) cannot be understood without knowing the utopias, neither can the utopias be understood without historical insight into the age."[45]

Through Mercier's vision of the future there opens a fresh new perspective for the formation of ideological climate and the first phases of the modern secular outlook. This starting point orients the analysis towards "traditional" intellectual history, in the sense that the main emphasis is on the filiation of the different currents of "enlightened" philosophy through Mercier's utopian vision and on the ways they molded his conception of happiness. For this reason the "standard accounts" – which tend to interpret the Enlightenment as a monolithic movement – have also been taken into consideration as a relevant point of reference. Without an acknowledgement of the standard interpretation of the Enlightenment, it would have been highly problematic to evaluate Mercier's position on the divide between tradition and innovation, or to set his social criticism in correct proportions.

In his vision of the twenty-fifth century world, Mercier provides one example of a "future of the past", thus revealing the contrafactual nature of historical processes. This refers to the fact that as a mirror image of latent aspirations, or "mental exercise of lateral possibilities", as Raymond Ruyer has expressed it,[46] Mercier's image of the future functions not merely as a reflection of the actual conditions prevailing in late eighteenth-century France, but at the same time also provides a prognosis of the possible course of events. As such it reminds us that like us, those living in the past also conceptualized reality as prospective. The future becomes concrete in their expectations, hopes, fears, conceptions and aims, with far-reaching effects on their entire behavior. In mapping alternate futures, the historian is not restricted to those possibilities which have been realized, i.e., the factual history, but can also access those potential outcomes which remained, for one reason or another, unrealized. This is a process which demands a reversal of the traditional understanding of the past; when one aims at deciphering the contrafactuality of events, the historian has to situate himself on the contemporary level and identify those situations where there were possible developments. It then remains his task to answer what alternative options were available, which of them was realized, and for what reason.[47]

By opening a vision of Paris and the world in the future, Mercier opens up the following questions: *What if* reality were different from the present conditions? Under what circumstances would that be so, and how could the miraculous

. . . .

45   Polak 1961, 316–318.
46   Ruyer 1988, 9.
47   Männikkö 1993, 264. See also Männikkö 1983, 33.

"what if" be contrived in practise? It is by this means that the survey of Mercier´s utopia stimulates the reader´s curiosity, making one speculate on different possibilities in the future, those invisible " what if" worlds ruled by different norms and ideals than those governing the actual conditions.

The most common way of exploring utopias has been to approach them either as literary fiction or as a political vision. Moreover, an emphasis has usually been placed in the connection between utopias and progress, and their social role.[48] The aim of this study does not diverge from these prevailing tendencies. It is necessary to note, however, that because utopias draw their substance from mythical stock of images deeply embedded in the collective imagination of the human race, it would be misleading to reduce them merely to political declarations. This explains why in recent decades the focus of scholarly interest has increasingly shifted toward exploring utopias as an intrisically *human phenomenon*. Ruyer's above mentioned launching of what he terms "the mental exercise of lateral possibilities" in his study *L'utopie et les utopies* (1950) provides a good example of this orientation.

One of the most ardent propagators of this approach to utopian mentality has been Roger Mucchielli, who writes in his classical study *Le mythe de la cité idéale* (1961) that "ideal cities seem to us to be other than simple imaginary portraits reducible to socio-cultural, historical or psychological factors. Beyond these influences... they purport to express the pure relationship of man to humanity in the form of a social order which loses... the character of a political solution and reveals its meta-empirical character".[49] The utopians, suggests Mucchielli, visualize a regenerated world in which miseries have disappeared by virtue of a "new mentality".[50]

After these reflections on the methodological questions, it is time to have a look at the research situation and at the sources which have been used. For the

. . . .

48 Levitas 1990, 9–11.
49 Mucchielli 1960, 7–8.
50 Ibid., 112. The precise definition of what is meant by the concept of "mentality" is not, however, a totally uncomplicated matter, and for this reason the more recent historians in the tradition of French *Annales*, to name Jacques Le Goff or Roger Chartier, have largely replaced it by such terms as "representations" or "collective imagination". Burke 1997, 162–182, passim. See also Le Goff 1992, xviii. When one aims to penetrate at the core of the "collective imagination"or "collective psyche" of a specific historical epoch, one comes to deal with "idea-forces", which according to Chartier means enlargement of the scope of the traditional history of ideas. He speaks about an "imagined social reality", which he sees as constituting a system of representations in close relationship with the "objective reality", which it is born to reflect, suggesting that "when ideas are... situated in their social settings and considered as much in terms of their affective or emotional charge as of their intellectual content, they become, like myths or value complexes, one of the ´collective forces by which men live their times´". Chartier 1988, 19–52, especially 29, 45. Concepts such as "idea-forces", "representations" or "collective imagination" are all useful when one aims at unlocking the concealed messages contained in a utopian text. Utopias are storehouses of collective desires, hopes and fears, and thus constitute systems of representations which are as real as the reality which they have been created to reflect. Starting from the premise that utopias are always closely related to the existing society in which they were produced, the only appropriate thing is to say that they are disguised representations of that same reality which they purport to contest.

purposes of this study, the raw material has been supplied by primary sources and a wide range of research literature. The main source is the three-volume version of *L'An 2440*, published in 1786. Even within Mercier's lifetime there were several editions of the novel,[51] and the textual evolution from one version to the next will be taken into consideration as far as it helps to explain changes in Mercier's personal ideas. In addition, the analysis uses a selection of Mercier's above listed printed works which are of relevance as regards the theme of happiness.

The value of a work of fiction such as *L'An 2440* as a historical source for cultural historiography cannot be denied. Works of fiction are, however, always bound by artistic tradition, and for this reason their status as a reflection of their time, or their relation to "reality", is to some extent problematic.[52] This is especially true of a utopian work, the themes of which have a tendency to repeat without major alterations from century to century.[53] The historian thus encounters the challenge of deciphering the complex networks through which a utopian work, in this case *L'An 2440*, reflects the "historical" reality of its society, and to what extent it should rather be read as a representative of a specific fictional genre, based on the repetition of a conventional pattern.

The second group of primary sources includes a selection of texts, novels and philosophical treatises, produced by other eighteenth-century French writers and philosophers, which have been used in locating Mercier and his work in the general cultural framework and the intellectual debate of his century. Considering that the epoch is distinguished by an unprecedented number of lengthy treatises on subjects ranging from religion to morals, philosophy and politics, the selection chosen in this study has been necessarily restricted within certain limits. Special concern is devoted to the works of Jean-Jacques Rousseau due to the fact that they were of prime importance for Mercier's development as a writer. Another writer who had probably served as Mercier's source of inspiration was the German philosopher Gottfried Wilhelm Leibniz (1646–1716).

In eighteenth-century France approximately fifty works were produced with titles such as *Essai sur le bonheur* or *Traité du bonheur*. Those works, especially devoted to the treatment of the theme of happiness, have not, however, offered many innovative perspectives because of their monotonous character, with some rare exceptions like Mme du Châtelet's *Réflexions sur le bonheur*. This being the case, the field of "*littérature d'imagination*" remained to be investigated if one wished to know what the eighteenth-century men dreamed about.[54]

As for the research literature, the examination of Mercier's utopian vision in a very wide cultural historical context has also imposed demands for the choice

. . . .

51   See Chapter II p. 36.
52   Simonsuuri 1980, 31–32. See also Virtanen 1987, 76.
53   See Chapter II, p. 47.
54   See also Mauzi 1994, 9–10.

of the source material. The research literature used can be divided into three different categories. The first category consists of investigations focused on various aspects of Mercier's literary work. The second group of secondary sources includes studies on the modern tradition of utopian and future-oriented thinking more generally. Finally, extensive use has been made of studies which shed light on various aspects, – political, social, economic and cultural, – of society in late eighteenth-century France.

The two last categories help to shed light on Mercier's utopian thought from a double perspective: Whilst the studies on utopias have assisted in the examination of the a-historical and mythical dimensions of *L'An 2440* and in evaluating its status in the tradition of modern utopian thinking, the wide selection of studies approaching eighteenth-century French society from various angles have proved their importance in contextualizing the multiple themes of *L'An 2440* in the wider historical setting of its age. Since Mercier treats in his utopia subjects of great diversity, from religion to politics, economics and gender roles, the use of a restricted selection of studies on the *ancien régime* would not have been adequate. In this context it would be pointless to list at length all the studies made use of.

Among the more important individual sources of inspiration, the study by Robert Mauzi, already referred to several times, so far offers the most comprehensive survey of the theme of happiness in eighteenth-century French literature, and has proved of immeasurable value. Mauzi focuses, however, on the idea of individual happiness (without neglecting the concept of "*sociabilité*" as its integral factor), but does not address utopias. Otherwise utopias have received ample attention as a field of academic enquiry. One of the most ambitious efforts in this field is the *Utopian Thought in the Western World* (1982) of Frank E. Manuel and Fritzie P. Manuel, which has served as one of the basic sources of inspiration for this study. As for the problem of time and future, F.L. Polak's *The image of the future* (1961) has offered many valuable insights for the better understanding of the development of modern future-oriented thinking.

The tradition of research specifically addressing Mercier and his work can be traced back to the early nineteenth century. Many of Mercier's contemporaries held hostile attitudes toward him, and nineteenth-century scholars and historians of literature reinforced this negative image, maintaining a tenacious view of Mercier as a ridiculous and in a pejorative sense "original" literary figure. Mercier's bad reputation is largely indebted to works such as Cousin d'Avalon's *Merciériana, ou Recueil d'anécdotes sur Mercier; ses paradoxes, ses bizarreries, ses sarcasmes, ses plaisanteries, etc, etc.* (1834) and Monselet's *Les oubliés et les dédaignés*, mentioned above. The titles of these works already reveal their malicious attitude toward their target.

Since the early twentieth century, this dismissive attitude has gradually been replaced by a more positive view of Mercier, and it has become a commonplace amongst more recent Mercier scholars to repeat the reproach that Mercier's importance was undervalued by earlier scholars. Léon Béclard, the author of the first full-length biographical work on Mercier, *Louis-Sébastien Mercier. Sa vie, son oeuvre, son temps* (1903), complains that Mercier has been "the victim of incredible and iniquitous rejection".[55] In his work of almost eight hundred pages, Béclard presents the first favorable portrait of Mercier. With his tendency to whitewash Mercier, however, Béclard fails to shed light on the complexity of Mercier's personality. Furthermore, Béclard's treatment ends at the year 1789; a biographical study of Mercier's final years is still lacking.

In his relatively recent study *Le Rêve laïque de Louis-Sébastien Mercier entre littérature et politique* (1995) Enrico Rufi campaigns against the tenacious myth of Mercier as "despised" and "forgotten", rejecting the persistent conception of him as an "extremist who should not be taken seriously".[56] In the same year a selection of writings by various authors was published under the title *Louis-Sébastien Mercier (1740–1814). Un hérétique en littérature* (1995), where Mercier's thinking is approached from a multiplicity of fresh, new perspectives. Here the label "*hérétique*" has been finally transformed from a pejorative into a positive label.

Almost twenty years earlier, another compilation of contributions from diverse scholars on Mercier had been published under the title *Louis-Sébastien Mercier précurseur et sa fortune* (1977). Here Mercier's value is acknowledged as a "precursor", and it is argued that he has left many traces for example in the German "Sturm und Drang".[57] The comprehensive critical bibliography compiled by Geneviève Cattin, included in this same collection, also makes one question Mercier's marginality. Mercier and his work have aroused considerable interest, especially in the German-speaking world.[58] Similarly, Rufi's bibliography of the large number of scientific treatises on *L'An 2440* and *Tableau de Paris*[59] is a further sign of Mercier's "revival".[60]

The awakened interest in Mercier and his work attests to the increasing interest in popular culture as a wider phenomenon. There is no doubt that literary works like Mercier's *L'An 2440*, produced by despised literary figures viewing their contemporary society from a marginal position, may reveal the polyphony of their epoch even more clearly than the canonized texts of the elites.[61]

The studies on Mercier display a tendency to follow one of two principal directions: Either he is seen as a "*philosophe*", or as an "*illuminé*" and a

. . . .

55   Béclard 1903, v.
56   Rufi 1995, vii.
57   Hofer 1977b, 8. For more detail, see Beriger 1977, 47–72.
58   Cattin 1977, 341–361.
59   Rufi 1996.
60   In addition to this, the many re-editions of Mercier's major works in the recent years testify to this. *L'An 2440* was fully reprinted in the 1970s. See Mercier, *L'An 2440. Rêve s'il en fut jamais*, prefaced by Alain Pons (1977); Mercier, *L'An deux mille quatre cent quarante. Rêve s'il en fut jamais*, prefaced by Raymond Trousson (1971, 1977, facsimile of the edition of 1799). See also Mercier, *Tableau de Paris* I–II. Édition établie sous la direction de Jean-Claude Bonnet. Mercure de France: Paris 1994. See also Mercier, *Le Nouveau Paris*. Édition établie sous la direction de Jean-Claude Bonnet. Mercure de France: Paris 1994. As for the purposes of this study, the analysis is based on the re-editions of *Tableau de Paris* and *Le Nouveau Paris*. They contain the integral text of Mercier's original works.
61   See also Collier 1990, 99.

Romantic thinker.[62] The most prominent study in the latter category is definitely Henry F. Majewski's *The Preromantic Imagination of Louis-Sébastien Mercier* (1971). In his study Majewski succeeds in illuminating the "irrational" and "mystical" side of Mercier's visionary thinking with a compelling talent not equaled by any other study on Mercier. My own examination of Mercier's ideas on spirituality and his images of disaster have been greatly inspired by Majewski's ideas. The great achievement of Majewski's groundbreaking study is in his provision of a more complex and complete image of Mercier's personality than for example Béclard was capable of. This helps us better to understand Mercier's position in relation to the cultural elites of his time, his marginality and his stance between tradition and innovation, scientific rationalism and Romanticism.

Among Mercier's voluminous literary output, *L'An 2440* and *Tableau de Paris* are the two works which have aroused most interest among the scholars. The *Tableau de Paris* is a monumental representation of Parisian society on the eve of the French Revolution, and provides an authentic documentation of immeasurable value for any historian exploring the life of all social layers in late eighteenth-century Paris. It is specifically with his *Tableau de Paris* that Mercier has taken his place as a precursor of such great nineteenth-century social realists as Victor Hugo and Honoré de Balzac. In *La poésie de Paris dans la littérature française de Rousseau à Baudelaire* (1961), Pierre Citron accords to *Tableau de Paris* a key position in the creation of the romantic "myth of Paris",[63] and the mythical dimensions of Mercier's Paris are also emphasized in Helen Patterson's work *Poetic Genesis: Sébastien Mercier into Victor Hugo* (1960).

As far as Mercier's utopian thought is concerned, Raymond Trousson is without doubt the most important scholar. Both his introductions to the new editions of *L'An 2440*, and the pages on Mercier's utopia in his study *Voyages aux pays de nulle part. Histoire littéraire de la pensée utopique* (1975),[64] have contributed a great deal to the understanding of *L'An 2440*. Bronislaw Baczko, one of the most important scholars of the utopian thinking of eighteenth-century France, also devotes some useful attention to Mercier in his study *Lumières de l'utopie* (1978) and in his articles. Moreover, our knowledge of the production, distribution and reception of clandestine novels like Mercier's *L'An 2440* has been considerably enriched by Robert Darnton.

Furthermore, Paul K. Alkon devotes some interesting pages to *L'An 2440* in his study *Origins of Futuristic Fiction* (1987),[65] as do Alexandre Cioranescu,[66] Raymond Ruyer[67] and the Manuels[68]. Mercier's invention is also treated briefly

. . . .

62   See also Rufi 1995, 28.
63   On Mercier's different views on Paris, see Citron 1961, 116–138.
64   Trousson 1975, 175–179.
65   Alkon 1987, 117–129.
66   Cioranescu 1972, 193–197.
67   Ruyer 1988, 209.
68   Manuels 1982, 458–460.

in works such as Krishan Kumar's *Utopia and Anti-Utopia in Modern Times* (1987),[69] Jean Delumeau's *Mille ans de bonheur. Une histoire du paradis* (1995),[70] Jean Servier's *Histoire de l'utopie*[71] and Gilles Lapouge's *Utopie et civilization* (1978).[72] In addition to those listed above, J.B. Bury's classical work *The Idea of Progress. An inquiry into its origin and growth* (1920) includes a treatment of the basic themes of *L'An 2440*.[73] By contrast, Robert Nisbet, surprisingly, ignores Mercier in his *History of the Idea of Progress* (1942).

In general, the prevailing attitude towards Mercier's *L'An 2440* has not been very positive. The birth of the modern future-oriented utopia is almost totally ignored, for example, in Marie Louise Berneri's *Journey through Utopia* (1950), and in Ian Tod's and Michael Wheeler's *Utopia* (1978). Among more recent studies, for example in Georges Minois' *Histoire de l'avenir. Des prophètes à la prospective* (1996), the emphasis is on the authoritarian aspects of Mercier's utopia.[74] Increasing attention has been paid in recent decades to the anti-utopian dimensions of many utopias,[75] which is a sign of disillusionment with utopias and "progress" following of the world wars of the twentieth century. In particular Theodor Adorno's and Max Horkheimer's *Dialectic of the Enlightenment* (1944), first published in the aftermath of the Holocaust, has opened our eyes to the self-destructive dimensions of the Enlightenment and to the fatal consequences of its teleological concept of rationality.[76]

Although interest in Mercier has been steadily increasing in recent years, there still to my knowledge exists no other overall cultural historical study focused on his utopian thought. At least two unpublished dissertations have been made on Mercier's utopian vision, both of them, however, approaching their subject from a literary perspective.[77] The same neglect concerns the future-oriented thinking of the eighteenth-century French Enlightenment in general.[78] It was thus high time for a critical re-examination of Mercier and his vision of the twenty-fifth century, together with a selection of his writings, which help to provide a fuller understanding of how the people of pre-Revolutionary France conceptualized their world, what they thought about the future and about the ways man would best be able to maximize his well-being and satisfaction this side of the grave.

. . . .
69   Kumar 1987, 38–39.
70   Delumeau 1995, 307–310.
71   Servier 1991, 203–207.
72   Lapouge 1978, 235–238.
73   Bury 1920, 192–201.
74   Minois 1996, 441–444.
75   See for example Berneri 1951; Kateb 1963.
76   Adorno and Horkheimer 1979, 3–42, especially 9.
77   Wiseman 1979; Denoit 1983.
78   Männikkö 1986, 32.

Louis-Sébastien Mercier, drawing by Pujos, engraving by Henriquez, 1787. Cliché Bibliothèque Nationale, Paris.

LOUIS SEBASTIEN MERCIER,

Ancien Professeur de belles-Lettres, Avocat en Parlement, Membre de plusieurs Académies.

Né à Paris.

II Louis-Sébastien Mercier and his Place in the Tradition of Modern Utopia

An Author in the Pursuit of Happiness: The Dialectics between "spleen" and "ideal"

It has been claimed that the feature which most unites the creators of utopias is their acute awareness of evil, which is the reason for their anger and disgust with society. Their sense of disappointment and frustration drives them to withdraw from present conditions into a fantasyland. In the eyes of their contemporaries they look like fools, or madmen, whose fancies could lead to destruction. Because the future rarely conforms to their fantasy, utopians are almost always tragic figures who die without finding fulfillment.[1]

Mercier was one of the utopian writers whom this definition characterizes exceptionally well. In the republic of letters of his age he was a "heretic", always pushed forward by a desire to break the rules. The questioning of given truths, literary, political or social, formed a crucial element in Mercier's literary action from the outset. He was all his life fighting against everything.[2] Mercier was an apostle of the theory of engaged literature, and he denied the autonomy of the esthetic sphere: he saw it as subordinate to considerations of moral and political order.[3] His rallying cry on behalf of a committed literature is expressed in the catchphrase "No masters, no models".[4] This rebellious character made of him a precursor of Romanticism and an *"homme révolté"*.[5]

Mercier's highly critical attitude to his contemporary society and its institutions made of him one of the most controversial among eighteenth-century French writers. In the eyes of his contemporaries he was famous for his "extravagances", eccentricity and paradoxes, even madness. As Rufi has correctly observed, works such as Cousin d'Avalon's collection of Mercier anecdotes, by transmitting to posterity the cliché of an eccentric personality, are responsible for this tenacious view.[6] Yet, even if too much emphasis should not be placed on Mercier's presumed "eccentricity" (in the pages that follow it will be put under critical re-examination), it goes without saying that his personality had many irritating features, which consolidated his place on the margins of the

. . . .

1   Manuel 1966a, xiii; Manuels 1982, 27.
2   Rufi 1995, 3.
3   Hofer 1975, 247; Rufi 1995, 192.
4   Bibliothèque de l'Arsenal, Fonds Mercier, Ms. 15081 (1.1.), f. 419.
5   Majewski 1971, 2–3.
6   Rufi 1995, 21–22.

During his life time, Mercier was often ridiculed for his deliberately provocative opinions. A caricature by an anonymous cartoonist. Cliché Bibliothèque Nationale, Paris.

Erostrate moderne, Écrivant sur les Arts.

literary elites. As Cousin d'Avalon reminded his readers, Mercier raised his voice against the philosophical heroes of his century such as Locke, Voltaire and Condillac. He spoke about corruption caused by art and regarded the system of Newton as ridiculous. The globe was, in his opinion, flat, and he believed that the sun revolved around it.[7] Owing to his opinions, for many years Mercier was the target of lampoons and scorn; the journals published caricatures, and he was nicknamed "*marchand de mercerie*".[8]

In the final decades of the eighteenth century, when Mercier's literary productivity was at its height, the hegemonic structure of the republic of letters itself, centered around some prominent philosophical figures, was in a state of turmoil. Darnton asserts that after the death of the great philosophers from Rousseau to d'Alembert between 1778 and 1785, the high point of Enlightenment was over.[9] Mercier was one of the lesser literary figures, whose task was to transmit the ideas first presented by literary and philosophical talents more distinguished than himself. Yet, this humble role did not satisfy his ambitions for long, and he was soon to distinguish himself also as one of the most critical descendants of the entire philosophical movement.[10]

With his desire to fight against academic dogmatism and the cultural hegemony dominated by a small elite of philosophers, Mercier emerges as a

. . . .

7 Cousin d'Avalon 1834, xvj–xix, 10.
8 Roy [s.a.], iii–iv.
9 Darnton 1982, 15.
10 Bonnet 1995, 11.

typical figure of the Low Enlightenment. It has been suggested that the feature uniting the figures of the Low Enlightenment was a bitter resentment towards the *philosophes*' monopoly of the cultural establishment. For this reason the anti-philosophical resistance, opening the world of the counter-Enlightenment, sheds at the same time new light on the Enlightenment itself.[11]

As Darnton has shown in many of his investigations, in pre-Revolutionary France the literary underworld formed a fascinating subculture of its own. In the final years of the *ancien régime* there had opened up an exceptionally wide gulf between the High Enlightenment and the French equivalent of "Grub Street", which constituted the lowest social layer in the hierarchy of the republic of letters. As a member of the bohemian literary underworld, Mercier was one of the "sentimental hack writers" or "gutter Rousseaus", who lived on the margins of the literary elite of his time, and who earned their living as best they could.[12] Darnton's reference to the archives of the Parisian police reinforces the image of Mercier as a bohemian, rather obscure character:

> "Mercier: lawyer, a fierce, bizarre man, who neither pleads in courts nor consults. He hasn't been admitted to the bar, but he takes the title of lawyer. Fearing the Bastille, he left the country, then returned and would like to join the police."[13]

In the hierarchical structure of the republic of letters Mercier's status was on the margins, but he did succeed in escaping from total penury. In this respect he did not differ much from other less successful writers, – the *"canaille de la littérature"*, as Voltaire so contemptuously expressed it, of the *ancien régime*, who lived on the fringes of the law, called themselves lawyers and took on odd jobs. To live decently by writing alone was still exceptional in this period, for the monarchy supported only writing which flattered the regime.[14]

The precariousness of existence which befell Mercier and other "gutter Rousseaus" living and working in pre-Revolutionary Paris was a consequence of the transformations which had begun to shape the production, diffusion and consumption of literature in the course of the eighteenth century. As historians of the book have pointed out, after mid-century literary production was increasingly professionalized and commercialized, which meant that there was a shift from the traditional patronage system toward operation in the market; books now became commodities endowed with commercial value and treated as cultural objects to be evaluated in monetary terms, which brought automation of literary activity, and with this, absolute freedom of creativity.[15] Although the term "intellectual" had not yet been coined, this was the new literary type which now emerged.[16]

· · · · · · · · ·

11   McMahon 1998, 77–112, especially 103.
12   Darnton 1982, 16; Darnton 1997, 117.
13   Darnton 1982, 26.
14   Darnton 1982, 10, 25; Chartier 1994, 48; Pomeau & Ehrard 1998, 26–27.
15   Chartier 1994, 37–38.
16   Darnton 1988, 141–142, 175.

Despite his legendary reputation as an *"intellectual engagé"* and an *"enfant terrible"* of eighteenth-century French literature, the exterior events of Mercier's life offer few dramatic events. Partly, at least, this can be explained by the fact that he does not reveal much of his personal life or intimate feelings in his voluminous production, nor even in his correspondence, – a fact lamented by Béclard, the first scholar who also had access to Mercier's unprinted papers.[17]

The main lines of Mercier's life are, however, well known. Apart from short periods of time, he spent his whole life in Paris, where he was born in 1740. His father was a dealer in small wares. The family was not rich, but did not live in poverty. Contrary to his father's wish to continue in the same career, Mercier from an early age was more interested in literature and the theater. He idolized the philosophical writer Jean-Jacques Rousseau. In his early thirties Mercier started his literary career as a writer of heroic poetry, which was currently a fashionable genre. In 1763 he left Paris for a while to take up a teaching post in Bordeaux, which did not satisfy Mercier's ambitious mind for long. Uncertain of his future destiny, he left Bordeaux in 1765 and decided to settle down in Paris as a freelance writer. A "polygraph" had been born, and literary works started to flow.[18]

In eighteenth-century France academic debate offered one of the ways to achieve notoriety, and in the 1760's Mercier produced a series of works in this style, which were collected in 1776 under the title *Éloges et discours académiques qui ont concouru pour les prix de l'Académie française et de plusieurs autres académies* (including, for example, *Le Bonheur des gens de lettres* (1763)).[19] This was also the period when Mercier wrote his novel of the American wilderness, *L'Homme sauvage* (1767), which reads like a gesture of respect for the fashionable cult of the primitive. It is the story of two North American Indians, the siblings Zidzem and Zaka, and their idealized existence amidst nature. As the narration proceeds, the innocent and virtuous life of these "noble savages" is, however, destroyed by the intrusion of cruel Spanish conquerors, and after many adventurous and tragic confrontations the natives are forced to abandon their paradise.[20]

. . . .

17   Béclard 1903, viii.
18   Trousson 1971, 10–12. See also Béclard 1903, 2–30, passim. Mercier's social position corresponds to the average status of birth of a man of letters in his period. As Darnton has shown, seventy percent of eighteenth-century French writers came from the Third Estate. Darnton 1988, 163.
19   Delon 1990, 6.
20   The authorship of *L'Homme sauvage* has aroused considerable dispute in the research literature, and Mercier's authorship has not been taken for granted. One argument is that the novel was not written by Mercier at all, but that his contribution was to make an adaptation of a novel which was actually written by Johann Gottlob Benjamin Pfeil. This view has been justified by arguing that the themes of *L'Homme sauvage* diverge to such an extent from those advanced in *L'An 2440* that it is improbable that they could have been produced by the same author. See for example Versins 1972, 582. Rovillain, by contrast, has convincingly demonstrated that Mercier was the original author of *L'Homme sauvage*. Rovillain 1930, passim. Béclard adopts the same view in his biography of Mercier. Béclard 1903, 45. For the purposes of this study the latter interpretation has been accepted, since there can be discerned no legitimate reason to suspect Mercier as the original creator of the novel. As is shown in Chapter VI, pp. 183–186, the contradictions between the view of the world in *L'Homme sauvage*

After these youthful experiments Mercier found his proper style in the drama, producing also a series of theoretical treatises on the state of the theater and literature of his century. He had made his first efforts in this career already in 1773, publishing a treatise entitled *Du Théâtre ou nouvel essai sur l'Art dramatique*, which was followed three years later by *De la Littérature et des Littérateurs suivi d'un Nouvel examen de la tragédie française* (1776).

Among other literary genres, the *"conte morale"*, made famous by Marmontel, enjoyed great popularity in eighteenth-century France.[21] Although Mercier personally distanced himself from Marmontel's manner of ridiculing the vices of his society instead of fighting against them,[22] he followed this literary fashion of his period by creating a series of moral allegories, *Songes philosophiques* (1768), *Les Songes d'un hermite* (1770) and *Songes et visions philosophiques* (1788). Their main purpose is to criticize human vices in a religious-mystical tone, creating fanciful wonderlands peopled by spirits, vampires, phantoms and other imaginary creatures. In these often hallucinatory visions, the stars fall and tombs open, to announce the end of the world. The major concern is focused on the question why the virtuous so rarely achieve happiness, and why evil forces win in the battle of life. Many of the titles of Mercier's *songes*, such as *"D'un Monde heureux"* or *"L'Optimisme"*, anticipate his great invention, *L'An 2440*. It is now time to take a closer look at Mercier's masterpiece and to provide a concise overview of its publishing history.

L'An 2440 is a prolix and lengthy novel, but its underpinning narrative structure is a very simple one: At the beginning of the story the anonymous narrator (probably an *alter ego* of Mercier himself, concluding from the fact that he is said to have been born in the same year as Mercier himself, 1740)[23] falls asleep after a moral discussion with an "English friend" about the corruption of big cities like Paris, and sleeps through the centuries, to end up in Paris in 2440. The "plot" (it is not, perhaps, exactly the proper word, for the structure of the novel, as Darnton has remarked, is rather "formless")[24] is a tour around the future Paris, where the time traveler is guided by a local inhabitant of this distant epoch, like Dante and Virgil. The element of surprise is generated from the realization that he is confronting a city which has undergone a total transformation during his long sleep. In response, the time traveler pities himself for the unfortunate lot of having been born on the earth in the century of misery:

> "Oh! si je pouvois partager le temps de mon existence en deux portions, comme je descendrois à l'instant même au cercueil! comme je perdrois avec joie l'aspect de mes tristes, de mes malheureux contemporains,

. . . .

and in *L'An 2440* is not problematic, since these two novels represent two successive phases in the evolution of Mercier's utopian thought and in his thinking about the conditions necessary for the achievement of happiness.

21   Delon, Mauzi & Menant 1998, 218–221.
22   Mercier, *Fictions morales I* 1792, vj–vij.
23   Mercier, *L'An 2440 I* 1786, 23.
24   Darnton 1997, 118.

pour aller me réveiller au milieu de ces jours purs que tu dois faire éclore, sous ce ciel fortuné, où l'homme aura repris son courage, sa liberté, son indépendance et ses vertus!"[25]

This setting forms the starting point for Mercier's utopia, which is based on a strict polarization between the author's contemporary society of the 1770's and the twenty-fifth century. Mercier's method is to emphasize the huge difference between the two temporal levels separated by a cleavage of almost seven hundred years by using critical footnotes, addressed directly to the contemporary reader, where he presents, with the voice of moral indignation, lengthy comments on the many abuses which he sees in his own society. As one scholar has observed, the entire novel can be interpreted as the description of a society through its own negation.[26]

This is a common practise in utopian literature, for most utopias have been used as tools of social criticism. For the creators of utopias, the existing society is typically in a state of total crisis, dominated by evil and injustice. As we have already seen, the point of departure is the sense of a rupture between the "ought" and "is", the ideal and the social reality.[27] Contrary to some other forms of ideal societies, utopias thus always attribute serious attention to the problems of the real world;[28] their aim is not a total carnivalization of the existing order of things. As Martin Buber explains it, utopias are not "fantasy-pictures", but the vision of "what should be" is inseparable from a critical relationship to the existing condition of humanity.[29] Instead of being merely "escapist nonsense", utopias form a significant component of human culture;[30] on these grounds, purely personal daydream should be excluded from the category of utopias as a narcissistic yearning.[31]

It was in the summer of 1768 that Mercier began to develop his novel of the brave new world of 2440. A letter to his friend Thomas, dated from that period (22 June 1768), verifies this fact: "Je travaille du long rêve de l'An deux-mille quatre-cent quarante."[32] Some time later, in an undated letter, Mercier mentions

. . . .

25 Mercier, *L'An 2440 I* 1786, xij–xiij.
26 The semantic polarities are further emphasized in Mercier's utopia by linguistic means, using the past tense, e.g. "*on ne voit point, on ne voit plus*", to express a grammatical negation of the existing social order. Ricken 1975, 301–303.
27 Baczko 1978, 30–31. See also Moos and Brownstein 1977, 24–25.
28 Davis 1981, 375 and passim.
29 Buber 1958, 7.
30 Levitas 1990, 1.
31 Manuels 1982, 7. For example Ruyer writes, however, rather mistakenly, that some utopias are "pure reveries" and "realisations of childish desires". Ruyer 1988, 6.
32 Bibliothèque de l'Arsenal, Fonds Mercier, Ms. 15078(2)b, f.4; Mercier, *L'An 2440* I (1786), 21. In point of fact, the idea of the future had captured Mercier's imagination already before the writing of *L'An 2440*. His collection of stories, *Les Songes d'un hermite* (1770), already contains speculative elements, utopian and Arcadian themes. There are also some novelties: premonitions about future war and dystopias, which would not begin to flourish for almost a century. Versins 1972, 581–583. Moreover, in the collections *Songes philosophiques* and *Songes et visions philosophiques*, the theme of the future is occasionally approached in a form of pedagogical allegory. For example, in the story "*Les Lunettes*", Mercier describes fantastic binoculars, which show simultaneously all the possible happiness and unhappiness

that he has reworked the text: "Depuis longtems, je m'occupe à refaire mon ouvrage intitulé l'an 2440 qui dans l'origine en 1770 n'avoit pas recu le développement dont il étoit susceptible."[33]

In this letter, Mercier mentions 1770 as the year when his utopia first saw daylight. He repeats this statement in the beginning of the edition of 1786 ("*Avis de l'auteur*") as follows: "J'ai publié la premiere édition de cet Ouvrage en 1770..."[34] Despite this, Trousson is not exactly sure whether Mercier's utopia was first published in 1770 or 1771, and regards it as possible that the novel might have appeared in the end of 1770.[35] In his article on the publishing history of *L'An 2440* Everett C. Wilkie Jr. suggests 1771 as the date of first publication: In his opinion several allusions in the work itself sustain the idea that Mercier was still writing the novel quite late in 1770, for example the fact that Mercier mentions the shortage of bread during the severe winter of 1770.[36]

L'An 2440 was soon to claim its place as one of the best-sellers of the eighteenth century. At least a dozen editions came out, which clearly testifies to its popularity.[37] From a careful survey of the best-seller lists of eighteenth-century publishers and reading habits, Darnton has established that the ideas of Enlightenment popularizers and vulgarizers like Mercier fascinated the French readers of that period much more than the works of the great philosophers. With his vision of the twenty-fifth century world Mercier opened a totally new, unforeseen, horizon.[38] During the eighteenth century the consumption of literature, by and large, steadily increased.[39]

Over the years, *L'An 2440* expanded from a rather modest one-volume version into a monumental edition of three volumes and almost a thousand pages. It appeared anonymously in one volume in 1771, 1772, 1773, 1774, 1775 and 1776. One version in two volumes was published in 1785; another, in three volumes, in 1786, 1787, 1793 and 1799.[40] The last of these versions is also the largest. It appeared after the French Revolution, in "Year VII" of the secular Revolutionary Calendar, beginning in September 1792, the day of the Republic's founding.[41] In this "An VII" edition, Mercier has rewritten the Preface, expounding on the French Revolution and the accuracy of the predictions he had made about its course in previous editions of the novel.[42]

· · · · · · · · ·

in the world. The different possibilities of future events are revealed to man at the same time: good and evil. It depends on man himself, which way is chosen. The value of anticipation is justified by preventive reasons: "...si nous pouvions lire dans le tems futur, nous éviterions les fausses démarches, source de nos malheurs..." Mercier, *Songes philosophiques* 1768, 108, 114.

33 Bibliothèque de l'Arsenal, Fonds Mercier, Ms. 15078(2)b, f. 48.
34 Mercier, *L'An 2440 I* 1786, v.
35 Trousson 1971, 34–35.
36 Wilkie 1984, 9.
37 Béclard 1903, 90; Wilkie 1984, 6; Darnton 1997, 115; Collier 1990, 89.
38 Darnton 1982, 140–141; Darnton 1990, 153; Darnton 1997, 73, 118–120.
39 For further reading, see for example Roche 1987, 197–233; Goulemot 1989, 363–395. See also Gossman 1972, 112–139, especially 134.
40 Trousson 1971, 71.
41 Kennedy 1989, 345–351; Rifkin 1989, 90–93; Darnton 1990, 5.
42 See also Wilkie 1984, 15.

L'AN
DEUX MILLE
QUATRE CENT QUARANTE.
Rêve s'il en fût jamais ;

SUIVI DE

L'HOMME DE FER,
SONGE.

Par L. S. MERCIER, ex-Député à la
Convention nationale et au Corps légis-
latif ; Membre de l'Institut national de
France.

Le présent est gros de l'avenir.
Leibnitz.

NOUVELLE ÉDITION
IMPRIMÉE SOUS LES YEUX DE L'AUTEUR.

AVEC FIGURES.
TOME SECOND

A PARIS,

Chez { Brosson et Carteret, Libraires, rue Pierre-
Sarrazin, n°. 7 et 13 ;
Dugour et Durand, Lib. rue et hôtel Serpente.

An VII.

Otherwise, it contains the same basic text as the final version first published in 1786.[43] Mercier asserts this by himself in the "new preliminary discourse" added to the final version of the novel:

> "Comme la malice et la malveillance pourroient insinuer que j'ai glissé dans cet ouvrage plusieurs phrases nouvelles et que j'aurois fait ainsi la prédiction après l'événement, j'atteste que j'ai réimprimé ces trois volumes sans en retrancher un seul mot, sans y ajouter un seul mot, sans déranger une virgule, tels enfin qu'ils ont paru en mars 1786."[44]

The great popularity of *L'An 2440* gave rise to a flood of imitations.[45] For example a 1785 edition has nothing in common with Mercier's novel other than the title. Mercier himself bitterly disapproved of these counterfeits:

. . . .

43 The many editions of Mercier's utopia can easily lead to confusion. Wilkie suggests that Mercier himself gave his approval only to the editions of 1771, 1786 and the An VII. Wilkie 1984, 15–16.

44 Mercier, *L'An 2440 I* An VII [1799], xxviii.

45 Not all of these imitations flatter their target, and it is obvious that some of Mercier's contemporaries found the extreme optimism of *L'An 2440* rather irritating: For example, Semival's brief parody in verse, entitled *L'Année 2440 ou Tout à sa place.* See Béclard 1903, 142.

"Je désavoue pleinement & entiérement les éditions, ou plutôt les contrefacons qui ont paru depuis 1770 jusqu'à ce jour. On y a joint des additions fautives qui ne sont pas de moi... "Ce n'est pas seulement une contre-facon défectueuse, informe, c'est une falsification faite avec la plus grande imprudence, car ce n'est qu'un pillage indécent de plusieurs chapitres de mes autres ouvrages ..."[46]

Various confusions to do with the publishing history, such as wild guesses about the authorship, can be explained by the fact that at the end of the *ancien régime* the book trade still rested on a rather unorganized basis. It is characteristic, as Béclard has noted, that *L'An 2440* was first published anonymously in Amsterdam.[47] This was not a rare practise in late eighteenth-century France; many of the best-known French works of that period first appeared in print outside France, and banned books were also smuggled into the country. Because of police censorship and the booksellers' guild monopoly, the writers of unorthodox views worked in an atmosphere of repression.[48]

As soon as Mercier's utopia was published, it was marked by the stigma of a forbidden book. Despite the great popularity that the novel enjoyed amongst readers (or precisely for this reason), Mercier's vision of the future was regarded by the authorities as a dangerous propaganda. It was classified in a typical category of illegal literature, the *livres philosophiques*, which was a general label covering a vast range of literary productions from utopian fantasies and theoretical speculations to pornography. Their common denominator was the fact that they challenged the legitimacy of the *ancien régime*.[49] Because *L'An 2440* was immediately banned in France, Mercier found himself in serious conflict with the authorities.[50]

The authors of clandestine literature also had to encounter the obstacles posed by literary criticism, which tended to support the official line of the authorities. For example, the author of a review of *L'An 2440* published in December 1771 in the *Correspondance littéraire, philosophique et critique* comments that the novel has been strictly banned, and as a consequence, very vividly researched, undoubtedly due to the fact that it could not be easily procured. The banning of the novel is alleged to be the sole reason for the success of Mercier's utopia, which is "not an interesting or attractive book".[51] As this shows, the "dangerous" nature of *L'An 2440* increased its popularity even further, reinforcing Mercier's reputation as a rebel.

By twenty-first-century standards, the "dangerous" character of Mercier's utopia is surprising. Set in the context of the French *ancien régime*, however, the image becomes more clear; under absolutism the legitimacy of the monarchy,

· · · · · · · ·

46   Mercier, *L'An 2440 I* 1786, v, *"Avis de l'auteur"*.
47   Béclard 1903, 90. See also Mercier, *L'An 2440 I* 1786, v.
48   Lough 1978, 175–177, 181–187. See also Roche 1988, 25–46. For more details, see Darnton 1990, 114–153.
49   Darnton 1997, 194–195.
50   Majewski 1971, 9.
51   *Correspondance littéraire, philosophique et critique*, Décembre 1771, 108–109.

assisted by the powerful Catholic church, was supposed to be beyond criticism. Mercier, as Darnton has observed, revealed the many abuses of Paris in the final decades of the *ancien régime*. By addressing his words directly to his contemporary readers in the footnotes of his utopia, Mercier establishes a confidential relationship between the writer and the reading public as a bulwark against the absolutist regime.[52]

The technique chosen by Mercier reveals the mechanisms of the process which had gradually in the course of the eighteenth century changed the status of the printed book from a cultural artefact authorized by royal *privilège*[53] into a commodity. Mercier proclaims his independence as a writer by raising his voice against the absolutist state, using at the same time all available means in order to please the reading public. With the commercialization and profession-alization of the book trade, as writers became more and more dependent on the fluctuations of the market instead of the system of patronage, they needed to please their readers as best as they could instead of flattering the government. This imposed new demands on the writers, since they had to keep the interest of the audience alive by satisfying its insatiable appetite for novelties.

In his novel Mercier makes ample use of the typical utopian method of establishing sharp contrasts between the categories of "ideal" and "spleen", or "is" and "ought", and the exaggerated manner in which he accomplishes this task reads as a deliberate act to startle his contemporary readers to face the rottenness of the society of the *ancien régime*. Daniel Roche has also drawn attention to the fact that for Mercier the inclusion of superficial realism through creating social tensions was a "trick of the time", and the image his writings convey is more exotic than familiar. His moralizing aim justifies the contrasts of light and shade, a taste for the picturesque, and an attitude which is a mixture of observation and pedagogy.[54]

The thoroughness with which Mercier accomplishes his task to function as the moral mouthpiece against the injustices which he confronted in his country is impressive. Bronislaw Baczko has noted that all utopias have a tendency for what he calls "global representation",[55] and in the pages of Mercier's utopia, too, all different aspects of life are dealt with in a sweeping manner. In the course of the story the time traveler visits many places, for example the royal library, the temple, a theater, a private home, and the funeral of an old peasant. He is also informed by his guide about the political, social and religious life of the future Parisians. In the final scene of the novel he travels from Paris to Versailles, now in ruins, which has lost all of its former prestige as the center of arbitrary power. After this the narrator awakens from his sleep back in his own century.

. . . .

52 Darnton 1997, 120.
53 Under the *ancien régime* books which had passed the watchful eye of the royal censor and thus officially approved for publication were stamped with a *privilège*. See for example Lough 1978, 180.
54 Roche 1987, 45–46.
55 Baczko 1978, 30.

Besides Mercier's wish to please the reading public, another obvious reason, less calculating perhaps, for his desire to create visions of a better world arose from his two-focal attitude to life, a simultaneous awareness of the miseries and injustices of the existing society, always balanced, nonetheless, by the hope that some day all the oppressive evils would be removed which now hindered man from enjoying happiness on earth. Béclard noted that sensitivity, enthusiasm, love for his fellow-men, a passionate belief in their happiness and indefinite perfectibility were the articles of the new faith which Mercier embraced.[56] In the preface to his *Fictions morales*, Mercier expresses this optimism when he declares that he has always been guided by the sentiment that man was born to rise from the slough of errors and shame in order to rise to the highest state of virtue. This is what he means by man's inborn capacity for perfectibility: "Ayant toujours été dominé par cette primitive et consolante idée, j'y ai assujetti presque tous mes ouvrages."[57]

The constant interplay between the "is" and "ought" thus explains Mercier's desire to see beyond current social, economic and political conditions; marginalized, isolated (at least in his own mind), angry and insulted – what else was there to do than to escape from the prison of mental and physical suffering to self-made paradises, dreams and utopias? It is expressly this interior duality which Majewski sees as the core of Mercier's escapism. In his view, through Mercier's work there can be traced a basic refusal to accept reality as it is, and "a movement away from the tragic limitations of life in the present, toward the world of the future, the dream of a more perfect existence". This same tension between repulsive reality and an idealized "lost paradise" runs as a basic motif through the whole tradition of Romantic literature.[58]

Feeling misunderstood by his contemporaries, Mercier found his intellectual masters from such great visionary thinkers as Plato, Mohammed, St. Augustine and Emmanuel Swedenborg.[59] He regarded himself as the descendant of a long reform tradition, which can be traced back to Plato's *Republic*. It is characteristic that in the beginning of *L'An 2440* he writes: "Pour moi, concentré avec Platon, je rêve comme lui."[60] Amongst the creators of utopias that Mercier admired, in *Tableau de Paris* he mentions the sixteenth-century writer Raoul Spifame;[61] another influence was Fénelon (1651–1715), the writer of *Les aventures de Télémaque* (1699).[62]

The chapter "*La Bibliothèque du Roi*" in *L'An 2440* illuminates Mercier's literary preferences further. The time traveler visits the royal library of 2440,

. . . .

56   Béclard 1903, 38–39.
57   Mercier, *Fictions morales I* 1792, XIV.
58   Majewski 1971, 18.
59   Ibid., 41.
60   Mercier, *L'An 2440* 1786 I, 3. In *Notions claires sur les gouvernemens*, however, Mercier dismisses the value of Plato's *Republic* and describes it merely as a "play of imagination". He considers it a "fatal" flaw in Plato that it suggests the possibility of a perfect government, thus ignoring the fact that men are always prepared to abuse the laws. Mercier, *Notions claires sur les gouvernemens I* 1787, 170.
61   Mercier, *Tableau de Paris II* 1994a, 94–98, passim. See also Béclard 1903, 591–592.
62   Bibliothèque de l'Arsénal, Fonds Mercier, Ms. 15078(2)b, f. 53.

where he is surprised to note that only a small amount of the literature produced in previous centuries has been preserved for posterity. He is informed by his guide that abridgments have been made of the most important books and the rest have been burnt. The works saved from destruction include those of Moïse, Plato, Plutarch and Virgil, and English writers, preserved almost in their entirety: in 2440 Milton, Shakespeare, Pope, Young and Richardson still enjoy wide fame. Among French writers, the works of Descartes, Montaigne (with some exceptions) and Fénelon have been carefully preserved, together with the the *Encyclopédie* and entire production of Rousseau. The destroyed works include Aristophanes, Lucretius (on the grounds of his dangerous morals), Boileau, all works dealing with scholarly disputes, and much of Voltaire.[63]

Curiously enough, Mercier makes no mention of More's *Utopia*, nor of other utopian writers, notwithstanding Fénelon's novel *Télémaque* and Marmontel's *Bélisaire* (1767),[64] which both contain utopian themes. The word "utopia" is never mentioned in *L'An 2440*, and Mercier does not himself call his novel a utopia. Most eighteenth-century philosophical writers held a rather hostile attitude towards utopias,[65] and Mercier may have consciously avoided all allusions to utopianism in order not to be labeled as a creator of unrealistic dreams whose projects should not be taken seriously.

Mercier's closest personal relationship among all the writers of his generation was with the pornographic and utopian writer Restif de la Bretonne (1734–1806),[66] and in modern research literature those two are often lumped together.[67] Like Mercier, Restif belonged to the literary proletariat of his age. Owing to his low birth, he too was excluded from the privileges of the *ancien régime* and from the Enlightenment elites. Both writers had complex mixed attitudes of admiration and jealousy to the recognized philosophers.[68]

Among the major philosophers of his century, Mercier most admired Jean-Jacques Rousseau.[69] Like Mercier, Rousseau began his intellectual career from social marginality.[70] Mercier succeeded on one occasion to meet his idol, who unfortunately believed that he was a police spy.[71] Amongst Rousseau's works, Mercier was particularly influenced by *La Nouvelle Héloïse* (1761) and the pedagogical treatise *Émile* (1762). Although in the course of time Mercier's early passionate adoration of Rousseau lost its hold, it reappears in his *De Jean-Jacques Rousseau considéré comme l'un des premiers auteurs de la Révolution* (1791).[72] Here Mercier explores his relation to Rousseau's political theory and sets out to formulate his own.

· · · · · · · · ·

63   Mercier, *L'An 2440 I* 1786, 320–367, passim.
64   Mercier, *L'An 2440 I* 1786, 348.
65   See Chapter II, p. 51.
66   Hofer 1977a, 16. See also Béclard 1903, 434–438, 723–747; Trousson 1971, 21.
67   See for example Delon, Mauzi & Menant 1998, 401–413.
68   Delon, Mauzi, Menant 1998, 402.
69   See for example Hofer 1977a, 13.
70   For more detail, see for example Baczko 1997, 177–198.
71   Monselet 1857, 59.
72   Bonnet 1995, XIV. See also Rufi 1995, 69–100.

In addition to Rousseau, Mercier was also profoundly influenced by philosophical writers of his century such as Diderot, Montesquieu and the abbé Prévost.[73] This admiration did not pass unnoticed by Mercier's contemporaries, as can be seen in titles mocking his lack of original ideas, such as "Rousseau's ape" or "caricature of Diderot".[74]

The malicious nicknames have been slow to die; for example André Le Breton writes in his study on the French eighteenth-century novel that Mercier was a nobody who stole his ideas from Rousseau and Diderot, *"traduites en français de cuisine"*. He labels Mercier a "pure vandal", whose novels were the most mediocre ones produced in the entire eighteenth century.[75] Cousin d'Avalon, for his part, proclaimed that Restif de la Bretonne, Dorat Cubières-Palmezeaux, and Mercier formed "a triumvirate of bad taste".[76]

Exclusion from elitist literary circles did not, however, undermine Mercier's high conception of himself as a professional writer, which he expressed by proudly calling himself *"le premier Livrier de France"*.[77] The hardships following on the publication of *L'An 2440* did not exhaust his creative energy. He now started to work on a still larger project: As a counterpoint to his imaginary city of happiness, Mercier now embarked on a vast panorama of contemporary Paris, *Tableau de Paris*, in which he sets out to reveal precisely those vices which he had earlier aimed at repairing in *L'An 2440*. It is an encyclopedic work, containing twelve volumes and over two thousand pages. As indicated above, *Tableau de Paris* is a comprehensive survey of eighteenth-century French society: its customs, fashions, social relations, literary and political life. *Tableau de Paris* is a precursor of modern journalism, where, for the first time in literature, the common people are elevated as the hero.[78]

The publication history of *Tableau de Paris* repeated that of Mercier's earlier book. After the appearance of the two first volumes in 1781, it was banned because of its criticism of social customs, politics, religion, and economics. With his republican sentiments and critical attitude toward royalism, Mercier succeeded in avoiding the Bastille only by fleeing to Neuchâtel in Switzerland (1782), where he spent three years in exile.[79]

Exile also had a positive impact on Mercier's development as a writer. The time spent in Switzerland was extremely important, for it was now that his romantic sentimentalism was awakened. He now experienced the pre-Romantic landscape in real life, and through his reading of Rousseau, Young, and Gessner.[80] The natural landscapes of Switzerland provided the inspiration for *Mon bonnet de nuit*, which is a bizarre compilation, even more formless than *L'An 2440* and *Tableau de Paris*, a sort of "private notebook", including short

. . . .

73   Hofer 1977a, 13, 15–16.
74   Patterson 1960, 35; Collier 1990, 89.
75   Le Breton [1898], 351.
76   Cousin d'Avalon 1834, XIX–XX; Monselet 1857, 82–83; Patterson 1960, 35.
77   Cousin d'Avalon 1834, 83; Patterson 1960, 35.
78   Hofer 1977a, 23.
79   Majewski 1971, 10. See also Patterson 1960, 37.
80   Majewski 1971, 10; Trousson 1971, 18–20.

essays on a variety of subjects (for example astronomy and anatomy, impressions of Swiss mountains and lakes, or allegorical visions, many of which were earlier published in *Songes philosophiques*).

Mercier returned to Paris from exile in 1785. After the final completion of *Tableau de Paris* in 1789 his fame began to grow, and Mercier now took his place as one of the most prominent literary and public figures of his century. He was the friend of Marat, Robespierre, Camille Desmoulins, Condorcet, Clootz, and Brissot.[81] Mercier also became a leader of a circle of pre-Romantics, which was occasionally visited by personages such as Restif, Grimod de la Reynière, and Olympe de Gouges. It was within this circle that Mercier became an enthusiastic admirer of occultism, esotericism and Freemasonry, and participated in several of the secret societies which spread up during the Revolution.[82] This shows that Mercier actually occupied a much more significant place in the literary life of his period than the general view of him as a capricious and complex personality has led us to believe.[83]

Taking advantage of this unexpected rise of social prestige Mercier now became more and more interested in the political events which were to lead to the Revolution. He continued his literary activities, publishing a two-volume *Notions claires sur les gouvernemens* (1787) and entered journalism, editing with Jean-Louis Carra[84] one of the most famous journals of the time, the *Annales patriotiques et littéraires de France* (1789–1791). Late on, Mercier collaborated on the Girondist journal *La Chronique de mois*, where he engaged in more and more virulent attacks against the Jacobins. In the autumn of 1792 the Department of Seine-et-Oise elected him as a deputy in the National Convention, and he now definitively broke his relations with the Jacobins in order to make common cause with the Girondins.[85]

Mercier's decision to break with the Jacobins was caused by the fact that despite his Revolutionary enthusiasm he was no extremist, and he was particularly disgusted by the September massacres. As a supporter of the more moderate Girondist party, he voted against the execution of Louis XVI, demanding perpetual detention instead. Mercier thus came to irritate the Jacobin leaders and became himself the target of persecution. In consequence, he was imprisoned by the Jacobins from 8 October 1793 to 24 October 1794. Only the fall of Robespierre on 9 Thermidor saved him from being executed.[86]

. . . .

81   Patterson 1960, 35–36.
82   Majewski 1971, 11.
83   Hofer 1977a, 13–36, especially 13.
84   Jean-Louis Carra (1742–93) started his Revolutionary career as an active member of the Paris Jacobin club, was elected to the Convention, then turned away from the Jacobins and began to work with the Girondins. He was executed on 31 October 1793. See for example Bosher 1988, xxix.
85   Trousson 1971, 22; Viguerie 1995, 1185. See also Béclard 1903, 645–646; Hofer 1975, 246–258, especially 252.
86   Hofer 1975, 253, 255; Majewski 1971, 11; Trousson 1971, 23–24. During his incarceration Mercier wrote a vast number of letters to his common-law partner, Louise Marchand, of which eighty-eight have been preserved. A collection of these letters ("Lettres de prison", 1793–1794) is contained in the re-edition of *Le Nouveau Paris*. See Mercier, *Le Nouveau Paris* 1994b, LXXIV–CLXXVII.

It is also possible that Mercier's "elastic" character had something to do with his survival. As his contemporary critics rather cynically observed, he was "a republican under the monarchy and became a royalist under the republic".[87]

Whatever his good intentions, Mercier's talent as a political reformer may not have been very considerable. His friend Reynière commented that as a legislator Mercier was a mere nonentity.[88] At any events, this did not hinder the tone of Mercier's criticism from sharpening further towards the end of the century. Scholars have noted that in his later years his extravagancies and paradoxes multiplied: Forgetting his earlier attacks against the Academicians in *L'An 2440*, in 1795 Mercier joined the Institute.[89] Another contradictory decision in this period was his acceptance of the position as Treasurer of the National Lottery (1797), an institution he had previously frequently criticized.[90]

In addition to his practical occupations, Mercier was now preoccupied by writing a sequel to *Tableau de Paris*, a six-volume *Paris pendant la Révolution (1787–1798) ou Le Nouveau Paris*, in which he revises his former observations on the city, which had undergone a total transformation. In this chronicle of post-Revolutionary Paris, all the participants in the Revolution are equally condemned: the members of the more moderate Girondist party as well as the cruel Jacobin leaders such as Darnton, Marat and Robespierre.

In addition to *Le Nouveau Paris*, which was to bring Mercier's chronicle of Paris to its conclusion, in this last phase of his life he produced a peculiar dictionary, *Néologie ou Vocabulaire de mots nouveaux* (1801), which is an attempt to regenerate the language in the same way as the Revolution had turned the old social and political order upside down. On the verge of death, Mercier's originality still took new forms. As a final "extravagance" he published in 1806 a work entitled *De l'impossibilité du système astronomique de Copernic et de Newton*, in which he attacks the Copernican world view as "impossible" and continues his derogatory attacks on idols of his age such as Locke, Newton and the encyclopedists.

Trousson recounts that in his old age Mercier no longer succeeded in retaining the attention of the public, which became more and more disenchanted with this old-fashioned and slightly mad old man. There was little brilliance in his last years. Mercier's memory was further weakened after his death by the spread of rumors that his brother, Charles-André, was the real author of *L'An 2440* and *Tableau de Paris*. For lack of proof, however, the matter remained unresolved.[91]

· · · · · · · · · ·

87 Tod & Wheeler 1978, 58.
88 See Desnoiresterres 1877, 189.
89 Trousson 1971, 24–25; Hofer 1975, 252.
90 Majewski 1971, 12.
91 Trousson 1971, 29, 31–32.

A Brief Overview of Modern Utopian Thinking

Utopias before Mercier

From the background of all utopian visions there can be found two tenacious myths: the Christian faith in a paradise, and the Hellenic myth of an ideal, beautiful city built by men without divine assistance. The ideal urban forms of life became a central preoccupation in the philosophy of the ancient Greeks, and especially Plato's (427–347 BC) *Republic*, which is a plan for a just and harmonious urban society, has continued to attract many later creators of utopias.[92]

Scholars of utopianism have often claimed that the Middle Ages was a static period in all respects, including that of utopian and future-oriented thinking. This interpretation cannot, however, be justified; the images of the terrestrial paradise, heavenly Jerusalem and millennium[93] incarnated the focal ideals of the Middle Ages, and the expectation of the coming Kingdom of God shaped the general mentality of the entire period. Moreover, despite the fact that medieval images of the future were characterized by a religious frame of reference and the main emphasis was on transcendent and eschatological goals, the same period prepared also the ground to ideas which in their further development turned into secular images of the future.[94] Thus, even if the Middle Ages could be considered as a barren period as regards utopian thinking in the sense that it did not leave to posterity any literary utopian works, its general mentality was, nevertheless, permeated by a deep-rooted utopian inclination as a general attitude to life.[95]

In the Renaissance, the focus of concern shifted more and more from the heavenly to the terrestrial paradise.[96] In that period, increased interest in a

. . . .

92 Manuels 1982, 16–17, 33, 64–65. See also Rihs 1970, 261, 264.
93 Millenarianism, or chiliasm, was originally confined to a prophetic conviction derived from the Apocalypse of St. John, where a detailed description is given about how the devil is bound for a period of a thousand years, during which the earth would be ruled by the just who had died and suffered for Christ. At the end of the thousand years the devil would be released for a brief period, and this would bring chaos and misery into the world. The transition to the millenium is depicted in images of catastrophe. Eventually God would intervene and cast the devil with its followers to a burning lake, while the rest would live in the "new heaven and new earth", the New Jerusalem, the Holy City. In the myth of the millenium, heaven is thus often blended with the image of the terrestrial paradise. The idea of a millenium led men to expect joy and justice already on earth. The Church, on the other hand, held that happiness was reserved for the afterlive. Tod & Wheeler 1978, 11–12; Keohane 1982, 27; Manuels 1982, 46; Cazes 1986, 48; Cohn 1993, 13; Delumeau 1995, 15–17, 316, 326.The term "Apocalypse", which means "revelation", refers to the scriptures which claim to reveal the last times ("eschatology"). The writer of the Apocalypse tells of a vision in which God has revealed His plan concerning the future of humanity. He believes that the world's end is relatively near and describes in symbolic language the events leading to it. See for example Minois 1991, 68–69.
94 Polak 1961, 163–164; Tod & Wheeler 1978, 17. See also Berneri 1951; Minois 1996, 293.
95 Mannheim suggests that in the post-medieval period, the Orgiastic Chiliasm (belief in a millennial kingdom on earth) of the Anabaptists represented the first form of a Utopian mentality. The orgiastic mentality was characterized by ecstatic outbursts and the belief that the fulfillment of utopian expectations could occur at any moment. The idea of the millenial kingdom on earth has always contained the seeds of revolution, which explains why its adherents were often persecuted by the church. Mannheim 1972, 190–197.
96 Tod & Wheeler 1978, 27.

beautiful urban environment shows in the profusion of ideal city models. The *"Città Felice"* depicted in Italian architectural treatises from the mid-fifteenth to the mid-sixteenth centuries represents one of the greatest moments of utopian creativity. Other well-known examples of such models include those planned by Leone Battista Alberti, Filarete (the composer of Sforzinda in the 1460s) and Francesco di Giorgio Martini. Their aim was to ennoble existing social relations by placing them in a more beautiful setting. In order to accomplish this, the creators of architectural utopias drew their inspiration from classical models, in particular from Plato and Vitruvius. They believed that an ideal city mirrored the soul of a just man, and the physical environment should be constructed in the same way as a well-proportioned human body. Correspondences with the heavens were also emphasized: the ideal city was regarded as a reflection of celestial harmony.[97]

With his work *Utopia*, which gave the name to the whole genre, Thomas More was the creator of the first modern literary utopia.[98] The term "utopia" is ambiguous by nature, in that it opens paths to two different interpretations. More forged the word to designate a country that does not exist ('outopia', no place). He also, however, alludes to the possibility that the island described in the novel "deserved to be called 'eutopia' " (the good place).[99]

As this reveals, the concept of utopia is Janus-faced by nature. Utopias tell at least as much about happiness as about its negation. The function of utopias is to offer representations of humankind's longing for a Golden Age, or a paradise, but this ardent wish is matched by a simultaneous awareness of the purely illusory nature of such beautiful images. This explains why the supreme importance of utopias is not so much to provide concrete programs of action, as to stimulate the social imagination, i.e., to make men understand that the world need not necessarily be a "vale of tears". As Ernst Bloch notes, the best state – "optima res publica" – was already set as a goal by More,[100] who repeats in his *Utopia* the idea that it is nature itself that requires man to pursue his proper happiness; it would be the extreme form of madness to pursue hard and painful virtue, suffer pain and to banish the sweetness of life:

> "When nature bids you to be good to others, she does not command you conversely to be cruel and merciless to yourself. So nature herself, prescribes to us a joyous life or, in other words, pleasure as the end of all our operations."[101]

. . . .

97 Manuels 1982, 150–180, passim; Rosenau 1983, 42–67, passim.
98 Cioranescu 1972, 20; Ruyer 1988, 3; Minois 1996, 293.
99 Manuels 1982, 1; Levitas 1990, 2. See also Rihs 1971, 272; Baczko 1978, 20; Tod & Wheeler 1978, 19; Frängsmyr 1981, 48; Rahkonen 1996, 37–42. According to James Holstun utopia is also "ou topos", i.e., "no place", because it is a "vagabond colonial paradigm", eager to replicate its social structures in any new waste ground and people it meets. Holstun 1987, 57.
100 Bloch 1989, 4.
101 More, *Utopia* 1964, 92–93.

More's *Utopia* is a representation of a communist society situated on an island somewhere in the middle of the South Pacific Ocean. According to the narrative pattern, which soon established itself as an immutable literary convention, the hero of the utopian story arrives by accident in an ideal community as a consequence of a shipwreck or some other exceptional event, becomes acquainted with the circumstances prevailing in this mysterious ideal commonwealth, and eventually returns to his own country, where he informs his audience about everything what he has learned and seen in his marvelous voyage.[102] A causal connection can be traced between these utopian tropes and actual voyages of discovery, as Kumar, for example, has reminded us. The new navigations intensified interest in exotic countries and populations, thus nurturing the utopian imagination.[103] Real-life expeditions of exploration, and the stories of travelers about exotic countries, also provided the inspiration for the "Extraordinary voyage" literary genre, which enjoyed wide popularity in France during the seventeenth and early eighteenth centuries. The distinguishing feature of the "Extraordinary Voyages" was their geographical realism, and in this respect they contrasted with the fictional geographical settings of the utopias.[104]

In his *Utopia*, More thus set a model imitated by the creators of utopias in the sixteenth and seventeenth centuries. Utopian themes are often transmitted from one generation to another, and older utopias give birth to new. Despite the fact that utopias contain a strong ahistorical and acultural aspect, they are, nevertheless, always found in a specific social and psychological context.[105] Utopias are, thus, at least two-layered by nature; at the same time as they function as mirror images of a specific social, political and economic setting, they also draw their substance from a mythical stock of images which is not bound to a specific historical context.

The most striking characteristic of the early modern utopias was insularity; the Morean utopias projected the ideal as really existing on some faraway island, as a society which could be imitated.[106] The "Isles of the Blessed" had, however, fascinated the human imagination since Greek antiquity. Dante, too, gave the terrestrial paradise the characteristics of an island, and in many medieval *récits* the mythical kingdom of Prester John is situated on an island. Distance further increased enchantment, and isolation preserved things in existence.[107]

. . . .

102 Manuels 1982, 2.
103 Kumar 1987, 23. See also Berneri 1951, 56; Tod & Wheeler 1978, 28. It would be, however, premature to conclude that the writers of utopias were simply inspired by the narrations of travelers. Rather, because the knowledge of distant countries was still rather vague when the first modern utopias were written, and in the lack of knowledge based on facts, the stories of the travels of discovery in the New World were often mixed with utopian fantasies. Both the New World and Utopia were seen as fictious, mythical places. See for example Davis 2000, 95–96.
104 Atkinson 1922, 7–26, especially 9.
105 Manuels 1982, 13–14.
106 Ibid., 5.
107 Delumeau 1992, 130–131.

The background to this preference for islands was a conviction that only a community saved from the disrupting influences of the outer world could attain perfection. The world of happiness was withdrawn within itself.[108] Furthermore, an isolated geographical space offered "a controlled experimental site in which to prepare for the conquest and reorganization of the world", as James Holstun puts it. From this perspective, the utopian affinity for islands and other isolated places reads not merely as a desire to flee from the world, but also as the wish to submit the world under a vision of perfect rationality.[109]

The utopias of the sixteenth century, existing in the eternal paradise of a static society, marked a transition from the medieval preoccupation with heavenly beatitude to the modern idea of an infinite progress.[110] It may not be mere coincidence that the birth of modern utopian literature occurred simultaneously with the breakup of the unified Christian world, the rise of the Reformation and the Renaissance. The secular nature of the modern utopia was evident from the beginning.[111]

The shift from the sixteenth to the following century brought a change in utopian models: the seventeenth century represents an intermediary phase between the "magic island" utopias toward a plurality of voices and wider variety in the geographical location of ideal societies. Some authors now also ventured onto other planets. The Islands of the Blessed had become a worn-out trope. The first interplanetary voyage narration was Francis Godwin's (1582– 1633) *The Man in the Moon* (1638), and the idea of a paradise situated on the moon also inspired for example Cyrano de Bergerac (1619–1655). On the other hand Margaret Cavendish, the first female utopian author, situated her utopia in an subterranean landscape in her novel *The Blazing World* (1668).[112]

Compared with their predecessors, the seventeenth-century utopias were able to abandon the narrative framework all together; the "pansophic"[113] utopias of Campanella, Andreae, Comenius and Leibniz, for example, are representations of Christian republics extending all over the earth.[114] The *Civitas Solis* (1602) of Tommaso Campanella and Francis Bacon's *Nova Atlantis* (1627) were the two most important utopian treatises of the early seventeenth century. *Civitas Solis*

. . . .

108 Trousson 1975, 19–20.
109 Holstun 1987, 55.
110 Clarke 1979, 5.
111 Kumar 1987, 22. Too much emphasis should not, however, be put on this secular character of modern utopianism. Far from breaking their bondage with the Christian image of the "Heavenly Jerusalem", in for example the philosophical-architectural utopias of the Renaissance the religious and aesthetic elements were fused. See Manuels 1982, 177.
112 Trousson 1975, 94–96.
113 "Pansophia" was one of Johann Amos Comenius's (1592–1670) projects for the elaboration of a new method for natural sciences. He wanted to construct a system of knowledge in which all branches of knowledge would be unified as a totality, a "pansophia". This system would serve as a "temple of wisdom", inspired by Francis Bacon's ideas concerning the organization of science. Behind this monumental idea of "pansophia" was the doctrine of universal harmony, which found its expression in theories focused around the notion of microcosmos – macrocosmos. Frängsmyr 1981, 57–58.
114 Manuels 1982, 2–3, 205–221.

is a description of a socialist ideal state led by a pope, and *Nova Atlantis* is focused on the theme of dominance over nature by scientific achievements.[115]

Utopia and its Forms in the Eighteenth-Century French Literature

In some epochs, utopias have represented only a marginal and isolated phenomenon, whereas in others utopian creativity has become more intense. The years immediately preceding the French Revolution have been occasionally called the Golden Age of Utopia, on the grounds of the exceptional propensity for utopian thinking in that epoch. At such times all things seem possible.[116]

It has been estimated that in eighteenth-century France there were produced as many utopian texts as in the two previous centuries put together.[117] Baczko suggests that during the period 1676–1789, if utopias are understood as the same thing as the "*voyage imaginaire*", the total number of new utopian works amounts to approximately eighty.[118] The period witnessed an unprecedented proliferation of various kinds of Utopias – Morean, Robinsonian, physiocratic, communist, sexual.[119] Utopias also began to arouse academic interest, the earliest contribution of which was a Latin dissertation by Henricus ab Ahlefeld, published in Cologne in 1704.[120] The main reason for this sudden flowering of utopianism was, without doubt, the exceptional variety of possible modulations that utopias offered for preachers of happiness.[121]

Another indication of the increased interest in utopian thinking in eighteenth-century France is the publication of a collection of texts (36 volumes, 74 different texts) compiled by Charles-Georges-Thomas Garnier (1746–1795) between 1787 and 1789, which is the first extensive collection of speculative fiction. The collection contains utopias, allegories, extraordinary journeys and scientific predictions. It is divided into three classes, of which the first one includes four divisions: 1) "Voyages imaginaires" ("romanesques", "merveilleux", "allégoriques", "amusants"), 2) "Songes et Visions", and 3) "Romans cabalistiques". In Garnier's compilation, Mercier's *Songes d'un hermite* and *Songes et Visions philosophiques* are included in the category "Voyages imaginaires romanesques".[122]

The first French utopia, an anonymous work published in 1617, bore the title *Histoire du Grand et Admirable Royaume d'Antangil*. It has also been described as the most boring of the French seventeenth-century utopias, for its author borrowed all his ideas from More. More's *Utopia* had a great influence also for

. . . .

115 Frängsmyr 1981, 37–47, 53–57.
116 Trousson 1975, 121; Baczko 1978, 18–19, 29; Manuels 1982, 14; Hudde and Kuon 1986, 9; Delumeau 1995, 302.
117 Manuels 1982, 6.
118 Baczko 1978, 47; Goulemot 1989, 378. In the eighteenth century the utopian novel was catalogued under the category "voyages imaginaires". Krauss 1970, 392.
119 Manuels 1982, 19–20. See also Baczko 1978, 37; Ruyer 1988, 187.
120 Manuel 1966a, ix; Manuels 1982, 10. The analytic study of utopias goes already back to the ancient Greeks, however. The belief that ideal cities demanded "critical examination" was first expressed by Aristotle in Book II of the *Politics*. Manuel 1966a, ix.
121 Trousson 1975, 128.
122 Versins 1972, 944–946; Baczko 1978, 43.

many other utopias produced in seventeenth- and eighteenth century France, such as *Histoire des Sévarambes, peuples qui habitent une partie du troisième continent communément appelé la Terre australe* (1677) or Fénelon's *Les aventures de Télémaque* (1699).[123]

Eighteenth-century French utopians assume a variety of attitudes to the conditions of the real world and to the need for reform. For the more conservative authors, existing society needed only minor corrections in order to attain at least a supportable state, whereas for the more radical utopians this was not sufficient. Some of them came to glorify the natural and virtuous lifestyle of the "savages" – a view advanced vigorously for example by Montesquieu in his *Lettres persanes* (1721) and Diderot in his *Supplément au voyage de Bougainville* (1772). In addition, there were anarchists like Morelly, the author of the communist treatises *Naufrage des Isles flottantes, ou Basiliade du célèbre Pilpaï* (1753) and *Code de la Nature (1755)*. Dom Léger-Marie Deschamps (1716–1774), the author of *Vrai système ou le mot de l'énigme métaphysique et morale*, can also be classified in this category of the most unorthodox constructors of utopias.[124]

Like these authors, Restif de la Bretonne was another typical representative of the more radical utopian thinking in pre-Revolutionary France. In addition to fictitious utopian stories like his long and complex novel, *Découverte australe par un homme volant, ou le Dédale francais* (1781), he wrote a number of treatises, collected under the general heading *Idées singulières* (1769–1789). This collection contains the following reform projects: *Pornographe* (1769), *Gynographes* (1777), *Andrographe* (1782), and *Thesmographe* (1789). Restif had also a habit of including miniature utopias in his other works; for example his novel *Paysan perverti* (1776) includes a description of the agricultural community of Oudon (lettre CCLXXXVIII, *Statuts du bourg d'Oudon*).[125]

The utopia of the eighteenth century was not always "serious". Instead of constructing a seriously intended alternative society, it often contented itself with making fun of vices. An example of this fantastic utopian orientation is Ludvig Holberg's (1684–1754) work *Nicolai Klimii iter subterraneum* (1741), where the hero falls into a deep cave and finds a subterranean world peopled by speaking and moving trees. Another very strange novel was Casanova's *Icosaméron* (1788), which is also a narration about falling into a subterranean world. The center of the earth is said be inhabited by little androgynous creatures ("*les Mégamicres*"), nourished by a fruit which preserves them from sickness, old age and the need for sleep.[126]

The geographical scope of utopias was now also widening, and by the eighteenth century there hardly existed any location which had not yet offered the site for an ideal commonwealth.[127] The unprecedented expansion of

. . . .

123 Berneri 1951, 174–176.
124 Trousson 1975, 132–155.
125 Ibid., 155–160.
126 Ibid., 123–124.
127 Berneri 1951, 176.

scientific exploration and the stories of travelers in exotic lands had a greater influence in the utopian literature than ever before. This led to the idealization of primitive peoples, as incarnated in the image of the "noble savage". Sentimental exoticism was followed by philosophical exoticism, and Voltaire and Montesquieu, for example, searched for their inspiration from oriental civilizations.[128]

The eighteenth century also witnessed the first anti-utopian experiments, born in reaction to the optimism of the Enlightenment.[129] A typical example of anti-utopian imagination in that epoch is provided by the Marquis de Sade (1740–1814) whose novel *Aline et Valcour* (1788) contains descriptions of two micro-utopias. The first of these shows the happy island of Tamoé, which is ironically opposed with the terrifying kingdom of Batua, where sexual despotism reigns and where vice has been set up as the ideal.[130]

This flourishing of utopian writing was, however, not capable of producing one unique masterpiece. Utopian creativity was passing through a kind of transition, for the utopian constellations of the Enlightenment had lost the coherence of earlier centuries, and future-oriented utopias had not yet been properly born. A sense of ambivalence was also typical of the attitudes toward utopias, as can be seen in the fact that despite the popularity of the genre, not all eighteenth-century philosophical writers gave their blessing to utopian dreaming. It now became customary to assume a sceptical, even hostile, attitude toward utopian thinking. The fact that there is no article on utopia in the *Encyclopédie*, and that old utopias were treated with contempt, testifies to this clearly.[131]

Moreover, the patriarchs of the Enlightenment had no predilection for utopias. This does not mean that their works were totally lacking in utopian excursions, and philosophers did on occasion incorporate utopian digressions in their works; the best examples of this practise are provided by the *"histoire des trogdolytes"* in Montesquieu's *Lettres persanes* and a sketch of El Dorado in Voltaire's *Candide*.[132]

How is it possible to explain this ambivalent attitude toward utopias? Why did the latter part of the French eighteenth century witness an unprecedented proliferation of different sort of utopias, while at the same time utopias were despised and neglected? Krishnan Kumar offers one possible solution to this apparent paradox when he argues that the period was characterized by an accelerated tempo of scientific and economic expansion, and for this reason utopias, which preserved their loyalty to older modes of thinking, became increasingly fragmented and marginal.[133]

· · · · · · · · ·

128 Rihs 1970, 331–350, passim. See also Ruyer 1988, 188.
129 Hudde & Kuon 1986, 10. See also Baczko 1978, 48–49.
130 Trousson 1975, 164–167.
131 Manuels 1982, 19, 414; Collier 1990, 86.
132 Manuels 1982, 413; Baczko 1997, 141.
133 Kumar 1987, 37.

The negative attitude toward utopian dreaming was, obviously, also due to its presumably "dangerous" nature. The possibility that utopias might contain seeds of revolt, invoking aspirations which were beyond realization, could never be totally ruled out. Judith Shklar suggests that this was the reason why for example Rousseau, one of the most "utopian" minds of the whole eighteenth century, did not apply the word utopia in his own work; he associated utopia with futile dreams of perfect cities: "Rousseau's sense of disaster was total, which led him to refuse the platonic hope that man could ever have sufficient knowledge in order to leave the 'cave'."[134]

Similar argumentation can be traced from the writings of the most optimistic philosophers of progress. For example Volney warns his contemporaries of the dangers of escapism in his treatise *Les ruines, ou méditation sur les révolutions des empires*, published in the first year of the French Revolution (1789), arguing that since desires cannot be satisfied on earth, man hopes for their fulfillment in another world. This beautiful illusion is, however, followed by a new disorder, since, enchanted by his imaginary world, man neglects reality, and comes to see his life as nothing but "a boring voyage, a painful dream".[135]

The pejorative view of utopias could also be argued to reflect a sense that wishful thinking was in contradiction with the credo of the age, the belief in the power of reason. On the other hand, this interpretation cannot be maintained if one bears in mind the fact that the drive toward rationalization is embedded in the utopian ideal of happiness itself. Bronislaw Baczko, for example, emphasizes that the ideal of happiness advanced by the creators of utopias is manifestly a *rational* ideal: the utopian, "other" society is thought to conform to reason.[136]

As we have already seen, therefore, contrary to what might be expected, utopian dreaming is not synonymous with "escapist nonsense"; there is always a strong social aspect involved.[137] Considering this fact, it is manifestly the rational tendency contained in most utopias which explains the sudden outburst of utopian energy on the eve of the French Revolution. The eighteenth-century French utopias embody the "cult of reason", which matured in the years immediately preceding the events of 1789. As Kumar notes, they give visible form to the long rationalist tradition: "Despite the scepticism of Enlightenment

. . . .

134 Shklar 1969, 8–9.
135 Volney, *Oeuvres choisies de Volney* 1836, 56.
136 Baczko 1978, 32.
137 If one accepts this definition, for example Mercier's moral allegories in *Songes philosophiques, Songes et visions philosophiques,* and *Les Songes d'un hermite* should be excluded from the category of utopias, since they contain many purely subjective and irrational elements, which do not draw their substance directly from the author's contemporary society. On the other hand, as is discussed in the chapter below on the significance of dreams in Mercier's utopian thinking, the *songes* are not "spontaneous" in nature. There is also a strong moralizing tendency involved; for Mercier allegory is merely a literary device for the proclamation of the critical message. The same point also applies to *L'Homme sauvage*; even if Mercier's description of primitive life could perhaps be classified as a social myth rather than a utopia proper, it pulsates, nonetheless, with the same utopian energy as *L'An 2440*.

philosophes, despite the exhaustion of the literary form of utopia, it was by a creative synthesis of certain elements of Enlightenment thought that utopia made itself once more as central to the intellectual life of the age as it had been in the sixteenth and seventeenth centuries."[138]

It would, thus, be inconceivable to locate the utopias of the eighteenth century in any other historical epoch. Both utopias and the ideological climate that shaped the prevailing tendencies of the whole project of the Enlightenment shared the same urge to break traditional mental structures through the critical analysis of their contemporary society. In no previous age in the history of Western civilization had utopian energies been released with the same power as in the images and visions of a more dignified earthly existence on the eve of the great Revolution.[139] The faith in the omnipotence of reason constituted a new religion, and, as Kumar puts it, "Progress was the recognition and realization of the reason that was immanent in the world."[140] In this new progressive atmosphere the ground was prepared for the emergence of the modern future-oriented utopia, which on the eve of the French Revolution came to represent an important subgenre of utopian imagination. A brief overview of the intellectual setting in which the modern temporal utopias such as Mercier's *L'An 2440* first came into being, will be provided in the pages that follow.

The Discovery of the Future

In the second half of the eighteenth century the creators of utopias started more and more to transpose the promised land, which Thomas More had conceived as an island in the South Seas, from space into time.[141] The shift of emphasis from classical spatial utopias toward projections in time entailed certain changes in the functions of utopian writing. Whereas from More's *Utopia* to the French Revolution, the main function of utopias was to represent criticism against existing society, with the birth of utopia set in the future, there took place a shift of focus from a spatial critique of the present to a temporal anticipation of the future. The modern future-oriented utopias mirrored the hopes and aspirations of the bourgeoisie.[142] Compared with the utopias produced in earlier epochs, the new utopian images were distinguished by advanced realism and a belief in the possible realization of utopian visions.[143]

Henceforward, the "ideal" and "real" were no longer two totally separate categories which could never meet, but two distinctive points on the same linear continuity. The idea of hope was now gradually changing: ideal societies were no longer located in some exotic or mythical geographical place beyond mysterious sea voyages, as pure abstractions without any hope of the beautiful image of happiness which they embodied being achieved. It is in this crucial

. . . .

138 Kumar 1987, 39.
139 Polak 1961, 243–244.
140 Kumar 1987, 39.
141 Bloch 1989, 3.
142 Lowe 1982, 46–47.
143 Hudde & Kuon 1986, 16.

aspect that Mercier's *L'An 2440* differs from all anterior utopian models: the place of happiness is now a concrete city, – Paris –, not a life beyond the grave or a paradisal enclosure in the middle of nowhere. The ideal of happiness is brought down from the celestial spheres and situated as an extrapolation of the historical process itself.

Although a future dimension has always been at least implicitly present in the utopian imagination, the ideals proposed by classical spatial utopias had been abstract models, without relevant points of contact with practical social and political realities. For example, in his *Utopia* More makes sceptical comments about the possible realization of utopian hopes in real life:"But I readily admit that there are very many features in the Utopian commonweal which it is easier for me to wish for in our countries than to have any hope of seeing realized."[144]

More's words confirm the notion of Habermas that the spatial utopias of the Renaissance, those produced by More, Campanalla or Bacon, do not yet communicate with history. Their authors had no doubts about the purely fictional character of their narrations, and mankind still lacked the means and methods for their realization. This situation does not change until Mercier transfers his island of happiness to the distant future.[145] Bearing this in mind, scholars from Trousson to Baczko suggest that Mercier's *L'An 2440* marks a "Copernican turn" in the history of utopian literature.[146] It has even been argued that "as a contributor to the Western utopian vision, Mercier rivals Thomas More in significance".[147]

Mercier thus wins the honor of being the author of the first genuine time-utopia.[148] In other words, in *L'An 2440* the "u-topie" is transformed into a "u-chronie".[149] The term "uchronia" is often used as a synonym for a utopian construction situated into the future. The word was invented by the French philosopher Charles Renouvier, who describes, in his *Uchronie* (1876), not the future but a different march of history.[150] In the beginning of his work Renouvier describes his method as follows: "L'ecrivain compose une uchronie, utopie des temps passés. Il écrit l'histoire, non telle qu'elle fut, mais telle qu'elle aurait pu être..."[151]

In the second half of the eighteenth century, interest in the far future began to steadily increase. For example, in 1771 the abbé Galiani confines to Mme d'Epinay his intention to "lancer un cour d'oeil prophétique sur l'état qu'aura

. . . .

144 More, *Utopia* 1964, 152.
145 Habermas 1987, 191.
146 Baczko 1974, 484; Trousson 1982, 279.
147 Alkon 1990, 62. See also Alkon 1994, 61.
148 Polak 1961, 294.
149 Baczko 1974, 484–485.
150 Hudde & Kuon 1986, 10. See also Manuels 1982, 4.
151 Renouvier, *Uchronie (L'Utopie dans l'histoire). Esquisse historique apocryphe du développement de la civilisation européenne tel qu'il n'a pas été, tel qu'il aura pu être* 1876, 10. According to this definition, the term "uchronia", as a synonym for a utopia situated in a future time is, to a certain extent, misleading. It reveals, however, the counterfactual nature of history; i.e., the idea that every historical moment is full of possibilities, of which some are chosen and some others rejected.

l'Europe dans cent ans d'ici". Trousson suggests that if Galiani's work had been completed, it would have been a genuine temporal utopia.[152] Playful experiments with the idea of what the world would look like after centuries had passed also made a breakthrough in the journals of the age. *Mercure de France* published between 1755 and 1756 a series of articles purporting to be "memoirs from the year 2335", written by a scientist not yet been born: "C'est donner un être à la possibilité, c'est réaliser les conjectures."[153]

In the course of the eighteenth century the idea of progress made its definitive breakthrough in utopias. Mercier's *L'An 2440* provides the first and most important fictional work in eighteenth-century French literature in which a belief in terrestrial progress is preached with exceptional fervor. As Bronislaw Baczko expresses it, Mercier's 2440 does not exist just in any future, but in the future which belongs to progress. In Mercier's novel the idea of progress commands the representation of time.[154]

As a "hymn to unlimited progress", Mercier's utopia can be classified in the same category with such works as Anne-Robert Jacques Turgot's (1727–81) *Discours sur les progrès de l'esprit humain* (1750) and Antoine Nicolas de Condorcet's (1743–94) *Esquisse d'un tableau historique des progrès de l'esprit humain* (1793).[155] Turgot and Condorcet were the most ardent apostles of progress in the late eighteenth century. They believed in the infinite perfectibility of man and society, anticipating a dynamic utopia, forever changing for the better with the help of human reason, and the continual amelioration of instruction and knowledge.[156]

Despite the triumphant march of the modern philosophy of progress in the course of the eighteenth century and the reflections of this new optimistic outlook in the formation of the future-oriented fictional utopias in late eighteenth-century France, the idea of how the world would look in some remote time ahead had already started to take its captive hold on the human imagination in the previous century. Over a century before Mercier, a Frenchman Jacques Guttin had published a peculiar novel named *L'Épigone*,

. . . .

152 Trousson 1975, 175.

153 *Mercure de France*, Juillet-décembre 1755, 159.

154 Baczko 1974, 485.

155 In Condorcet's treatise the history of humankind is divided into ten different phases, the last of which is situated in a far future. The content of Condorcet's tenth epoch of progress has many similarities with Mercier's ideal society of the year 2440. In his preface to the new edition of Mercier's utopia, however, Alain Pons draws attention to a distinction between Mercier's and Condorcet's attitudes towards the future. Both were oriented toward the future, but for Condorcet the tenth period of the history of humanity, which he thought to begin in the end of the eighteenth century, was possible only in the light of the knowledge drawn from the preceding periods. Condorcet never forgets that he was a mathematician and a specialist in the calculation of probabilities. Pons 1977, 18–19. In this crucial respect Mercier's utopian discourse turns out to be less rational, more imaginative. As will be pointed out later in this study, his awareness about the mechanisms through which successive phases rise in the course of historical development was not as clear as Condorcet's.

156 Elliott 1982, 471; Delumeau 1995, 316. See also Polak 1961, 293.

histoire du siècle futur. This novel, which contains an embryonic projection in time, had been published in 1659.[157]

As Cioranescu points out in an article on Guttin's novel, *L´Épigone* is a very ordinary story of adventure, based on the traditional pattern of shipwreck. The only peculiar thing is that the action of the novel is situated in a far future time. Its author is, however, incapable of making any difference between the present and the future. In other words, the fact that the action takes place in the future does not give inspiration to any particular idea.[158]

The interest in future-oriented utopias was not restricted solely to French soil; for example, two English works in the new genre were published: *The Memoirs of the Twentieth Century* (1733) by S. Madden, which is a vision of Europe in 1997, and *The Reign of George VI, 1900–1925* (1763), an anonymous description of an ideal sovereign and the relations between the European powers.[159] Yet, as I.F. Clarke has reminded us, the honor of discovering the "true potentialities" of the futuristic fiction belong to the French – first to Mercier, and after him to writers such as Cousin de Grainville, the writer of *Le Dernier Homme* (1805), and Félix Bodin, whose work *Le Roman de l'avenir* was published in 1834.[160]

The breakthrough of "uchronia" has been explained by many different factors, such as the accelerated tempo of modernization and urbanization, which was finally to break down the static order of things and create an optimal ground for a more progressive temporal orientation. Paul Alkon's observation that Guttin's *Épigone* was the only representative of futuristic fiction before the invention of Newcomen's steam engine (1712),[161] supports this view.

Moreover, there were purely literary reasons: the writers of utopias were tired of the old trope, for the genre had exhausted its traditional sources. The utopians had already dreamed long enough of the Islands of the Blessed, of Africa, of "terre australes", of subterranean countries, moon, sun and other planets.[162] Now, when all possible geographical locations had been used, a new dimension – that of the future – provided a fresh perspective. From now on, the future was conceived as a new temporal horizon, into which it was practical to project the dream of a happier world.

The many playful experiments with temporal fiction in the course of the seventeenth and eighteenth centuries reveal that Mercier's *L'An 2440* was not born out of nothing. As the first genuine utopian model situated in a remote future century, it mirrors the most innovative and actual debates of its time. As a "polygraph", keenly observing and commenting on the new philosophical ideas circulating in pre-Revolutionary Paris, Mercier adjusts his utopia to respond to

· · · · · · · · ·
157 Trousson 1975, 174; Alkon 1994, 21, 59.
158 Cioranescu 1974, 442–448, passim. About Guttin and his novel, see also Alkon 1987, 3–44.
    See also Versins 1972, 398–400.
159 Trousson 1975, 174–175.
160 Clarke 1979, 23.
161 Alkon 1990, 43.
162 Trousson 1975, 174.

the intellectual currents of the society in which it was produced. Deliberately or not, with his vision of the future Mercier announced the dawn of the modern era in the history of Western utopian thinking. It is quite possible, as Kumar suggests, that "Mercier did not himself fully realize the new zest for the future characterizing his time and which came to change the nature of utopian thinking in an irreversible manner."[163]

It would be a misconception, however, to presume that all eighteenth-century French writers or philosophers were equally optimistic as regards the future as were the most ardent propagators of this new outlook from utopians like Mercier or Restif de La Bretonne to more "serious" progressive thinkers, such as Condorcet or Turgot. It has been asserted that it was rather on the contrary; in their contemplation of the future, Frenchmen remained rather pessimistic, for their view of the world was still limited by the cyclical conception of time.[164]

Despite the prevalence of cyclical and static interpretations of the future, new winds had already started to blow. In his fairly recent work *Histoire de l'avenir. Des Prophètes à la prospective* (1996), Georges Minois points out that in pre-Revolutionary France, images of the future were in a state of turmoil. Divination, astrology, religious prophesy and interpretation of biblical scriptures existed side by side with the first steps of modern scientific methods; the illuminist Swedenborg (1688–1772) belongs equally well to the eighteenth century as the mathematician Pierre Simon marquis de Laplace (1749–1827). The traditional methods of prophecy and astrology, which still formed an element of popular culture, were gradually rejected by the cultural elites, whose demand for rationality and efficiency were in ascendance. The progress of sciences, politics and economics was manifested as an extending desire to dominate an increasingly desacralized spatio-temporal environment. For Cartesians, time flowed in an irreversible direction, and the future was an unknown world waiting to be explored.[165]

Dreams – A Means of Escapism

Mercier most often casts his utopian visions in the guise of a dream. *L'An 2440* is in its entirety a narrative of time travel accomplished in a state of dream: as was noted above, at the beginning of the story the narrator falls asleep as a young man in Paris of the eighteenth century, sees a vision of the urban paradise of the future, and awakens at the end of the novel to return to his own time. Moreover, the dream functions as a motif in many of Mercier's "*songes*" (for example "*Songe d'un monde heureux*") or "*rêves*", both terms which Mercier uses to characterize his works.[166]

· · · · · · · ·
163 Kumar 1987, 39.
164 Manuels 1982, 19; Kumar 1987, 42–43. See also Gay 1970, 100; Ehrard 1994, 772–774.
165 Minois 1996, 453–454.
166 See also Pons 1977, 21; Wiseman 1979, 9.

Mercier uses the trope of a dream because it offers unrestricted possibilities to create images of a better life. There thus exists a close interrelation between happiness and dream, and Mercier leaves no doubt that dream is a better state than the state of consciousness: "Dormir, voilà donc notre félicité".[167] Dream functions as the necessary key which unlocks the doors leading to Mercier's mysterious and often hallucinatory fictional worlds. Frequently he uses the technique of dream as an introduction to some fantastic condition beyond the present moment. For example, in the story *"Le rêve singulier"* he begins as follows: "Mes paupières venoient de se fermer, quand je crus apercevoir une figure gigantesque, dont l'aspect m'effraya."[168]

It is characteristic that the hero of Mercier's utopia is on the verge of falling asleep, and feels cheated when he is disturbed and forced to return to that chaos (the contemporary society) from which he imagined he had already liberated himself: "Tu m'ôtes un songe dont je préférois la douce illusion au jour importun de la vérité. Que mon erreur étoit délicieuse, et que ne puis-je y demeurer plongé le reste de ma vie!"[169]

As a "soft illusion" or "delicious error", as Mercier expresses it, dream functions as a means of escapism from ugly reality, as a detachment from physical and mental torture, as a voyage in space and time. This confirms Majewski's suggestion that for Mercier dream was "a positive means to arrive at superior knowledge about the universe". In Mercier's view "Man is but a prisoner to reason in this life and is only truly free when his dreams reveal the richness of the irrational world".[170]

The following excerpt from *Mon bonnet de nuit* tells quite a lot about the importance of dreams for Mercier: "Le sommeil est presqu'un rêve céleste".[171] It has been suggested that Mercier thus establishes a strong relation between truth and sleep, its vehicle, thus asserting that "conscious life does not always reveal truth, but that sleeping and dreaming do". In practise this meant that for Mercier the state of dream was a kind of secular equivalent for divine revelation, since he regarded dream as a moment in which he personally received instruction and enlightenment from God.[172]

There seems to exist a conjunction between Mercier's conception of dream and his vision of the night as the optimal time for the imagination to fly. It was expressly during the night that he preferred to create his "visions" or "meditations"; as Mercier himself put it: "La nuit est la bienfaitrice commune

· · · · · · · ·

167 Mercier, *L'An 2440 I* 1786, 4.
168 [Mercier], *Les entretiens du Palais-Royal* 1786b, 174. In addition to giving wings to the imagination, dream provided a convenient vehicle for discharging oneself from responsibility; when everything is said to have occurred merely in a dream, it was possible to imply that the creator of the dream vision did not even himself subscribe to all his wild ideas. This was, possibly, a deliberate effort on Mercier's part to avoid censure. If so, as noted above in the chapter devoted to his personal life, this strategy did not prove very effective.
169 Mercier, *L'An 2440 I* 1786, 7.
170 Majewski 1971, 49.
171 Mercier, *Mon bonnet de nuit I* 1784, 1.
172 Wiseman 1979, 1, 15.

de tout ce qui respire: c'est pendant son regne qu'il y a une plus grande somme de bonheur répandue sur la terre..."[173] He was fascinated by such works as Young's *Night Thoughts* or Milton's *Paradise Lost*. In his *Le Bonheur des gens de lettres* Mercier suggests that the Milton ought to be read during the night, which is the most favorable time for the imagination to work.[174] As night falls, Mercier is carried away in his imagination to Milton's poetic universe, begging the English poet to lead him to the paradise of Eden, where he could see the "majestic beauty of Adam". He asserts his readers that when one lets oneself be guided by the imagination, "l'infortune fuit, les rayons de l'espérance dorent la perspective du bonheur".[175]

It is noteworthy that it was, above all, the more "obscure" side of existence from which Mercier drew his supreme inspiration. In addition to dreams and night as their nurturing ground, he also felt a special inclination toward death, the brother of sleep.[176] Moreover, Mercier's interest in esoteric thinking such as Freemasonic rituals and the occult mysticism of Swedenborg also explains his interest in dreams. As Majewski suggests, for Mercier dream provided the means to re-establish lost contact with the spiritual world, and dream was for him a spiritual voyage, often guided by a specter or a spirit.[177] Alternatively, the guide can be also a real person, as is the case in *L'An 2440*.

Helen Patterson refers to the same point when she speaks about Mercier's illuminist theory according to which dreams are our "true reality". She argues that Mercier was the first man of letters who exploited *illuminisme* in literature and who popularized the ideas of the *illuminés* in his works.[178] Moreover, both Rousseau's *Rêveries*[179] and Dante's *Inferno* and the related ancient tradition of dreams may have served as Mercier's additional sources of inspiration.[180]

Despite the fact that the history of literature provides innumerable examples of dream pictures, dreams are not an easy object to study from a historical viewpoint. Yet there is no use in assuming a pejorative attitude toward the language of dreams, loaded with secret messages. As mirror images of man's unconscious fears or desires, dreams have a power to reflect the mentality of a historical period in a very comprehensive manner. As Peter Burke suggests, "repressed wishes, anxieties and conflicts are likely to find expression in the

· · · · · · · · ·

173 Mercier, *Mon bonnet de nuit I* 1784, 6. The great importance that Mercier accorded to night as the source of creative inspiration also shows in the fact that when he describes in his *L'An 2440* the rites of initiation to the mysteries of the universe, this secret act is described as taking place, expressly, during the night. For him night was the optimal time to enlarge one's consciousness and to build a contact between man and the universe. For more detail on this theme of initiation, see Chapter IV, pp. 88–89.
174 Gillet 1975, 399–402.
175 Mercier, *Le Bonheur des gens de lettres* 1766, 37–38, 46, 48–49.
176 See Chapter X, pp. 287–293.
177 Majewski 1971, 49.
178 Patterson 1960, 41. The vogue of illuminism, which fascinated educated minds in pre-Revolutionary Paris, can be defined as an occult source of romanticism, which entailed a return to the utopian aspirations of the Middle Ages. See for example Ruyer 1988, 210.
179 Wiseman 1979, 11.
180 Krauss 1970, 394, 398.

latent content of dreams, and may help historians reconstruct the history of repression".[181]

For the purposes of a utopian author like Mercier, one could scarcely imagine a more appropriate intellectual vehicle than the vision of dream. The only adequate way to approach the utopian dreams as created by Mercier is to treat them as reflections of irretrievable conflicts. They tell of anxieties and frustrations, secret wishes and hopes prevailing in a period of transition. This reflects the common truth that the level of interest in dreams rises, specifically, most often in periods of crisis. When social and political unrest intensifies, the popularity of dreams, mystical and illuminist under-currents correspondingly increases. It has been suggested that in the second half of the eighteenth century, a growing sense of restlessness, frustration and melancholy was also directly reflected in French literature; the sentiments of malaise and escapism now entered in the scene.[182]

As a "non-rational" means to create order in the seeming chaos of the world, dreams seemed, however, to fit only uneasily to the dominant eighteenth-century spirit characterized by the demand of rationalism. Despite the fact that the "plots" of Mercier's dream visions are often complex and bizarre, not even he was capable of detaching himself from the rational tendency of his age. Philippe Berthier draws attention to the fact that the dreams imagined by Mercier are too "rational" and "controlled" to serve as valuable guides to the labyrinth of the unconscious world of their inventor. In his view Mercier's dreams contain too many literary reminiscences, in particular those drawn from Milton, Dante and the Apocalypse. Mercier never forgets his moralizing and didactic purposes; what is at issue is always a "philosophical" lesson.[183]

In Mercier's utopian vision of the twenty-fifth century the supreme importance of dream lies in the fact that it provides a framework for the voyage in time. It is a bridge which connects the imaginary with the real, thus constituting an easy way to pass from present misery to the happiness of the future. Pierre Versins remarks that dream is, in general, an important theme in *conjecture*. It is a "literary" tool, a framework which makes it possible to access the unbelievable.[184]

In view of this fact, it is important to note that compared with the dream visions in Mercier´s *Songes et visions philosophiques*, in the context of *L´An 2440* the theme of a dream takes on a different, emphatically secular, role. As Paul Alkon has also pointed out, there is no prophetic element involved, which means that in Mercier´s utopia of the future, dream is not represented as a mystic experience. What is at issue is not a religious revelation, but a perfectly naturalistic explanation of hopes projected into the future. Mercier further enhances the naturalistic character of his dream by letting the hero of his novel

. . . .
181 Burke 1997, 29.
182 Bousquet 1964, 67.
183 Berthier 1977, 304–308. Cf. Wiseman 1979, 15–16.
184 Versins 1972, 749.

at times comment that he may have forgotten some details of his promenade around the ideal Paris, since one so easily forgets something when one is trying to remember dreams afterwards. In Alkon´s view, such losses could scarcely be possible if a supernatural prophetic vision had served as a framework for Mercier´s utopian vision.[185]

The hero of the "Rip-van-Winkle-like account"[186] of *L'An 2440* is argued to have been the first true time-traveler in literature.[187] Mercier may thus have invented the device of the sleeper or dreamer as a means of time travel, which in later utopias – e.g. those written by Bellamy, Morris and Wells – became conventional. It is to be assumed, however, that this technique was already well established long before Mercier invented it. For example Kumar is convinced that a late eighteenth-century readership would not have been impressed by this "clumsy literary contrivance".[188]

The theme of time travel is also related to that of longevity.[189] This is due to the fact that dream, as a realizer of the most miraculous fantasies, also has the capacity to enlarge the scope of man's personal characteristics. In *L'An 2440* this can be seen in the profound transformation of the protagonist's physical appearance during his dream of almost seven hundred years. After falling asleep the narrator becomes aware that his hands and legs are trembling. A look into the mirror reveals that his face is full of wrinkles, the hair has turned white, the whole figure is pale. When walking he has to lean on a cane.[190] Edward Bellamy (1850–1898) applies a similar pattern in his novel *Looking Backward 2000–1887* (1887), where the hero, Julian West, falls into a state of hypnosis, from which he awakens in the year 2000 in Boston, which has undergone a total transformation.[191]

. . . .

185 Alkon 1987, 123.

186 Patterson 1960, 41.

187 Clarke 1979, 26. See also Polak 1961, 294.

188 Kumar 1987, 39. The Dream Vision is only one of the techniques which have made possible the passing from reality to an ideal condition. In more recent experiments, for example in *The Time Machine* of H.G. Wells (1866–1946), the hero travels first into the future, then into the past, with technology. Before Wells, Restif de la Bretonne had sent his main character in his novel *Les posthumes* (1802) into the future. Versins 1972, 867. In modern science fiction, experiments with time have assumed more and more fantastic forms. On these techniques, see Versins 1972, 867–870.

189 Versins 1972, 867.

190 Mercier, *L'An 2440 I* 1786, 19–20.

191 In comparing the dream structure of Mercier's *L'An 2440* with Edward Bellamy's novel *Looking Backward 2000–1887*, Raymond Ruyer traces a certain difference between these two: whereas Mercier's time traveller gets older during his long sleep, Bellamy's hero preserves his youth in the state of a dream. Ruyer 1988, 206. From this it can be inferred that Bellamy seems to have accorded a greater value to the aspects of eternal youth and immortality than Mercier. By emphasizing the emblems of advanced age in his time traveler, Mercier, for his part, shows his respect for the virtues of age. The significance of old age in *L'An 2440* will be dealt with in Chapter VI, pp. 175–176 of this study.

III The City of Purity

What is the meaning of the lived environment for man's happiness in Mercier's view? This is a relevant point of departure of the whole inquiry, taking into consideration that Mercier's ideal society of the future is not just any fictitious geographical place, but a concretely existing city of Paris. As a specific phenomenon, the city plays a crucial role in his all major writings, and the classical juxtaposition between city and countryside forms one of the leading themes both in *L'An 2440* and *Tableau de Paris*. The luxury and vice prevailing in the huge metropols also inspired Mercier to create fantasies of their destruction as a consequence of some devastating catastrophe.[1]

Mercier was acutely aware that there are better possibilities of realizing happiness in a beautiful than an ugly environment. In *L'An 2440* the capital of France has miraculously changed into a city of light, greenery, purity and hygiene. As the time traveller of the novel walks in the Parisian quarters of his youth, he is pleased to observe that the city has undergone a total transformation. Positive changes have taken place everywhere; the streets are broad and beautiful, dominated by perfect order. Noise no longer disturbs the ears, and fast-driving carriages do not threaten the safety of the passengers. The general impression of the city is very pleasing indeed: "La ville avoit un air animé, mais sans trouble et sans confusion."[2]

Mercier's utopian Paris of the future fulfills all the basic criteria of an ideal urban environment as it has been represented through the centuries. Rosenau suggests that the feature uniting all images of ideal cities is the idea of betterment, either on earth or beyond the grave. To quote her definition, "the ideal city represents a religious vision, or a secular view, in which social consciousness of the needs of the population is allied with a harmonious conception of artistic unity."[3]

Mercier's ideal city of the year 2440 forms a glaring counterpoint to eighteenth-century Paris, which he compares with a voluptuous Babylon.[4] An analogous division between the city as a representation of either Heaven or Hell has been characteristic of Christian thought, and a bifocal vision of the city as corruption or as perfection has long been maintained in Western culture.[5] For example, to St. Augustine (354–430) this conflict between two Cities, the one ruled by egoism and self-love, the other by love of God and man, was the motive

. . . .

1   For a closer view, See Chapter IX, pp. 253–265.
2   Mercier, *L'An 2440 I* 1786, 21.
3   Rosenau 1983, 2. See also Vercelloni 1996, 3.
4   See for example Mercier, *Tableau de Paris I* 1994, 24.
5   Pike 1981, 7–8. As indicated above, the earthly and celestial images of Jerusalem were much alive particularly during the Middle Ages. Lapouge 1978, 65, 70; Rosenau 1983, 26.

power of history.[6] Basically, in the background to all later ideal cities, although called by diverse names, such as City of the Sun, "Thelema", or "Hygeia", there can be traced the image of the New Jerusalem and the associated concept of the millenium.[7]

The image of the City of God did not fade even in the Age of Reason, and it has been suggested that the "Heavenly City of the Eighteenth-century philosophers" has many features in common with the New Jerusalem.[8] In a view reminiscent of St. Augustine, the philosophers of that epoch were convinced that man was subjected to the laws of Babylon, bearing, however, in his heart nostalgia for the City of God. This image sees the two cities as separated by a profound gulf.[9] It is expressly this eternal cleavage between two cities, the struggle between good and evil, Abel and Cain, on which the dramatic tension of Mercier's utopian vision is based. The beautiful city of the twenty-fifth century, reminiscent of the "City of God", forms a glaring counterpoint to eighteenth-century Paris, the city ruled by the "laws of Babylon".

Mercier uses often harsh images in order to underline the moral and physical corruption of eighteenth-century French society. He writes for example as follows: "Le génie de mon siècle me presse et m'environne; la stupeur règne; le calme de ma patrie ressemble à celui des tombeaux".[10] He sees his contemporaries as monstrous creatures with no breath of life: "Autour de moi, que de cadavres colorés qui parlent, qui marchent, et chez qui le principe actif de la vie n'a jamais poussé le moindre rejetton!"[11]

In Mercier's utopia, the ultimate metaphor of collapse and decay is a painting of a vile prostitute in the imaginary art gallery of the year 2440, symbolizing France on the eve of the Revolution. This obscene figure, decorated by diamonds and pearls, is the emblem of double morals, wickedness and selfishness:

> "Elle avoit a chaque main deux longs rubans couleur de rose, qui sembloient un ornement; mais ces rubans cachoient deux chaînes de fer auxquelles elle étoit fortement attachée."[12]

Her luxurious dress is torn and soiled by filth, and behind the prostitute hungry children are devouring a piece of black bread. There are castles and marble palaces in the background, but the half-cultivated contryside is full of miserable

. . . .
6   Nisbet 1970, 69. For more detail, see for example Lapouge 1978, 64–73.
7   Girouard 1989, 348.
8   Tuveson 1972, xii and passim. This phrase refers to the title of Carl Becker's classical study *The Heavenly City of the Eighteenth-century philosophers* (1932), the leading theme of which is to argue that far from being onesidedly cold rationalists, eighteenth-century Enlightenment thinkers were greatly indebted to the Christian framework and the code of values set by it. Becker 1965. This question will be returned to in the later chapters of this study.
9   Servier 1991, 220.
10 Mercier, *L'An 2440 I* 1786, xij.
11 Ibid.
12 Mercier, *L'An 2440 II* 1786, 71–72.

and starving peasants.[13] Simon Schama argues that this image conveys "an impression of enduring hopelessness, a world that needed to be blown up if it was ever to be substantially changed. Institutionally torpid, economically immobile, culturally atrophied and socially stratified, this "old regime" was incapable of self-modernization."[14]

It is undoubtedly no pure coincidence that Mercier uses a female figure to represent the incarnation of vice. In the light of his misogynic view of women[15] this causes little suprise. Mercier's image of a vile prostitute is reminiscent of the biblical "harlot of Babylon"; in the Revelation to John, the vast, luxurious, and voracious city of Babylon is described by feminine attributes as "arrayed in purple and scarlet, and bedecked with gold and jewels and pearls".[16]

It is clear that for Mercier eighteenth-century Paris could not provide a worthy place for man's dignity. Many of his writings convey a strong impression of the overwhelming presence of death in his contemporary society. Images of the dead haunted his imagination, and this is one of the themes to which he incessantly returns.[17] Mercier conceived of human life as a great book of death, and he saw man as a destructive creature.[18] In *Tableau de Paris* the metaphor of omnipresent death rises as the symbol of the whole city. Mercier characterizes Paris as a great corpse, and creates fantastic images of its gigantic skeleton.[19] This obsessional attitude toward death in many of its diverse forms seems to mirror the way in which eighteenth-century people were still forced to live a precarious life under the oppressive shadow of sudden and unexpected death, which could lurk behind any corner. Accidents, public executions, violent men and savage animals made life hazardous throughout.[20]

Putrid odours and inadequate hygiene were part of the everyday reality in pre-Revolutionary Paris. Death circulated in the atmosphere with the odours of corpses and decaying carcasses, and the remains of the dead, buried in the churches, tortured the senses. Indignation was also expressed about the presence of slaughterhouses inside the city. Moreover, the cesspools aroused anxiety, and the accumulation of excrement challenged the city's very existence.[21] The post-1760 period, in particular, witnessed aroused concern

. . . .

13   Mercier, *L'An 2440 II* 1786, 72–73.
14   Schama 1989, 184.
15   A more detailed treatment of this theme is provided in Chapter V, pp. 140–151, passim.
16   *The Holy Bible*, Revelation to John 17:4.
17   Majewski 1971, 123–124.
18   Favre 1978, 402. The significance of death in Mercier's *Tableau de Paris* has aroused interest amongst some historians of death; for example in Robert Favre's paramount contribution *La mort dans la littérature et la pensée francaises au siècle des lumières* (1978) and in John McManners' *Death and the Enlightenment. Changing attitudes to death among Christian and unbelievers in eighteenth-century France* (1981) Mercier's name is mentioned quite often. A comprehensive study of the theme of death in Mercier's work is, however, still lacking; so far, only sporadic allusions have been made. A brief overview on the mutual relation of happiness and death in Mercier's utopian visions will be provided in the final chapter of this study.
19   Citron 1961, 119.
20   McManners 1981, 14, 59–88, passim.
21   Corbin 1986, 27–34.

with problems of health and hygiene, which can be seen for example in the fact that after 1777 it became forbidden to bury the dead within the cities.[22]

All of these features aroused Mercier's anger, too. In the chapters of *Tableau de Paris* the narrow and obscure Parisian streets function as stages of violence and blood, there are funeral processions incessantly rolling through the city, and the smell of rotting corpses fills the churches.[23] Moreover, Mercier also complains about the poor construction of the sewers in eighteenth-century Paris, as a result of which they could easily overflow into the neighbouring wells and cause food-poisoning. What is even more incredible, protests Mercier, is the habit of anatomy students to steal corpses, cut them to peaces and throw the remains into the ditch. He also refers to the insupportable smell of the remains of skinned horses.[24] All in all, the general lack of hygiene seemed to make all advances in the betterment of living conditions impossible:

> "Des rues étroites et mal percées, des maisons trop hautes et qui interrompent la libre circulation de l'air, des boucheries, des poissonneries, des égouts, des chimètieres, font que l'atmosphère se corrompt, se charge de particules impures, et que cet air renfermé devient pesant et d'une influence maligne."[25]

The omnipresence of death, sickness and general misery haunted eighteenth-century Parisian society also in the form of unhygienic hospitals, which seemed to promote sickness instead of curing it. A turn for the better began in 1774, however, when six new hospitals were built in Paris.[26] In Mercier's dream, a similar kind of reform has been executed: the widely feared hospital of *l'Hôtel Dieu* has been divided into fifty separate hospitals, and "ce dépôt effroyable et commun, ce rendez-vous de toutes les maladies" has been transferred to the countryside.[27]

In Mercier's mind the concepts of moral corruption and of physical degeneration were closely intertwined.[28] For example in the article *"Boucheries"* in *Tableau de Paris*, he paints a scene of a butchering of a bull, with the blood flowing down the street and soiling the shoes of passers-by. The target of criticism here is the custom, mentioned above, of locating slaughterhouses in the middle of the city.[29] In Mercier's city of 2440, by contrast, the slaughterhouses are transferred out of the cities: "...nous nous

. . . .

22   Rudé 1985, 16. See also Ariès 1994, 69–70.
23   See for example Mercier, *Tableau de Paris I* 1994a, 115.
24   Mercier, *Tableau de Paris I* 1994a, 116–121.
25   Ibid., 114.
26   McManners 1981, 33, 54.
27   Mercier, *L'An 2440 III* 1786, 104–106, especially 105.
28   In Majewski's opinion Mercier heralds the nineteenth-century novel, for example Balzac, through his talent for discerning the constant inter-relationships between physical and moral phenomena, milieu and personality: "Mercier was aware of the need to situate man with more precision than in the past in the complexities of his concrete social and political milieu. He understood that he cannot know himself and his society without knowing in depth the political and social structure which has formed him." Majewski 1971, 118.
29   Mercier, *Tableau de Paris I* 1994a, 112.

épargnons le spectacle du trépas."[30] The urban environment is "purified" in the same way in More's *Utopia*, also, where the slaughterhouses are situated outside the city walls.[31] It has been argued that this feature unites the whole tradition of ideal cities: it is important that the city be purified both in the spiritual and in the physical meaning of the term. For similar hygienic reasons, hospitals are often located outside the city walls. A city which aims to be pure, rejects all wickedness which could infect it and threaten its happiness and beauty.[32]

In Mercier's eyes eighteenth-century Paris was not only a city of corruption and death, it was also a place of glaring contrasts. For him the continual conflicts between the poor and the rich formed an inexhaustible source of moral indignation, constituting the foundation of his social critique. It is characteristic that before falling into his sleep of 672 years, the time traveller of *L'An 2440* speaks with his "old English friend", who is complaining of this contradictory nature of Paris, describing it as a mixture of greatness and deprivation: "Votre capital est un composé incroyable. Ce monstre difforme est le réceptacle de l'extrême opulence et de l'excessive misère: leur lutte est éternelle."[33]

As we have already seen, from Mercier's ideal city of the twenty-fifth century, all cacophonous elements whatsoever have been eliminated. Paris in 2440 constitutes a critical contrast to the inadequate hygiene, crowding, and conflicting voices characterizing the capital of France in the second part of the eighteenth century. The atmosphere of general confusion, chaos and darkness has given place to symmetry, perfect harmony and organized supervision of the public space. As evidence of this, every street corner has a guard, who controls the public order and the passage of traffic.[34] The streets are fully lit by day and night, and no longer occupied by prostitutes alluring passers-by into debauchery.[35]

Baczko suggests that the light in which Mercier's future Paris is bathed, also has a symbolic dimension: the city no longer has anything to hide, either physically or morally.[36] Mercier's imaginary ideal urban environment is a representation of a totally transparent and open society, where all frontiers between public and private life have been obliterated. There exists no space for secrets or privacy. The contrasted pair of light and darkness thus function as significant metaphors in Mercier's different descriptions of Paris; darkness, symbolizing the great city as "hell", and light, symbolizing its "heavenly" nature, are also symbols of corruption and happiness respectively.

All in all, the concept of transparency is essential for the proper under-standing of Mercier's utopian vision of the future. The demand for total

. . . .

30   Mercier, *L'An 2440 I* 1786, 214–215.
31   More, *Utopia* 1964, 77–78.
32   Baczko 1978, 301.
33   Mercier, *L'An 2440 I* 1786, 8.
34   Mercier, *L'An 2440 I* 1786, 31.
35   Mercier, *L'An 2440 I* 1786, 295–296.
36   Baczko 1978, 321.

transparency is underscored in *L'An 2440* by many different symbols; for example, in 2440 the temple has a glass roof.[37] Mercier also uses many expressions which refer to looking and seeing. He relates, for example that the children of the future are trained in the spirit of universal ideology to regard the universe as a single family, " which is gathered under the eye of the common father".[38] On another occasion he emphasizes the overwhelming transparency of his ideal society as follows: "Notre oeil ne s'arrête point à la surface."[39]

The dream of visual control over the lived environment is essential also in *Tableau de Paris*, where at times Mercier applies a depth perspective. He prefers to look over his home town from high places, such as the bell tower of Notre Dame.[40] In one of his essays, *"Oiseau"*, Mercier explains his desire to be a bird because of the wide scope of a bird's vision: "Que j'aimerois à planer sur les villes & sur leurs clochers."[41] The great significance that Mercier accords in his various writings to the power of looking and seeing exemplifies the interpretation suggested by Vercelloni that the problem of total visual control lies at the core of the philosophy of the Enlightenment.[42]

In addition to light, a second symbol of purity and transparency in *L'An 2440* is water. In Mercier's vision, every street corner has a fountain which rinses the pavement.[43] Moreover, airiness and spaciousness are represented as essential factors contributing to the comfort of the lived environment. As a contrast to the narrow and dark Parisian apartments of his own day, Mercier created in his imagination fantasies about elegant buildings, with terraces on a roof: "de sorte que les toîts, tous d'une égale hauteur, formoient ensemble comme un vaste jardin: et la ville, apercue du haut d'une tour, étoit couronnée de fleurs, de fruits et de verdure."[44]

With its fountains and terraces, Mercier's future Paris revives the archetypal image of the garden of Eden. As Jean Delumeau has pointed out, both the biblical and the Greco-Roman traditions posit a strong quasi-cultural link between happiness and gardens. The features best typifying this paradisal tradition have been the myth of a favoured era when the generosity of nature is symbolized by water, a springtime climate, the absence of suffering, and peace between humans and animals.[45]

The impression of total transparency and openness prevailing in Mercier's ideal city is furthered also by the fact that the city is dominated by numerous public places, monuments and statues, the function of which is to give moral lessons. For example, one of these statues represents humanity, in front of which the other statues – described as female figures – kneel in order to repent

. . . .

37   Mercier, *L'An 2440 I* 1786, 151.
38   Mercier, *L'An 2440 I* 1786, 300.
39   Mercier, *L'An 2440 I* 1786, 37.
40   Mercier, *Tableau de Paris I* 1994a, 34–36.
41   Mercier, *Mon bonnet de nuit I* 1784, 29–30.
42   Vercelloni 1996, 116.
43   Mercier, *L'An 2440 I* 1786, 52.
44   Mercier, *L'An 2440 I* 1786, 53.
45   Delumeau 1992, 15.

of their sins committed against humanity.[46] It is by this means that the entire public space of Mercier's urban paradise, – the squares, monuments, temples and statues –, is constructed as a forum for an educational programme, the principal aim of which is to teach how one should live one's life in conformity with the demands of virtue. All those public monuments form a "book about morality", and the entire space is "speaking",[47] as Baczko puts it. Darnton draws a similar conclusion when he remarks that the metaphor of "open book" is one of the key concepts in Mercier. He notes that in *L'An 2440* reading and writing sustain all civic life, which is organized around notions of the book (the soul as a book, the city as a book, the book of nature): "Seeing, unmasking, penetrating surfaces has become the primary duty of the citizens".[48]

This means that Mercier's version of the "*Città Felice*" is nothing but a "screen" onto which an ideal of "happy rationality" is projected. Every promenade is a virtual lesson about moral and civil virtues. To a certain extent everything is simultaneously reality and symbol.[49] Because of its symbolic dimensions, Mercier's ideal city also has extensions as a universal, global model. Even if the object of description is a specific city, the city image simultaneously expands as a vision of urban space which is not confined to a specific time or space. The streets and squares which the time traveller of *L'An 2440* becomes acquainted with are not localized, but are situated in an abstract space.[50] In this sense, Mercier's utopian Paris is not so much a representation of the capital of France but of a universal, archetypal image of "the City". As such it is an embodiment of an invisible idea of a perfect urban environment, the memory of which each and every man bears in his heart as the memory of the "Heavenly Jerusalem" or the paradise on earth.

As an image of a universal vision of an ideal urban environment, Mercier's future Paris is reminiscent of the Christian "pansophic utopias" of the seventeenth century and their attempt to encompass the whole world.[51] The prefix "pan" suggests an association with the principle of the "panopticon", which Foucault has traced to the evolution of disciplinary power in the course of recent centuries, and the construction of "observatories", telescopes and other means to use power through observation, which permitted detailed control over individuals.[52] In the same way, the entire society of Mercier's imaginary year 2440 constitutes a sort of "panopticon", a world dominated by total surveillance and discipline through the power of looking and seeing.

Mercier's future Paris, this city of total transparency, liberated from physical and moral corruption, breathes the same rationalistic spirit as the whole of eighteenth-century philosophy. It is a representation of a society dominated by

. . . .

46 Mercier, *L'An 2440 I* 1786, 189–190. This is yet another proof of Mercier's misogynist atti-
    tude. It is probably no mere coincidence, that the sinners, begging for mercy, are women.
47 Baczko 1978, 323.
48 Darnton 1997, 135–136.
49 Baczko 1978, 299–300.
50 Ibid., 323.
51 See Chapter II, p. 48.
52 Foucault 1975, 173–176 and 197–229, passim.

the power of the "totalizing gaze", and as such it embodies the basic ideals of the project of modernity, which according to David Harvey was based on the Baconian dream concerning the rational ordering of space and of time as one element of the overall domination over nature.[53] Owing to the fact that the same tendency toward extreme rationalization has been characteristic for the entire tradition of utopian thinking, ideal societies have most often been situated in an urban environment. Northrop Frye suggests that in contrast with Arcadia, which emphasizes the integration of man with his physical environment, a utopia is a city for the reason that its aim is to express man's mastership over nature.[54] Ruyer draws a parallel conclusion when he argues that utopias are essentially urban because the city is a manifestation of the domination of man. In his view the special emphasis put in utopias on the triumph of symmetry symbolizes the inorganic, non-living nature of utopias. As he sees it, utopias are "anti-naturalist" by nature, because they prefer symmetry and uniformity.[55]

Mercier's utopia scarcely challenge the correctness of these arguments; as *L'An 2440* clearly demonstrates, the basic utopian ideal is rational control over the environment by man himself. Frye and Ruyer overemphasize, however, the rational content of utopias. As it will be pointed out in the subsequent chapters of this study, the ideas of the integration and mutual co-existence between man and the rest of created beings (the attribute that Frye restricts to Arcadia) also occupy a prominent place in many utopias, in particular in those centred around the figure of the "noble savage".[56] This leads to the logical conclusion that Ruyer's assumption about the "anti-naturalist" nature of utopias is untenable. It would be more accurate to note that in the context of the modern utopian literature the tendency is not to annihilate the "natural" elements from the lived environment, but rather to subordinate them to serve the purposes of systematic rational organization, based on the harmonious co-existence of agrarian and urban way of life. Utopia thus does not aim at the negation of rurality at the expense of urban forms of life, but at the disenchantment of arcadian nature.[57] *L'An 2440* amply exemplifies this disenchantment, with its desire to integrate bucolic elements in an urban setting: the fountains, terraces of the roof, the stress on co-existence between men and the rest of created beings, all point in this direction.

Although eighteenth-century Paris was not equal in size with London, which was approximately twice as large, the population of the city experienced considerable growth throughout the century. Many country-people, attracted by the many temptations offered by a big city, decided to settle there, and also a more positive developmental curve as regards mortality now took place; the

. . . .

53   Harvey 1990, 249.
54   Frye 1966, 41.
55   Ruyer 1988, 43, 45. See also Eaton 2000, 119–131, especially 119.
56   See Chapter VI, pp. 181–187.
57   Holstun 1987, 32, 70, 73.

growth of births in ratio to deaths led to a veritable demographic explosion.[58] The second half of the eighteenth century was also a period characterized by the execution of many large-scale building projects. This furthered even more the spatial expansion of Paris, which evolved into a melting pot and a monstrous city devouring the agrarian supplies of the other parts of the kingdom. The proximity of the countryside offered a contrast both to the social misery and to the luxury characterizing the living conditions of the big city.[59]

The enormous size of Paris was also one of Mercier's major concerns. He writes, for example, that by examining the individuals of different nationalities swarming in this immense capital, one can study the entire human species.[60] Despite the fact that in *L'An 2440* demographic expansion has been transformed into a purely positive phenomenon, since by 2440 the population of France has increased by half since the eighteenth century,[61] in *Tableau de Paris* the capital of France in the final years of the *ancien régime* is proclaimed as "un chef démesuré pour le corps de l'Etat" and a "*gouffre*", into which the human species disappears.[62] A metropolis whose limits have expanded to monstrous proportions, invokes the image of a brute devouring its innocent victims, a sort of Moloch.

Mercier's labeling of Paris as a "*gouffre*" was obviously inspired by Rousseau's *Émile*, where the same term is used as a symbol of urban corruption:

> "Les villes sont le gouffre de l'espèce humaine. Au bout de quelques générations les races périssent où dégénèrent; il faut les renouveler, et c'est toujours la campagne qui fournit à ce renouvellement."[63]

Mercier also pays attention to the anonymity of the inhabitants of big cities as a consequence of the dissolution of social networks: "Nous sommes, pour ainsi dire, condamnés dans cette ville immense à nous voir sans nous connoître..."[64] This description of the urban landscape as a place of isolation, where the individual is excluded from community, became common in the course of the following century.[65] By the romantic epoch it had become customary to describe hell as a subterranean world or a city.[66] The "infernal" character of big cities is vividly recalled when Mercier observes Paris from the tower of Notre-Dame; Paris appears to be dressed in a veil of "eternal smoke",[67] and this smoke floating on the metropolis reminds him of the eternal fire of Hell, announcing at the same time the melancholy darkness and pollution of industrialized cities. As Majewski so accurately puts it, "Hell" is no longer beyond the grave, it is here

. . . .

58   Rudé 1974, 35–38.
59   Roche 1987, 9–35, passim.
60   Mercier, *Tableau de Paris I* 1994a, 23.
61   Mercier, *L'An 2440 I* 1786, 31, 61.
62   Mercier, *Tableau de Paris I* 1994a, 32.
63   Rousseau, *Émile ou de l'éducation* 1904, 32.
64   Mercier, *Tableau de Paris I* 1994a, 237.
65   Pike 1981, xii.
66   Bousquet 1964, 202, 257.
67   Mercier, *Tableau de Paris I* 1994a, 34.

and now, in decadence, corruption, misery and suicide. The traditional image of hell is replaced by the "malheur" of the modern city, "a new symbol of man's misery".[68]

All this testifies to the fact that the extensive growth of London and Paris turned the city into an anti-utopia. In *Tableau de Paris* the capital of France on the edge of the great Revolution often seems to be such an "anti-utopia", a nightmarish jungle of people surrounded by vice and crime: a pressing, apocalyptic atmosphere hangs over this urban "hell".

One of the consequences of the unforeseen demographic and spatial growth of Paris in late eighteenth-century France was to engender many proposals concerning the need to "embellish" the city.[69] Ideal images usually emerge most powerfully in periods of social change, and in that epoch the optimistic vision of a perfect environment was realized in various designs. For example Voltaire refers to the need to reorganize Paris in his essay *"Les embellisements de Paris"* published as early as 1749, and the subject of urban planning is also dealt with in Morelly's treatise *Code de la nature* (1755).[70] Cities thus became an object of debate, and it was quite natural that Paris occupied in these debates the first place. The success of such works as Mercier's *Tableau de Paris* was a manifestation of the growing interest in the city as a social space in that epoch.[71]

The novel approach to city planning which emerged in the course of the eighteenth century was characterized by a shift of emphasis from religious to social considerations. J.-F. Sobry's *De l'architecture* (1776) was the first work which took into consideration the needs of the members of the socially lower strata such as the inhabitants of lodging houses, the need for large staircases and windows, high ceilings and good drainage.[72] Social compassion, so typical for the eighteenth-century's utilitarian philosophy,[73] was thus harnessed to serve the purposes of practical urban planning, progress and general well-being.

The reorganization of the urban space was also one of Mercier's major concerns, i.e., the public good and the well-being of the members of all social classes instead of individual luxury.[74] In the preface to *Tableau de Paris*, Mercier expresses this clearly:

> "J'ai fait des recherches dans toutes les classes de citoyens, et n'ai pas dédaigné les objets les plus éloignés de l'orgueilleuse opulence, afin de mieux établir par ces oppositions la *physionomie morale* de cette gigantesque capitale".[75]

L'An 2440 throbs with this same egalitarian spirit. Mercier predicts that when public celebrations are organized in the city of the future, they will be directed

. . . .

68   Majewski 1971, 132.
69   Delon 1990, IV–VII. See also Bruneteau & Cottret 1982, 39–43.
70   Rosenau 1983, 2–3, 91–92.
71   Baczko 1978, 308.
72   Rosenau 1983, 92–93.
73   For a more fully treatment of this theme, See Chapter V, pp. 124–131.
74   Bruneteau & Cottret 1982, 45.
75   Mercier, *Tableau de Paris I* 1994a, 13–14.

above all to the people.[76] The public squares are always situated in front of some important edifice (palace of justice, theatres, temples). This is evidence of the power of the people, creating an impression that all these edifices belong to it and that it is the master of those political and civic institutions.[77]

Mercier's attitude demonstrates the changed idea promoted by the philosophers of the Enlightenment concerning man and his relation to the authorities as representatives of public power. Harvey traces back to the Age of Renaissance a continuous line of development related to the reorganization of space and time, based on new premises in the sense that the aim of organization was gradually shifting from reflecting the glory of God to celebrating the liberation of man himself.[78] This more egalitarian view on the re-organization of the urban space reached its final breakthrough in the French Revolution; in the pre-Revolutionary period, the function of the public space was exclusively to promote the power of the monarchy and aristocracy.[79]

In his article devoted to Mercier's role as the precursor of modern urban planning, Anthony Vidler suggests that among the men of letters and architects of his century Mercier was the one who created the most coherent picture of the "Heavenly City of the Enlightenment". In Vidler's view, in *L'An 2440* Mercier produces a complete synthesis of the various different projects which had been elaborated during the thirty years preceding the Revolution. As such Mercier's utopia forms a part of a long tradition of projects devoted to the renovation and rationalization of urban space, and there can be traced similarities in particular between Mercier's utopian urban space and the architect Pierre Patte's project concerning the ideal street (1765).[80] Mercier's ideas are also, on the other hand, linked with urban reconstruction in the nineteenth century, and one can find echoes of them even in Le Corbusier's projects for Paris after 1918.[81]

In particular, in the chapter "*Le Nouveau Paris*" in *L'An 2440*, Mercier deals with questions relating to the need for reorganization of urban space and architectural reform. In this chapter he refers to many reform projects actually represented in his epoch. He dreams that in 2440 the construction of the Louvre will have been completed, and all Parisians will have free access to it.[82]

. . . .

76   Mercier, *L'An 2440* I 1786, 48.
77   Ouellet & Vachon 1973, 84. Mercier advances this theme of the "city of man" in *Tableau de Paris*. He develops the idea of an ideal urban environment by dreaming how beautiful Paris would be, if Louis XIV, instead of having built Versailles for himself, had built Paris for the people. In that case Paris could be called as "*la Ville des hommes*". The pavements would be as large as in London, and the city would have only one big temple. Mercier, *Tableau de Paris II*, 1994a, 775–780.
78   Harvey 1990, 249.
79   Outram 1989, 4.
80   The work of Pierre Patte signifies an important phase in the evolution of eighteenth-century urbanism. He argued for the enlargement of the streets and facilitation of traffic. He identified the essential goals as being to protect pedestrians from accidents, to increase the number of fountains, and to improve the sanitation. Baczko 1978, 312–316. As mentioned above, all these reforms have been implemented.
81   Vidler 1995, 223–243, passim. See also Baczko 1978, 320.
82   In this respect Mercier's wish seems to anticipate the events of the near future. As mentioned, up to 1792 Louvre had been a royal palace, serving at the same time as a gallery. Several ministers, from Colbert to Angiviller, had hoped to make it into a national library or a museum,

Between it and the castle of Les Tuilleries there is an immense square, where public ceremonies take place. The old houses have been demolished from the bridges,[83] and the Bastille has been replaced by the "temple of clemency".[84]

Compared for example with the models of ideal cities from the Renaissance period, characterized by a striving for an unchanging ideal and formal perfection,[85] L'An 2440 offers a much more practical and dynamic image of an ideal city. Contrary to the previous utopian models, Mercier's future Paris is no more a mere platonic, universal idea, a pure abstract, but a practical prognosis waiting to be realized. In this crucial sense it differs considerably for example from the mythical ideal city of Eldorado, the description of which is contained in Voltaire's *Candide* (1759). In Voltaire's fantasy-city the public edifices are described as reaching to the clouds, the market places are decorated with a thousand colonnades and fountains of pure water and sugar cane juice continually flow in the vast squares.[86]

It is easy to note how much the image of an ideal city as it is promoted in models like Voltaire's "Eldorado" is indebted to the "Heavenly Jerusalem" described in the Revelation to John, which is told as being built of pure gold, and the foundations of its walls embellished with beautiful stones.[87] In contrast to this, in Mercier's ideal urban environment all signs of exterior luxury and adornment have been rigorously excluded; the streets are not made of gold, and the fountains do not flow with wine or other precious liqueurs, but pure, refreshing water. The basic values are now utility and practicality. Mercier's Paris is planned as a glorification of the dignity of the common man – not that of the king or the rich and the powerful.

Mercier's ideal city is also more concrete than Voltaire's Eldorado or many other prior utopian cities owing to the fact that it is not cut off from the rest of the world. Voltaire, for example, emphasizes the hermetic isolation of his Eldorado; this ancient kingdom of the Incas is surrounded by high mountains, which explains how the land has succeeded in conserving its innocence and felicity.[88] The predication of isolation as a necessary condition of happiness is also emphasized, for example, in Fénelon's novel *Les aventures de Télémaque*, which comprises a description of the wonderland of Bétique. Bétique has

· · · · · · · · ·

but the dream was never realized during the old regime. The seizure of the Tuileries, the in-carceration of the royal family, the abolition of the monarchy, and the nationalization of royal property settled the question. The Louvre was now opened as a public, national mu-seum under the Republic on the anniversary of the overthrow of the monarchy, 10 August 1793. See for example Kennedy 1989, 220–221.

83 Mercier, *L'An 2440 I* 1786, 43, 45.
84 Mercier, *L'An 2440 I* 1786, 49–50.
85 Pfeifer 1979, 180.
86 Voltaire, *Oeuvres completes de Voltaire*, t. quarante-quatricme, 1787, 283.
87 *The Holy Bible*, Revelation to John 21:18–19. It is noteworthy, however, that in the "Heavenly Jerusalem", gold does not function as a symbol of ostentation or vanity. Instead, it emphasizes the supernatural glory of the celestial city in the same way as Mercier's utopian Paris bathes in bright, transparent light and purity.
88 Voltaire, *Oeuvres completes de Voltaire* 1787, 280, 284.

preserved its inviolability, because nature – the sea on one side and high mountains on the other – separates it from other peoples.[89]

It is appropriate to end this chapter with the conclusion that in the urban landscape of Mercier's future Paris, the mythical image of the "Heavenly Jerusalem" and the concrete problems related to modern urban planning are fused together in a coherent whole. The representation of an ideal city as imagined by Mercier is at the same time an attempt to reanimate the memory of the archetypal and immutable image of an ideal city, as a model closely reflecting the contemporary realities of its time. For its part, Mercier's vision of an ideal city helps one to better understand the captive hold of the image of the "Heavenly Jerusalem" on the human imagination throughout the centuries, and, consequently, its far-reaching impact upon practical projects of urban reform.

. . . .

89   Fénelon, *Les aventures de Télémaque* [1864], 194.

IV The Spiritual Side of Happiness

The Cult of the Heart

Despite the fact that *L'An 2440* discloses a vision of a secular future, Mercier´s ideal Paris is a representation of a society dominated by a deep-rooted religious spirit. Belief in an omnipresent God forms one of the most important cornerstones on Mercier's utopian society. In *L'An 2440* God is elevated as the "eternal source of happiness"[1], and there is no love without religion. As Mercier's utopians conceive it, atheism is the worst evil in the world: "Le coeur qui n'aima point fut le premier athée."[2]

As this quotation reveals, it would be totally misleading to assume that eighteenth-century people had no religious sentiments. Quite the contrary; despite the existence of vehement materialists like d'Holbach, La Mettrie or Helvétius, atheism confronted energetic opposition.[3] The spiritual life of the eighteenth century was not characterized by rejection of faith, but by a new ideal of faith and religion, and it was renewal which was now demanded from religion itself. A flow of accusations was directed against the Catholic church, its dogmas and prejudices, which in the eyes of the philosophers seemed to constitute the most severe obstacle for the possibility of happiness.[4]

In eighteenth-century intellectual discourse, the demand for man's right to search and find the optimal condition of life already this side of the grave was thus closely intertwined with attacks against traditional Christianity. The philosophical conviction that it was man's own task to control his destiny for the sole purpose of a better life on earth seemed to be incompatible with the Christian pretension to direct thoughts away from this life into a mythical and possibly non-existent paradise. Moreover, in concentrating all thoughts on the idea of personal salvation, Christianity was accused of turning the mind away from the love of other men.[5] Many of the eighteenth-century French philosophers shared the conviction that Christianity was a "historical disaster", and around 1750–1760 the conflict between faith and reason had matured to the point of divorce.[6]

. . . .

1   Mercier, *L'An 2440 I* 1786, 158.
2   Ibid., 94.
3   Rudé 1985, 134–135; Trousson 1993, 249–257, especially 249. Even the materialists and atheists believed, rather cynically, perhaps, that the common people was in need of religion – if for no other reason, at least so that the fear of Hell would keep the *"canaille"* under discipline. Ehrard 1994, 400.
4   Cassirer 1966, 193–195; Gagliardo 1968, 15.
5   Crocker 1969, 3; Mauzi 1994, 180–181, 204, 206.
6   Woloch 1982, 233; Trousson 1993, 216. See also Mauzi & Menant 1977, 50–51.

The need for the reformation of religious practises formed also one of Mercier's major concerns. Despite his deeply religious mind, he emerges as a typical representative of his century in the sense that traditional Christianity as such with its rigorous doctrines could not provide for him a satisfying solution. As one scholar has noted, *L'An 2440* is pervaded by anti-clerical elements, and Mercier's attacks against Christianity increase even further in later editions of the novel.[7] But could there be any genuine possibility to solve the problem posed by the apparent contradiction between man's desire to find happiness already on earth and his spiritual vocation? Could any reconciliation be reached between those two orientations?

In the chapter "*Le Temple*" of *L'An 2440* the time traveller takes part in the religious worship, which provides Mercier a good opportunity to criticize the dogmas of traditional Christianity. In his scenario, by the middle of the third millennium the understanding of religion has undergone a radical change. In Mercier's imaginary Paris of the future, religious worship forms a part of men's everyday activities, but it is purified from all exterior decoration. The atmosphere in the temple is described as extremely solemn, and the heavens are described as proclaiming the unity and goodness of the Creator. In the profound silence prevailing in the temple, the time traveller is occupied by a feeling of "sacred terror"; it is as if the divinity had descended into the temple and filled it with its invisible presence. There are no intermediaries between man and God. It is the immediate contact that counts, for "c'est l'ame qui sent Dieu". All that man needs is "une morale pure, et point de dogmes extravagans".[8]

In the same way as the spokesmen of the Protestant Reformation like Luther and Calvin, who had insisted on a return to the "pure piety and pure practise of primitive Christianity",[9] Mercier too dreamed of a return to the origins: "Notre Religion est celle d'Enoch, d'Elie, d'Adam. C'est bien là du moins la plus ancienne. Il en est de la Religion comme de la Loi; la plus simple est la meilleure."[10]

The religious practises followed in Mercier's ideal city directly mirror the rise of new spiritual doctrines, in particular Deism, in the course of the eighteenth century. Deism, which had been gradually developed in seventeenth and early eighteenth century England, advocated that there should be no dogmas, bibles, or miracles. God ought to be adored as the Creator of the world, which was believed to be governed by universal and immutable laws. The adherents of Deism believed that after having created the world, God had withdrawn from it and left it entirely self-sufficient like a great clock.[11] As a rigorously intellectual system, Deism condemned mysteries and secrets, in order to bring religion into the "clear light of knowledge".[12]

. . . .

7   Bowman 1975, 430–431.
8   Mercier, *L'An 2440 I* 1786, 151–153, 160.
9   Gay 1968, 18.
10   Mercier, *L'An 2440 I* 1786, 159.
11   Coates, White & Schapiro 1966, 253; Gay 1968, 14; Gagliardo 1968, 11; Trousson 1993, 201.
12   Cassirer 1966, 235.

From the background of this idea of nature as a law-bound system can be traced the accomplishments of the scientific revolution of the two previous centuries, which had introduced a new vision of reality as a kind of "machine".[13] In the formation of the non-organic and rational worldview, the philosophy of Descartes and his placing the central areas of human knowledge on "clear, distinct, and certain" foundations, was of immeasurable importance. He held that God had created nature and its laws, sustaining them by recreating the world from moment to moment. Owing to God's eternal and immutable intellect, the laws of nature were unchanging and intelligible to human understanding.[14] Seen from this standpoint, nature was no longer conceived as an occult force, inaccessible to human reason.[15]

This was a typical attitude amongst the French eighteenth-century philosophers. For them Nature constituted "an orderly, stable mechanism, run by universal, automatic, and immutable laws that operated smoothly, infallibly, and benevolently".[16] The definition given for the concept of "nature" in the *Encyclopédie* provides a good example of this argumentation: "l'ordre & le cours naturel des choses, la suite des causes secondes, ou les loix du mouvement que Dieu a établies."[17]

In his utopia, Mercier faithfully echoes the common intellectual habit of his age when he argues that in order to find happiness the only thing man needs to do is to follow the laws of nature, through which God manifests Himself. It is the "law of nature" that constitutes the principle of uniformity as the supreme norm of conduct:

> "La loi divine qui parle d'un bout du monde à l'autre, est bien préférable à ces réligions factises, inventées par des prêtres... "La loi naturelle est une tour inébranlable; elle n'apporte point la discorde, mais la paix et l'égalité."[18]

Mercier writes, also that the "natural law", so "simple and pure", is not surrounded by "shadows or mysteries".[19] This statement mirrors the general conception that "the eighteenth-century philosophers tried to demonstrate that the kernel of all the great religions of the world could be reduced to a few simple

. . . .

13 Merchant 1983, 193.
14 Descartes, *Discours de la méthode...* 1898, 64, 69; Merchant 1983, 194–195, 203; Toulmin 1990, 9, 13–14, 34, 72. As such, the identification of order in the apparent chaos of nature contained nothing unforeseen. It is most often associated with the formulation given it by Thomas Aquinas in the thirteenth century. As its derivatives, later theories of natural law have led to long-lasting disputes about the status of Protestant natural law (mainly embodied in the person of Hugo Grotius, "the father of modern natural law") vis-à-vis Thomism. See for example Becker 1962, 37–38; Haakonssen 1996, 15 and passim. For further reading, see also Finnis 1980; Saastamoinen 1995. The concept of "natural law" forms an integral concept in Mercier´s utopian vision, which will be returned to in subsequent chapters of this study.
15 Ehrard 1994, 63.
16 Coates, White & Schapiro 1966, 191–192.
17 *Encyclopédie XXII* 1780, 228.
18 Mercier, *L'An 2440 I* 1786, 186–187.
19 Mercier, *L'An 2440 I*, 1786, 187.

ethical principles, which could just as well have been derived from the laws of Nature, and without the useless and expensive ceremonies, rituals, dogmas, and priesthoods that had made organized religion burdensome to mankind".[20]

For Descartes, "reason" had meant an unchangeable intellectual tool which could be conceived as absolutely identical in all human beings,[21] and in eighteenth-century philosophical discourse this static conception of Cartesian reason became fused with the idea of a universal and static human nature, which was adequate in all places and at all times.[22] Deism preached universal morality, according to which "God had engraved on everyone's heart a moral code; everyone knew instinctively good from evil."[23] Amongst the eighteenth-century philosophers David Hume (1711–1776) was one of the few who considered the whole idea of a "human nature" as a mere fiction.[24]

The skepticism of Hume was alien to Mercier; he was a typical representative of his age, in the sense that he was firmly convinced that there existed an identical human nature and a common yardstick of righteous morals to be followed by all men in all epochs and cultures. He believed that the "law of nature" automatically told to man what is right and what is wrong, and for this reason the possibility to find happiness already on earth was a relatively uncomplicated matter: "La loi naturelle... est gravée dans tous les coeurs en caractère ineffacables..."[25]

In other words, it was the "law of nature" as the manifestation of God's will, which planted in each and every man a natural instinct toward happiness. In this respect no differences could be discerned between different cultures or peoples, because the voice of God spoke equally to all men: "O amour de Créateur! qui a imprimé dans le coeur de l'homme la nécessité d'être heureux; par là, tout marche sous ta main invisible..."[26]

What was at issue in this new religious attitude was the attempt to create a new kind of synthesis between reason and religion, i.e., between religion and the advances made in science and philosophy. The adherents of deism believed that Nature was an equal with the Bible as a source of revelation in revealing God's grandeur. Locke's pamphlet, The *Reasonableness of Christianity* (1695), was a cornerstone of this new outlook.[27]

Similarly, by emphasizing the overwhelming presence of God in the religious worship of his utopians, Mercier embraces the idea that the whole of nature

. . . .

20 Gagliardo 1968, 15.
21 Descartes, *Discours de la méthode 1898*, 47. See also for example Elias 1993, 62.
22 Hampson 1981, 109.
23 Coates, White, Schapiro 1966, 253; Hampson 1981, 104.
24 Becker 1965, 55; Cassirer 1966, 243. Cassirer believes that eighteenth-century thinkers had too much confidence in the power of reason to share Hume's scepticism in relation to natural religion. This explains why Hume's ideas remained isolated in that epoch. Cassirer 1966, 246–247.
25 Mercier, *L'An 2440 I 1786*, 187.
26 Mercier, *L'Homme sauvage 1767*, 64–65.
27 Woloch 1982, 233–234.

constitutes a kind of bible, filled with the handprint of God.[28] Among Mercier's writings the primitivist utopia *L'Homme sauvage* is most deeply penetrated by the idea that nature can be read as a book which proclaims the greatness and goodness of God. Following the fashionable Deist credo of his age, he describes God as the "first and eternal cause", pointing to the order and harmony of the universe as proof of God's existence. Everything in nature is a manifestation of divinity: "...tout me donnoit une preuve invincible de sa haute sagesse..."[29]

Again in *L'An 2440* Mercier reiterates his admiration for the religious life of the savage peoples:

> "Un sauvage errant dans les bois, contemplant le ciel et la nature, sentant, pour ainsi dire, le seul maître qu'il reconnoît, est plus près de la véritable religion qu'un chartreux enfoncé dans sa loge et vivant avec les fantômes d'une imagination échauffée."[30]

By emphasizing the purely spiritual nature of religious life as it is practiced among the utopians living in Paris in 2440 or among the Indians, Mercier seems to imitate the model set by Rousseau, to whom, it has been suggested, belongs the merit of having given affective content to natural religion in eighteenth-century France.[31] In Mercier's imaginary year 2440, religious worship has many features in common with that of the *"profession du foi du Vicaire Savoyard"*[32] set out in Rousseau's *Émile* (1762), but with two exceptions: there are no mentions of Christ, and Mercier believes in *"métempsychose"*[33]. Rousseau refers to this new ideal of "natural" religiosity as follows:

> "Les plus grandes idées de la divinité nous viennent par la raison seule. Voyez le spectacle de la nature, écoutez la voix intérieure. Dieu n'a-t-il pas tout dit à nos yeux, à notre conscience, à notre jugement?"[34]

It is characteristic, also that whereas Mercier speaks about the "soul that feels God", Rousseau speaks about the "cult of the heart": "Le culte que Dieu demande est celui du coeur..."[35]

In eighteenth-century France the principal target for criticism was revealed religion,[36] and Mercier advances the same view in his utopia; he is not willing to accept religion based on a Revelation which is reserved solely for the few: "Nos prêtres ne se disent point exlusivement inspirés de Dieu: ils se nomment nos

. . . .

28 In point of fact, Mercier represented the Romantic image of nature as God's temple long before Chateaubriand or Lamartine. Majewski 1971, 41.
29 Mercier, *L'Homme sauvage* 1767, 122–123.
30 Mercier, *L'An 2440 I* 1786, 152.
31 See for example Chaunu 1982, 245.
32 Rousseau, *Émile ou de l'éducation* 1904, livre IV. See also Darnton 1997, 129; Collier 1990, 93.
33 Bowman 1975, 431–432. On metempsychosis, See Chapter V, pp. 94–95.
34 Rousseau, *Émile ou de l'éducation* 1904, 349.
35 Ibid., 349.
36 See for example Coates, White, Schapiro 1966, 195.

égaux..."[37] In 2440, every virtuous man can be a priest, and universe is his temple.[38]

The view that the relation between man and God should be private and intimate, without any intermediary links, was related to the idea that the only guiding principle in religious matters should be toleration.[39] This central Deist conception posited that dogmas and rites divide people, while natural religion unites them.[40] Similarly, in Mercier's utopia the idea of the purely spiritual nature of religion is intertwined with a demand for toleration: "Que chacun t'honore à sa manière et selon ce que son coeur lui dictera de plus tendre et de plus enflammé: nous ne donnerons point de bornes à son zèle."[41] Here he echoes such treatises as Locke's *Letter Concerning Toleration* (1689)[42] and Turgot's edict of toleration (1775), according to which man's religious belief should never be subjected to the control of political authorities.[43]

The "Universal Plan of Harmony"

With the rise of "natural religions", the traditional image of a revengeful and vindictive God began to change in a more positive direction. It was replaced by a new vision of His role as a kind of "super-Newton" or an "original law-maker", who had created a world-machine which functioned perfectly according to the laws of nature through which God had set the world in motion. God now became referred to by names such as the "Supreme Being", the "First Cause", or the "Architect of the Universe". This new concept of a beneficent Deity was thus compatible with the Enlightenment's optimistic belief in a harmonious natural order run by natural laws. The following two implications sustained this changed image of God: 1) God's creation is good, evil is the imperfection of man; 2) Man can, however, dominate the natural order by discovering its laws.[44]

For Mercier, too, the belief that the world was ruled by a "benevolent" God was axiomatic. It forms one of the underpinnings of his whole idea of happiness, and from Mercier's different writings can be drawn several examples to support this focal thesis. For example, in *L'An 2440* he writes as follows: "L'homme sensible sera ému du spectacle de la nature, et reconnoîtra sans peine un Dieu bienfaisant..."[45] In one of his "*songes*", Mercier characteristically calls God a "tender father", whose "supreme goodness" he adores in silence.[46] This

. . . .

37   Mercier, *L'An 2440 I* 1786, 159–160.
38   Mercier, *L'An 2440 I* 1786, 187.
39   Mornet 1933, 39–41; Cassirer 1966, 223–247, passim; Woloch 1982, 235.
40   Ehrard 1994, 451.
41   Mercier, *L'An 2440 I* 1786, 157.
42   See for example Gay 1968, 17.
43   Koselleck 1988, 149.
44   Polak 1971, 73, 103–104. See also Coates, White & Schapiro 1966, 254; Ehrard 1994, 401–402.
45   Mercier, *L'An 2440 I* 1786, 103.
46   Mercier, *Songes philosophiques* 1768, 14, 42.

seems to be borrowed directly from Rousseau's *Émile*, where it is stated that nothing is more manifest than the goodness of God: "...la bonté dans l'homme est l'amour de ses semblables, et la bonté de Dieu est l'amour de l'ordre ce qui existe, et lie chaque partie avec de tout."[47]

As these extracts clearly reveal, it became now a common practise to assume that the supreme concern of the providential God, who manifests His will through the "natural laws", is the happiness of man. In addition to Mercier, other creators of utopias were also eager to adopt the same view. For example, in Morelly's egalitarian utopia *Naufrage des isles flottantes, ou Basiliade du célèbre Pilpai* (1753) it is told that "l'Etre suprême s'irritât jamais contre les humains".[48]

In the minds of the eighteenth-century Deist philosophers, the idea of God's "benevolence" was related to a conception that the whole creation was animated by the same benevolence. All the pejorative, Hobbesian views of nature were now rejected. Instead of being a hostile and unpredictable force, Nature, governed by immutable and benevolent laws, was revealed to be man's "friend". In this belief, everything that was "natural" was considered good, and what was artificial was decadent. From this it was only one step to the assumption that because man himself formed an integral part of nature, also the old conception of his depravity should be rejected as unworthy of human dignity.[49]

As we have already seen, the rejection of the doctrine of original sin and the theme of fallen nature are evidence of a new faith in progress and terrestrial happiness.[50] It was expressly the idea of original sin that was the common target uniting the different tendencies of the philosophy of the Enlightenment.[51] For example, Voltaire vituperated against Pascal's view of man as a "fallen king", claiming that submission to organized religion was a betrayal of man's "true estate". This "rebellious pagan spirit", as Peter Gay puts it, signified a severe blow to the Christian concept of man.[52] In *L'Homme sauvage* Mercier vigorously propagates this new, more dignified view of humanity and man's original goodness, proclaiming that "*l'homme est né bon*".[53]

In the formation of this principle of benevolence or *bienfaisance*, the philosophy of Leibniz was of decisive importance. It was due to Leibniz that the word *optimiste* was added to the French language.[54] The extremely optimistic credo of Leibniz culminates in the words contained in his treatise *De l'origine radicale des choses* (1697): "Et je juge que dans l'univers il n"y a rien qui soit plus vrai que le bonheur, ni plus heureux et plus doux que la vérité".[55] His focal

. . . .
47 Rousseau, *Émile ou de l'éducation* 1904, 335.
48 [Morelly], *Naufrage des isles flottantes I* 1753, 9.
49 Cassirer 1966, 201; Coates, White & Schapiro 1966, 191–192.
50 Trousson 1993, 210.
51 Cassirer 1966, 201.
52 Gay 1970, 170–171.
53 Mercier, *L'Homme sauvage* 1767, 11.
54 See for example Hampson 1981, 79–81.
55 Leibniz, *Oeuvres I* 1972, 344.

philosophical theme was the idea that when God created the world, he chose the "best of possible worlds": "Il suit de la perfection suprême de Dieu, qu'en produisant l'univers il a choisi le meilleur plan possible..."[56]

The proposition of Leibniz that this is the "best of possible worlds" became a commonplace among eighteenth-century optimists. In his philosophical system, the dogma of "sufficient reason" was evidence for the fact that the world was constituted on the principle of logical necessity and for this reason it was the best that God could have created. According to this view the existent universe was "logically inevitable in its least detail", and it could never be equalled by any other alternative universe.[57]

According to Leibniz' optimistic rationalism, the benevolence of God and his laws assured the happiness of man in this life and hereafter. Because of the "perfect order" of the universe, everything was planned for the supreme happiness of man. In his *Principes de la nature et de la grâce fondés en raison* (1714) Leibniz clearly expresses this crucial idea:

> "Et outre le plaisir présent, rien ne saurait être plus utile pour l'avenir, car l'amour de Dieu remplit encore nos espérances, et nous mène dans le chemin du suprême bonheur, parce qu'en vertu du parfait ordre établi dans l'univers, tout est fait le mieux qu'il est possible, tant pour le bien général, qu'encore pour le plus grand bien particulier..."[58]

As regards the major themes of this study, Leibniz is an important philosopher in the sense that Mercier's utopian vision is profoundly influenced by the theory of "universal harmony" by Leibniz. Already a most superficial overview on Mercier's major writings reveal how much they are indebted to Leibniz, and for example in *Le Nouveau Paris* Mercier shows his respect toward this great philosophical ancestor by mentioning Leibniz' treatise *Théodicée* as "*le plus beau des livres*".[59]

L'An 2440 can in its entirety be approached as a fictional representation of the focal Leibnizian thesis that the supreme truth in the universe is happiness. Moreover, already in one of his allegorical moralities, characteristically entitled "*D'un Monde heureux*", Mercier explicitly advances the Leibnizian belief that "everything is well":

. . . .

56 Leibniz, *Principes de la Nature et de la Grâce/Monadologie* 1996, 229.
57 Lovejoy 1950, 166, 169, 181, 208.
58 Leibniz, *Principes de la Nature et de la Grâce/Monadologie* 1996, 233.
59 Mercier, *Le Nouveau Paris* 1994b, 873. In the same context Mercier expresses his repulsion for Voltaire's *Candide*, because it attacks the "consoling dogma of Providence". The philosophy of Leibniz has often been interpreted in a naive and simplified manner; Mauzi, for example, criticizes the practise, typical of Voltaire, of reducing the optimism of Leibniz to the famous phrase "*Tout est pour le mieux dans le meilleur des mondes possibles*". Mauzi 1994, 549–554, especially 549. Mercier, for his part, had no higher ambitions. As an ardent popularizer of philosophical and intelletual doctrines he was perfectly content, both in *L'An 2440* and in many of his moral allegories, expressly to revive the Leibniz' argument that "everything is for the best in the best of possible worlds", which has now become a common cliché. For the purposes of the present study the invocation of the main lines of the philosophy of Leibniz thus serves well enough.

"L'intelligence a découvert, a conduit, & soutient cette vaste harmonie; ses desseins sont fixes & immuables... "Il t'est utile de croire, & de croire que le tout est bien. Il t'est utile d'honorer ton Créateur, de mettre ta confiance en sa suprême bonté..."[60]

Mercier continues to develop similar ideas also in the allegory "*L'Optimisme*", which reflects in every detail the optimistic rationalism of Leibniz. In this pedagogical morality he regrets the fact that it is so often the good people who have to suffer. But there is no use for sorrow, because "Providence regulates everything".[61] It is not man's task to question the intentions of God, since everything is destined to advance his supreme happiness. The final sentence of "*L'Optimisme*" sums up in a nutshell the essence of the eighteenth century's optimistic credo that whatever happens, human life is maintained by "la vérité immuable, éternelle, qui ordonna le cours des événemens pour sa plus grande gloire, pour la plus grande félicité de l'homme".[62]

With his argument concerning the *perfectly sufficient universe* ("the best of all possible worlds"), created by omnipotent God, Leibniz adopted a position diametrically opposed to Newtonian physics. The main reason for the disagreement between Leibniz and Newton was their different view of God and His role in the universe. According to Newton the "watch" would stop if the watchmaker (God) did not refix it from time to time. The God of Newton was, thus, a free agent, whose periodic intervention was necessary if the "laws of nature" were to function at all. In comparison with this Newtonian God, the God of Leibniz seemed to be a simple watchmaker, who was the prisoner of his own laws.[63]

All of Mercier's major writings which are of any importance for the present study convey a strong impression that as regards the conflict between Newton and Leibniz, he was an ardent adherent of the latter. Following in the footsteps of Leibniz, Mercier believed in a cosmic determinism based on the omnipotence of God. For example in "*L'Optimisme*", he advances a firm conviction that there exists a pre-established and immutable order, which God has planned in His infinite wisdom and goodness, the rationality of which man must not question. Mercier did not believe that the divine plan was in need of God's subsequent interventions, once He had created it. Contrary to Newton and his adherents, he did not question the Leibnizian assumption that already in the beginning of the world God had known in a perfectly sufficient manner what was best for man. As Mercier expresses it in his allegory of a happy world: "Crois-tu que la suprême sagesse ait abandonné quelque chose au hasard? Crois-tu que son plan soit tracé d'une main chancelante & incertaine?"[64]

. . . .

60   Mercier, *Songes philosophiques* 1768, 204–205.
61   Mercier, *Songes philosophiques* 1768, 17. For a more detail on this theme "persecuted virtue", See Chapter VII, pp. 190–193.
62   Mercier, Songes philosophiques 1768, 44.
63   Hampson 1981, 78; Trousson 1993, 214; Ehrard 1994, 135, 146–150. See also Coates, White & Schapiro 1966, 222–225; Gay 1970, 140–145; Rifkin 1989, 202–203.
64   Mercier, *Songes philosophiques* 1768, 203.

As has been stated earlier in this study, Mercier's dislike of the system of Newton, the hero of his age, formed part of his so called "madness".[65] One should not forget his passionate attacks against Newton in *De l'impossibilité du système astronomique de Copernic et de Newton* (1806), where Mercier sets out to put forward reasons for the "impossibility" of Newtonian science. From the philosophical labyrinth of this bizarre treatise can be traced an idea that Mercier abominated Newton's system on the grounds that it reduced God's role and His will to purely arbitrary dimensions:

> "Un Dieu dont la puissance éclate si magnifiquement dans ses oeuvres miraculeuses, un Dieu dont la parole anima le soleil, serait-il réduit à mettre un peu plus ou un peu moins de poudre attractive dans ses ouvrages?"[66]

As this passage reveals, Mercier's hostility toward the system of Newton was grounded expressly on its cold materialism. He detested the way it reduced God's sole purpose to that of a simple watchmaker, whose principal role was to repair the machinery from time to time in order that the "machine" would continue in full motion. As Mercier conceived it, it was not the God of Leibniz, but on the contrary that of Newton, who was the powerless victim of the laws which He had Himself created; for Mercier, the Leibnizian presumption that God had already in creating the world known without the slightest doubt what was best for man, was a sufficient proof of His infinite wisdom and perfection.[67]

Considering Mercier's highly personal and intimate conception of man's relation to God, it causes no great difficulty to understand why he found alien Newton's idea concerning God's mechanical intervention in the physical world. As Darnton also suggests, in a sense Mercier's profound spirituality went beyond Deism: Instead of winding up the universe and letting it run according to Newton's laws, the God of Mercier's utopians "sees into the blackest souls and intervenes to maintain the moral order".[68] This is a typically Leibnizian way of conceiving things; disagreeing with Newton, Leibniz claimed that "God acts at the present time, not through mechanical interventions in nature, but by acts of grace directed toward individual human beings."[69]

. . . .

65 See Chapter II, p. 44.

66 Mercier, *De l'impossibilité du système astronomique de Copernic et de Newton* 1806, 142–143.

67 Mercier's admiration for the system of Leibniz can be traced clearly for example from the following statement: "Les loix du mouvement, dit Leibnitz, qui ne sont pas d'une nécessité absolument géométrique, mais qui sont un effet du choix & de la sagesse de Dieu, ces belles loix sont une preuve merveilleuse d'un Etre intelligent & libre, contre le système de la nécessité absolue et brute de Straton & de Spinosa." Mercier, *Mon bonnet de nuit I* 1784, 260–261.

68 Darnton 1997, 129. See also Majewski 1971, 41.

69 Toulmin 1990, 113.

The "Two Infinities"

The eighteenth century was a great time of scientific discovery, and science seemed to promise an intellectual tool to resolve the old mysteries. Amongst the educated elites there existed a widespread belief that man could analyze and master the "divine plan" through his reason. Bacon, Newton and Locke were the heroes of the philosophers, whose logic was based on the argument that "when science advances, superstition retreats".[70] New tools of experimental science like telescope and microscope increased their confidence even further.[71]

The chapter of *L'An 2440* entitled *"Communion des deux Infinis"* provides ample evidence of the fact that Mercier was anxious to share the profound interest of his contemporaries in the accomplishments of the scientific revolution of the seventeenth and eighteenth centuries. In this chapter, one of the most important of the entire work, Mercier describes the rites of initiation into the secrets of the universe. The time traveller hears from his guide that at a certain age, when they have reached sufficient maturity, the young men of Paris in 2440, – women are not mentioned – , are taken to the observatory for one silent night. In the silence of the observatory the "abyss of infinity" is exposed to their eyes through the lens of the telescope.[72] After the telescope, another, even more amazing, universe is revealed for Mercier's young men, through the microscope, which helps them better understand the relativity of spatial relations.[73]

The chapter "two infinities" gives a vivid example of Mercier's "insistence upon antithesis", as Helen Patterson puts it. She notes that "Mercier cherished quasi-mystical beliefs in the one-ness of the universe, and held that awareness of contrast is the first secret of art because it reflects the great antithesis inherent in nature". Patterson proposes that originally this telescope-and-microscope approach to the two infinities of firmament was represented in the *"Deux infinis"* of Pascal's *Pensées*. The pantheistic conception of the *communion* of these two infinities, and of divine strands linking up within the great whole of Creation phenomena of the utmost diversity and apparent divergence (moral as well as physical) would seem, however, to be peculiar to Mercier and later to Victor Hugo.[74]

In Mercier's 2440 utopia, great emphasis is put on the view that the main function of the telescope is, above all, to reveal the immensity of the works of the Creator. The suggestion is that everything in nature and in the universe is filled with the handprint of God:

. . . .

70   See for example Gay 1970, 126–166, passim. See also Coates, White & Schapiro 1966, 234. For more details, see Hankins 1985.
71   Hampson 1981, 73; Chaunu 1982, 202.
72   Mercier, *L'An 2440 I* 1786, 172–173.
73   Mercier, *L'An 2440 I* 1786, 175.
74   Patterson 1960, 101, 260–261.

"Jeune homme! voilà le Dieu de l'univers qui se révèle à vous au milieu de ses ouvrages. Adorez le Dieu de ces mondes, ce Dieu dont le pouvoir étendu surpasse et la portée de la vue de l'homme, et celle même de son imagination. Adorez ce Créateur, dont la majesté resplendissante est imprimée sur le front des astres qui obéissent à ses loix."[75]

As Mercier's words clearly reveal, for him there could never be any doubt about the fact that the "laws of nature" were always subordinated under the "law of God". Far from constituting an autonomous force, for him the laws of nature always derived and emanated from the divinely ordained system.

In the utopian society imagined by Mercier the main purpose of scientific discoveries is to widen the scope of human understanding concerning God's intentions as regards man's future destiny, i.e. to help man in his process of spiritual perfectibility. The suggestion is that through technological improvements man's senses would receive a new extension.[76] Mercier expresses the hope that gradually in the course of time man's knowledge would be completed: "il y a tant de merveilles accumulées qui dormoient dans son sein, maintenant exposées au grand jour; la nature enfin est si éclairée dans ses moindres parties..."[77]

Mercier was, undoubtedly, firmly convinced that experimental science could open the gates of a new terrestrial paradise by comparatively simple means; everything rests in the bosom of Nature, and man has only to search for it. As Mercier wished it to be, in the future the progress of science would lead to the elimination of all life's hazardous elements.[78] The underlying idea is that by eliminating the totally unpredictable elements from human life, the telescope has the power to liberate man from the old mysteries and ignorance, and to bring all secret corners of the universe under the bright light of reason: "Le télescope est le canon moral qui a battu en ruine toutes les superstitions, tous les fantômes qui tourmentoient la race humaine."[79]

In statements like these, Mercier promotes an attitude typical of many of his contemporary philosophers and encyclopedists, who, it has been suggested, saw themselves as scientists, worshipping God only because of the perfection of nature and its laws which were being revealed by their discoveries.[80] This testifies to the fact that the scientific revolution of the seventeenth century marked no break with the Christian view of the world.[81]

This self-confidence was greatly indebted to Francis Bacon (1561–1626), who had put forward the idea that science is a tool of mastery over nature. In his treatises *Advancement of Learning* and *Nova Atlantis* this ancestor of a modern, materialist understanding of progress advances the idea that men were justified

. . . .

75   Mercier, *L'An 2440 I* 1786, 173–174.
76   Manuels 1982, 516.
77   Mercier, *L'An 2440 I* 1786, 181–182.
78   Mercier, *L'An 2440 II* 1786, 35–37.
79   Mercier, *L'An 2440 I* 1786, 173.
80   Pollard 1971, 42.
81   Gay 1970, 140; Chaunu 1982, 18; Trousson 1993, 213–214.

in extending their command over Nature as a way of achieving comfort and happiness. Nature was now transformed from a teacher to a slave.[82] In eighteenth-century France in particular the *encyclopedists* followed in Bacon's tracks.[83] They saw in Bacon's method of scientific experimentalism an ideal to aspire to, which did not contradict with their basically religious view of the world.[84]

Mercier's according of a prominent place to scientific inventions was also founded on a Baconian ideal concerning the formula "knowledge is power". For his utopian men it is self-evident that man occupies a privileged position amongst created beings, and that he was the master of the whole of creation. Although man was a "fallen king", his original and basic goodness made it perfectly justified that he should regain his lost dignity:

> "Nous ne marchons qu'au flambeau de l'expérience. Notre but est de connoître les mouvemens secrets des choses, et d'étendre la domination de l'homme, en lui donnant le moyen d'exécuter tous les travaux qui peuvent aggrandir son être."[85]

Accordingly, in Mercier's scheme the increase of knowledge means emancipation from ignorance and the fears caused by it. And, because fear is an antithesis of happiness, the telescope has the power to increase the sum of human happiness. By revealing the immensity of the universe, the telescope constitutes a magic bridge between man and the whole cosmos. In consequence, Mercier's young man of 2440 feels animated by an unprecedented joy of living:

> "Je sens que mon être s'est aggrandi depuis que Dieu a daigné établir une rélation entre mon néant & sa grandeur. Oh! que je me trouve heureux d'avoir recu l'intelligence & la vie! J'entrevois quel sera le destin de l'homme vertueux!"[86]

In this context Mercier makes a distinction between the pleasures *"qu'il doit à l'esprit"* ("spiritual pleasures") and *"plaisirs matériels"* ("material pleasures"). He clearly wishes to point out that in the hierarchy of pleasures, spiritual ones are of much higher value than those which man receives from the senses alone:

> "Pourquoi la puissance du Créateur ne pourroit-elle pas prolonger, fortifier cet heureux état? L'extase qui remplit l'ame du juste méditant

. . . .

82 Toulmin & Goodfield 1965, 109; Tod & Wheeler 1978, 53–56; Cohen 1985, 147. For more details, see for example Merchant 1983, 164–190.
83 Dubos 1961, 35, 37; Tod & Wheeler 1978, 56.
84 This rests on the idea that the function of science is above all to foster knowledge of God, a position not alien to Bacon; the scientific order, or society, called "Salomon's House" described in *Nova Atlantis*, is "dedicated to the works and creatures of God" –, and it is sometimes also called, revealingly, the "College of the Six Days' Works". Bacon, *The Advancement of Learning and the New Atlantis* 1906, 255.
85 Mercier, *L'An 2440 II* 1786, 39–40. See also Mercier, *Mon bonnet de nuit III* 1786a, 22: "N'avons-nous pas la faculté d'apprendre à connoître la nature, à voir dans ses productions merveilleuses les traits de l'infinie perfection?"
86 Mercier, *L'An 2440 I* 1786, 178.

sur le grands objets, n'est-elle pas un avant-goût du plaisir qui l'attend lorsqu'il contemplera sans voile le vaste plan de l'univers?"[87]

The exquisite joy, or the "ecstasy which fills the soul" as Mercier calls it, is based on the profound inner sentiment that the immensity of the universe which is exposed to man's eyes, through the lenses of the telescope, contributes to the enlargement of his scope of understanding. This joy, born from purely intellectual passion, reminds one of the philosophy of Benedictus de Spinoza (1632–1677), who describes how "the Mind can undergo great changes, and pass now to a greater, now to a lesser perfection. These passions... explain... the affects of Joy and Sadness". By Joy, Spinoza understands the *"passion by which the Mind passes to a greater perfection"*, and by Sadness, the *"passion by which it passes to a lesser perfection"*.[88]

In facing the immensity of spatial relations, Mercier's young men in 2440 are animated by the same cosmic emotion which Bernard Le Bouvier de Fontenelle had described earlier in his *Entretiens sur la pluralité des mondes habités* (1686). In this treatise, focused on the dialogue between a marchioness and a "man of the world", the latter is explaining the Copernican revolution in the natural sciences and the significance of observation. He is describing the enlargement of the limits of the universe, and how he feels liberated from the oppressing chains of the static conception of the world, as follows:

> "Quand ce Ciel n'étoit que cette voûte bleue où les Étoiles étoient clouées, l'Univers me paroissoit petit et étroit; je m'y sentois comme oppressé. Présentement qu'on a donné profondeur à cette coûte,en la partageant en mille et mille Tourbillons, il me semble que je respire avec plus de liberté, et que je suis dans un plus grand Air, et assurément l'Univers a toute une autre magnificence."[89]

Entretiens sur la pluralité des mondes habités was the most important writing in the early eighteenth century which promoted a new view of the world based on the Copernican theory of the solar system. Fontenelle believed that there existed a plurality of worlds and also other inhabited planets than Earth.[90] Paul Hazard sees the enlargement of man's spatial horizons described in Fontenelle's treatise as a kind of initiation; the marchioness of the story enters into the communion of the faithful instead of belonging to a group of pagans or heretics.[91]

The idea of initiation is also one of the key concepts in *L'An 2440*. In Mercier's utopian vision, the way the telescope changes man's ideas about the limits of the universe can be conceived as a form of initiation to a higher level of consciousness. François Labbé suggests that Mercier presents in his novel the theme of initiation in a manner closely reminiscent of descriptions of

. . . .

87   Mercier, *L'An 2440 I* 1786, 174–175.
88   Spinoza, *The Collected Works of Spinoza* 1985, 500–501.
89   Fontenelle, *Oeuvres complètes II* 1991, 98.
90   Lovejoy 1950, 130.
91   Hazard 1961, 103–106.

Freemason rituals. He pays special attention to this chapter devoted to the "two extremes", arguing that in the eighteenth century there were numberless Masonic writings where the initiation of new apprentices is described in a similar way. In Mercier's utopia, as in Masonic lodges, society is directed toward moral perfection (religion is identified with the practise of virtue) and initiation opens a path leading to wisdom.[92]

Mercier's enthusiasm for esoteric and irrational cults, such as Freemasonry and illuminism, also helps to explain why the Newtonian "clockwork" God was not good enough for him. Between 1778 and 1783 he was himself a member of a Freemason lodge called the "*loge des Neufs Soeurs*", which was the most influential of the eighteenth-century Masonic lodges in France, founded by the philosophes and encyclopedists in 1769.[93] Labbé presumes that when *L'An 2440* was published, Mercier already knew the ceremonies of the lodges and their philosophy, and for him the fact of having "seen the light" was much more than a fashionable concession.[94]

In his fascination with Freemasonry, Mercier joined ranks with many of his educated contemporaries. It has been asserted that Freemasonry played a very important role in eighteenth-century France. The Masons' popularity increased considerably in the course of the century: whereas in the 1730's there were only five or six lodges in France, by 1789 there were approximately seven hundred.[95] The advanced interest in Masonic rituals reflects a shift of emphasis in religious attitudes toward the end of the century. Various kinds of supernatural phenomena and pseudo-science, such as mesmerism, magnetism and hypnotism, now began to captivate the human imagination. Faith became visionary and prophetic.[96]

Many of Mercier's moral allegories are peopled by angels, vampires, phantoms and other irrational creatures, which reflects his pre-romantic imagination. He believed that the universe was animated by invisible forces, the existence of which could not be explained solely by cold reason. This is vividly expressed in the following statement from *Tableau de Paris*: "Nous sommes dans un monde inconnu."[97] These words exemplify Majewski's reading that for Mercier the universe had lost its rational stability, and there is room in his view for the mysterious, the irrational, the obscure. He found the systems of Newton and Locke so repulsive expressly for the reason that their oversimplification of the complexity of the existence eliminated its mystery and destroyed faith in God and immortality.[98]

. . . .

92   Labbé 1978, 43–44.
93   Servier 1969, 412; Labbé 1978, 42, 49.
94   Labbé 1978, 42.
95   Mornet 1969, 192–193; Bluche 1993, 116.
96   Didier 1976, 118–119. See also Bousquet 1964, 68; Darnton 1995; Delon, Mauzi & Menant 1998, 154–161.
97   Mercier, *Tableau de Paris II* 1994a, 1573. In the same context Mercier expresses his belief in the existence of angels, because it is easier to have confidence in one unique God, "seul moteur et conservateur de l'univers" (p. 1574).
98   Majewski 1971, 25, 61.

The irrational and "pre-logical" side of Mercier's thought is also shown in his repeated characterization of man in *L'An 2440* as "un abrégé de l'univers … lié à tout ce qui existe".[99] This idea of man as an "abridgment" of the universe describes a theory according to which man is a "microcosmos", an image of the universe in miniature. According to this view, everything in nature became a symbol, allegory. All things had a double meaning. It was thought that the "plan of nature" was the same, whether its object was man or the world. This idea of organic analogy between the human body, or microcosmos, and the larger world, or macrocosm, was much alive for example in the age of the Renaissance.[100] Foucault argues that resemblance, similitude and analogy played a constructive role in Western culture down to the end of the seventeenth century,[101] but the biological metaphor of the life-cycle has survived even longer, in one form or another.[102]

In this context it is interesting to note that the organic theme is essential in many thinkers whom Mercier named as his sources of inspiration or who had an undeniable influence on the formation of his utopian vision. To name individual examples, a metaphysical belief in a real connection between the universe and man can be found from philosophers such as Paracelsus, Giordano Bruno, Leibniz and Swedenborg.[103] Both in Swedenborg's mystical visions, and in the mind of many other late eighteenth-century thinkers who had been inspired by "illuminism", such as Restif de la Bretonne, Mesmer and Saint-Martin, one of their main ambitions was to reveal "the relations which exist between God, man and the universe". They hoped to find unity in the universe, and the principle of analogy offered them the possibility to establish a relation between visible and invisible, between man and the universe, microcosmos and macrocosmos.[104]

In his classic study *The Great Chain of Being* (1933), Arthur O. Lovejoy suggests that the common proposition of the eighteenth-century optimists that "this is the best of possible worlds" was closely related to the revival of the originally platonic and Aristotelian doctrine of the "Great Chain of Being". The theory of the Great Chain of Being was based on an idea that the universe was composed, following the principles of continuity, plenitude and gradation, of a limitless number of links ranging in hierarchical order from the humblest form of existence to the "Absolute Being". Along with the term "Nature", the "Great Chain of Being" was a fundamental concept of the eighteenth century.[105]

The "monadology" of Leibniz provides the most complete visualization of this theory of the Great Chain of Being in the philosophical system-building of the seventeenth century. For him the whole universe was constituted of vital, dynamic units, "monads", which formed a continuous and uninterrupted chain

. . . .

99   Mercier, *L'An 2440 II* 1786, 234.
100 Le Flamanc 1934, 59–60; Toulmin & Goodfied 1965, 66– 67; Merchant 1983, 5.
101 Foucault 1966, 32.
102 Nisbet 1970, 8, 10.
103 Frängsmyr 1981, 29. See also Delon, Mauzi & Menant 1998, 158.
104 Delon, Mauzi & Menant 1998, 157–158.
105 Lovejoy 1950, 59, 183–184.

from the minor creatures up to the most spiritual beings like angels and God. Based on the theory of analogy, the function of each single monad was to mirror the entire universe.[106]

When Mercier creates an analogy between man, the microcosmos, and the universe, macrocosmos, he gives a very high status to man's uniqueness: "Eh! quel animal, en fait de jouissances, a été plus favorisé que l'homme?"[107] As an "abridgment" of the universe, each and every human being is revealed to be a Leibnizian "monad", a universe in miniature; he is constructed of the same stuff as the stars are made of. By breathing new life to the ancient microcosmos-macrocosmos metaphor, Mercier implies that the whole universe constitutes an immense, living organism, shaped in the same way as one individual human body. By this means he embraces the Leibnizian notion of a vital and dynamic universe, rejecting at the same time the Newtonian mechanic metaphor of the universe as a machine.

As an ardent apostle of the "Cult of the Heart" Mercier never lost his belief in something "divine" in man's destiny. Already in his *Le Bonheur des gens de lettres* he writes that nature has given man a sensible soul, and that there exists an intimate relation between man and the universe.[108] It was expressly this belief, in the existence of an immortal and spiritual soul, which constituted one of Mercier's focal religious arguments. Opposing the materialists of his age, he followed the tradition of Descartes and Pascal in conceiving of man's grandeur as dependent upon the mind or spirit, completely distinct from matter[109]:

> "...il ne faut que rentrer en soi-même pour sentir qu'il y a quelque chose en nous qui vit, qui sent, qui pense, qui veut, qui se détermine. Nous pensons que notre ame est distincte de la matière, qu'elle est intelligente par sa nature."[110]

As the cited passage reveals, for Mercier the knowledge of some basic truths, for example the notion of God, was an idea engraved in the mind *a priori*. This reads as an antithesis to the philosophy of John Locke and its focal principle that man is born as a "blank sheet". In his *An Essay concerning Human Under-standing* (1690) Locke reduces the origin of all ideas to sensations, attacking the Cartesian doctrine that all men had innate ideas engraved in their minds already in the moment of birth.[111] He denied the possibility that there could exist any innate ideas, on the ground that discovering the truthfulness of moral Principles requires "Reasoning and Discourse". He did not conceive these as natural Characters engraved in the mind. Locke suggests, however, that nature

. . . .
106 Coates, White & Schapiro 1966, 224–225. According to Leibniz each monad is "*un miroir vivant*", "*représentatif de l'univers*". Leibniz, *Principes de la Nature et de la Grâce/ Monadologie* 1996, 224.
107 Mercier, *L'An 2440 II* 1786, 233.
108 Mercier, *Le Bonheur des gens de lettres* 1766, 36.
109 Majewski 1971, 42.
110 Mercier, *L'An 2440 I* 1786, 160–161.
111 Sagnac 1946, 82; Coates, White & Schapiro 1966, 179; Crocker 1969, 14; Hampson 1981, 75, 98.

had put into man a desire for happiness, and an aversion to misery, which were innate and universal principles "in all Persons and all Ages"; but they were merely "Inclinations of the Appetite to good, not Impressions of truth on the Understanding".[112]

As noted above, Mercier's image of man was not confined to these purely material dimensions; subscribing firmly to the Cartesian dictum concerning "innate ideas", for him man was much more than the sum of his sensorial experiences. Contrary to the suggestion of Locke, Mercier did not believe that the desire for happiness could be reduced merely to an instinctual drive. It has been explained that Mercier's thinking differed from that of Locke precisely in the sense that according to Mercier one had to think in order to sense, whereas according to Locke one had to sense before thinking.[113]

Mercier's assumption that man forms an integral part of a much larger totality than himself led him later to turn against Descartes as well. In *Le Nouveau Paris* he abandons the admiration which he had in his youth shown toward Descartes in his treatise *Éloge de Descartes*, now accusing Descartes of lack of respect toward nature. In his opinion Descartes had not sufficiently understood the fact that there exists a "*souffle de la divinité*" in man. Founding his criticism on the same argument, Mercier repeats his attacks against the sensualist theories of Locke and Condillac: "...ils n'ont point senti la liaison intime de l'homme à l'harmonie universelle..."[114]

Similar reasons led Mercier to condemn the materialist philosophy of Paul Henri Thierry D'Holbach (1723–1789), the author of what he considers one of the most dangerous treatises produced in the eighteenth century, *Système de la nature* (1770). He accuses it of destroying the order and harmony of nature, arranged by infinite Intelligence.[115] In contradiction to Mercier's highly spiritual idea of man, D'Holbach denied that man had any reason to believe that he is a privileged being in nature: "...il est sujet aux mêmes vicissitudes que toutes ses autres productions."[116] Nor did he believe that man has inborn ideas; man could have ideas only from exterior objects, and only through experience was man able to understand what is useful or a nuisance.[117]

The materialism of d'Holbach meant the final blow in the criticism directed against traditional religion and its gradual substitution by scientific rationality in the second half of the eighteenth century. d'Holbach was the most prominent figure in a circle of materialists who drew their inspiration from Epicurean philosophy, promoting a new idea of morals based on the leading position of passions. They conceived the world in a state of continuous, aimless and random flux, and according to d'Holbach "there was no divine purpose and no master-plan".[118]

. . . .

112 Locke, *An Essay concerning Human Understanding* 1979, 66–67.
113 Leterrier 1995, 310.
114 Mercier, *Le Nouveau Paris* 1994b, 858–877, passim.
115 Mercier, *Tableau de Paris I* 1994a, 1376–1382.
116 [d'Holbach], *Système de la nature I* 1771, 95.
117 Ibid., 168, 171.
118 Coates, White & Schapiro 1966, 234; Mauzi & Menant 1977, 56–57; Hampson 1981, 94.

With his belief in the "universal plan of harmony", Mercier already, to a certain extent, belonged to an obsolete world. In the course of the eighteenth century the "universal music of the spheres" had already began to lose its spell on the human imagination, and it has been suggested that the acceptance of the cosmology of Leibniz would have meant "a return to the demonology of the Middle Ages".[119] Even in the sixteenth century Francis Bacon had criticized the projection of order in things on the basis of resemblance, pointing out that similitudes are mere *idols*.[120]

The ancient metaphor of analogy started to break down when it was realized that the earth did not lie at the center of the universe, and that the sublunary world was not a mirror image of heavens above. At times, the vision of the immensity of the universe opened by the telescope, and, at the other extreme, the microscope, could lead to sentiments of life's meaningless and insecurity.[121]

As we have seen, in Mercier's case the recognition of the "infinite universe" did not lead to frustration or speculations on the precariousness of human existence in the middle of the great unknown.[122] On the contrary; instead of disturbing his focal belief in the harmonious relation between man and the universe, it rather consolidated it. As Mercier represents it in his vision of the future, only the awareness of the immensity of the universe can create a solid uniting bond between man, the microcosmos, and the macrocosmos, God's temple. And, if the infinity of the spatial dimensions should sometimes fill man's heart with despair, he could always find consolation through the lens of the microscope in order to remind himself that in the scale of being there were always creatures much lower than himself.

Mercier found consolation from the idea that the earth was not a lonely planet amidst a total emptiness, but formed a link in the well-ordered cosmic chain. His utopian Parisians turn out to be ardent admirers of Fontenelle, for amongst them the idea of the "plurality of inhabited worlds" constitutes an unquestioned dogma:

> "Nous pensons ensuite que tous les astres, & que toutes les planetes sont habités... Cette magnificence sans bornes, cette châines infinie de ces differens mondes, ce cercle radieux devoit entrer dans le vaste plan de la création. Eh, bien! ces soleils, ces mondes si beaux, si grands, si divers, ils nous paroissent les habitations qui ont été toutes préparées à l'homme..."[123]

. . . .
119 Coates, White & Schapiro 1966, 225.
120 Foucault 1966, 65, 68.
121 Brumfitt 1972, 92. See also Sagnac 1946, 80; Lovejoy 1950, 238–239.
122 This interpretation will be put under critical re-examination in later chapters of this study.
123 Mercier, *L'An 2440 I* 1786, 162. Mercier also reiterates this idea for example in one of his philosophical-religious treatises, entitled *"De Dieu"*. In this sublime vision of God's greatness, the belief in a well-organized universe, now called a *"grande horloge"*, is emphasized as follows: "Tous ces astres épars, subordonnés les uns aux autres, font fuir l'image du chaos: tout est ordre & harmonie, parce que tout est nombre, poids & mesure. Oui, tous les globes que le téléscope découvre sont habités". Mercier, *Mon bonnet de nuit IV* 1786a, 44–45.

As this excerpt reveals, for Mercier the philosophical idea of the "plurality of inhabited worlds" serves as the basis for an anthropocentric conception of the world and man's place in it. He had no doubts about the fact that in the Great Chain of Being man was the masterpiece of God. Yet, as noted above, in Mercier's vision the "imperial", Baconian, attitude to nature has not, however, totally replaced the Arcadian theme, based on the holistic conception of man and his relation to the cosmos and on the idea of the harmonious co-existence between humans and the rest of the creation. It has been argued that on the eve of the Industrial Revolution this constituted a common practise: Arcadian idealism coexisted with imperial tradition.[124]

In his vision of the future Mercier also uses the theory of the "plurality of inhabited worlds" to illustrate his views concerning the immortality of the soul and life beyond the grave. He imagines that in the moment of death the souls are separated from the body and begin their glorious march toward God. Basing his arguments on the theory of the "plurality of inhabited worlds", he dreams as follows:

> "L'ame humaine monte dans tous ces mondes, *comme à une échelle brillante & graduée*, qui l'approche à chaque pas de la plus grande perfection. Dans ce voyage, elle ne perd point le souvenir de ce qu'elle a vu, & de ce qu'elle a appris..."[125] (my emphasis)

It was in a similar manner that the idea of the soul was understood amongst the majority of eighteenth-century French theologians. They believed in the existence of a platonic, immortal and spiritual soul, which had existed long before the body and which would continue to exist after its death.[126]

In Mercier's utopia the transmigration of souls from planet to planet is referred to by the term "metempsychosis". In the course of this process the souls ascend through the cosmos into more and more luminous spheres along the Great Chain of Being until the final assimilation with God, the source of ultimate happiness and perfection:

> "Cette marche progressive, cette ascension dans différentes mondes... cette visite de la création des globes, tout me paroît répondre à la dignité du Monarque qui ouvre tous ses domaines à l'oeil fait pour les contempler... tu parcourras le sein immense de la nature, jusqu'à ce que tu ailles te perdre dans de Dieu..."[127]

It is by this means that Mercier revives the ancient Pythagorean theory of the perfectibility of beings in time, through successive lives in increasingly more spiritual spheres. As Majewski has pointed out, Mercier's idea of the transmi-

. . . .
124 Worster 1985, 30–31.
125 Mercier, *L'An 2440 I* 1786, 162, 165–166.
126 McManners 1981, 148–149.
127 Mercier, *L'An 2440 I* 1786, 165–166.

gration of souls from planet to planet differs, however, from Pythagorean doctrine, in one specific aspect: "Instead of a closed circle Mercier sees life as a spirally, spiritual evolution toward perfectibility and final union with God"[128]: "...mais ces ames tournoient sur le même cercle, & ne sortoient jamais de leur globe. Notre métempsychose est plus raisonnée."[129]

In Mercier's utopian vision the ultimate stage of man's spiritual perfectibility is a synonym for a state of consciousness where all differences between the individual "I" and the whole universe have been dissolved. In addition to being indebted to various mystic-religious doctrines based on the idea of purification through successive reincarnations, Mercier's poetic vision of the transmigration of souls and the yearning for unity between man and a larger entity than himself anticipates Romanticism and the romantic idea of love. To cite Irving Singer on this issue, for the Romantics "love is a metaphysical craving for unity, for oneness that eliminated all sense of separation between man and his environment, between one person and another, and within each individual". In its purest form this idea is embodied in the "ladder of love" of Coleridge, derived from Plato, according to which "we rise from sensuality to affection, from affection to love, and from love to the pure intellectual delight by which man becomes worthy to conceive... our marriage with the Redeemer of mankind."[130]

Relative and Absolute Perfection

One of Mercier's most often repeated statements was that the glorifying of man's privileged position in the creation should not, however, give reason for pride; rather on the contrary, since the function of the microscope and telescope is to reveal to man that his position in the scale of being is somewhere "in between": "Etres foibles que nous sommes, placés entre deux infinis, opprimés de tout côté sous le poids de la grandeur divine..."[131]

By underscoring man's "middle position", Mercier reflects a common eighteenth-century idea that man is the "middle link" in the Great Chain of Being in the sense that he is "at the point of transition from the merely sentient to the intellectual forms of being". The idea that man was lower than any spiritual being, and that there were numerous successive hierarchies above him, gave reason for humility.[132]

This is the view most ardently propagated by the English poet Alexander Pope, in whose treatise *An Essay on Man* (1733) the theory of the Great Chain

. . . .

128 Majewski 1971, 46–47. Pythagoreanism has had an important impact on the subsequent history of perfectibility. The focal issue in this oriental doctrine is the idea of contemplation of the (mathematical) order of the universe, and purification by wisdom as an end result of this contemplation. The underlying suggestion is that in identifying itself with the order of the Universe, the soul would be able to perfect itself in order to eventually escape from the cycle of transmigration. See for example Passmore 1972, 38–39.
129 Mercier, *L'An 2440 I* 1786, 164–165.
130 Singer 1987, 288.
131 Mercier, *L'An 2440 I* 1786, 175–176.
132 Lovejoy 1950, 189–190.

of Being finds one of its most visible manifestations of the early eighteenth century. According to Pope it would be an absurdity to expect the same perfection in the moral world as in the natural, and for this reason it is better to remain in the "middle position" in the scale of living creatures:

> "Placed on this isthmus of a middle state,
> A being darkly wise, and rudely great..."[133]

As a kindred soul of Pope, Mercier was convinced that even if man spent all his life in trying to find out the secrets of nature, the final causes of God would always remain a mystery to him. In *L'Homme sauvage* he expresses very clearly this idea concerning the "hidden" nature of God's purposes: "Il veut être caché, il ne se manifeste que par ses oeuvres..."[134] Thus, even if man had every right to feel himself to be under the protective guidance of Providence, God does not ever reveal all his plans at one and the same time. It has been suggested that this was a view typically promoted both by the adherents of Cartesian and post-Cartesian philosophy and by those of Newton: The creator of an "infinite" universe going progressively further. He is a hidden and remote God in the creation, accessible, however, to consciousness. The idea contained in this view of God was that it would be impossible for man ever to attain to an understanding of the "final causes". Paradoxically, this remote God existed in the center of all intellectual activity.[135]

In one of Mercier's brief treatises ("*Platon*") included in *Mon bonnet de nuit*, this idea that there always exists an insurmountable gulf between man's mediocrity and God's intellect, is expressed more clearly, perhaps, than in any other of his writings:

> "Dieu est tout ce qu'il doit être, son essence est une & nécessaire; mais l'être fini ne peut atteindre que successivement la plénitude de son existence... "L'homme est un être fini par sa nature, il est donc impossible qu'il soit parfaitement heureux: il faut qu'il éprouve des peines, des chagrins."[136]

Also in this respect Mercier seems to echo faithfully the ideas of Leibniz, who promotes in his *Principes de la nature et de la grâce fondés en raison* an analogous view that the amount of human happiness is even at its best doomed to remain merely on a mediocre level compared with the absolute happiness and perfection destined solely for God. Pains and sufferings form an integral part of man's destiny[137]:

> "Il est vrai que la suprême félicité...ne saurait jamais être pleine, parce que Dieu étant infini, ne saurait être connu entièrement. Ainsi notre

. . . .

133 Pope, *An Essay On Man* 1993, 281.
134 Mercier, *L'Homme sauvage* 1767, 118.
135 Chaunu 1982, 17; Ehrard 1994, 127–129.
136 Mercier, *Mon bonnet de nuit I* 1784, 262.
137 This is a crucial issue, to which we will return later in Chapter VII, pp. 191–193.

bonheur ne consistera jamais, et ne doit point consister dans une pleine jouissance, où il n'y aurait plus rien à désirer, et qui rendrait notre esprit stupide, mais dans un progrès perpétuel à nouveaux plaisirs et de nouvelles perfections."[138]

As the words of Leibniz suggest, the fact that man's happiness on earth can never be complete is not entirely to be regretted; on the contrary: the suggestion is that instead of complete repose it is rather ceaseless activity, "perpetual progress", that forms the essence of human happiness. Otherwise man would be in danger of falling into a state of lethargy and boredom.[139]

Lovejoy suggests that the idea of an immense distance between man's understanding and the universe was a commonplace in the eighteenth century. For this reason men's climbing along the chain of creatures towards God was considered endless. Furthermore, it implied that men needed only some simple truths in order to survive.[140] Mercier advances in his utopia a similar assumption concerning the "simplicity of the truths" destined for man; it is characteristic that when the time traveller of the novel asks from his guide how the future Frenchmen have reached their freedom, he is told that it has happened very easily: "Il ne faut qu'un soleil pour l'univers. Il ne faut qu'une idée lumineuse pour éclairer la raison humaine."[141]

In Mercier's visionary writings the notion of man's imperfect nature is closely associated with the dogma of humility. For example, in his allegory "L'Optimisme", he demands that men should admit the limitations of their understanding, since only God can possess ultimate truth: "L'aveugle esprit de l'homme, ne voit rien que dans le présent, la Providence seule connoît l'avenir."[142] Mercier returns also to this theme in L'An 2440, where he reformulates his earlier idea that man is always separated from God by an enormous gulf and that the only proper thing to do is to fatalistically accept one's lot, which is written in God's cosmic plan:

> "Il est un terme à nos connoissances; nous ne pouvons savoir ce que Dieu sait. Que l'univers vienne à se dissourdre! pourquoi craindre? quelque révolution qui arrive, nous tomberons toujours dans le sein de Dieu."[143]

As the passages quoted from Mercier's writings reveal, faith in a Leibnizian God did not leave much room for voluntarism. His texts all contain the same message, focused on the certainty that because of his inevitable imperfection, man should not hope for reaching the happiness reserved only for beings

. . . .

138 Leibniz, *Principes de la Nature et de la Grâce/Monadologie* 1996, 233.
139 This is not the proper place to provide a full-scale analysis of the theme of the significance of temporal evolution, as this theme is dealt with in Mercier's utopian vision (for a more thorough survey, see Chapter VIII, pp. 208–252.
140 Lovejoy 1950, 9, 246. See also Mauzi & Menant 1977, 58.
141 Mercier, *L'An 2440 I* 1786, 184.
142 Mercier, *Songes philosophiques* 1768, 30.
143 Mercier, *L'An 2440 I* 1786, 189.

superior to himself. It did not matter how unswervingly he tried to better his condition, there would always be a great gulf separating the harsh realities of man's terrestrial journey from the world of absolute perfection.

The reconciliation of God's omniscience with the assumption of man's free will is not an easy problem to solve. By reserving predictive activity solely for God, Mercier seems totally to rule out the human agent as the moulder of his own future destiny. And yet, as will be pointed out later in this study, one of the cornerstones of his whole utopian scheme is the idea that it was, above all, man himself whose task it would be to construct the new paradise on earth.[144]

How can this apparent paradox be explained? In order to clarify this kind of confusion, suggests Bertrand de Jouvenel, in eighteenth-century philosophical discourse a sharp distinction was made between the concepts of "prévision" and "prévoyance". Whereas the former was used to describe complete knowledge of the future (reserved only for God), "prévoyance" was considered a human capacity, referring to a forecasting facility in the sense of forming opinions about what the future might possibly bring.[145]

From the background of Mercier's warnings that man should not try to transgress the limits imposed by his own limited understanding, can be traced the ancient idea of hubris. It has been explained that by this term the ancient Greeks meant an effort to imitate gods, i.e., to be presumptuous, to get above oneself. It was founded on an assumption that perfect happiness was for the gods alone. To set oneself up as being godlike, whether in respect to happiness or any other respect, was believed to be severely punished.[146]

Notwithstanding his insistence upon man's "mediocre" nature, Mercier never gave up his belief that man was capable of perfectibility, at least in theory: "Si l'homme étoit trouvé dans l'impossibilité d'améliorer son sort, que lui auroit servi l'intelligence qui le distingue des brutes?"[147] In thus commenting he expresses the optimistic creed of his time, which was characteristic of many other writers and philosophers in eighteenth-century France. The major part of the philosophers of that epoch shared a hypothesis according to which humans pass from the darkness of primitive barbarism and have the capacity to gradually elevate themselves toward wisdom.[148]

Mercier's underlining of man's exceptional capacity for perfectibility compared with the "brutes" is once again a quest to purify man from his "fallen" nature and to emphasize his unique position as the masterpiece amongst created beings. Also in this sense Mercier adopted a position different from the materialistic philosophers of his century. For example in his treatise L'Homme machine (1747) the materialist La Mettrie vigorously contests the view according to which only man could have the conscience of good and bad: "La

. . . .
144 See Chapter VIII, p. 230.
145 De Jouvenel 1967, 15–16.
146 Passmore 1972, 29. See also Polak 1961, 28.
147 Mercier, Notions claires sur les gouvernemens I 1787, 26.
148 Rihs 1970, 9.

Nature nous a tous crées uniquement pour être heureux; oui tous, depuis le ver qui rampe jusqu'à l'aigle qui se perd dans la nue."[149]

Mercier's implication seems almost to be that the imperfect nature of man was, in a sense, the very reason which forced him incessantly to aspire toward a better condition. He did not believe that man's knowledge of the universe or of the intentions of God could ever be "complete"; in spite of his efforts man could never find a totally rational intellectual system, which could provide a final explanation for everything which exists. Following in the footsteps of Leibniz, Mercier was convinced that if man felt himself perfectly happy already in the present moment, he had no need of aiming at higher and higher forms of happiness and perfection: "Nous sommes nés pour connoître & pour perfectionner notre entendement; ce désir dévorant de connoître, est le plus noble attribut de l'homme..."[150] These words reflect Majewski's suggestion that despite the fact that for Mercier nature was "infinite in variety and fundamentally inexplicable to man's reason", he was endowed with an overwhelming *ardeur de connaître*.[151]

Mercier's definition of man as a "feeble creature, situated between two infinities", cited above, reveals the Janus-face nature of man as half beast, half God. It comprises the idea that man has a unique capacity to have visions of a better and more beautiful existence, but is at the same time forced to recognize his mediocrity in relation to the absolute perfection of God and other beings more spiritual than himself. In the final resort, there was no easy way to explain away the contradiction between the "ideal" and the "spleen". Lovejoy refers to this same contradiction, which characterized the whole of eighteenth-century philosophical terminology: the definition of man as the "middle link" emphasized "the peculiar duality" and the "tragicomic inner discord" of man. Torn by conflicting desires, man was now seen as a creature not in harmony with himself, which was considered to be the reason for his "unhappy uniqueness." The tragic element was born from the awareness that even if man occupied a middling position in the scale of creatures, he nonetheless had a capacity to feel disappointment at his condition.[152]

The words of Lovejoy describe the same idea which F.L. Polak refers to by the term "split man". By this he means the specific human capacity to conceive the existence of "The Other", because man's mental structure has a specific "dividing property" which enables him to be at the same time a citizen of two worlds, this world and an imagined world: "Deep in the human soul there is an

. . . .

149 La Mettrie, *L'Homme machine suivi de L'art de jouir* 1921, 103.
150 Mercier, *De la littérature et des littérateurs* 1970, 11.
151 Majewski 1971, 26.
152 Lovejoy 1950, 198–199, 205. A certain clarification is in order here. As Lovejoy himself observes, the recognition of man's disharmonious nature was not due primarily to the notion of the Chain of Being. Elements drawn both from Platonism and from Christianity and their habit of posing a sharp opposition between "flesh" and "spirit" had made of this dualistic theory of human nature a commonplace in Western thought. Lovejoy 1950, 198. In conjunction with Mercier's utopian vision it forms an important dichotomy, to which we will frequently return in the chapters that follow.

aching nostalgia, an unsatisfied yearning, an ineradicable longing for perfection, for a meaningful life with a happy ending, and for immortality."[153]

Man's constant desire to expand his narrow spatial and temporal horizons can thus be seen as a positive form of "restlessness". This tendency was only one of the many features which Mercier shared with his master, Rousseau. It has been explained that for Rousseau the term "restlessness" meant a desire to break the physical limits, and can be considered as a proof of the immateriality of the human being. For Rousseau "restlessness" was a superior form of unity – expansive unity.[154] In the same way as Mercier, Rousseau too was acutely aware that in his pursuit of happiness man was doomed to chase an illusion. Regardless of men's efforts, the inner content of happiness would remain a mystery, after all. The following words drawn from *Émile* express this clearly:

> "Il faut être heureux, cher Émile: c'est la fin de tout être sensible; c'est le premier désir, que nous imprime la nature, et le seul qui ne nous quitte jamais. Mais où est le bonheur? qui le sait? Chacun le cherche, et nul ne le trouve. On use la vie à le poursuivre et l'on meurt sans l'avoir atteint."[155]

. . . .

153 Polak 1961, 16–18.
154 Deprun 1979, 133.
155 Rousseau, *Émile ou de l'éducation* 1904, 546.

V Social and Political Aspects

The Desacralization of the Images of Public Power: Governmental Reform

In eighteenth-century France the critical spirit which was shaking the religious foundations was simultaneously also reducing the respect for other institutions, including the monarchy.[1] Throughout the century the philosophers of the Enlightenment raised their voices to challenge the old assumption that the King was the possessor of both secular and also spiritual power. The pamphleteers of the literary underworld were occupied by this same iconoclastic aim to tarnish the sacred aura of the crown.[2] Similarly, in that epoch the utopian novel emerged as an imaginative response to absolutism and to the anxiety caused by the destruction of traditional political forms.[3]

Utopian authors such as Restif de la Bretonne, Morelly and Dom Deschamps shared a common conviction with prominent philosophers like Rousseau, Montesquieu and Voltaire that the divine mission entrusted to the state should be eliminated. The rationalists wanted to "secularize" the state by preserving its institutional form. For them, Reason replaced Heaven. The question was: to whom does the sovereignty then belong?[4] Utilitarian philosophy, which began to challenge the theory of natural law, now made its entrance on the political scene. Bentham, Hume, Beccaria and other adherents of this new perspective were convinced that the institutions of human society should no longer be seen as creations of God, but rather as the accomplishments of human reason in its pursuit of happiness. In this new climate of opinion they drew their justification only from their utility.[5]

Like many creators of utopian societies before and after him, Mercier too was highly concerned with political and social issues, and the need for political reform is one of the major concerns in his vision of the twenty-fifth century. By creating an image of an utopian counter-world he sets out to lay the basis for an ideal political system, which would optimally meet the demands of a more just society, i.e., one under which man would be able to find supreme individual happiness, and yet live as a member of a social and political order. One of Mercier's leading arguments was that if one wished to ameliorate the society,

. . . .

1   Mornet 1969, 202.
2   Darnton 1990, 11–12.
3   Goulemot 1989, 378.
4   Rihs 1970, 10–11.
5   Gagliardo 1968, 12; Gay 1970, 459.

only a thoroughly reformation of the existing social and political relations of power would be adequate: "il faut qu'il soit renversé de fond en comble, car si la régénération n'est pas complette, elle devient nulle ou même funeste."[6]

Marcel Dorigny, who has traced the evolution of Mercier's political thinking in the years preceding the Revolution of 1789, notes that Mercier's entire production published from the 1770s until the outbreak of the Revolution indicates that he was resolutely engaged in resisting the political regime inherited from Louis XIV and Louis XV, and pleading for a total reform of the French political system. During that period he was constantly searching for a form of government compatible with his conception of individual liberties and human rights.[7]

Mercier was profoundly convinced that the society of estates of the *ancien régime* could not provide decent and equal conditions for all men. In his utopia Mercier directs his criticism against eighteenth-century court society and its characteristic abuses of power; in 2440 the only form of nobility which is acknowledged is that based on the nobility of character and actions. In his ideal state, members of the upper social classes are no longer permitted to despise the workers ("*roturies*"[8]) by reducing them to the state of slavery solely on the basis of birth. Their old prerogatives have been taken away, and the avidity, cruelty and self-love of eighteenth-century Frenchmen are treated with contempt: "L'orgueil criminel des nobles...fut puni; et comme il dégénéroit en pitoyable vanité, il fut encore livré aux ris moqueurs."[9] In 2440 the prejudices that used to separate men have fallen, and the future Frenchmen regard all men as their brothers and friends.[10]

In his utopia Mercier gives a reversed, albeit to some extent oversimplified image of the situation prevailing in the final years of the *ancien régime*. In addition to other privileges enjoyed by the members of the nobility (for example more lenient treatment before the law, hunting rights, non-participation in manual labor, a monopoly over the highest offices in the army, court and in the Church, exemption from the payment of taxes),[11] the right of political participation was limited only to the aristocracy.[12] Under Absolutism not even the most wealthy members of the middle classes had any say in state politics. Being thus ruthlessly excluded from the domain of political decision-making, the struggle of the middle classes was directed into two directions: against the monarchy which denied them political rights and imposed obstacles to material and intellectual progress, and against the privileged orders and their desire to

. . . .

6   Mercier, *De Jean-Jacques Rousseau considéré comme l'un des premiers auteurs de la Révolution II* 1791, 248.
7   Dorigny 1995, 246, 248, 263. See also Hofer 1975, 257.
8   The label "*roturier*" refers to the members of the "third state", or "*tiers état*". See for example Lough 1961, 98. See also Mercier, *Tableau de Paris II* 1994a, 1526: "Qu'on est heureux d'être né roturier! On est dispensé d'être valet de prince..."
9   Mercier, *L'An 2440 III*, 1786, 151–159, especially 159.
10   See for example Mercier, *L'An 2440 III* 1786, 12.
11   Goubert & Roche 1984 I, 16–17, 124–126.
12   Fralin 1978, 15.

maintain their privileges.[13] Yet, in the course of the eighteenth century the strict hierarchy of orders was gradually lessening its hold.[14]

As in most of Continental Europe, representative political systems were practically non-existent in eighteenth-century France. The Estates-General had not met since 1614, and they could assemble only if summoned by the King. The lack of a regularly meeting national representative body posed a problem for the nobility, for it was now more difficult to resist the demands of both the King and the bourgeoisie. A solution was found in the *parlements*, which were the regional courts of France. As final courts of appeal the *parlements* had extensive juridical powers; for instance, when new royal decrees were promulgated, these had to be registered by the *parlements*. The *parlements* could also refuse to register a decree, in which case it could, nevertheless, be registered by a legal procedure (the *lit de justice*). The consequence for continual resistance to royal authority was exile to some other part of the country. The most influential of the *parlements* was that in Paris, which declared that in the absence of the Estates-General it represented the entire nation. In practise this meant that it defended the interests of the nobility against the monarchy and the bourgeoisie.[15]

Under Louis XIV the *parlements* had yet not had the courage to resist the King, but under the following weaker governments intensified confrontation developed between the King and the *parlements*. With their claims concerning the right to interfere and oppose the government, the *parlements* formed the most persistent opposition to the crown.[16] Thanks to the *parlements*, from 1752 onwards a persistent political opposition to the government existed for the first time in a continuous fashion.[17]

This was, in its main lines, the institutional setting and the political climate in France in the latter eighteenth century. It was in this tense political atmosphere that Mercier's utopia first saw daylight. In his novel he does not, however, succeed in giving an exhaustive answer to the question under what kind of political organization man's life would be arranged on the optimal basis. Mercier contents himself with rather vaguely stating that the form of government prevailing in his ideal society of 2440 is not monarchist, democratic or aristocratic, but "reasonable and made for man".[18] In this respect he is in fact a very typical representative of his age, for the majority of Mercier's contemporaries shared the same uncertainty as to which way to follow in order to attain social perfection.[19]

. . . .

13 Lough 1961, 95–96.
14 Rudé 1985, 73, 77.
15 Cobban 1957, 62–63; Fralin 1978, 16–18. See also Hibbert 1982, 27–29; Le Roy Ladurie 1996, 429–436.
16 Cobban 1957, 63; Doyle 1988, 69, 157–167; Furet 1988, 43; Mandrou 1977, 306–309. See also Palmer 1962, 41–44.
17 Doyle 1988, 76–77; Le Roy Ladurie 1996, 383–404, especially 390. See also Habermas 1989, 67.
18 Mercier, *L'An 2440 II* 1786, 98.
19 Dorigny 1995, 249.

On the eve of the revolution it was generally agreed that the best prospects probably lay in some form of representative system. There was, however, no unanimity about the precise form of such representation.[20] In *L'An 2440* Mercier sets forth his own version of an ideal representative system. The imaginary governmental reform executed in his utopian society is based on a model for the distribution of power: the "Estates" ("*états assemblés*") assemble once every two years to pass legislation. Governmental power is dedicated to a Senate which administers the laws. Finally, the King oversees the execution of the laws. The Senate is responsible to the King, and the King and the Senate are responsible to the Estates. All issues are decided by a plurality of votes.[21]

Darnton suggests that the political system imagined by Mercier sounds like an "impossible amalgam of institutions from the Old Regime": Mercier's "Estates" resemble the Estates-General, and the Senate appears to be like an improved version of the *Parlement* of Paris.[22] This comment is just; Mercier has mixed together diverse elements from different political traditions without, seemingly, any clear image of what he is aiming at. Yet, even if his image of an ideal political organization may look like an "impossible amalgam", it does anticipate the actual course of events in the near future, since in 1788 the *Parlement* of Paris registered the declaration convoking the Estates-General in the same form as the last time when they had met, in 1614. The summoning of the Estates-General was a decisive step, for it meant the abandonment of absolute monarchy.[23]

Mercier's dream of all political decisions being made on the basis of equal votes, did not, however, correspond with the situation in 1788; when the Paris *Parlement* insisted that the Estates-General should be composed as they had been in 1614, they meant that each of the three orders (the clergy, nobility, the Third Estate) was to have an equal number of delegates. This meant that the clergy and nobility could always defend their privileges against the Third Estate. As a consequence, the *Parlement* lost its popularity with the middle class, which had come to see it as a bulwark against despotic government.[24] One year before the convocation of the Estates-General, in 1787, Mercier had criticized a revival of the estates in his *Notions claires sur les gouvernemens* as follows: "L'ancienne composition de nos Etats généraux seroit très vicieuse aujourd'hui, parce que les représentans du peuple pourroient être subjugués par la ligue facile des deux premiers ordres."[25] Twisting the actual state of events, in his utopian vision the representatives of the third estate have gained equal status with other orders in the National Assembly.[26]

Mercier argues that under the *ancien régime* royal authority was merely the instrument of personal ambition for certain privileged individuals. There had

. . . .

20 Doyle 1988, 92–93.
21 Mercier, *L'An 2440 II* 1786, 112.
22 Darnton 1997, 130.
23 Cobban 1957, 131–134; Hibbert 1982, 39.
24 Hibbert 1982, 40.
25 Mercier, *Notions claires sur les gouvernemens I* 1787, 223.
26 Mercier, *L'An 2440 III* 1786, 167.

been a "monstruous and contentious marriage" between the crown and the aristocracy.[27] This comment reflects a change in attitude: by the 1780s the absolutist regime had lost all of its appeal in public opinion.[28] The intensification of general discontentment with absolutism shows in the increase of "subterranean" turmoil under the veil of official politics; in particular the harsh tone of the *libelles*[29] reflects the fact that the person of the King was no longer beyond criticism; in the *libelles* circulating in the streets of Paris, the monarchy was accused of having degenerated into a despotism. In the most insulting slanders Louis XV was represented as a king who had lost two wars and who let Madame du Barry dominate him and the whole kingdom "by applying the tricks that she learned in the brothel".[30]

Sex and tyranny were thus connected in a way that leaves no doubt that on the eve of the Revolution political corruption was seen as related with the degeneration of morals in general. It may not be too far-fetched to suggest that Mercier may have had the King's mistress of ill repute, Madame du Barry, in mind when he created his image of the vile prostitute, the symbol of eighteenth-century France, in his *L'An 2440*.

Mercier's anger toward the absolutist system did not, however, lead him to total rejection of kingship. In his utopian vision, France remains a monarchy even in 2440; King Louis XXXIV sits on the throne. Mercier's views on monarchy are, however, somewhat contradictory. In the "*Nouveau discours préliminaire*" of his novel, he argues that the King is "le plus ridicule ouvrage de l'homme en société".[31] The hereditary form of monarchy is now harshly condemned: "L'inviolabilité des rois et leur trône héréditaire sont donc des absurdités si révoltantes, que la raison ...ne conçoit plus que des hommes se soient soumis à de pareilles erreurs."[32]

These statements make one wonder what made Mercier preserve monarchy – in a hereditary form[33] – in his ideal state. This apparent paradox may, however,

. . . .

27 Mercier, *De Jean-Jacques Rousseau considéré comme l'un des premiers auteurs de la Révolution II* 1791, 231. See also Mercier, *Notions claires sur les gouvernemens I* 1787, 216.
28 Doyle 1988, 88.
29 The *libelles* formed a subgenre of forbidden books in pre-Revolutionary France. They were slanderous attacks on public figures, which "pulsated with Rabelaisian energy", as Darnton puts it. As such they formed a continuity for the scandalous literature which had been collected around public figures for centuries. No one had, however, considered it a threat to the state before the eighteenth century when the tone of the *libelles* became gradually more and more threatening. Darnton 1997, 198–216, passim. Mercier, for his part, wanted to distinguish himself from the writers of *libelles*, whom he calls in *Tableau de Paris* as "l'écume de la basse littérature". Mercier, *Tableau de Paris II* 1994a, 25–29: Ch. "*Libelles*". Mercier's aversion towards *libelles* can be explained, as also Darnton suggests, by the fact that he did not want to be identified with the producers of these humbler forms of literaty activity. Darnton 1997, 228. As noted above, Mercier, who had a rather unrealistic self-image as "*le premier livrier de France*" had a high esteem of himself as a professional writer.
30 Darnton 1997, 213. See also Schama 1989, 210–211; Bluche 1993, 118; Le Roy Ladurie 1996, 386, 393. About the desacralisation of the image of the royal family in eighteenth-century France, see also Farge 1995, 67 and passim.
31 Mercier, *L'An 2440 I* An VII [1799], xiij.
32 Ibid., xiv.
33 Mercier, *L'An 2440 III* 1786, 128.

be due to the fact that he added the "new preliminary discourse" in the version published in "Year VII" after the Revolutionary upheaval and after the dethronement of the King, whereas the basic text was retained intact from the 1786 version to that of 1799 – as Mercier himself points out at the beginning of the later edition.[34]

Furthermore, it is important to note that in Mercier's terminology a clear distinction is made between an absolutist monarch and a monarch whose power is restricted by legal measures: "Nous avons conservé la monarchie, mais limitée par des lois fixes..."[35] He did not aim at the abolition of the King, but at denying the traditional concept of the "divine rights" of the monarch. This could be accomplished by restricting the scope of royal power within reasonable limits: when laws reign, nobody, not even the King, is above them. This ensures that the King has "all the power to do good, but he is not capable of doing evil".[36] The benevolent nature of the ideal King guarantees his position as a "happy prince": happy, because he works for the well-being of his people, gaining satisfaction from the knowledge of contributing to public happiness.[37]

Mercier's belief that the main duty of the future king would be to advance the general well-being of his people is consistent with utilitarian philosophy. In his utopia he desacralizes the traditional image of the King, stressing his role as a man, whose power is of human, not of divine origin. Mercier emphasizes the "commonness" of his imaginary monarch; for example, the social status of the King is merely that of "first citizen". Moreover, even if the kingship is hereditary, the heir to the crown does not know his true origin in his early years. As part of his education, he lives amidst the peasants, dressed in their simple fashion, and is required to learn all the agrarian and artisan professions. By this means he has the capacity to identify with the lives of the common people.[38]

The humble character of the sovereign can also be seen in the fact that he chooses his wife from among the common people. It is also stated that the needs of the monarch of 2440 are no more extensive than those of the least of his subjects. The person of the king is, thus, no longer in any sense of the term 'intact' or protected; if the young prince commits some offense, it is published in the newspaper the following day.[39] As these examples reveal, Mercier's utopia provides ample evidence to illustrate the general erosion of belief by the end of the eighteenth century in the religious legitimation of monarchical rule, the belief that monarchs were chosen by God.[40]

Mercier's ideal monarch of 2440 is a typical "enlightened" or "virtuous despot". In his investigation into the theory of enlightened despotism in

. . . .

34   See Chapter II, p. 37.
35   Mercier, *L'An 2440 III* 1786, 126. Darnton suggests that in praising limited monarchy as the best form of government in contrast both to democracies and despotism, Mercier follows Montesquieu. Darnton 1997, 127.
36   Mercier, *L'An 2440 II* 1786, 116, 126.
37   Mercier, *L'An 2440 II* 1786, 112–113.
38   Mercier, *L'An 2440 II* 1786, 132–134.
39   Mercier, *L'An 2440 II* 1786, 143–146.
40   See for example Outram 1995, 109.

eighteenth-century Europe, John G. Gagliardo suggests that its focal principle was the idea that a sovereign prince was only *primus inter pares* ("first among equals"), merely the "first nobleman" of the realm. In practise this meant that the role of the public power should not be limited merely to protective or police functions, but also had an obligation to foster the general well-being of the people. In other words, "the power exercised by the monarch was not a personal attribute, but belonged to the state and was merely utilized for the public good by the monarch as the executor of the state".[41]

One of the leading arguments for enlightened despotism was the appeal to reform imposed from above, which implied the rejection of popular sovereignty.[42] Mercier, too, believes that the initiative for reform should always come from the government, not from the people. He writes:

> "La révolution s'est opérée sans efforts, et par l'héroïsme d'un grand homme. Un roi philosophe...plus jaloux du bonheur des hommes que de ce fantôme du pouvoir... offrit de remettre les États en possession de leurs anciennes prérogatives..."[43]

In order to advance the general well-being of his people, Mercier's King does not claim to possess alone all the wisdom which is needed for this demanding task. For this reason he does not hesitate to consult with his advisors:

> "Le monarque ne manque point d'inviter à sa court cet homme cher au peuple. Il converse avec lui pour s'instruire; car il ne pense pas que l'esprit de sagesse soit inné en lui. Il met à profit les lecons lumineuses de celui qui a pris quelque grand objet pour but principal de ces méditations."[44]

The time traveler of *L'An 2440* is informed by his guide that "c'est de l'éducation des grands que dépend le bonheur des peuples",[45] and the same view is also reiterated in *Notions claires sur les gouvernemens*, where Mercier argues that it is possible to find an equilibrium between power and freedom only if there exists an intimate accord between the rulers and the educators.[46] This idea, that a close alliance should be established between monarchs and philosophers, formed part of the theory of enlightened despotism and the associated educational program. In eighteenth-century Europe, monarchs invited to their courts tutors and advisors from the world of art, literature, and philosophy. The new community of interest between the Enlightenment and despotism thus created a new and direct alliance between power and philosophy.[47]

. . . .

41 Gagliardo 1968, 93–94.
42 Dorigny 1995, 257.
43 Mercier, *L'An 2440 II* 1786, 109. The last phrase of this quotation is revealing in the sense that in it Mercier expresses manifestly his desire of the convocation of the General Estates.
44 Mercier, *L'An 2440 I* 1786, 38.
45 Mercier, *L'An 2440 II* 1786, 132.
46 Mercier, *Notions claires sur les gouvernemens I* 1787, 1.
47 Gagliardo 1968, 21–23. The "enlightened despotism" was supported by many of the leading philosophers, for example Voltaire. See for example Lough 1961, 12–13; Coates, White, & Schapiro 1966, 278.

The image of a "philosopher-king" has, however, much older origins. It is already found in the ideal state in Plato's *Republic*, where the ruler must have wisdom and the task of the king's auxiliary is to assist him. Plato took it for granted that no man could achieve perfection except as a member of a perfect society, ruled by philosopher-kings.[48] In his *Notions claires sur les gouvernemens* Mercier refers explicitly to the political theory of Plato as a model to be imitated: "Quand Platon a dit que les républiques seroient heureuses, si les philosophes étoient Rois...il a défini le vrai Gouvernement."[49] Over the centuries, the idea of a "philosopher-king" has also fascinated other utopian writers, who often describe their ideal states as having been created by the action of an enlightened individual; Utopus in More's *Utopia*, or Séverius in *Vairasse d'Alais's Histoire des Sévarambes* (1702), for instance.[50] The mythical figure of the "good prince" is also met in Marmontel's *Bélisaire* (1767): "plus un prince est aimé de ses peuples, plus leur bonheur lui devient cher".[51]

One of the most important books in which the classical theory of enlightened despotism was revived in the early Enlightenment was Fénelon's (1651–1715) *Les aventures de Télémaque*. Polak labels it as a "Mirror for Monarchs", by which he means an utopian image in which the the heir to a throne is transformed into a philosopher-king through rational education.[52] Fénelon's fictional kingdom of Salente is ruled by the wise king Idoméne: wise because he acknowledges his human weaknesses and his need for assistance from a mentor: "Heureux le roi qui est soutenu par de sages conseils!... "Mais doublement heureux le roi qui sent son bonheur, et qui en sait profiter par le bon usage des sages conseils!"[53]

There are good grounds to believe, however, that the idea of enlightened despotism remained for the most part a utopian ideal, without much support from the actual sovereigns of Europe. In point of fact, few French intellectuals acted as close advisors to governments, and despite the growth of public opinion in the course of the eighteenth century, power remained largely within the aristocracy. Subsequently, the whole concept of enlightened despotism has become the target of critical attack, in particular since 1945. Anachronism has been one charge, for the term was not used by any of the eighteenth-century rulers themselves.[54]

Despite the fact that in Mercier's vision of the future the "philosopher-king" has voluntarily surrendered his power to the ancient estates of the realm, it is probable that not even he had any illusions as regards the irresoluble paradox between utopian ideal and reality. Mercier was painfully aware of the fact that the rulers in the real world were often driven by totally other interests than the

. . . .

48   Passmore 1972, 43. About the theory of philosopher-king in Plato, see also Martin 1981, 4–5.
49   Mercier, *Notions claires sur les gouvernemens I* 1787, 116.
50   Goulemot 1989, 378.
51   Marmontel, *Bélisaire* 1821, 92.
52   Polak 1961, 250–252. See also Manuels 1982, 388–391.
53   Fénelon, *Les aventures de Télémaque* [1864], 250.
54   Dorigny 1995, 97, 102.

well-being of their people. He especially abhorred Louis XIV, who, as Darnton observes, represented for Mercier the image of a despot, "surrounded by flatterers" and "sunken in luxury".[55]

Using the technique of creating reversed images of the society of the *ancien régime*, Mercier projects in his utopia that the frightening emblems of the arbitrary use of power have collapsed. *L'An 2440* ends with a scene where the time traveler walks in the ruins of the demolished palace of Versailles, where he meets an old man in tears, who reveals his identity: he is the phantom of Louis XIV, and divine justice has made him to contemplate his deplorable deeds forever and ever... The encounter between narrator and the despot's ghost comes to a sudden end when a snake falls from a column, bites the time traveler and he awakens.[56]

The same critique toward despotism is also found in Mercier's allegory "*De la Royauté & de la Tyrannie*". In this story he makes a comparison between monarchy and tyranny, emphasizing the virtues of monarchy when it is assisted by Justice and Peace. The co-regents of Tyranny, on the other hand, are personifications of Cruelty, Violence, Injustice, and Fanaticism. On the radiant throne of monarchy sits a majestic woman dressed in white, and her gaze protects the empire, bringing happiness and abundance; her reign is described as from the Golden Age. Tyrants, by contrast, are to be destroyed, and the rejection of despotism is further accentuated by dramatic natural metaphors: whereas the kingdom rises toward fresh air, the empire of the tyrant exists amidst thunderstorms and snow.[57]

Mercier's writings thus provide ample evidence that he had no intention of challenging the legitimacy of monarchy as such, and especially the myth of Henri IV captivated his imagination.[58] Similarly, although many eighteenth-century philosophers had republican sympathies and a hatred of despotism, they often defended monarchy.[59] This also explains why Mercier's utopian vision does not envisage the sovereignty of the people. In *Notions claires sur les gouvernemens*, for instance, he reveals himself as an eager adherent of representative political systems, attacking democracy as "the worst of governances".[60]

. . . .

55 Darnton 1997, 127.
56 Mercier, *L'An 2440 III* 1786, 202–209. This last scene of the novel contains symbolism that reminds of the Christian myth of the paradise; the time traveller is doomed to awaken and to return to the unhappy eighteenth century as a consequence of the bite of a snake. As in the biblical account of the expulsion from the paradise, the snake functions also in *L'An 2440* as a metaphor of evil.
57 Mercier, *Songes philosophiques* 1768, 150–163.
58 Darnton 1997, 126–127. In Mercier's city of the future for example *Le Pont-Neuf* is repabtized as "*le pont de Henri IV*". Mercier, *L'An 2440 I* 1786, 44. See also Mercier, *L'An 2440 I* 1786, 202: "Henri IV a été le meilleur des rois..."
59 Crocker 1969, 29. See also Mauzi, Delon, & Menant 1998, 83.
60 Mercier, *Notions claires sur les gouvernemens I* 1787, 337. See also Dorigny 1995, 258. After the outbreak of the Revolution Mercier denied, however, his former view. In his treatise on Rousseau he writes (in 1791) that the democracy is the sole legitimate constitution, and that the monarchy is nothing but moderated despotism. Mercier, *De J. J. Rousseau considéré comme l'un des premiers auteurs de la Révolution I* 1791, 55–56.

Mercier's negative attitude to popular government was based on the assumption that the members of the lower social orders were too "passionate" by nature to be capable of contributing to important political decisions or even to take care of their own lives.[61] It is against this background that he explains the need for a representative political system: "Un Gouvernement populaire est tumultueux, indiscret, lent, car le peuple ne connoît pas ses véritables intérêts; il lui faut des représentans."[62] Since in Mercier's opinion the violence and unpredictability of the passionate masses represented a severe danger to the maintenance of public order, they needed to be severely controlled.[63] This reveals his basically patronizing attitude toward people of lower social origins; in Mercier's eyes they were like children in need of guidance.[64]

The majority of eighteenth-century French philosophers shared the same scepticism regarding the common people. Democracy had few adherents, and in general the masses were thought to be unfit to rule because of their poverty, ignorance, and superstition.[65] Even Rousseau, who did not totally rule out the possibility of the sovereignty of the people, remained deeply ambivalent about its political potential.[66] In point of fact, none of the French philosophers used the word "democracy" in a favorable sense before 1789.[67] They developed no systematic program of large-scale reform, and political questions play a relatively unimportant role in their work. They were reformers, not destructors. Their aim was to temper the French monarchy, which had become absolute and arbitrary, by the use of intermediary powers.[68] Not even the extremists guillotined by Robespierre were "communists" in the modern sense of the term; the Terror only intensified with the appearance of radicals such as Babeuf, the author of the first communist document, *Manifeste des Egaux* (1796).[69]

In *De Jean-Jacques Rousseau, considéré comme l'un des premiers auteurs de la Révolution*, however, Mercier is prepared to approve of popular uprising, when he writes that insurrection is a legal means of an oppressed people: "C'est le premier, le plus beau et le plus incontestable droit des peuples outragés."[70] In this treatise on Rousseau, published two years after the outburst of the Revolution, Mercier also argues that increasing popular discontent may

. . . .

61 Mercier, *L'An 2440 II* 1786, 104–105.
62 Mercier, *Notions claires sur les gouvernemens I* 1787, 338.
63 Ibid., 317.
64 It is noteworthy, however that Mercier made a clear distinction between the pejorative term "populace" and the "people". Whilst the "populace" seems to appear as synonymous with the "mob", the last mentioned contains more positive connotations, and in Mercier's view there existed an alliance between the people and God. Mercier, *De J.J. Rousseau considéré comme l'un des premiers auteurs de la Révolution I* 1791, 131.
65 Coates, White & Schapiro 1966, 278; Crocker 1969, 29. See also Bosher 1988, 33–45.
66 Fralin 1978, 72. See also Cobban 1974, 190.
67 Palmer 1959, 13–20, especially 14.
68 Gagliardo 1968, 16. See also Sagnac 1946, 89; Cobban 1974, 188.
69 Lichtheim 1969, 20–25, passim.
70 Mercier, *De Jean-Jacques Rousseau considéré comme l'un des premiers auteurs de la Révolution I* 1791, 60–61. See also Mercier, *Notions claires sur les gouvernemens I* 1787, 195. See also Mercier, *L'An 2440 III* 1786, 44: "...autant que la guerre civile est quelquefois nécessaire, parce qu'elle seule peut rétablir les principes constitutifs".

eventually lay the way for the violent turnover of the existing structures of power: "De l'oppression du pauvre nait le mécontentement, du mécontentement la haine du prince ou de sa cour, de la haine du prince l'insurrection générale."[71]

Yet, even if Mercier seems to espouse the cause of the common people in social compassion, a pejorative attitude toward the masses is dominant for example in *Parallèle de Paris et de Londres*. In this text, based on a comparison of Paris and London (most often to the advantage of the latter), Mercier writes that whereas in London the people is always its own master, in Paris there is immediately an "infernal disorder" when the people is not supervised by the authorities.[72] All in all, his attitude toward the uneducated masses is somewhat ambiguous. As Jean-Louis Vissière points out, Mercier avoids extremes; he does not give an idyllic image of the people, but does not make it a "scarecrow", either.[73]

On several occasions, in contrast to the unhappy social and political conditions of eighteenth-century France, Mercier offers England and its representative form of governance.[74] It may not be mere coincidence that in the beginning of *L'An 2440* it is an "old English friend" with whom the narrator is talking before he falls asleep, and who presents critical comments on the corruption of big cities.[75] Moreover, it is characteristic that in the chapter "*Quel est le Peuple le plus heureux*" of *Notions claires sur les gouvernemens*, Mercier praises England as the happiest nation in the world, on the grounds that in his view it was the most enlightened country, having succeeded in removing the vestiges of despotism and established human liberties. He argues that Englishmen had been able to liberate themselves from the abuses of royal authority for the reason that the great had made common cause with the people.[76]

Mercier shared this *anglomanie* with many other eighteenth-century French philosophers, who vigorously praised the English political system for its achievement of civil and political liberty. The main reason for this admiration was the "Glorious Revolution" of 1688, which had liberated the British people from the oppression of a hated ruler and launched an age of prosperity and progress.[77] Admiration for England's political system was not, however, totally unreserved,[78] and in Mercier's case *anglomanie* came to an abrupt end in the Revolutionary period, when – as his treatise on Rousseau reveals – England had ceased to be a model and turned out to be the land that Mercier most detested, an image of an aristocratic tyranny.[79]

. . . .

71   Mercier, *De Jean-Jacques Rousseau considéré comme l'un des premiers auteurs de la Révolution II* 1791, 292.
72   Mercier, *Parallèle de Paris et de Londres* 1982, 108.
73   Vissière 1973, 123–137, especially 123.
74   See also Dorigny 1995, 259.
75   Mercier, *L'An 2440 I* 1786, 7–18. See also Chapter III, p. 66.
76   Mercier, *Notions claires sur les gouvernemens I* 1787, 201–215, passim.
77   Coates, White & Schapiro 1966, 294; Lasky 1976, 583; Mandrou 1977, 315; Sher 1990, 101.
78   See for example Baker 1987, 45–55. The eighteenth-century French philosophers had often a controversial attitude as regards to England. To get a more vivid idea of what was at issue, see for example Montesquieu, *De L'Esprit des loix I* 1749, 121–129: "De la constitution d'Angleterre".
79   Gillet 1995, 375–395, especially 389.

Another, even more alluring "living utopia" was found from America, which was widely admired among radical thinkers in late eighteenth-century France. The revolt of the American colonies against British rule in 1776, in which the French monarchy intervened in the side of the insurgents, confirmed America's position as a "natural society", where the wildest dreams could come true.[80] Mercier thus expresses the feelings of many of his contemporaries when he praises the American War of Independence as an important manifestation of public spirit.[81]

Man and his Relation to Society

The Principle of Uniformity as the Basis of Collective Well-Being

Amongst political reformers of the eighteenth century, it became customary to discharge man from responsibility for the wickedness of the world and to blame the evil social order instead. With the replacement of the older conception of man's original depravity, there emerged a secular conception of salvation.[82] The denial of man's "fallen" nature gave birth to a new assumption that men's hope of attaining perfection was not necessarily linked with God, but rather with their fellow-creatures. Henceforward, "perfection" was defined in moral rather than metaphysical terms, and read with a new meaning as "doing the maximum good". This new moral psychology led to the suggestion that men could be infinitely improved by the help of social mechanisms and education.[83]

Mercier was also a typical representative of this common attitude prevailing among his educated contemporaries inasmuch as he put his confidence in men's original goodness[84] and their malleability through appropriate education. In L'An 2440 he criticizes his contemporaries for considering men as wicked, without realizing that abominable and cruel laws had made them so.[85] Mercier was convinced that no man was wicked by nature, and just as corrupt social and political institutions could undermine men's original goodness, equally education could restore them to the path leading to virtue: "L'homme n'est méchant que parce qu'il se trompe sur ses véritables intérêts."[86]

A necessary premiss for the assumption that men are malleable through education is that they are willing to co-operate, and for the eighteenth-century French "enlighteners" the guarantee of this derived from their belief in man's inborn goodness. It has been suggested that educated thinkers of that century had adopted profound respect for social institution, and now regarded man as primarily a sociable being. For them, it was society which makes man. The

. . . .

80 Coates, White & Schapiro 1966, 294–295; Mandrou 1977, 291–292; Woloch 1982, 309; Doyle 1988, 94; Schama 1989, 27.
81 Mercier, *Notions claires sur les gouvernemens II* 1787, 337.
82 Coates, White & Schapiro 1966, 192.
83 Passmore 1972, 169–170, 190.
84 See Chapter IV, p. 81.
85 Mercier, *L'An 2440 II* 1786, 125.
86 Mercier, *L'An 2440 II* 1786, 110.

moral good was the well-being and utility of society.[87] This belief that man was destined by nature to be a "social animal" was also consistent with the denial of any contradictions between individual and collective happiness.[88]

Mercier was one of those thinkers most ready to embrace the idea that man is sociable by nature. It forms one of the most focal themes in his major writings, and for example in *Mon bonnet de nuit* Mercier argues that absolute independence is impossible for man, because he is a feeble creature dependent on everything that surrounds him; he is strong only when he is united to society: "...c'est de la dépendance réciproque des citoyens que naît le véritable esprit de liberté."[89]

The same belief in man's inborn sociability forms the cornerstone of collective life in Mercier's utopian society. In the ideal world of 2440 nobody can reach happiness by himself, without a close bond with the surrounding society. In Mercier's vision, the men living in the future have learned to respect each other, and reciprocal rights and duties determine their behavior towards their fellow creatures. It is now everyone's duty to think and act in ways that do not offend the feelings of others. Correspondingly, every man has the right to expect to be treated in this same human way by others. In Mercier's eyes one of the worst abuses prevailing in eighteenth-century French society was that society's incapability of connecting public happiness with the happiness of everyone.[90] The society of estates was built on competing privileges and prerogatives, rather than on the concept of "union" on which every legal constitution should be founded: "C'est en politique le synonyme de création..."[91]

In Mercier's ideal society the optimal reconciliation between the personal happiness of the individual and the collective well-being of the whole community is reached through the elaboration of a social contract. This social contract forms the basis of the principle of uniformity and imposes common values and norms on all the citizens, without exceptions. The relationship between the community and individual is defined as follows: "Nous avons concilié ce qui paroissoit presque impraticable à accorder, le bien de l'Etat avec le bien des particuliers".[92] Individual and society thus form an inseparable totality: "Le bonheur général de la patrie est fondé sur la sûreté de chaque sujet en particulier..."[93] Mercier explains that the social contract ensures the maintenance of equality and uniformity, because it is based on the sovereignty of the law, not that of one individual: "Les lois règnent, et aucun homme n'est au-dessus d'elles..."[94] The law is an expression of the general will ("*volonté générale*").[95]

. . . .

87   Sagnac 1946, 83; Cassirer 1966, 342.
88   Mauzi 1994, 141; Pomeau & Ehrard 1998, 84.
89   Mercier, *Mon bonnet de nuit I* 1784, 383–384.
90   Mercier, *L'An 2440 II* 1786, 122–123.
91   Mercier, *De J. J. Rousseau considéré comme l'un des premiers auteurs de la Révolution II* 1791, 237–238.
92   Mercier, *L'An 2440 II* 1786, 122.
93   Mercier, *L'An 2440 II* 1786, 116–118.
94   Mercier, *L'An 2440 II* 1786, 116.
95   Mercier, *L'An 2440 II* 1786, 107.

Mercier's idea of happiness based on a contract is borrowed directly from Rousseau's political theory as it is represented in *Du contrat social* (1762). In his treatise, Rousseau advances his famous thesis that society can be properly governed only on the basis of common interest. For this reason he proposes the elaboration of a social pact, which gives to the body politic absolute sovereignty over all its members. This social pact, which is an act of the "general will", establishes between the citizens an equality which engages all under the same conditions and the same rights. Rousseau writes that in the same way as nature gives to each man absolute power over all his members, the social pact gives to a body politic absolute power over all its members, and this same power, directed by the "general will", bears the name of sovereignty. When the people are subject under such conventions, they obey nothing else but their own will. In practise this means that the sovereign power never has the right to charge one subject more than another. The commitments that bind man to a social body are obligatory for the sole reason that they are mutual. The "general will", which is always right and tends always to the public good, is an act of sovereignty and it creates the law. Because the laws are acts of the "general will", not even the prince is above them.[96]

The "general will", in contrast to the "will of all",[97] thus emerges when the members of the community have given themselves completely to the service of the public good. It is "a standard independent of human will", a common faculty which addresses all men equally. Appealing to it, every citizen can protect himself against the pain caused by social conflicts such as divergent opinions. Expressed in a biological metaphor, it could be argued that like the individual, the body politic also naturally aims at self-preservation, and for this reason the happiness that it offers to man represents his security.[98]

The content of the general will is most clearly expressed in Rousseau's argument that "one cannot offend the members of the social pact without at the same time offending the whole body politic". When the individual enters into a social contract, he surrenders his natural liberty, but gains civil liberty.[99] Echoing his master almost word by word, in Mercier's utopia of 2440 infractions of the laws and the "general interest" which forms the basis of all justice constitutes ipso facto an offence against each and every member of the body politic.[100] As we have seen, this rule also applies to the King. Not even the ruler has the right to put in jeopardy the general well-being of the whole community. The fact that his possible misconduct is publicized in the press gives visible proof of this. At any event, individual aspirations are ranked only

. . . .

96 Rousseau, *Oeuvres complettes de J.J. Rousseau II* 1793, 36–50. On Rousseau's social contract – theory, see for example Shklar 1969; Fralin 1978; Trousson 1989, 83–103.
97 Rousseau argues in his *Du contrat social* that "Il y a souvent bien de différence entre la volonté de tous et la volonté générale: celle-si ne regarde qu'à l'intérêt commun: l'autre regarde à l'intérêt privé, et n'est qu'une somme de volontés particulières..." Rousseau, *Oeuvres complettes de J.J. Rousseau II* 1793, 42.
98 Shklar 1969, 166–167, 196–197, 202; Fralin 1978, 86.
99 Rousseau, *Oeuvres complettes de J.J. Rousseau II* 1793, 30.
100 Mercier, *L'An 2440 II* 1786, 119–120.

of secondary importance, when the general well-being of the whole community is at stake.

From this it is to be inferred that in Mercier's utopia the content of the "general will" is conceived as a "moral consensus about the well-being of society as a whole".[101] It constitutes a new source of authoritative power in a transformed political culture, an authentic public sphere within the monarchic state itself, a synonym for public opinion. It offers a response to a contemporary need, for, as Jack R. Censer notes, what eighteenth-century French thinkers were yearning for was a unified public space in which "one true opinion... might hold sway". As a consequence, by the 1770s public opinion had become a powerful political force, limiting the government's freedom of action. [102]

Public opinion was now seen as an impersonal and anonymous "tribunal" and an ultimate "court of appeal", a new abstract source of legitimacy. As such, its authority was universal and its empire extended to men of all estates and all conditions. Public opinion was thought to have independence which discredited traditional authority, a capacity to judge everything, which required the displacement of inherited authority. In principle, public opinion replaced religious and secular power by restoring to men the ownership over their own decisions. This did not however change the fact that men still continued to appeal to some transcendental authority.[103]

As such, the idea of a reform of social relations on the basis of a contract was not new. Various kinds of social pact theories had been elaborated already long before Rousseau,[104] and despite their differences and an absence of specific political reforms, most eighteenth-century French philosophers accepted some version of the social contract, which they hoped could provide a solution for the problem of how men would live in society pursuing their interests without ending up in conflicts and eventually in a state of total chaos. In addition to the model put forward by Rousseau in his *Du contrat social*, where the social contract is justified by arguing that the aim of collective action should be to improve the conditions of life for all, some echoed the *Leviathan* (1651) of Hobbes, which postulated that men formed a civil society out of fear. A third group followed Locke, who had suggested in his treatise *Of Civil Government* (1690) that men came together because they wanted to protect their natural rights (life, property, liberty).[105]

. . . .

101 Darnton 1997, 130. See also Dorigny 1995, 257.
102 Censer 1994, 211.
103 Doyle 1988, 81–83; Ozouf 1989, 419–434, passim. See also Baker 1987, 41, 44, 55, 61–62; Habermas 1989, 89–102.
104 Rousseau's version of the social contract differed, however, in one crucial respect from the preceeding tradition. Contrary for example to Hobbes, Rousseau insisted that a social contract is absurd and contradictory, if it is based on exterior coercion; he thought that the unity could never be attained through coercion, it had to be founded on liberty. On the other hand, liberty did not exclude submission. But in his theory this submission does no more mean a submission of individual will to another individual subject. See Cassirer 1966, 335–336.
105 Gagliardo 1968, 12–13, 16.

According to the utilitarian philosophy based on the catch-phrase "the greatest happiness of the greatest number", which was embraced by the majority of the eighteenth-century philosophical writers, the means justified the ends and man should consider all his actions in the framework of the well-being of the whole community.[106] The Revolutionaries of 1789 adopted the same position. For them it was self-evident that humanity was necessarily marching towards a goal, and the sacrifice of individual rights for the collective good became insignificant compared with the immense idea of a destiny. They conceived the Republic as a society regulated by the public spirit, in which the individual realized his own potentiality only by identifying himself with the community as a whole.[107]

The list of writings produced in eighteenth-century France in which the attainment of personal happiness is considered as possible only in institutional terms, is endless. In this context a few examples will be sufficient to illustrate the prevalence of this theme. For example Mably argues in his treatise *Du Développement des progrès et des bornes de la raison* that nature has constituted man in such a manner that he cannot find his particular happiness in any other way than through the general happiness. The love of the public good is the "first law".[108] Helvétius formulated the same thing as follows: "Toute sage législation qui lie l'intérêt particulier à l'intérêt public et fonde la vertu sur l'avantage de chaque individu est indestructible."[109]

The desire to abolish all differences between the personal happiness of one individual and the collective well-being of the whole society has for centuries also been one of the leading themes in utopian thinking. For utopian writers, the happiness of all has to mean the same thing as the happiness of everyone.[110] The "invisible city" depicted in the myth of the ideal city is, actually, a kind of a mythical "social bond" uniting the citizens, who have lost their individual characteristics in order to become "pure social beings".[111]

According to Mucchielli, in the history of ideal cities the desire for uniformity is revealed in many different aspects, which can be grouped under the following sub-categories: 1) the unity of spirit, 2) concord, 3) co-operation. The first of these aims at the abolition of all dissidence between different beliefs. That means that everything that concerns one man, also concerns his fellow creatures. The idea of concord, for its part, means that citizens living in the harmonious City have no sentiments of rivalry or competition; they have no warlike sentiments either, or sentiments of revenge, envy or hate. The third aspect, co-operation, implies that the activity of everyone is made totally to serve the City. This excludes idleness.[112]

. . . .

106 Hampson 1981, 123–124.
107 Hampson 1989, 240–241; Ozouf 1989, 573.
108 Mably, *Collection complète des oeuvres de l'abbé de Mably XV* 1794–1795, 17–20.
109 Helvétius, *Collection des plus belles pages* 1909, 244.
110 Cioranescu 1972, 32. See also Mucchielli 1960, 99, 180.
111 Mucchielli 1960, 175–176.
112 Ibid., 184–191.

The points listed by Mucchielli are all means which the creators of utopias, including Mercier, have regarded as necessary for the maximization of happiness. Strictly speaking, happiness is not, however, the major concern in utopias. Their principal aim is to find a perfect order, and in this sense they differ for example from the myth of the Golden Age, where men's happiness is the major concern, whereas the utopias are concerned with nothing else but the happiness of the state. As a consequence, in utopias the happiness of individuals is a by-product.[113] Kumar sees this as a purposeful reaction against individualism, since the utopias from the sixteenth to eighteenth century regarded it as their primary function to reintegrate society around a new moral and social order: "The threat seemed to be not too little but too much freedom and change, and so the new order must be stable and unchanging."[114]

Paul Ricoeur argues that eventually all utopias have to deal with the problem of authority. The eternal problem in utopias is how to end the relation of subordination, the hierarchy between rulers and ruled. Ricoeur distinguishes two principal ways through which utopians have attempted to solve the problem of power. The first alternative is to abandon rulers altogether. The other suggestion has been the institution of a "moral rational power".[115] This division is approximately analogous with the distinction by Ernst Bloch between two kinds of social utopias, in which the best possible communal living conditions are determined either through freedom or through order.[116]

L'An 2440 belongs definitively to the category of utopias where the problem of man and his relation to society is based on strict order and on the elimination of individual freedom. In Mercier's utopian society, the focus of political power, formerly incarnated in the figure of a powerful king, has been depersonalized and replaced by a moral consensus focused around the notion of a social contract in the way described above. What counts is no longer political power as such, but "moral rational power", to apply the terminology of Ricoeur. In other words, in Mercier's utopian model the question of the best way of living is, above all, a moral rather than a political issue.[117]

In Mercier's ideal state the "general will", or "public reason", which constitutes the supreme norm of righteous conduct, is said to be founded on natural law. In the chapter *"Le Professeur en Politique"* in *L'An 2440*, where Mercier explains the system of government, he illustrates this idea by writing that "tout système politique doit être posé sur le droit naturel".[118] The law of nature constitutes the source of virtuous moral conduct, and is equally applicable to all nations, cultures and epochs. In contrast to the excessive number and confusion of

. . . .
113 Cioranescu 1972, 53.
114 Kumar 1987, 36.
115 Ricoeur 1986, 298–299.
116 Bloch 1989, 9.
117 As will be shown with more detail in Chapter VII, pp. 202–204, the replacement of political absolutism by a moral concept of a social pact does not, however, lead to a less oppressive system of power.
118 Mercier, *L'An 2440 II* 1786, 337.

statutes in the eighteenth century, in Mercier's future justice is said to manifest itself in the voice of Nature; nature is the "sovereign legislator, the mother of virtues and everything that is good on earth".[119]

The notion of Natural law as sketched for example by seventeenth-century thinkers such as Grotius or Hobbes has been defined as "a synonym for a moral norm which obligated all human beings regardless of their religion or nationality, and consisted of rules which were considered indispensable for the maintenance of peaceful and ordered social life between individuals".[120] Mercier recalls this anterior tradition of natural law when he argues that in his ideal society, natural law forms the basis of human happiness expressly for the reason that it guarantees equal rights and duties for everyone. Life is very simple when uniformity reigns:

> "Le droit naturel est le droit de l'homme, à son plus grand bonheur possible. Il veut être heureux et il lui est impossible de ne pas le vouloir. Jamais homme n'a fait convention avec un autre qu'à raison d'une jouissance mutuelle".[121]

In Mercier's scale of preferences there was no difference between the "law of nature" and the "law of society". In *Notions claires sur les gouvernemens* he clearly states that regardless of the form of government, the most important thing is that there exists an equivalence between the law of nature and the law of society: "Que les loix de la société ne contredisent pas les loix de la nature, car elles en sont la perfection."[122]

One of Mercier's leading propositions was that in order for the world to be transformed as a place of general happiness and well-being, it first needs to be purified from all moral and physical evils. This illuminates the point explored in Chapter III, why his future Paris appears as a transparent city, clean in every sense. The message is that only when the jungle of contradictory laws, voices and practises is abolished, can man see the laws of nature in all their shimmering glory. Mercier was convinced that man would be able to find happiness, if he could restore the political and institutional chaos to the original state governed by the law of nature: "Les lois de la nature nous environnent, c'est le tumulte du monde qui nous empêche d'entendre ses lecons: ôtez ce que les hommes ont édifié, il restera ce que la nature a fait."[123]

The focal idea in this extract illustrates Nisbet's idea that the central theme of the philosophy of nature in the eighteenth century was that "Nature was ever present, and could be made visible if only enlightened political action would remove the underbrush of convention and historical tradition that hid nature and its laws". Nature was seen as a kind of an ideal-type that would *manifest itself*

. . . .

119 Mercier, *L'An 2440 I* 1786, 108.
120 Saastamoinen 1995, 13.
121 Mercier, *L'An 2440 II* 1786, 337. See also Mercier, *De J.J. Rousseau considéré comme l'un des premiers auters de la Révolution II*, 296: "L'*unité* est nécessaire dans la *loi*: la nature est une; les devoirs sont les mêmes".
122 Mercier, *Notions claires sur les gouvernemens I* 1787, 59, 66.
123 Mercier, *L'An 2440 II* 1786, 337.

provided only that corrupting circumstances did not obtrude. For this reason the most necessary thing was to eradicate everything that hindered the knowledge of nature.[124]

Servier refers to the same idea when he suggests that human organization came now to be seen as founded on the same laws as the universe. Yet at the same time, it was realized that the universe is harmonious, while human life is not. In its present condition humanity seemed not only to be alienated from nature's plot but it seemed even to contradict its aims. Original sin was reintroduced into eighteenth-century thinking under a new label: social disorder. Only wise constitutions would permit the rediscovery of man, through the accumulated vices, as nature had formed him. It was necessary to reintegrate him into the universe by giving him the laws appropriate for his microcosm.[125]

From the background of this chain of reasoning can be found the primordial idea of "Cosmopolis", which can be traced back to the ancient Greeks, in whose thinking it was customary to conceptualize the world as divided between two orders, which they termed the Order of Nature ("cosmos") and the Order of Society ("polis"). In their terminology the first was used to describe the astronomical universe with its pre-ordained laws of nature. The second order, that of society, referred to the human-dominated world, at times broken by the misconducts of the despots and dissidences of opinion. The dream of reachieving harmony, i.e., to fit the Order of Society to that of Nature, has frequently re-emerged in various cultural settings.[126]

Mercier had already developed this theme in *L'Homme sauvage*, where he praises a life spent amidst the natural landscape. In the beginning of the story Zidzem tells about his happy childhood with his sister Zaka in the solitude of the mountains of Xarico, living peacefully, following the simple laws of nature. All this changed with the arrival in the Americas of the cruel and avaricious Spanish conquistadores. In the aftermath of the barbaric confrontations a few Indians succeeded to find shelter in the mountains, where they formed a new people. Despite having lost everything, they felt happy because they were free. The government was entrusted to one of their members, Xalisem, who ruled according to simple laws. The aim of these laws was to unite people instead of dividing them, and to make the particular interests to submit under the general interest. The universal law was the law of public security.[127]

The message of *L'Homme sauvage* is that the "state of nature" does not necessarily mean living in a state of chaos, without laws or desire for mutual organization. Mercier returned to this theme later, in *Notions claires sut les gouvernemens*, rejecting the Hobbesian idea that the state of nature is a state of war.[128] As Mercier saw it, even primitive man tends toward union, and there

. . . .

124 Nisbet 1970, 141–142.
125 Servier 1991, 219. See also Polak 1961, 235–236.
126 Toulmin 1990, 67.
127 Mercier, *L'Homme sauvage* 1767, 25–32, passim.
128 Mercier, *Notions claires sur les gouvernemens I* 1787, 25. In this sense Mercier differs sharply for example from Helvétius, who shared the idea of Hobbes that the "state of nature"

could not exist any antinomy between the state of nature and the state of society. For Mercier, it was *nature* which reveals the law of society, and it was nature which tells under which conditions the society accords with its proper *raison d'être*.[129]

In this integral aspect Mercier differed quite sharply from Rousseau, who preferred the "state of nature" to the civil state. In Rousseau's opinion the social pact was planned for corrupted man, who had fallen from his original state of happiness. Rousseau regretted the loss of this primordial happiness, but argues that it cannot be restored. For him the purpose of the social contract was to re-establish the regularity of the social state into which man had degenerated.[130]

Rousseau preferred the "state of nature" to life in society above all because he believed that in a state of nature man was independent. In his treatise *Discours sur l'origine et les fondements de l'inégalité parmi les hommes* (1754), he argues that from the moment man realized that he needed the help of other people, equality disappeared, personal property was introduced and work became necessary.[131] Again, in *Émile* Rousseau sees self-sufficiency as a precondition of happiness, proposing that this imagined state of independence had existed before prejudice and institutions had altered man's "natural inclinations": "Quiconque fait ce qu'il veut est heureux, s'il se suffit à lui-même: c'est le cas de l'homme vivant dans l'état de nature."[132]

It has been suggested that Rousseau's true originality lay precisely in his rejection of the common eighteenth-century premise according to which man could accomplish his destiny only by living in society. According to Rousseau, not all men possessed a primitive instinct of sociability. As he understood it, there existed in the state of nature no harmony between the personal interest and the common interest.[133]

As regards the assumption about man's natural propensity for sociability, Mercier follows a more conventional path than Rousseau. Like most of his contemporary philosophers, he was convinced that if excluded from the social community, man would be inevitably doomed to unhappiness. Contrary to Rousseau, Mercier did not believe that life in society could offer merely "secondary" happiness compared with the perfect harmony prevailing in some mythical "state of nature".[134]

Mercier never gave up his his view that man can find happiness only through communion with a larger totality than himself. As has been shown in the Chapter on the "two infinities", the dream of a cosmological unity between man

. . . .

was a state of war: "L'homme de la nature est son boucher, son cuisinier, ses mains sont toujours souillées de sang. Habitué au meurtre, il doit être sourd au cri de la pitié." Helvétius, *Collection des plus belles pages* 1909, 220.

129 Béclard 1903, 766–767, 771.
130 See for example Rihs 1970, 53.
131 Rousseau, *Discours...* 1992, 232.
132 Rousseau, *Émile ou de l'éducation* 1904, 65.
133 Cassirer 1966, 333–334, 342.
134 A more fully treatment of this theme related to the "state of nature" is provided later in this examination (See Chapter VI, pp. 181–187.

and the universe was crucial for him; in Mercier's view the tranquility of the soul is born from the deep inner sentiment that man has established an intimate relation with his individual "I" and the whole planetary system. Correspondingly, Mercier's utopians can maximize their feeling of personal happiness only through the knowledge that they are related with a mythical bond to a social community by being bound by the social contract. In this crucial respect they resemble people living in medieval and pre-modern societies, when dissimilarity was regarded with fear.[135]

In the Middle Ages the spheres of the public and private were not yet clearly distinguished and no one had a private life;[136] similarly, in Mercier's ideal state individuality can exist only through the institutionalization of the individual. This means that an individual can exist only within society and by absorption into the social macrocosm. He is initiated into his community like a Christian in his religious community. In Mercier's utopian world the rites of initiation for the attainment of full membership of the community are secular acts of initiation into the mysteries of the universe, reminiscent of Christian's baptism. The process depicted in L'An 2440 is analogous to that described by Gurevich, who writes that there exists a vast gulf between a "carnal" human being and someone transformed through the act of initiation into the community of the faithful and who through this act acquires the chance of salvation, adopting the norms of the Christian community.[137]

This provides an explanation why Mercier's utopians have not chosen the life of Robinson Crusoe, living in a state of solemn solitude in the middle of the oceans or amidst the wilderness without laws and without mutual respect. The purpose of their life is not limited only to self-preservation, finding food and shelter. Mercier's conceptions related to man's social role in community and his idea of an "ideal citizen" will be explored in the following Chapter.

The Citizen and his Role as a Mouthpiece of Social Virtues

In Mercier's opinion the ancient Greeks and Romans had known how to think and act like citizens, because they had known how to reconcile the public and the particular good and to appreciate the value of union. For this reason they could well provide examples of political virtues for the eighteenth century as well.[138] This was a widespread view amongst educated men living and writing in France in the late eighteenth century, which witnessed a great revival of the

· · · · · · · · ·

135 See for example Hautamäki 1996, 22–37, passim.
136 Ariès 1989, 9.
137 Gurevich 1995, 89–90.
138 Mercier, *De J.J. Rousseau considéré comme l'un des premiers auteurs de la Révolution II* 1791, 236–237. It has to be admitted, however, that Mercier's admiration for the ancient ancestors seems to have been confined within certain, rather restricted, limits: they were rather ideal types without much practical bearing. This can be concluded from Mercier's statement that despite the fact that the foundation of society remains the same, the face of history changes. From this it follows that "Il seroit presque aussi ridicule alors de vouloir remonter à des usages antiques et barbares, que si on vouloit faire des loix qui ne seroient exécutées qu'à l'époque future de cinq ou six siecles." Mercier, *De J.J. Rousseau considéré comme l'un des premiers auteurs de la Révolution I* 1791, 74–75.

worship of classical models. To be more specific, it was not so much in the sphere of politics, but in the sphere of morality and customs that the ancient republics fascinated the imagination; republican ideals, – a republican idea about "right moral" and the republican concept of "virtue", a republican friendship, a republican sense of duty, a republican pride –, survived even in the heart of a monarchical state.[139]

If one tries to give a brief and clear definition of what eighteenth-century writers understood by the word *vertu* when they used it in a political context, it can be reduced to the following: simplicity, self-government, and the citizen's voluntary sacrifice of his personal interests to the service of the collectivity.[140] As we have already seen, the last mentioned of these was of special importance in the philosophical discourse of that century; inspired by the Roman Stoics[141], the inheritors of the republican tradition insisted upon the notion of a public good which is preferred to individual desires. Accordingly, "virtue in the individual is nothing more or less than allowing the public good to provide the standard for individual behavior".[142]

The most prominent propagators of the republican concept of virtue amongst eighteenth-century French philosophers were Montesquieu and Rousseau. In Montesquieu's treatise *L'Esprit des loix* (1748) the underlying principle that best characterizes the republican societies is suggested to be virtue. It is identified with patriotism, which requires one to prefer the public interest to one's proper interest.[143] Similarly, for Rousseau the ancient republics of Sparta and Rome, like contemporary Geneva, had a social function to perform, because from them it was possible to draw an image of the perfectly socialized man.[144] This same conception of virtue became an integral component in Revolutionary discourse; despite its puritan aspects, for the Revolutionaries of 1789 virtue was, above all, a virile force; it meant willingness to fight for the patriotic trinity of values – liberty, equality, fraternity.[145] In this process, a shift took place from *homme* to *citoyen*.

Solitude thus does not provide the best possible nurturing ground for virtuous activity, and it is easy to note how closely the eighteenth century's cult of "sociability" was related to a horror of being left alone, of being excluded from the sacred community constituted around the elaboration of the social contract. The same horror of loneliness also explains the great revival of utopian thinking in pre-Revolutionary France; in the utopian ideal image of a coherent and all-

. . . .

139 Venturi 1971, passim.,especially 70–72.
140 Hampson 1981, 209. See also Venturi 1971, 72.
141 For the Roman Stoics the idea of social service had been the *summum bonum*. See for example Hibler 1984, 41.
142 McIntyre 1987, 236–237.
143 Montesquieu, *De L'Esprit des loix I* 1749, 15–20, 27, 32–33.
144 Shklar 1969, 12–32, especially 12–13.
145 Darnton 1990, 10. The same moral code – that the practise of virtue and doing one's duty are the necessary ingredients of happiness (eudaemonia) – is preached in Aristotle's *Nicomachean Ethics*: "If happiness consists of virtuous activity, it is only reasonable to suppose that it is the activity of the highest virtue..." Aristotles, *Nicomachean Ethics* 1897, 334–335.

encompassing social organization, each and every citizen forms a functional unit of the collectivity, and social usefulness is the highest virtue of all. Against this idealization of perfect social order, it is not difficult to see why the bee is one of the animals most favored by the creators of utopias.[146] With their ceaseless activity the utopian cities have invoked the image of a beehive at least since Thomas More.[147]

In *L'An 2440* Mercier follows in the footsteps both of earlier creators of utopias and of Montesquieu and Rousseau in the sense that in his utopian society a socially active citizen is elevated on a pedestal. The entire life and behavior of the utopians is directed toward fulfilling one's duties as virtuous members of the social community of which they form a part. Because they are bound together by the social pact, the code of honor imposed on them demands above all the capacity of self-sacrifice, altruism and brazenness in the face of dangers. The suggestion is that under ideal circumstances man is always prepared to sacrifice his own interests for the general well-being of his community. As Mercier formulates it: "Il faut que chaque particulier fasse le sacrifice d'une portion de ces forces, afin que la liberté de tous ne soit pas en danger."[148]

Mercier distinguishes two different paths which both contribute to man's journey towards higher and higher level of perfection: " ...il eut été inutile à l'homme de perfectionner son ame, si elle n'eût pas dû s'élever, soit par la contemplation, soit par l'exercise des vertus..."[149] This makes one conclude that the utopians living in his future Paris are a mixture of Christian saints and pagan heroes. They are personifications of a moral hero, "saintly", "wise", or "superhuman", which are all attributes for a specific human type which Mucchielli suggests has been constantly repeated in representations of ideal cities through the centuries. A feature best typifying it is the exclusion of everything reminiscent of an individual style of existence. A moral hero is a "regenerated man" living in a "regenerated city", and he is entirely engaged in social action.[150]

In Mercier's utopian society, a contempt for passions and their subordination under cold reason and reflection is the means for the attainment of moral perfection. He suggests that when the general well-being necessitates it, man

. . . .

146 Lapouge 1978, 208. It is highly questionable if a life spent as a hermit could under any circumstances be called an utopian condition. Robinson Crusoe provides an classic and often cited example of the fact that in solitude, – at least if it is not freely chosen, – life can be only deeply frustrating and unhappy. Therefore, on his solitary island Robinson Crusoe constantly laments his hard lot, longing only for escape back to his former conditions before the shipwreck. See for example Clayes and Sargent 2000, 180–181. Against this background it is easy to note that the literary genre named "robinsonade" differs from utopia in the crucial respect that whereas nobody ever dreams of leaving utopia, in the robinsonade it is quite the contrary. Both in robinsonade and in utopia, solitude is abhorred, and social life is seen as the optimal human condition.
147 Trousson 1975, 24.
148 Mercier, *L'An 2440 II* 1786, 338–339.
149 Mercier, *L'An 2440 I* 1786, 163.
150 Mucchielli 1960, 196, 198–200.

has to learn to control even his natural fear of death.[151] If he can accomplish this, he has made a great advance in the process of moral perfectibility: "Développe toutes tes forces, méprise la mort; il n'appartient qu'à toi de la vaincre et d'augmenter ta vie qui est la pensée."[152] This shows that the conquest over physical pain is elevated as one of the beneficial virtues in Mercier's imagined society. In his work on the culture of pain, William B. Morris names this propensity as one of the crucial elements in the Stoic outlook; the Stoic wise man never forgot the moral purpose of all his actions, and for this reason he lived according to reason, despising the passions. This moral purpose required an attainment of an absolute conquest over pain, a victory of mind over body.[153] It is expressly in this fashion that Seneca, one of the leading Stoics, formulated the idea of happiness; in his view only the man who through his reason is free from desires and fears, can be called happy.[154] In the seventeenth century in particular Descartes and his followers strongly supported the Stoic outlook of Seneca, arguing that man's greatest felicity depends on his right use of reason. According to the Cartesian view, when reason governs the passions, man's condition is the best possible.[155]

Despite the strong hold exercised by the idealization of Cartesian rationalism over recent centuries, in particular in the Enlightenment project, the philosophy of the modern age also contains strong threads emphasizing feeling and instinct. The mathematician Blaise Pascal (1623–1662), for example, posed in antithesis to reason intuition and the "voice of the heart". The whole philosophy of modern times has been characterized by a struggle between reason and sentiment (reason and intuition).[156]

This tense antagonism between reason and sentiment forms a leading thread throughout Mercier's major writings; it is precisely the contradiction between these two seemingly opposite forces that forms the complexity of his utopian vision and the "eccentricity" of his personality. Despite his admiration of the Stoic attitude to life, as an apostle of the "Cult of the Heart" and as the creator of visions of the "mysterious universe" Mercier did not believe that cold rational reasoning could provide a sufficient means to access happiness on earth. In

. . . .

151 More about this theme concerning the conquest of the fear of death by cold rational reflection, See Chapter VII, p. 195.
152 Mercier, L'An 2440 I 1786, 163–164.
153 Morris 1993, 160–164.
154 Sénèque, La vie heureuse 1995, 26. Mercier also explores the value of the Stoic attitude to life in one of his essays contained in Mon bonnet de nuit, where he refers to the words of Seneca according to which "virtue is something austere, but it fortifies the soul". He gives his support to Seneca by reasoning that pleasure is less compatible with human nature than sorrow; man is too feeble to support sorrow for a long time. Sorrow is less dangerous than the pleasures, because the latter much too often degenerate into libertinism. Mercier, Mon bonnet de nuit I 1784, 245–251: "Douleur".
155 Coates, White & Schapiro 1966, 185–186. Too much emphasis should not, however, be set on Descartes's denial of passions. According to the formulation of Descartes the passions are beneficial in the sense that they promote man's good as natural beings. See for example James 1999, 100–101.
156 See for example Hautamäki 1996, 16–19.

addition, man needed to place his trust in his sentiments and in his "inner voice". Mercier was convinced that every human being had an inborn capacity to feel compassion toward his fellow creatures. In his terminology this sentiment of social compassion is synonymous with the concept of "*attendrissement*", which he describes as a special emotional feeling of tenderness of heart, "le sentiment le plus heureux dont l'ame humaine soit susceptible..."[157]

In this respect Mercier follows in the traces of Rousseau, in whose *Émile* those who lack the capacity for tenderness are condemned as totally unnatural:

> "L'homme qui ne connaîtrait pas la douleur ne connoîtrait ni l'attendrissement de l'humanité ni la douceur de la commisération; son coeur ne serait ému de rien, il se serait pas sociable, il serait un monstre parmi ses semblables."[158]

Like Rousseau, who saw pity as a natural sentiment, which, by moderating the operation of self-love in each individual contributes to the mutual conservation of the whole species,[159] Mercier envisaged that in the future pity would be "the most beautiful and worthy gift which nature has given to man".[160] In *Mon bonnet de nuit* he advances the view that the sentiment of pity and the capacity for compassion are the preconditions for a feeling of happiness founded on the knowledge that one has contributed to the happiness of those less fortunate. In other words, only a person who has the capacity to identify with his fellow creatures could attain happiness.[161] The following passage expresses this focal theme in a nutshell:

> "L'homme est doué d'une sympathie qui le fait entrer dans les intérêts de ses semblables. C'est par cette passion généreuse qu'il est touché de ce qui les frappe, & qu'il ne peut rester spectateur indifférent de leur peine: il en est récompensé, car le plaisir le plus doux accompagne fidélement la pitié. Comme ce n'est pas raisonnement, mais un instinct, don sacré de la main bienfaisante du Creáteur, il pénetre intimiment l'ame..."[162]

The last phrase reveals that Mercier thought that the propensity for pity was an inborn human characteristic, pre-dating rational reflection. The suggestion is that it constitutes a "law of sentiment" which applies equally to all men in the same way as the scope of the "law of nature" speaks to all men without exception. Against the background of this kind of argumentation there can be traced the fact that Mercier's thinking was not encumbered by anthropological pessimism, for he was always spurred by a firm conviction that man has an inborn capacity for virtue. By vigorously rejecting the notion of man's "fallen"

. . . .

157 Mercier, *Mon bonnet de nuit II* 1784, 7.
158 Rousseau, *Émile ou de l'éducation* 1904, 68.
159 Rousseau, *Discours...* 1992, 214.
160 Mercier, *L'An 2440 I* 1786, 215.
161 Mercier, *Mon bonnet de nuit III* 1786a, 115.
162 Mercier, *Mon bonnet de nuit I* 1784, 10.

nature,[163] he seems to contend that a vicious man is in war against his "true self". It is then easy to argue that it was a natural propensity in each man to prefer the well-being of his fellow-creatures to his own; otherwise there would prevail an irresoluble disharmony between man's will and his actions.

Mercier's belief in man's inborn capacity to make morally correct choices is reminiscent of the philosophy of Immanuel Kant (1724–1804). Kant asserts that in order to be virtuous it is not sufficient that man does the "right thing", but he must also act out of the right motive, which means respect for the moral law. For Kant the rational part of man's mind, not God, presented duty as an imperative, what he called a "categorical imperative"[164]:

> "The moral law commands me to make the highest possible good in a world the ultimate object of all my conduct. But I cannot hope to effect this otherwise than by the harmony of my will with that of a holy and good Author of the world; and although the conception of the *summum bonum* as a whole, in which the greatest happiness is conceived as combined in the most exact proportion with the highest degree of moral perfection... includes *my own happiness*, yet it it is not that this is the determining principle of the will which is enjoyed to promote the *summum bonum*, but the moral law, which, on the contrary, limits by strict conditions my unbounded desire of happiness."[165]

A penetrating analysis on the impact of Kant's moral philosophy on Mercier's thinking is not possible within the scope of this study. It merits mention, however that Mercier was one of the first defenders of Kant's philosophy in France. When he was released from prison after the Revolution, he was appointed a member of the *Institut* (1795–1814), where his original ideas aroused attention, attacking the sensualists, empiricists and Epicureans, whom he named "*idéologues*", and proclaiming a return to "innate ideas". Resorting to Kant, Mercier set out to prove the independence of "moral man" and the absolute value of the imperative laws of man's own conscience, affirming the existence of a moral instinct over the sensations. By this means he criticized the interest of his contemporary Frenchmen in the "machine-man" and their treatment of truth, virtue and Stoic dignity as meaningless.[166]

Despite Mercier's despair when he was forced to witness the increased popularity of materialist philosophies in his contemporary society, even a superficial overview of the essays, novels and treatises produced in that epoch reveals that many educated Frenchmen did sincerely believe in the existence of a moral instinct as an inborn capacity in each man, and it became now customary to draw an equation between the concepts of virtue and happiness. For example, in her treatise on happiness Madame du Châtelet (1706–1749)

. . . .

163 See for example Mercier, *L'Homme sauvage* 1767, 178; Mercier, *L'An 2440 III* 1786, 155: "...la bonté de l'homme, inhérente à sa nature..."
164 Coates, White & Schapiro 1966, 190; Passmore 1972, 219; Hampson 1981, 197. For more details, see for example Williams 1968, 1–12 and passim.
165 Kant 1996, 150–174, passim, especially 156.
166 Leterrier 1995, 295–316, passim.

clearly expresses the idea that without virtue there could be no happiness, either: "...il faut être vertueux, parce qu'on ne peut être vicieux et heureux. J'entends par vertu tout ce qui contribue au bonheur de la société."[167]

Even the materialistic philosophers of that epoch, such as d'Holbach, shared the same opinion. He had no doubts about the fact that man is "sociable" by nature:

> "Ainsi la vertu est tout ce qui est vraiment & constamment utile aux êtres de l'espece humaine vivans an société... "L'homme vertueux est celui dont les actions tendent constamment au bien-être des ses semblables..."[168]

In its purest form the principle of generalized sympathy as a natural propensity in each man is met in the thinking of the Scottish philosopher David Hume, who represents his theory of sympathy and its normative significance in his works *A Treatise of Human Nature* (1739–40) and *An Enquiry Concerning the Principles of Morals* (1751). In the last work he draws a contrast between "natural pleasures", those retained from the reflection of having done one's part toward mankind and society, and the "empty amusements" of luxury and expense. These natural pleasures, indeed, are really "without price".[169]

These examples are sufficient to testify to the fact that among eighteenth-century writers there prevailed a widespread unanimity that virtue consisted of according advantage for the happiness of the others over one's own. Sociability was conceived as the art of how to please, based on an assumption that by contributing to the happiness of others, one made them love oneself in return. The aristocratic ideal of the *"honnête homme"* of the previous century now gave way to the larger but equally abstract idea of human nature. Contrary to the moral of *"l'honnête homme"*, who had not needed other men in order to be himself, sociability implied that one cannot imagine himself separated from others. To put it briefly, the alliance between virtue and sociability was based on an formula "to make happy in order to be happy".[170]

All this overwhelming talk about the virtue of social compassion and of the special tenderness of heart as man's natural propensity formed a part of the eighteenth-century cult of sentimentality[171] and the belief in the power of *bienfaisance* as its integral element, discussed above.[172] The term *bienfaisance*, invented by Abbé de Saint-Pierre,[173] formed the basis for the assumption of benevolence as an inborn propensity. It was given in the eighteenth century approximately the same meaning as the Christians had given to charity.[174] Originally, the theory of the inner moral instinct had been presented at the end

. . . .

167 Châtelet, *Discours sur le bonheur* 1997, 42.
168 [d'Holbach], *Systême de la nature I* 1771, 145.
169 Hume, *An Enquiry concerning the Human Understanding* 1894, 278–284.
170 Mauzi 1994, 216–217, 580–583, 603–607.
171 For more detail, see Campbell 1987, 138–160, especially 139–142.
172 See Chapter IV, p. 81.
173 Gay 1970, 37, 43–44; Mauzi 1994, 606; Pomeau & Ehrard 1998, 84.
174 McIntyre 1987, 232.

of the seventeenth century by Anthony Ashley Cooper, better known as the third Earl of Shaftesbury. Shaftesbury was convinced that doing good for its own sake, irrespective of the hope of reward, was one of the major pleasures of life.[175]

With the publication of Rousseau's novel *La Nouvelle Héloïse* (1762), the secular cult of sensibility made its final breakthrough. It popularized the idea of the compatibility of happiness and virtue, and the idea that one who cries because of others must be good. The novel purifies and elevates the soul by teaching the "gospel of the heart".[176] *La Nouvelle Héloïse* testifies better than any other literary work produced in eighteenth-century France that the age of the philosophers was at the same time a period of *"hommes sensibles"*.[177]

An extremely profound sense of pity often leads to tears of emotion. As Anne Vincent-Buffault points out in her history of tears, one visible manifestation of the eighteenth century's "cult of sensibility" was the fashion of crying in public. The *"scène larmoyant"* is characteristic for the pathetic sentimental novel of that epoch. Crying was no longer regarded as indecent, since it embraced the entire humanity. The propensity to cry over the misfortunes of strangers or humanitarian principles was now considered natural, it was the affirmation of a new sensitivity to unhappiness and pain: "Tears circulated like a universal language all over the surface of planet."[178]

Vincent-Buffault's allusion to tears as a "universal language" is a sign that crying in public was no longer a privilege of the nobility. The meaning of tears now underwent a transformation. As has been suggested, for a long time they had been tolerated because they were a public sign of a specific elitist sensibility.[179] From Mercier's writings can be traced this new idea, for him the tearfulness was, rather, a sign of a nobility of the soul, not that of birth. For example in the chapter of *L´An 2440*, devoted to the mysteries of the universe it is told that in the silence of the observatory, "le jeune homme ému... pleure de joie".[180]

. . . .

175 Hampson 1981, 99; Häyry & Häyry 1997, 55–56. See also McManners 1981, 53.
176 Trousson 1989, 105–124, passim. See also Schama 1989, 29.
177 Mauzi & Menant 1977, 61. Despite the success of Rousseau's novel, the honor of launching the word "sentimental" in the French language belongs to Lawrence Sterne's (1713–1768) novel *A Sentimental Journey* (1768), which was translated in French in 1769. Daumas 1996, 151.
178 Vincent-Buffault 1986, 39–44. I am not here suggesting, however, that there is no evidence of public crying in the preceding centuries. The supreme change that took place in the course of the eighteenth century was, however, that "tearfulness" now won the status of a cult or an "art", a constitutive part of secular and social sentimentalism, which meant that more importance was given to tears, both as a literary mannerism and as a component of social play, than before.
179 Revel 1989, 188–189.
180 Mercier, *L'An 2440 I* 1786. Tears can thus flow from the experience of exceptional beauty, as is also the case in one of Mercier's most sentimental essays, entitled *"Ma Fenétre"*, where he is contemplating in front of the Swiss mountain scenery, the reflections of moonlight silvering the lake of Neuchâtel; the melancholic musing is transformed into a kind of mournful consolation: "C'est alors que l'ame tombe dans une douce mélancolie, & que les idées qui naissent, vous subjuguent & vous arraches des larmes". Mercier, *Mon bonnet de nuit II* 1784, 414–415.

Mercier's utopians of 2440 are not ashamed of crying in public, which is consistent with the ideal of total transparency and publicity. As a visible sign of social compassion, the function of tears is now to unite men of all social strata in the name of reciprocal brotherhood, freedom and equality. Regardless of social class, all men have now only one and undivided cause, that of "suffering humanity". For example, when describing the execution of a murderer,[181] instead of focusing on the spectacle of cruelty and bloodthirstiness among the execution audience, Mercier emphasizes the compassion, tenderness, affection and tearfulness of the spectators towards the criminal mind.[182]

As this reveals, from the viewpoint of the new cult of social sensibility, tears and joy were often intertwined; by bemoaning the hard lot of the less fortunate, one could gain pleasure leading to the sentiment of happiness. The sentimental conviction that all men were good by nature led to the belief that men were expected to share each other's pain. The idea of the outcast's pain conferred a new humanity on marginal figures.[183]

The special emphasis on the virtue of social compassion also led to the glorification of friendship. The communication of hearts through the sharing of emotion was seen as "the most gentle of sentiments".[184] Mercier's short essay devoted to this subject, *Amitié*, characterizes this new sentimental orientation; he sees friendship as a feeling close to love, proclaiming that disinterested friendship exists even amongst criminals. The idea of genuine friendship contains the element of sacrifice: a true friend prefers to preserve his firmness even on the scaffold rather than reveal the names of his accomplices. This romantic ideal finds its most beautiful expression in Mercier's words: "Qui ne regarde que soi ne peut vivre heureux. Qui rapporte tout à soi sera seul. Qui vit seul est privé des délices du sentiment; car le sentiment n'est que la réaction de deux coeurs qui sont unis."[185]

Mercier's conception of disinterested friendship proclaims the dissolution of all borders separating people from each other. He anticipates the romantic idea of love as a synthesis and sympathy of the souls. The sublime feeling which underpins this elevated conception of friendship is akin to the religious-mystical sentiment of union with the divine which Mercier's utopians feel when they see the face of their Redeemer through the telescope. It has been suggested that this was a typical attitude for the Romantics, who thought that love enabled man to know the universe by means of endless yearning for oneness with another person, or with humanity, or with the cosmos as a whole.[186]

It is easy to observe how much the eighteenth-century dogma of mutual caring, loving and social compassion toward the whole of humankind was indebted to

. . . .

181 For a fuller analysis, See Chapter VII, pp. 194–195, 201–202.
182 Mercier, *L'An 2440 I* 1786, 128–130.
183 Morris 1993, 205–213.
184 Vincent-Buffault 1986, 32–34.
185 Mercier, *Mon bonnet de nuit I* 1784, 82–86, especially 84.
186 Singer 1987, 285–287.

the Christian moral code. Moreover, it has been claimed that Deism contributed a great deal in the formation of the modern cult of sensibility. In its sense of the fraternity of the whole of humanity, it fostered a new sympathy for man. Many Christians agreed with the Deists that the welfare of man and the duty to serve society was equally important as the worship of God. The conviction of the importance of social utility became one of the most frequently repeated ideas of the century.[187]

For Mercier there was no doubt that there should not be any contradiction between religious dogma and social utility, and it was above all the moral code of Christianity which appealed to him: "Oui, la morale est la seule religion nécessaire a l'homme: il est réligieux dès qu'il est raisonnable; il est vertueux dès qu'il se rend utile..."[188] It was expressly in a similar form that the meaning and function of religion is conceived in most utopias produced in eighteenth-century France. Their aim is to integrate religion into a whole of the good life on earth, to blend the City of God and the City of Man.[189]

Similarly, in his treatise on Rousseau Mercier clearly formulates this Christian precept focused on the love of one's neighbor:

> "Cette loi naturelle qui nous dit: de ne faire à autrui que ce que nous voudrions qu'il nous fît, et ce précepte divin qui nous ordonne d'aimer notre prochain comme nous-mêmes, n'ont-ils pas leur fondement dans l'évangile? L'évangile n'oblige-t-il pas l'homme à priser tout autre homme autant que lui-même; voilà la loi qui parle également à tous les hommes..."[190]

The dogma of social compassion, the spirit of universal love and fraternity – the dominant position of these themes gives ample testimony to the fact that despite its secularizing tendency, *L'An 2440* has not broken with the Christian inheritance. This sustains the Carl L. Becker's challenge to the traditional view of eighteenth-century philosophers as one-sidedly cold rational thinkers. In his view they were much less emancipated from the medieval Christian thought than it is usually supposed. The philosophers demolished the Heavenly City of St. Augustine "only to rebuild it with more up-to-date materials".[191]

It is noteworthy, however, that the most cynical eighteenth-century French philosophical writers ended up questioning the entire habit of identifying happiness and virtue, arguing that the rewards of virtue were often purely illusory: Was it not hypocritical to claim that an evil or vicious man would automatically be doomed to unhappiness? Why could it not be otherwise? Was it not at least equally probable that man might enjoy insulting other men, and draw pleasure from the sight of their sufferings? And, since man does do some

. . . .

187 Hampson 1981, 104–105.
188 Mercier, *L'An 2440 I* 1786, 187.
189 Polak 1961, 256.
190 Mercier, *De J.J. Rousseau considéré comme l'un des premiers auteurs de la Révolution II* 1791, 281.
191 Becker 1965, 29, 31.

virtuous deed, how could one be sure that it was not spurred by some purely egoistic motive?

In his treatise *"De L'homme"* for example, Helvétius rejects the thesis that all men are good. He argues that if men feel social compassion, it is because they have a personal interest to pursue. In his view, the benevolence that man shows toward other men always exists in direct proportion to the benefit that he expects to get himself. In other words, it is utilitarian morals which push him forward, and "love for other men" is, in the final resort, always based on self-love: "La compassion n'est donc point en nous un sentiment inné."[192]

In his *Système de la nature* d'Holbach draws a similar conclusion, advancing an opposite line of argumentation in relation to the tradition of altruism. Being absolutely convinced of men's purely egoistic motives, he explains the needfulness of a social pact:

> "Mais comme la nature de chaque homme le porte à chercher à tout moment son bien-être dans la satisfaction de ses passions ou de ses caprices passagers, sans aucune égard pour ses semblables, il fallut une pacte qui le ramenat à son devoir..."[193]

To continue the list further, the materialistically oriented philosopher La Mettrie was also an eager supporter of this cynical attitude. In his *Anti-Sénèque* (1750) he advances the idea that from the viewpoint of happiness good and evil are things quite different in themselves. It is even possible that one obtains greater satisfaction from doing evil than doing good, which explains why so many scoundrels are happy and shows that "there is a kind of individual felicity which is to be found, not merely without virtue, but even in crime itself".[194]

Virtues and Passions: Happiness through Coercion

To find an optimal reconciliation between men's instinctual drives and social constraints is not always an uncomplicated matter. In early-modern thinking the inability to control one's emotions was regarded as a punishment for the original sin; the inward chaos was a consequence of man's disobedience.[195] It appears that despite their denial of original sin, in this respect the philosophers of the Enlightenment did not make a decisive break with tradition. Mauzi asserts that in eighteenth-century France the passions were thought to constitute the severest obstacle for the whole doctrine of happiness.[196]

. . . .

192 Helvétius, *Collection des plus belles pages* 1909, 217–218.
193 [d'Holbach], *Système de la nature I* 1771, 152.
194 Hampson 1981, 123.
195 James 1999, 13.
196 Mauzi 1994, 437. During that century, however, a shift took place in the meaning of the word "passion". For example, in his *Pensées philosophiques* Diderot still employs it in the same way as Descartes; the word designates, in a very general manner, all affective states. Gradually the "passions" assume their modern sense, designating in particular violent and exclusive sentiments, which obsess the soul and attach it to just one object. In this way, the *passions* (the principle of torments and interior division) became opposed to the sentiment, which realized, in "soft euphoria", the unity of the consciousness. Mauzi 1994, 437. On the other hand, for example in his *Entretiens sur le fils naturel* Diderot alludes to the conception

The possible consequences of passionate outbursts was one of Mercier's major concerns, too. In his utopia he expresses his fear that they might constitute a threat, which could eventually put in jeopardy the whole social order and lead the world into a state of chaos and "moral anarchy". This idea is clearly formulated in the scene of *L'An 2440* where the time traveler remarks that the happiness prevailing in 2440 must be the end-result of a very long and difficult journey. The Parisian of the future agrees: "Les passions humaines sont de terribles obstacles."[197]

Rousseau had drawn a similar conclusion earlier in his *Du contrat social*, where he writes: "...car la volonté particulière tend par sa nature aux préférences, et la volonté générale à l'égalité".[198] Montesquieu, for his part, contends that as a limited creature, man incessantly violates the laws which God has established, and is subject to ignorance and error and to a "thousand passions".[199] Diderot echoes this common view of his time by emphasizing the inconsistency of virtue and passion in his treatise *Entretiens sur le fils naturel* as follows: "Le goût de l'ordre... c'est le germe d'l'honnêteté et du bon goût; il nous porte au bien, tant qu'il n'est point gêné par la passion..."[200]

The issue of passions and their significance for the happiness or unhappiness of man is, however, far from uncontroversial. There exists a certain ambivalence in the ways the passions have been dealt with by different philosophers. Instead of being solely painful and destructive impulses, they have also been seen as necessary to man's survival and well-being.[201] The philosophers of the eighteenth century did not propose a total denial of passions as a remedy for man's assumed depravity; most of them agreed that man was most rational when the passions were in balance rather than if they were subordinated or suppressed.[202] The reconciliation of enjoyment and virtue was not thought to be a very burdensome problem, as long as artificial passions were not replaced by natural passions.[203] For example Mably was an anxious propagator of the positive effects of the passionate impulses: "Car les passions sont l'ame du monde; elles nous ont été données pour développer les facultés de notre ame, et par conséquent pour nous enseigner le chemin du bonheur."[204]

Mercier was no exception to this attitude. Despite his sceptical attitude towards the passionate movements of the masses[205] or women[206], he did not, in the final resort, subscribe to the idea that all passionate impulses would only

. . . .

of passion in this "modern", exclusively obsessive meaning of the term: "La passion s'attache à une idée principale. Elle se tait, et elle revient à cette idée, presque toujours par exclamation." Diderot, *Oeuvres* 1951, 1219.

197 Mercier, *L'An 2440 II* 1786, 130–131.
198 Rousseau, *Oeuvres complettes de J.J. Rousseau II* 1793, 37.
199 Montesquieu, *De L'Esprit des loix I* 1749, 3.
200 Diderot, *Oeuvres* 1951, 1238.
201 James 1999, 14.
202 Coates, White & Schapiro 1966, 186.
203 Mornet 1969, 55.
204 Mably, *Collection complète des oeuvres de l'abbé de Mably X* 1794–1795, 247.
205 See Chapter V, pp. 110–111.
206 See Chapter V, pp. 146–147.

increase the sum of human unhappiness. In *L'An 2440* he proclaims that "pleasure is necessarily not a monster", and that virtue and passion do not automatically exclude each other.[207] Amongst the Parisians of 2440 it is customary to believe that passions have a decisive role to play for the perfectibility of man:

> "Loin de songer à détruire les passions, moteurs invisibles de nôtre être, nous les regardons comme un don précieux qu'il faut économiser avec soin. Heureuse l'ame qui possède des passions fortes! elles font sa gloire, sa grandeur et son opulence."[208]

Mercier also, nonetheless, readily accepted the view that not all passions promoted man's happiness, and some passions would do more damage than good. For example, in a brief treatise contained in *Mon bonnet de nuit*, entitled "*Sagesse*", he suggests that great passions could form a threat to wisdom, whilst the "soft passions" should not be disapproved of, for they were necessary and created by nature: "Vivre sans desir, mépriser les sensations agréables, se rendre impossible, c'est renoncer à notre état d'intelligence, pour tomber dans celui d'un individu isolé..."[209]

What passions, according to Mercier, are beneficial and what, by contrast, destructive for man's happiness? In his ideal society of the twenty-fifth century all passions which aim solely at the satisfaction of individual desires, or "particular interests", are condemned as immoral and shameful. In practise this means that only those passions are accepted which aim at promoting patriotic virtues and the general well-being of the whole community in the name of universal compassion. As a consequence, all warlike sentiments and violent confrontations between men have been eliminated, due to the fact that all means to be distinguished from the mass are ruled out and the sole criterion of distinction between men is based on the practise of virtue. Virtuous behavior is rewarded: any brave man who has saved the life of another citizen from a danger, or prevented a public disaster, is allowed to bear a "brocaded hat". Not even the heir to the throne is allowed to bear this symbol of honor, if he commits an error or has not done anything to deserve it.[210]

Mercier's discrediting of all social hierarchies except those based on virtue testifies to the fact that in his imaginary society the idea of glory is totally detached from its connection with personal merit. If the sole motive for doing some good work is vanity and selfishness, the pursuit of glory becomes worthless. This reads as a sign of a change in the mentality of the French eighteenth-century society itself. Mauzi suggests that heroic morals had identified happiness and glory, whilst henceforward glory could be nothing more than a composite of happiness. In the course of the century the heroic

. . . .

207 Mercier, *L'An 2440 I* 1786, xi.
208 Mercier, *L'An 2440 II* 1786, 175–176.
209 Mercier, *Mon bonnet de nuit I* 1784, 323–326.
210 Mercier, *L'An 2440 I* 1786, 38–39.

conception of glory was thus replaced by a new idea, in which the idea of glory was now set in relation with the ideas of happiness and virtue. This new meaning given to glory was a consequence of the recognition that a harmony between happiness and glory, in the sense traditionally understood, was not always possible. In the terminology of that epoch, such glory was often confounded even with inhumanity or barbarism. As its opposite, real glory was seen as the public conscience of a virtuous man, whose priority was to search for his own happiness through the happiness of others. Instead of serving the apotheosis of an individual, the idea of glory was mobilized to profit the social order.[211]

The "brocaded hats" granted to exceptionally virtuous citizens in Mercier's future city reads as a deliberate attack against the aristocratic code of honor. It is the author's symbolic way of stating that such things as birth, material possessions or victories on the battlefield should play no part in deciding man's value as a moral creature. The general aversion which he felt towards the privileged members of his contemporary society shows, for example, in his condemnation of the cruel amusement which the noblemen draw from the killing of animals (the prerogative of hunting),[212] and the "gothic chivalry" which was visibly manifested in the custom of wearing always an offensive weapon as a mark of honor.[213] In addition, Mercier criticizes the seigneurs of his century and their ruthless habit of rolling in the Parisian streets with enormous speed.[214]

These examples are sufficient to demonstrate the fact that in Mercier's view the noblemen of his time lacked the precious gift of "*attendrissement*"; they did not care for the feelings of their fellow-creatures, all they cared about was the ostentatious representation of the symbols of social power. They had no self-constraint, no desire whatsoever to control their passing caprices or passionate impulses. With this attitude Mercier seems to contradict what Norbert Elias has called "court rationality", by which he designates the gradual replacement of the customs of medieval warrior society by more "civilized" conduct, starting from the sixteenth-century court society of Paris. Elias's leading thesis is that contrary to the warrior societies characterized by "savage joys" and uninhibited satisfaction of pleasure, the individual living in a court society was largely protected from the attacks of physical violence, but at the same time he was himself forced to suppress in himself passionate impulses. As a consequence of this "civilizing" turn, the threat to individual life was depersonalized and subjected to strict norms and laws. When individuals could no longer manifest their passions directly toward other people, the struggle became concentrated within the individual himself; constraints between people were transformed into self-constraints. This meant enforcement and constraint on the affects, self-discipline and self-control.[215]

. . . .

211 Mauzi 1994, 484–485, 495.
212 Mercier, *L'An 2440 I* 1786, 219–220.
213 Mercier, *L'An 2440 I* 1786, 24–25.
214 Mercier, *L'An 2440 I* 1786, 34.
215 Elias 1982, 5–8, 229–243. See also Campbell 1987, 161–167.

Despite their apparent dissimilarities, Mercier's utopian society retains many features from court society: what is essential is the avoidance of all emotional excess, and ascetic self-control. The organizing principle in both is the same desire to direct one's forces for the continuous struggle against violent confrontations, in order that society would not lapse into a state of moral chaos. Yet, as stated before, the "*honnête homme*" of court society lacked one faculty which Mercier appreciated above anything else: the inborn capacity for social compassion. For him, self-interest could cause nothing but social disorder, and vanity is severely condemned.[216] From this line of thought can be found, by implication, a distinction between "*amour de soi*" and "*amour-propre*". In his *Émile*, Rousseau explains that whilst *amour de soi* finds its fulfilment from the satisfaction of real needs, *amour-propre* can never be fully satisfied, because it demands that others prefer us to themselves. As a consequence, whereas soft and affective passions are born from the love of oneself (*l'amour de soi*), hostile passions are born from *l'amour-propre*.[217]

Mercier was not, however, totally blind to the fact that men would not, probably, even in the remote future be "assez parfait pour faire le bien, pour le seul honneur d'avoir bien fait".[218] From this it follows that in order for them to learn their "true interests", a social pact must be established. The implication is that men, blinded by the temptations of passions, do not always know what is best for them. For this reason they need guidance in order to remain in the right path: "... dès que les esprits sont éclairés sur leurs véritables intérêts, ils deviennent justes et droits."[219] The principle that underpins this line of thought is akin to that promoted by Rousseau in *Du contrat social*: "...que quiconque refusera d'obéir à la volonté générale y sera contraint par tout le corps: ce qui ne signifie autre chose sinon qu'on le forcera d'être libre..."[220]

The idea that men could be "forced to be free" is based on the view that happiness is one "skill" or an "art" among many, which could be learned through proper education. According to Mauzi, this *didactic* conception of happiness, i.e., the desire to elaborate, for all men equally, an art of how to be happy has formed one of the most ancient dreams of humankind. For eighteenth-century thinkers, the discovery of happiness, its reduction to an easily learnable formula, appeared at the same time necessary and possible.[221]

This idea of happiness is, however, somewhat problematical inasmuch as the coercion practiced in the name of eudaemonia eventually leads to the elimination of liberty, due to the fact that the idea of a categorical obligation does not make sense.[222] It has been shown that Rousseau's *Émile* clearly

. . . .

216 See for example Mercier, *L'An 2440 III* 1786, 159.
217 Rousseau, *Émile ou de l'éducation* 1904, 239–240, 292.
218 Mercier, *L'An 2440 I* 1786, 40.
219 Mercier, *L'An 2440 II* 1786, 130–131.
220 Rousseau, *Oeuvres complettes de J.J. Rousseau II* 1793, 28.
221 Mauzi 1994, 514–515.
222 Telfer 1980, 126, 133.

illustrates the conflict between the concepts of freedom and order which ensues from this: the commitment is to "natural" feeling, but the education of Émile for freedom is based on the most rigid discipline. The whole educational programme is extremely coercive, and feeling is subordinated to rational control. The message is that feeling is wild and unmanageable if it is not properly socialized. Like Shaftesbury or Kant, Rousseau also considered feeling only as supplementary to reason, being convinced that only when dominated by reason, could feeling become virtuous.[223]

This is the same dilemma which the creators of utopias have over the centuries been forced to encounter: How to find a satisfying solution for the antagonism between freedom and order? Is it genuinely possible to teach men to be happy? As scholars devoted to utopian thought have pointed out, in most utopian novels the elimination of the danger of "moral anarchy" is executed by a total sacrifice of individuality. The populations of utopias are uniform beings with identical needs and reactions; they have no sentiments, desires or passions, because passions are manifestations of individuality. The uniformity is reflected in every detail of life, from clothing to schedule, from moral behavior to intellectual interests.[224] Because in most utopias everything is organized by the state, privacy is eliminated. It is regarded as a means of cutting oneself off from others, a kind of "moral pathology".[225]

In other words, there are no contrasts in utopias. This means the absence of certain character-types as incongruous with the idea of a utopian society: beggar, soldier, tyrant.[226] One searches in vain for these categories in Mercier's ideal state, too. In a purified city there is no room for marginal human groups, representatives of social extremes or for anyone who would form a deviance from the all-encompassing norm of uniformity and from the image of an "ideal citizen" shaped according to this general mould. There are neither despots, nor physically or mentally handicapped persons. Due to the fact that their entire life is devoted to the art of perfecting their skills in the art of becoming obedient and socially useful citizens, Mercier's utopians have no psychological complexity or awareness of individuality.

The utopian city is "made of iron", as Lapouge expresses it. Eventually the uniformization of individuals ends up in their negation. The utopians tolerate nothing but that which is uncorrupted, a sort of "dead-alive", and the utopians are only cogwheels in a machine. Each one of them, without roots and without future, anonymous like a number, is nothing but a function, a tool. In a "crystal society" there exists no hazard, there are only necessities. Utopia purifies life from its pathetic nature, convulsions, excrements, infirmity and almost from death. One could scarcely imagine a greater cruelty than to deprive man of the right for unhappiness.[227]

. . . .

223 Bell 2000, 2, 26–27, 33.
224 Berneri 1951, 4–5; Lapouge 1982, 15. See also Mucchielli 1960, 198; Kateb 1963, 220.
225 Goulemot 1989, 379–380.
226 Kateb 1963, 226–227.
227 Lapouge 1982, 15.

This monotonous uniformity of most utopias led Cioranescu to use the metaphor of death to characterize the utopian vision of man and his relation to society. He writes that because utopian societies are composed of interchangeable subjects, their atmosphere is extremely monotonous. Both social and personal life seem to be devoted to a sort of "virtuous and solemn boredom", which strongly resembles "the happiness of the dead". This happiness is the only preoccupation and *raison d'être* of the state. Because for the writers of utopias the happiness of all means necessarily the happiness of everyone, the place of individual in the collective has been traced in advance.[228]

The dramatic metaphor "happiness of the dead" also illustrates Mercier's future "paradise", which Lapouge describes by such attributes as "gray" and "melancholic".[229] Owing to its extreme "reasonableness" the atmosphere prevailing in this society of 2440 seems to be petrified in a state of eternal repose and immutability. There is no humor, no laughter, no passions (except those born from a profound sense of patriotism and the good conscience attained through the knowledge that one has filled one's code of honor as a citizen). As the time traveler is informed by his guide, there are no purely coincidental events, either; the word "hasard" has been eliminated from the language, since the utopian men regard it as a synonym for ignorance.[230] In a word, *L'An 2440* is a representation of a condition in which the individual will and free choice are totally broken. This makes of Mercier's utopian society a kind of "necropolis"[231], a city of the living dead.

Béclard has compared *L'An 2440* with the virtuous "moralities" of the fifteenth century; in both cases all sentiment of real life has been eliminated. Mercier's creatures are not human beings.[232] Because thinking and behavior are totally directed by a norm of uniformity, the population is reminiscent of an army of obedient tin soldiers, a group of mechanical dolls. Eighteenth-century thinkers felt a special fascination for automata,[233] and the mechanical doll is just as obedient, malleable and dispassionate as the "ideal citizens" in Mercier's utopian society. To continue even further these metaphors related to artificial human models, one can trace points of contact between the anonymous and faceless puppets of Mercier's "theater of allegory" and the actors of classic tragedy. In Greek drama a *persona* or face-mask made possible the concealment of one's true face.[234]

Against this mechanistic image of man, it appears to some extent ironic that Mercier seems to have regarded himself as a great apostle of individual liberty

· · · · · · · · · ·

228 Cioranescu 1972, 31–33.
229 Lapouge 1978, 237.
230 Mercier, *L'An 2440 II* 1786, 36–37.
231 The utopian cities are sometimes situated under the surface of the earth. These subterranean cities are "necropoles", where all life is absent, and the creatures inhabiting these cities traverse a "zone of death". They are not occupied by time; these cities are characterized by eternity, in which everything is simultaneously present. Roudaut 1990, 49–58.
232 Béclard 1903, 132.
233 Lapouge 1978, 242.
234 Gurevich 1995, 90.

and human rights. At least on one occasion he implies that God has bestowed man with free will for the reason that if man was not free, his heart would feel neither pleasure nor repentance, he would be dominated solely by blind instinct: "Il créa l'homme pour être heureux, mais il veut qu'il tende au bonheur librement, & par l'usage de sa volonté. C'est la prérogative qui le distingue de la brute".[235]

The view that happiness is above all an inner sentiment can be traced also from Mercier's didactic story entitled "*Seged*", which is contained in his collection of moral stories *Les Hommes comme il y a en a peu, et les génies comme il n'y a en a point* (1768). In this story the problem of happiness is approached in a more amusing, fairy-tale manner. It tells about the king of Ethiopia, who decides to retreat into a "palace of voluptuousness" for ten days. He pursues total liberation from fear, sorrow and discontentment by ordering that all his desires must be immediately satisfied. The king makes extensive efforts in order to find happiness: he invites all kind of artists to his enchanted island and declares that nobody is allowed to appear before the king with a sad look on his face. But this plan is doomed to fail, and the king learns by experience that without freedom there can be no happiness, since nobody can order himself to be happy.[236]

In *L'An 2440*, however, Mercier has forgotten the moral lesson of "*Seged*" that "eudaemonia through coercion" is not possible. As in Rousseau's *Émile*, there exists an irresoluble tension between freedom and order. In trying to create an image of an ideal human type who has emancipated himself from the enslavement of passions by using his reason, Mercier ends up in producing monsters subordinated under the burden of over-exaggerated demands of rationality and virtue. The intellectual experiment aiming at the noble liberation of man from the double tyranny of religious and political authorities is thus doomed to fail, because they have been replaced by equally rigorous and coercive system of power, based on the social pact as the supreme source of legitimacy.

Mercier's image of an "ideal citizen", purified from all conflicting aspects of existence, reveals that an experiment aiming at the reconciliation of happiness and virtue can never completely succeed. As has been suggested, happiness and virtue remain irreconcilable, because there exists no sure way to satisfy simultaneously the demands of the mind and the body. For this reason the utopian vision of a moral world is incapable of allowing man the tragic meaning of life.[237]

. . . .

235 Mercier, *Les Songes d'un hermite* 1788a, 311–312.
236 Mercier, *Eloges et discours philosophiques* 1776a, 165–179. The same story is also to be found in Mercier's collection *Fictions morales*, with some slight modifications, under the title "*Où est le bonheur?*". Mercier, *Fictions morales II* 1792, 1–28. In point of fact, "*Seged*" is a translation of Samuel Johnson's (1709–1784) two essays in *The Rambler*, numbers 204 and 205. Number 204 (first published on Saturday, 29.2.1752), is titled in collected editions of *The Rambler* "The history of ten days of Seged, emperor of Ethiopia". Number 205 (first published on Tuesday, 3.3.1752) is titled "The history of Seged concluded". Johnson 1969, 296–305.
237 Wunenburger 1995, 525–526.

By assuming that the happiness of one individual follows as a natural and automatic by-product of the well-being of the whole community, Mercier seems to ignore the difficulty that individual and collective happiness are not necessarily compatible. In other words, "nature" and "virtue" are not automatically one and the same thing. If it is supposed that the individual's "inner voice" always functions in perfect harmony with the "general will", man loses all his personal features as a unique human being. This philosophy, based on a didactic conception of happiness, leads to a very one-sided and distorted image of man and his needs.

It is this same deficiency for which Alisdair McIntyre has criticized the whole Enlightenment project. To paraphrase his point, despite the fact that the eighteenth-century moral philosophers purported to free the individual from the constraints of hierarchy and teleology, they replaced these by a new teleology, or by some new categorical status. The first of these options was typically based on utilitarian doctrines, whereas the second was indebted to the philosophy of Kant. Both attempts were doomed to fail, for the notion of the "greatest happiness of the greatest number" is only a pseudo-concept without any clear content.[238]

It is thus justified to argue that the whole concept of collective or public happiness is highly questionable: What is this "public felicity" in the first place? It is ultimately nothing but an abstract ideal, without relevant contact points with actual realities. As Ruyer puts it, in utopias happiness is given to the collectivity rather than to the individual, but the happiness of collectivity as such signifies nothing.[239] Due expressly to the fact that the utopians' prior values prioritized not happiness but *order*, utopia would be a place where man could not be happy.[240] The whole idea that the utopian condition is automatically synonymous with a state of happiness is thus reversed. This question will be raised subsequently in conjunction with the problem of evil.[241]

Not all eighteenth-century preachers of happiness were equally blind to the illusory aspects of the concept of *"le bonheur publique"* as Mercier, however. Shklar has shown that even Rousseau clearly realized that happiness is the most individual and personal of feelings, and he was well aware of the complexities embedded in his moral psychology. He based this knowledge on the following arguments: 1) Happiness could not be attained, for man was "born to suffer"; 2) Happiness cannot be taught; 3) Happiness is dependent on man's character and dispositions, and for this reason it differs greatly from individual to individual; 4) Because there exists no identity of feeling and need among individuals, public control is untenable as a concept; there is no abstract or collective notion of happiness dissociable with the individual feelings.[242]

. . . .

238 McIntyre 1987, 62, 64.
239 Ruyer 1988, 52.
240 Davis 1981, 375.
241 See Chapter VII, pp. 202–204.
242 Shklar 1969, 194.

Before Rousseau, Antoine-Francois Prévost was one of the few writers of the eighteenth century who was acutely aware of the fact that there could exist a contradiction between the individual and collective happiness, i.e., between nature and society.[243] Prévost's novel *Le Philosophe Anglais, ou Histoire de monsieur Clevelend, fils naturel de Cromwell* (1731–1739) contains a description of a "happy island" which turns out, however, to be an anti-utopia. Prévost has little sympathy with the patriarchal simplicity prevailing in this island, ruled in accordance with strict protestant discipline, where the relative equality is revealed on closer scrutiny to be incompatible with the spirit of true freedom. Prévost tells us that this extremely egalitarian society protects itself from the disorder caused by jealousy by using the drawing of lots to determine wives. Despite its simplicity, this practise is condemned as oppressive when the result contradicts the choice of the heart. There thus exists a conflict between the social order and individualism.[244]

The Issue of Gender

At least as much as on social and political roles, human happiness is dependent on one's gender and the expectations imposed by gender roles. The theme of the present chapter is to explore how the concept of gender is related to the idea of happiness in Mercier's utopian vision.

In the chapters *"Les femmes"* and *"De la grande loi domestique"* of *L'An 2440*, in which Mercier treats problems concerning femininity, marital relations and child caring, he advances very strongly the idea that man and woman live separate lives, they are born to fill different duties and tasks in society, and for this reason the kind of happiness reserved for them is also essentially different by nature. In eighteenth-century French society, he is concerned about the decline of masculine power and the growth of women's arrogance in terms of a desire for expensive jewels and clothes. In his imaginary world of the twenty-fifth century, this "disharmony" of sexual power, which Mercier found so alarming in his contemporary society, has been reversed. He propagates the importance of reinforcing the dominance of the husband in relation to his wife and children. Mercier dreams that in the future the wives, who have dared to make fun of their husbands, will have been restored under strict discipline and obedience, and the male has become in his home *"un maître, un juge absolu"*.[245]

If Mercier's hopes had been rewarded, in the world of 2440 women would live their lives totally subordinated to their husbands. In his imagined utopian community, patriarchal power knows no limits. The demand for equality of spouses was in Mercier's opinion a grave error. As he saw it, there are biological

. . . .

243 Baczko 1978, 49; Ehrard 1994, 769–770.
244 Prévost, *Le Philosophe Anglois, ou Histoire de monsieur Cleveland II* 1736, 127–135; Pomeau & Ehrard 1998, 274–275.
245 Mercier, *L'An 2440 III* 1786, 19–29, especially 23.

reasons, which can be drawn directly from "nature", supporting this argument: Mercier explains in his utopia that because of her "dependent and precarious nature" woman can not under any circumstances be a rival with man; subordination is thus a "law of nature": "Il est de la nature éternelle des choses, qu'un sexe soit subordonné à l'autre."[246]

These words illustrate the general dependence of eighteenth-century writers on natural-law theorists of the preceding century, such as Bodin or Grotius, who had argued that the husband should be the sovereign within the domestic commonwealth.[247] Joan Landes has suggested that for many intellectuals of that epoch the categories of gender became almost completely polarized: despite the fact that the French Revolution came to shatter the monologic discourse of absolutist France, the bourgeois emphasis on universal reason was at odds with particularism, of which sexual difference was one form. In this situation, two contradictory solutions were available: either women would have to be subsumed within the universal, or treated as different by nature.[248] As the above quoted extracts from *L'An 2440* clearly demonstrate, it was to the latter alternative that Mercier was inclined.

Mercier strongly emphasizes the idea that in his utopian society the women are above all mothers and wives. In her role as the guardian of virtuous morals the ideal woman does not consume cosmetics, tobacco or alcohol, stay up late, sing licentious chansons, or associate freely with men. Patience, modesty and tenderness are the basic characteristics of an ideal woman. Instead of vanity, music and dancing, the women of the future use their time in trying to learn how to please their husbands and rear their children.[249] Chastity is thus the supreme value of the ideal woman inhabiting Mercier's "city of purity", and the same admiration of a "non-carnal", almost spiritual, womanhood has been shared by many other utopian writers. To name individual examples, Campanella, for example, seems to have been almost obsessed by the idea of female chastity; in his utopia *Civitas Solis* women who dare to beautify themselves by artificial means or use high heels are punished by death. The ideal is a woman who has reached her beauty by physical exercise,[250] which is reminiscent of the Stoic ideal of a disciplined and well-shaped human body.

In his utopia Mercier leaves no doubt about the fact that in his mind domestic happiness was one of the most important values and major blessings in human life. In this respect he follows in the footsteps of More, who in his *Utopia* sets up the model of a patriarchal and monogamous family. Scholars of utopianism, for example Marie Louis Berneri, point out that in this respect the creators of utopias have assumed very divergent attitudes. Some of them have imitated the tradition of Plato[251] and abolished the family institution and monogamy

. . . .

246 Mercier, *L'An 2440 III* 1786, 20.
247 Traer 1980, 49–50.
248 Landes 1988, 105. Cf. Berlanstein 1997, 156–160.
249 Mercier, *L'An 2440 II* 1786, 161–162.
250 Campanella, *La cité du soleil* 1993, 121.
251 In the *Republic* of Plato, child-rearing is a communal practise: parents do not know their children, nor children their parents. Plato, *The Republic of Plato* 1991, 101, 136.

altogether. A third group of utopianists retains family institutions, but hands the upbringing of children over to the state.[252] Mercier's vision of an ideal family differs sharply from these radical communist utopias, based on the communal upbringing of children or sexual promiscuity. Instead he takes a decisive step toward a modern nuclear family model by emphasizing women's role as the guardians of virtuous morals, whose duties are limited to the domestic sphere in the private sector of life.

Mercier's vision of a rigorous distinction between the feminine and masculine spheres of life reflects the contemporary tendencies in eighteenth-century French society. As a consequence of a gradual process of "deprivatization", which Philippe Ariès has traced as far back as the late seventeenth century, public affairs were no longer confounded with private interests. The zone thus liberated was filled by the family, which began to assume new functions; instead of being simply an economic unit, it now became a focus of private life.[253]

This new orientation was directly influenced by the fashionable cult of sentimentalism, insofar as it now became customary to increase the expectations of sentiment in family relationships and to argue that marital partners ought to choose one another freely, not out of compulsion but out of mutual affection and esteem. Among the literary elites, a new, more positive status was accorded to the institution of marriage as a means to personal happiness. The consolidation of the image of a "happy family" was thus started, and attacks against "arranged marriages" multiplied.[254]

Passionate love was not a major preference for this new bourgeois sensibility. Even if affection between partners was regarded as acceptable, the traditional juxtaposition between "profane" and "sacred" love was far from being abandoned in the French novels of the eighteenth century. Erotic passion, dangerous and unpredictable, was often sacrificed in the name of a stable, emotional but non-passionate love.[255] Rousseau's novel *La Nouvelle Héloïse* provides a classical example of this sacrifice of passionate love on the altar of duty as this theme is dealt with in the literature of that epoch.[256]

Mercier's fashion to make a strict division in his utopia between men's and women's domains of life lays ground for the assumption that the idea of happiness is closely dependent on gender and on the expectations imposed by gender roles. The focal idea of *L'An 2440* concerning sexual roles is that a woman cannot reach happiness as an autonomous, independent creature: women's happiness is always bound to external factors. Mercier's woman of the future does not fulfil the role of an individual subject, as a free agent, but that of an object. The happiness accepted for woman is under all circumstances

. . . .
252 Berneri 1951, 6.
253 Ariès 1989, 7–8, 10.
254 Traer 1980, 49; Charlton 1984, 171–173.
255 Charlton 1984, 173–175; Delon, Mauzi & Menant 1998, 23.
256 About different interpretations concerning the mutual relation of duty and passion in *La Nouvelle Héloïse*, see for example Singer 1987, 303–343.

relational only – relational in regard to man, who is a "master", an "absolute judge" in his home, as Mercier puts is. It is thus woman's duty to accept the limits of her personality. The relationship between man and woman is constructed on the basis of subordination and masculine dominance, and the characteristics expected of a woman are humility, obedience and self-denial. As a consequence of this, the only possible sort of "happiness" allowed for women is exclusively determined on patriarchal terms.

By stressing the "natural" role of woman as mother and wife, Mercier proclaims himself as an ardent supporter of Rousseau. His ideas on a distinctive "feminine destiny" and on the biological differences between the sexes are drawn directly from Rousseau's *Émile*, where Rousseau gives a description of the characteristics of Émile's future life mate, Sophie (livre V: "*Sophie ou la femme*"). Rousseau's leading idea is that the differences between the genders are not due to the environmental or cultural factors; because of biological determination, the feminine condition is tightly bound by what he calls a "*destination particulière*": "...la femme est faite spécialement pour plaire à l'homme."[257]

Amongst French eighteenth-century writers, Restif de la Bretonne also shared these conservative ideas of Rousseau and Mercier as regards "ideal femininity". For example, in his work *L'Andrographe* (1782), he comes to the conclusion that the will of man is always "total", whereas the will of woman remains merely relational and dependent on conditions. Restif could not imagine woman as acting other than in relation to man, because the object of feminine desire always lies outside woman's own personality – in man. Because of this, Restif concludes – following the masculine logic of his century – there is an insurmountable gulf separating the mental lives of a man and a woman:

> "Enfin l'âme de la Femme est si peu ressemblante à celle de son Chef, qu'elle est substantiellement dépendante; une Femme ne peut être solidement heureuse, que par sa liaison avec l'Homme, & sa dépendance de ses volontés..."[258]

These words of Restif reveal a similarity of opinion to that propagated by Mercier; whereas the latter describes man as an "absolute judge", Restif refers to his dominant position by the term "chef". The same sort of reasoning is advanced again in Restif's comedy of five acts entitled *L'An 2000* (1790), where he follows the fashion set by Mercier to locate a utopia in a remote future. All that seems to interest Restif in the year 2000 are questions related to gender roles and marriage. The events are focused on the festivities of the New Year at the beginning of the third millennium, and in the course of the celebration a decision is to be made about two marriages. The young women are veiled, and the young men are allowed to choose the wives that they find most pleasing. The

· · · · · · · · · ·
257 Rousseau, *Émile ou de l'éducation* 1904, 431.
258 Rétif de la Bretonne, *Idées singulières IV* 1782, 6–7.

women can refuse only in the event that the suitor has not shown his talents as a civic hero.[259] As this shows, in the imagination of the utopian writer a virtuous and pleasant wife would be a reward for the practise of virtue.

Occasionally Restif's fantastic utopias concerning the subordination of women led to a dream of their enslavement in an oriental fashion. The hero of his novel *Les Posthumes* (1802), Multipliandre, expresses the wish that he could restore patriarchal customs and have twelve wives, who would do all the work in the family. The sole purpose of women would be to produce children. Restif reiterates at the same time his previous idea that women are such as they are made; jealous and egoistic if they are not mastered, soft and happy when they are powerfully dominated.[260]

Over the centuries, special emphasis has been put on women's close association with nature.[261] Mercier's, Rousseau's, and Restif de la Bretonne's views about "natural" femininity offer perfect illustrations of this tenacious belief. Man, on the contrary, has been seen more as a cultural being, not so much bound to his gender. As Rousseau, the most ardent proponent of this view in eighteenth-century France, expressed it: "Le mâle n''est mâle qu'en certains instants, la femelle est femelle toute sa vie... tout la rappelle sans cesse à son sexe..."[262]

As has been noted previously in this study, the emancipation of mankind from the burden of original sin formed an important starting point in eighteenth-century debates devoted to the pursuit of terrestrial happiness. It has been suggested that the change in the ideas of femininity was directly related with this changed idea of nature. In the centuries characterized by a belief that the whole of nature was dominated by sin and evil, a special emphasis was put on the "fallen" nature of women. When it was contended that nature is benevolent and good, this also provided a radically more favourable view of woman.[263]

In particular in the pastoral tradition the interrelation between the concepts of "nature" and "femininity" has played a striking role. Here nature was symbolized as a benevolent and nurturing female, and the Arcadian image rendered nature passive and malleable. It contained at the same time the implication that nature could be used as a commodity and manipulated as a resource. The Scientific Revolution of the seventeenth century thus undermined the female image of the earth, which was a central trope in organic cosmology.[264]

Mercier's vision of ideal femininity is based on the same bucolic metaphor. His vision of woman as biologically determined is basically grounded on an organic view of nature; like "mother-earth", Mercier's utopian "ideal woman"

. . . .
259 Restif de la Bretonne, *L'an deux mille* 1790, 23–26 and passim.
260 Restif de La Bretonne, *Les Posthumes IV* 1802, 132–133.
261 Charlton 1984, 158.
262 Rousseau, *Émile ou de l'éducation* 1904, 435.
263 Charlton 1984, 158.
264 Merchant 1983, xvi, 8–9, 28.

is passive, receptive, caring, maternal and "non-passionate".[265] This view of nature or femininity is no longer burdened by the stigma of original sin, which shows particularly well in Mercier's description of the earth as a "nurturing mother". Another sign of this more positive tendency is the fact that in 2440 the throne of the king is surrounded by a figure representing a woman nursing her child.[266]

Mercier's glorification of such attributes as passivity, obedience and chastity as the characteristics best typifying an ideal woman constitutes one aspect of his general aversion towards passions. His emphasis on "non-passionate" womanhood reflects the Cartesian dichotomy between reason and emotions. As has already been noted above, in the philosophy of Descartes calculation was enthroned as a virtue, which meant the repudiation of emotions. To cite Toulmin on this issue: "In this social sense, "emotion" became a code word for sex: to those who valued a stable class system, sexual attraction was a main source of social disruption... What began as a theoretical distinction in Descartes... turned into a practical contrast between (good) rationality and (bad) sentiment or impulsiveness."[267]

Although Descartes' presumed hostility toward all passions should not be over-emphasized, this "Cartesian" chain of reasoning can be traced from Mercier's utopia in a surprisingly dogmatic form. In Mercier's mind the growth of feminine power would mean a dangerous threat, because he saw it as a phenomenon parallel to the tottering of the social balance in its entirety. The utopian image of humble, obedient and passive femininity reflects, obviously, Mercier's secret fear with regard to the possible growth of feminine power. In the chapter "Mariage" in Notions claires sur les gouvernemens he writes that women are the main beneficiaries of the institution of marriage – an advantage which they should repay with submission and tenderness. Because society is based on marital duties, a disobedient or rebellious wife constitutes a severe threat to the happiness of the whole country. How could the fatherland maintain its happiness, if disorder prevails in families? Mercier rhetorically asks.[268]

Mercier's anxiety concerning the possible decline of patriarchal power can be interpreted as a counter-reaction to an assumed corruption of morals, the signs of which he saw in the society of his time. It may also be, as the Manuels suggest, that Mercier's and Restif de la Bretonne's secular tendencies can be read as expression of anxieties of petits bourgeois who had to face the fact that their women had begun to adopt and ape the licentious ways of the upper social classes. Mercier found a solution for this burdensome problem in the image of Roman republican virtue with its chaste and noble women, who had been

. . . .

265 It is easy to note how much Mercier´s ideal women of the future resemble the Virgin Mary, and it may not be too far-fetched to suggest that Mercier had in his mind the image of the mother of Christ when he created the vision of women´s desirable characteristics. Obedience, chastity and humility are the attributes also customarily related to the image of the Virgin.

266 Mercier, L'An 2440 II 1786, 89–90.

267 Toulmin 1990, 134–135.

268 Mercier, Notions claires sur les gouvernemens II 1787, 245.

subordinated to their husbands in law but who had achieved a full partnership in virtue.[269] In confronting the moral disorder of the aristocracy the bourgeoisie of the eighteenth century emphasized the family relations and domestic virtues.[270]

This is one of the themes to which Mercier returns in several different contexts: the expansion of women's active role in life could form a threat to the social balance, and owing to their overwhelmingly passionate nature it was important to hold them under control. This tenacious need to hold women in their subordinated position makes one to suspect that Mercier was not yet emancipated enough from traditional thinking, according to which femininity was a synonym for danger and sin. It is a well-known fact that the age-old fear that women are sources of corruption was too deeply rooted to be easily discarded,[271] and that popular notions about women's dual nature were still much alive throughout the eighteenth century.[272]

Mercier's fear that the increase of women's hidden power could mean a mortal blow to the social *status quo* itself implies that any woman who does not accept the normative role imposed on her is simply "unnatural". The suggestion seems to be that a woman who gives herself to the caprices of passions is a "monster", an abnormal creature – like the painted prostitute in the imaginary art gallery of 2440. As an example of this kind of reasoning, in criticizing the lack of social compassion in contemporary society Mercier pays special attention to women's extraordinary cruelty as spectators at public executions:

> "J'ai frémi, non du forfait du criminel, mais du sang-froid horrible de tous ceux qui l'environnoient... "O honte de ma patrie! les yeux de ce sexe qui sembloit fait pour la pitié, furent ceux qui resterent le plus longtemps attachés sur cette scène d'horreur."[273]

The ideas of Renate Kartz-Matausch shed further light on Mercier's stereotyped image of women's exceptional cruelty and bloodthirstiness. In her article "*La légende des femmes révolutionnaires au XIXe siècle*" she describes how historians, e.g. Michelet, aimed to provide evidence of women's special inclination to violence, cruelty, and sadism as spectators and executors of the French Revolution. The main point which Kartz-Matausch makes is to demonstrate that it has been customary amongst historians to see a metaphorical connection between the unchained "populace" and the female figure. She

. . . .

269 Manuels 1982, 537–538.
270 Krauss 1970, 397.
271 Gay 1970, 33.
272 Mack 1984, 3–4.
273 Mercier, *L'An 2440 I* 1786, 122. A certain paradox emerges here in the sense that in his utopia Mercier represents male and female as a gendered dualism (social reason versus feeling), but at the same time he advances the view that women have a more natural inclination toward sentiments of social compassion than men. The female personality thus appears to be constructed of two opposite poles, i.e. of uncontrollable and dangerous passions in need of being subordinated under masculine reflection, and of an instinctual knowledge directed toward everything which is good and decent. This illustrates the ambivalent attitude toward women still prevailing in late eighteenth-century France: women were at the same time both witches and angels.

suggests that fear of the power of the masses goes hand in hand, at least implicitly, with fear of the power of women. As "collective hysteria", as a "wind of madness", the masses of women involved in the revolutionary activity aroused fear. Women's collective appearance on the stage of the revolution created a new mythic configuration: the "madwoman", "woman-hyena", or "woman-ogress" who represented the opposite of the image of a nourishing woman, the source of life and love. Historians thus express a fear that women might be capable of breaking the laws which keep them in their subordinated position.[274]

Allusions to women's "madness" refer to a general habit of classifying the inclination to exaggerated sentimentality and hysterical behaviour as feminine attributes. It has often been maintained in the tradition of Hippocrates that women are more "restless" than men. Women's "sensibility" has been seen as a reason for their "perpetual agitation".[275]

It was expressly this negative sort of "restlessness" which according to Mercier and many other eighteenth century's male writers caused so much trouble to women themselves and to the surrounding society. It was precisely this characteristic which was presumed as an inborn feminine attribute and which predestined women to a subordinated position in relation to men. The message conveyed by *L'An 2440* is that women are passionate creatures in the same way as children, savages, or unchained masses, and due to their unpredictable nature, they need to be "tamed" and "domesticated" under masculine reflection. Mercier seems to suggest to his readers that women incarnate the image of a "monster" or a "woman-hyena" if they refuse to accept the antisexual and antipolitical gender role imposed on them. According to this logic, a "passionate" woman is a "demon" or a "witch", whereas a "virtuous" one is an "angel". The symbolic division between the "harlot of Babylon" (the macabre image of the lustful and shameless prostitute in the art gallery of Paris in 2440) and the purely "spiritual", nourishing woman, has lost nothing of its ancient appeal.

Mercier was probably well aware that the floodgates would be opened for female emancipation, if women were allowed to earn their own living. In point of fact, in the course of the eighteenth century an increased number of women began to earn an independent living in various branches of cultural production.[276] It was thus the gradual increase of women's influence in the public sphere of life that aroused the greatest fear amongst male writers like Mercier. As a radical counter-reaction he envisages that in 2440 women would be also economically totally dependent on their husbands. Mercier thought that this could be best accomplished through the abolition of dowry: "Vous saurez que les femmes n'ont d'autre dot que leurs vertus et leurs charmes." The

. . . .
274 Kartz-Matausch 1990, 247–256.
275 Deprun 1979, 97.
276 Outram 1995, 89–91. See also Mack 1984, 7–9.

underlying idea is that when women receive their whole subsistence from their husband, they will be more predisposed to fidelity and obedience.[277] Conversely, in Mercier's future the husband is allowed immediately to reject a disobedient wife. The most valuable feminine characteristic is the capacity to please, precisely for the reason that the husband can refuse a wife who has not known how to please him.[278] It will not cause great surprise to note that Mercier does not say a word about women's rights if they are not pleased with their husbands; one can only assume that no such rights exist.

In Mercier's utopian vision women's exclusion from the labour markets gives the final blow to their potential aspirations for self-improvement and mastery over their own lives. Mercier envisages that in the remote future women will have been liberated from the duty of carrying heavy burdens, because as a weaker sex they have been born to fill lighter and "happier" duties, which are for the most part situated inside the domestic sphere:

> "Rendues aux devoirs de leur état, les femmes remplissoient l'unique soin que leur imposa le Créateur, celui de faire les enfans, et de consoler ceux qui les environnent, des peines de la vie."[279]

This quotation gives a good picture of how the idea of a specific "feminine destiny" provided a practical pretence when eighteenth-century male writers wanted to legitimate women's exclusion from independence. It shows characteristically how the concept of "nature" was used to serve a double purpose: this new family image was consolidated by arguments about what woman "naturally *is*" and how she could be "liberated" to be her "true, natural self".[280] On the other hand the resort to "nature" or "biology" was a convenient means to imprison women within a straitjacket of virtue by imposing strict constraints on their opportunities for advancement in the public sector of life. In other words, whereas in the centuries stigmatized by original sin "nature" had been used as a legitimating proof of women's viciousness, it was now being used, on the contrary, as evidence of their high moral standing, which was now regarded as a natural propensity. In both cases the end result remained the same: the subordination of women.

By appealing to the irrevocable roles of the sexes, eighteenth-century French philosophers aimed also at justifying their right to set limits to women's education and self-improvement. In *Émile* Rousseau argues for a different upbringing for boys and girls from this starting point: it is necessary for women to learn a wide range of skills, "mais seulement celles qu'il leur convient de savoir".[281]

. . . .

277 Mercier, *L'An 2440 II* 1786, 150–151.
278 Mercier, *L'An 2440 III* 1786, 23.
279 Mercier, *L'An 2440 I* 1786, 32. Mercier's fears concerning the increase of women's power shows particularly clearly in his special concern about actresses and their supposed "dangerous" qualities. This concern highlights the condemnation of their prominence and influence in eighteenth-century French society more widely. Berlanstein 1997, 155–156. This too is borrowed directly from Rousseau, who protested loudly against "Public Women". For a more detailed analysis on this subject, see Landes 1988, 66–89.
280 Charlton 1984, 157.
281 Rousseau, *Émile ou de l'éducation* 1904, 438–439.

With the exception of rare adherents of the Lockean theory of the *tabula rasa*, who reasoned that because personality is a "blank sheet" man was not predestined either by his psychological or biological characteristics, most philosophers of that epoch maintained an equally sceptical attitude as regards the equal upbringing of the sexes. Amongst the philosophers of the French Enlightenment, Condorcet was the most prominent figure who questioned "natural differences" between the sexes. For him females are born "blank sheets" as much as males, and in the same way as males, women too are shaped by their experience and education.[282] In his *Esquisse d'un tableau historique des progrès de l'esprit humain* Condorcet formulates this idea as follows:

> "Parmi les progrès de l'esprit humain les plus important pour le bonheur
> général, nous devons compter l'entière destruction des préjugés qui ont
> établi entre deux sexes une inégalité de droits funeste..."[283]

Mercier does not offer in his utopia a clear idea about women's opportunities for education in the future, but presumably he shared Rousseau's opinion in this matter; the novel conveys an impression that women's education should not be as many-sided as that accorded to men. This can be concluded for example from the fact that the mystery of the "two infinities" is revealed only to men.[284] As an ardent enemy of the philosophy of Locke, the idea of equal education on the basis of "tabula rasa" was alien to Mercier. It is more realistic to presume that the "ideal woman" is in need of education only to the extent that it supports her role as a wife and a mother. In this respect, too, pleasing comes before other skills.[285]

Women should not, however, be totally unlearned, because as guardians of "righteous morals", they are in charge of the elementary teaching in the early years of their children. It is the task of the mothers to open their children's souls toward virtue.[286] In this focal aspect the influence of women is not restricted solely within the private domain; bearing the responsibility of the preliminary instruction of the future citizens, they have a highly respectable role to play in a semi-public domain between private life and the public sphere.

. . . .

282 Charlton 1984, 163. See also Badinters 1988, 296–297. On women's education in the eigh-
     teenth century, see also Browne 1987, 102–121.
283 Condorcet, *Esquisse d'un tableau historique des progrès de l'esprit humain* 1795, 346.
     About Condorcet's views on the "women question", see for example Landes 1988, 112–117.
284 See Chapter IV, p. 85.
285 Mercier's attitude to the question of women's education does not seem, however, to be
     totally onesided. For example in *Le Bonheur des gens de lettres* he writes that the exclusion
     of women from literary cultivation is unjust. In this text he appears almost as modern as
     Condorcet, demanding equal education for both sexes: "Je m'éleverai contre cette coutume
     barbare qui étouffe dans les jeunes personnes de votre sexe les germes précieux des plus rares
     talens. Pourquoi ne pas donner une égale éducation à des esprits également doués de raison?"
     Mercier invokes the question whether women's exclusion from education is due to blind
     prejudice, or to hidden jealousy and fear that women might surpass men. Mercier, *Le
     Bonheur des gens de lettres* 1766, 32–33. This "emancipatory" view appears to contradict
     the non-progressive and reactionary attitudes advanced in *L'An 2440.*
286 Mercier 1786, *L'An 2440 II*, 155. See also Mercier, *Mon bonnet de nuit II* 1784, 162–163.

Apart from some allusions to the education of young people, *L'An 2440* does not contain many references to childhood in general. *Mon bonnet de nuit* devotes to this theme, however, a brief analysis under the heading "*Enfance*". In this short essay Mercier underscores the special innocence of children, demanding parents to let their children enjoy the pleasures of their age.[287] This reads as an appeal on behalf of the idea that children should not be treated as "adults in miniature"; instead, an autonomous and unique importance should be accorded to them. The influence of the "cult of sentimentality" and "tenderness", in particular that of Rousseau's *Émile*,[288] is clearly revealed in Mercier's highly idealized image of childhood.

Despite his well-meaning intentions, Mercier is totally incapable of creating a sentiment of tenderness or mutual affection between members of the same family in the chapters of *L'An 2440* devoted to private life in the imaginary Paris of the future. Instead of a sentimental idyll, he offers an image of Spartan austerity. The "ideal women" in Mercier's 2440 are locked into an iron cage of virtue, which forces them to follow a norm imposed on them *a priori*. They are obliged to fit their entire existence into a pre-ordained mould of so-called "happiness", according to the same line of reasoning by which in the utopian community of 2440 the citizens are "forced to be free". Following this same logic, the gender roles also are arranged on the basis of contract between a master and a slave.

The subordination of women in Mercier's utopia accurately characterizes the inner contradictions contained in the bourgeois conception of virtue. By reinforcing the mechanisms of patriarchal power and the importance of strict gender roles, the novel comes to reveal in an exemplary manner the coercive nature of the eighteenth-century ideal of happiness. Basically the issue can be reduced to the unresolved conflict between the concepts of "freedom" and "order", or "virtue" and "nature". Paul Hoffmann highlights this apparent paradox when he writes that the utopia of the eighteenth century does not proclaim liberation for women in regard to their nature, but describes a state organized according to "nature defined a priori as the source of moral norms".[289]

David Coward draws a parallel conclusion in his analysis focused on the images of womanhood in Restif de La Bretonne's works *La Famille vertueuse* (1767) and *Les Gynographes* (1777). Coward describes Restif's conception of femininity with the term "the totalitarianism of happiness", which refers to the fact that in Restif's novels love ceases to be a private affair and becomes a

· · · · · · · · ·

287 Mercier, *Mon bonnet de nuit I* 1784, 283–286.
288 The focal theme of *Émile* is a particular idea that children should be allowed to live their childhood in the full meaning of the term. Several passages in Rousseau's work illustrate this idea, for example the following one: "Pourquoi voulez-vous ôter à ces petits innocents la jouissance d'un temps si court qui leur échappe..." Rousseau, *Émile ou de l'éducation* 1904, 57. For more detail, see Ariès 1973.
289 Hoffmann 1995, 447. Hoffmann's view is based on Émilie Schomann's dissertation *Französischen Utopisten des 18. Jahrhunderts und ihr Frauenideal* (1911).

political instrument. The liberty of women resides in conformity to a strict code extending even over the private life.[290]

Against this background it is appropriate to pose the following question: did writers such as Mercier, Rousseau or Restif de la Bretonne sincerely believe that they were pursuing the supreme best for women, and that they were advancing the liberation of women? Or was it rather a misogynist "conspiracy", the aim of which was to keep women in their subordinated position? For example Charlton rejects the first alternative, when he argues that when the philosophers attributed for women a role as mothers and wives, they were rejecting the older conception of the lustful woman, haunted by her insatiable sexual desire.[291]

To a certain extent this view sounds acceptable. There is no use denying that eighteenth-century French writers were "emancipating" women to fulfill a more positive and morally more valuable role as guardian spirits of their homes and as servants of their husbands and children. The greatest deficiency in this scheme, however, was the fact that women were "liberated" only to fill the social and sexual role imposed by the males. Women's authentic voice was silenced, and the new pattern of feminine happiness was not planned to please women but men. The resort to "nature", "biology" and particular "feminine destiny" was a sufficient legitimation for the "dictatorship of happiness", which meant in practise women's total exclusion from the public sphere.

There are well-grounded reasons to suggest that as regards the "women question" Mercier belongs to the most austere wing of eighteenth-century French utopian writers. Much more radical and fantastic, even genuinely feminist, themes had already been put forward in the pages of utopian literature in previous centuries. Aristophanes had anticipated that women would some day get the right to vote. Also the ancient legend of the Amazons, women subordinating men, has been alive through the centuries. Some writers had given their blessing to sexual equality, and for example in Ludvig Holberg's novel *Nicolai Klimii iter subterraneum* (1741) there prevails a total equality between men and women. Louis Rustaing de Saint-Jory, for his part, creates in his *Les femmes militaires* (1735) a vision of an island where the women are obliged to take up arms side by side with men in order to defend their liberty.[292]

In addition, various experiments with sexual alternatives formed one branch of utopian imagination in eighteenth-century French literature, from Diderot's promiscuous communism to de Sade's pornographic hedonism. Writers like de Sade and Choderlos de Laclos (1741–1803) shared the view that all lasting sentimental and legal ties should be abolished, and sex without love was the perfect relationship. For these preachers of sexual liberty in many of its forms, happiness meant following one's instinctual drives without any exterior constraints of whatsoever.[293]

. . . .

290 Coward 1992, 12.
291 Charlton 1984, 158–160, 166–167.
292 Versins 1972, 315–316.
293 Manuels 1982, 536–537.

Many of these playful experiments with sexual alternatives drew their inspiration from the new interest in foreign and exotic societies in that epoch which moulded European conceptions about marriage practises and family relationships. Especially Bougainville's (1729–1811) depictions of the open and natural sexual relations of Tahiti encouraged the questioning of conventional sexual morality. It was from the newly found "New Cythera", or Tahiti, that the ideal of free love found its application in real life. In the South Seas the institutional arrangements were subordinated to the perfect fulfillment of erotic passion. The exotic dream concerning the sexual liberation of both sexes seemed to promise new possibilities for sexual fulfillment for the individual. Approached from this new perspective, Christian monogamy was seen as merely hypocritical.[294] The full-scale fulfillment of erotic passion was thus now conceived as one essential component in man's right to enjoy the maximum amount of happiness already on earth.

Diderot's *Supplément au voyage de Bougainville* (1772) provides the most illuminating example of an eighteenth-century sexual utopia, the purpose of which is to expose the double morals embedded in the European concept of marriage institutions. Criticizing the abuses prevailing in his society, Diderot preaches the virtues of total sexual promiscuity, letting an old Tahitian speak on his behalf:

> "...nous somme innocens, nous sommes heureux; et tu ne peux que nuire à notre bonheur. Nous suivons le pure instinct de la nature... "Ici tout est à tout... "Nos filles et nos femmes sont communes."[295]

Despite the fact that Diderot's sexual communism would presumably have been too daring for Mercier, in his *L'Homme sauvage* he introduces an erotic theme by developing an incestuous relationship between the main characters of the novel, Zidzem and Zaka. Here Mercier seems to give his blessing to sexual gratification outside wedlock, and not even incestuous relationships are condemned as "unnatural". It is rather on the contrary; like Diderot in his *Supplément au voyage de Bougainville*, Mercier here suggests that everything that derives from "nature" is virtuous and innocent. After the arrival of the white conquerors, however, the natives learn to know that measured against the European standards they have committed the most abominable crime which can be imagined.[296]

It is easy to note a conflict between the sexual morals preached in *L'Homme sauvage* and in *L'An 2440*. Whereas in the former, virtue and passion are seen as perfectly compatible, the moral lesson of *L'An 2440* is that erotic passion can only lead man astray from the path leading to virtue, and the optimal relation between sexual partners is attained only through the total subordination of passionate impulses under the command of virtue. In the final resort, the erotic theme in *L'Homme sauvage* appears to be nothing more than a literary device.

. . . .

294 Manuel 1966b, 78–79; Manuels 1982, 535–536.
295 Diderot, *Oeuvres complètes de Denis Diderot I* 1818, 485, 468–460.
296 Mercier, *L'Homme sauvage* 1767, 286.

VI The Role of Material Prosperity

The Question of Luxury and Scarcity

Egoism, greediness and self-interest have through the centuries been regarded as mortal sins, and various kinds of vice form a constant theme also in Mercier's allegorical visions. Moral condemnation is to be read already from the titles of his allegories, such as *"L'Egoisme"*, or *"La Cupidité."* For example, in the former story a phantom in a white dress leads the narrator in a dream state under a subterranean vault to a dark and somber place filled with coffins, and peopled by greedy people, crying out loudly: "Que m'importe autrui? il faut vivre pour soi: je vis pour moi, pour moi." After this dramatic outcry they fall silently back into their graves. The narrator awakens from his nightmare covered with cold sweat.[1]

Mercier's allegory of the vice of selfishness serves as a good introduction to the theme of the present chapter, focused on the material aspects of happiness. What is at issue here is to provide answers to the following central questions: What was Mercier's idea of material prosperity? Did he regard wealth as a precondition of happiness, or was it rather its opposite?

It is hard to overlook how prominent a place these questions occupy in the philosophical essays and treatises produced in France in the final years of the *ancien régime*. Even a preliminary review of the literature of that epoch provides ample evidence that the intellectual elites were profoundly concerned about the moral aspects related to the unequal distribution of wealth and the consequences of the lust for luxury. There was wide discussion as to whether luxury was compatible with virtuous morals, or rather represented its antithesis.

The legitimation of consumption and luxury were made the focus of debate also in England in the same period and the camps were divided between the preachers of virtuous morals who readily condemned ostentatiousness and lust for luxury in the name of constraint and virtue, and those who justified consumption for the sake of utilitarian purposes, following the utopian writer Bernard de Mandeville (1670–1733), who had in the early eighteenth century represented his rather cynical thesis concerning the close link between private vice and public benefits.[2] As Mandeville conceived it, selfishness and excess were the driving motives of commercial society: "C'est d'Ailleurs une Vérité

. . . .
1   Mercier, *Mon bonnet de nuit II* 1784, 333–340. This allegory on egoism gives a good picture of the anti-utopian side of Mercier's visionary thinking.
2   Campbell 1987, 28–29.

généralement reconnue que l'Avarice & l'Orgueil sont les principales Causes de l'Industrie, du Commerce, & de la Richess de tout un Peuple."[3]

Mandeville´s famous allegorical poem, the *Fable of the Bees* (1723), which was translated into French in 1740, had a far-reaching impact for the debate whether luxury should be approved of or condemned. Insisting on the leading role of passion in the conduct of civilized society, Mandeville argues the importance of luxury as a necessity. He thus attacks the idea of communal existence based on a purely Christian code of values, proclaiming that it is not possible to equate moral principles with dogmas of social utility. In a critical response to Mandevillian cynicism, the voice of moral indignation was raised by the Christian economists and the members of aristocracy alike, albeit for dissimilar reasons. The Christians wished to uphold the social hierarchy on the grounds that consumption should be arranged on the basis "to each according to his status", and that men should not expect to gain equal access to material comforts this side of the grave. The upper social strata, for their part, criticized material expansion because they were afraid of social mobility and the possible ensuing confusion of ranks.[4]

The importance of the debate regarding the benefits or evils of consumption and luxury in pre-Revolutionary France can also be seen in the fact that between 1736 and 1789 over one hundred works dealing with this theme were published. Moreover, it is revealing that the Academie Française announced a competition under the rubric "The advantages and disadvantages of luxury". Voltaire, too, had his word to say on this subject in many of his writings, such as the *Dictionnaire philosophique*. Joining the camp of Mandeville, he chose to support luxury, on the grounds that its denial would mean condemning society to a state of permanent stagnation.[5] Mercier can hardly have been unaware of this prominent polemic over luxury in the society of the *ancien régime*, and it is directly reflected in the pages of *L´An 2440*.

This heightened interest in economic matters was typical of a period of transition; starting from the early sixteenth century, the Western societies underwent a gradual transformation in material culture, which smoothed the path towards the commercial revolution, or the "rise of the commercial capitalism": expansion of markets, increased concern for comfort in buildings and furniture, specialization in certain fields of production, commercialization of agriculture, and revolution in communications.[6]

Despite these visible signs of economic expansion, in the eighteenth century France was still an agrarian society, based on very traditional mercantile activity. Notwithstanding the rise of the middle classes and the expansion of trade and industry, on the eve of the French Revolution industrialization was far less widespread compared with the economic development of England in the

. . . .

3   [Mandeville], *Pensée libres sur la religion, l'eglise et le bonheur de la nation I* 1722 17.
4   Roche 1998, 563; Roche 2000, 75.
5   Roche 1998, 567–568; Roche 2000, 75–76.
6   Burke 1997, 244–250.

same period.[7] There thus existed a confrontation between a traditional agrarian way of life and the rise of modern commercialism.

Questions concerning the acceptability of luxury and consumption in general have formed one of the most focal themes also for the creators of ideal societies. The issue of the optimal satisfaction of needs has over the centuries formed a basic concern in utopias, as for example J.C. Davis points out. In their search for social order and harmony, utopianists have attempted to project an economic system which would optimally satisfy the "legitimate needs" of the people. According to Davis all forms of ideal society have to solve the problem of the supply of satisfactions, but utopias are more "realistic" than the others, since they accept the basic problem for what it is: "limited satisfactions exposed to unlimited wants".[8] The constructors of utopias have thus not ended up totally ignoring the question of material prosperity, due to the fact that "since Utopia belongs to the realm of the real world, not of myth, it can never ... start from the natural sufficiency of goods which characterizes the Garden of Eden."[9]

As a utopian writer, Mercier is no exception to this general rule. Like many prior and subsequent creators of utopian societies, he too devotes many pages in *L'An 2440* to the question of material well-being and consumption. Before a more detailed analysis of the ways in which Mercier deals with this problem in his utopia, it is worth refreshing one's memory that recognition of the economic imbalance prevailing in eighteenth-century French society formed a starting-point for his moral indignation and for his very desire to create visions of a happier and more beautiful existence somewhere beyond the harsh everyday realities. It is common for Mercier to complain that the tension between the richest and poorest in society is becoming more and more pressing every day. The insatiable lust for luxury and the desire for the public symbols of power amongst the rich and the powerful were in his opinion to be blamed for this unjust situation:

> "Ainsi la distance qui sépare le riche du reste des citoyens s'accroît chaque jour, et la pauvreté devient plus insupportable par la vue des progrès étonnants du luxe qui fatigue les regards de l'indigent. La haine s'envenime, et l'État est divisé en deux classes; en gens avides et insensibles, et en mécontents qui murmurent."[10]

Mercier's dramatic emphasis on the huge social cleavage separating the rich and the poor in contemporary society mirrors the fact that in the final years of the *ancien régime* the economic structure of France was still characterized by a big gulf between the aristocracy and the rest of the community. As we have already

. . . .

7   Hibbert 1982, 34;
8   Davis 1981, 19, 37.
9   Finley 1990, 185.
10   Mercier, *Tableau de Paris I* 1994a, 51. The same extract is to be found from Mercier's *De la littérature et des littérateurs*. Mercier, *De la littérature et des littérateurs* 1970, 83. See also Mercier's article "*Nécessiteux*" in *Tableau de Paris*: "L'horrible inégalité des fortunes, qui va toujours en augmentant, un petit nombre ayant tout, et la multitude riens..." Mercier, *Tableau de Paris I* 1994a, 667–678.

seen, the nobility enjoyed almost total exemption from taxation.[11] The nobility's exemption from taxes was inherited from the feudal past, and since the Middle Ages payment of taxes had been regarded as sign of inferior status.[12] Towards the end of the century the polarization separating the richer and the poorer members of the French society became even more striking.[13]

The bad treatment of the peasants formed one of the most barbaric abuses of power in France under the *ancien régime*. Because of the unjust basis of taxation, many burdens fell on the peasants' shoulders. It was the peasant's obligation to pay direct taxes in money, and in the course of the century there also grew up the practise of imposing on the peasants the *corvée royale*, which meant forced labor on the making of roads.[14]

Mercier harshly criticizes in *L'An 2440* the inhuman treatment of peasants. It is characteristic that in the art gallery of 2440 the painting representing the eighteenth century is peopled with starving peasants.[15] Mercier also expresses clearly how disgusted he is at the unequal taxation; he envisages that in 2440 the paying of taxes is organized, for the most part, on a voluntary basis. There are two boxes in the corner of the streets, into which the citizens can put money. One is for the state: in it the utopians are expected to put a fifth of their incomes. Those who have nothing are liberated from paying taxes. The other box is reserved for voluntary donations, which are to be used for useful purposes.[16]

In one of his allegorical stories, entitled "*L'île du Sang*", Mercier imagines that he is transported to an horrible island called "the island of Blood". The island is governed by an absolute tyrant who drinks his subjects' blood.[17] This story, filled with anti-utopian elements and saturated with gothic, "romantic", horror, has many similarities with the terrifying kingdom of Batua with its cannibal rites depicted in de Sade's novel *Valmor et Lydia*.[18] Both Mercier's and de Sade's stories can be read as allegories of the bottomless viciousness and wickedness of persecutors and tyrants. In eighteenth-century France, because of their greed, the tax-collectors, the *fermier générals,* were largely hated[19] as disgusting creatures who suck the elixir of life from the veins of other people. The bloodthirsty tyrant of Mercier's allegory symbolizes these greedy tax-collectors. At the same time this monstrous figure is, quite naturally, a metaphor for despotic kings, such as Louis XIV.

Mercier's critical attitude to the unjust institution of taxes reflects a certain change in the general mental atmosphere in the second half of the eighteenth century. There was a tendency toward more equal taxation, and in practise by

. . . .

11   Lough 1961, 122–123. Cf. Darnton 1990, 232.
12   Gossman 1972, 8.
13   Roche 1987, 76, 78.
14   Lough 1961, 53. See also Cobban 1957; Gossman 1972, 36–39.
15   See Chapter III, pp. 63–64.
16   Mercier, *L'An 2440* II 1786, 177–202, especially 179–184.
17   Mercier, *Les Songes d'un hermite* 1788b, 362–369.
18   [Sade], *Valmor et Lydia, ou voyage autour du monde de deux amans qui se cherchoient* An VII, passim., especially 74: "Cette chair étoit avalée crue, aussi-tôt qu'elle étoit coupée; mais avant de la porter à la bouche il falloit se barbouiller le visage avec le sang qui en découloit."
19   See for example Lough 1961, 87–90; Doyle 1988, 188–189.

1789 the *corvée royale* hadbeen replaced by money payments.[20] The *vingtième*, created by the edict of 1749, was intended to affect everybody without exception, and replaced the previous tax, the *dixième*.[21]

As could be expected, the new taxes often aroused strong opposition on the part of the privileged orders. They were not prepared to give up their "natural prerogatives" without resistance. The efforts of Turgot, who was the last of the reforming ministers under Louis XVI and who moved in philosophical circles, to bring change to the situation, give a vivid example of this. Pressure from nobility against Turgot's fiscal reform concerning the abolition of the *corvées* led to his resignation,[22] and only after prolonged resistance did the Parlement of Paris approve the *vingtième*. The resistance of the clergy was even more bitter, which led Louis XV to exempt the church from the tax. This further increased the unpopularity of the king, and widened the breach between the people and the *ancien régime*.[23]

The rather naïve solution offered by Mercier for the problem of taxation in his vision of the twenty-fifth century reveals that concrete and practical solutions to reform the unjust economic situation were still difficult to find. Mercier's only solution to the fiscal difficulties of his society seems to be a well-intentioned conviction that after several centuries, men would have learned to behave in an altruistic manner, always acting in accordance with the precepts of social compassion and always preferring the happiness of others to their own. The organization of taxation on a voluntary basis dependent on good will clearly testifies to this.

By and large, in Mercier's fantasy the economic relations between the higher and lower social strata have undergone a dramatic change like a carnival hurly-burly. The money-owning class has miraculously become unprecedentedly generous, tender and caring, when faced with the misery of the less fortunate. Despite the fact that in *Tableau de Paris* Mercier has no illusions when it comes to the moral or social virtues of the rich or aristocrats, who are usually described as exceptionally selfish opportunists, with no pity towards the suffering of either men or animals,[24] in the far future the rich keep their tables always set for those in need.[25]

Mercier accorded hospitality a very high value,[26] and in his future society food is sanctified in the spirit of universal love. Gathering for a common meal functions as a symbolic act the purpose of which is to break down social

. . . .

20 Lough 1961, 54; Schama 1989, 85–86. For more on the evolution of the system of taxation in eighteenth-century France, see for example Meyer 1985, 497–504. See also Roche 1998, 290–294.
21 Cobban 1957, 58; Gossman 1972, 55; Doyle 1988, 45–46; Le Roy Ladurie 1996, 383.
22 Gossman 1972, 62–64; Nisbet 1986, 96.
23 Mandrou 1977, 307–308; Le Roy Ladurie 1996, 383–386. See also Lough 1961, 179, 185.
24 Mercier, *Tableau de Paris* I 1994a, 147–149 and 653–654.
25 Mercier, *L'An 2440* I 1786, 216–221.
26 Mercier's views on hospitality, see also ch. "*Les dîneurs en ville*" in *Tableau de Paris*. Mercier, *Tableau de Paris* I 1994a, 150–153.

barriers. In the private home it is the task of the father to bless the bread before meals,[27] which reinforces the patriarchal structure of Mercier's ideal society. According to Mucchielli, the same Gospel spirit characterizes the entire tradition of ideal cities. The theme of hospitality, praised both by Greek and by Gospel texts, is related to the eschatological theme of a shared meal.[28]

In 2440, as Mercier imagined it, the question of luxury is no longer a burdensome problem; it has been solved by channeling the riches of the fortunate to benefit the less fortunate too, and thus the enjoyments of the rich also guarantee the well-being of the poor. At the same time he criticizes the eighteenth-century custom of using luxury for the building of expensive public monuments meant for amusement and pleasure.[29] As many as possible get their share of the pleasure of luxury as it passes from the upper classes to the lower. The reasonableness of the mutual sharing of luxury items is explained by utilitarian reasons: "La félicité nationale dépend de la félicité de plusieurs particuliers; il faut qu'ils jouissent pour qu'ils apprennent à faire jouir leurs semblables..."[30]

These words clearly demonstrate that Mercier approached the question of luxury strictly from the viewpoint of public utility; as he conceived it, luxury can be justified only if it contributes to the advancement of the general well-being in the spirit of social compassion. Following this line of thinking, man is supposed to become happier himself, when he helps those in need. Because the leading theme of L'An 2440 is that the happiness of one individual is always the same as the well-being of the whole community, the individual cannot have independent needs; otherwise man would cease to behave in a virtuous manner, losing his only purpose of existence, which is defined through his social utility as an active member of the human "beehive".

In Mercier's utopian society, nobody is permitted to consume more than he actually needs. The consumption of luxury items is accepted in so far as they are not used for the satisfaction of unnecessary or artificial desires. The right desires, Mercier implies, must be such that their satisfaction abolishes the most elementary needs, such as the experience of hunger. Using a future Parisian as his mouthpiece, he formulates this focal idea as follows:

> "Notre luxe est raisonné; il n'appartient point à l'orgueil, au faste, au misérable plaisir de la représentation; il tient aux commodités de la vie: notre luxe n'est pas coûteux; il ne s'égare pas au-delà des jouissances réelles..."[31]

All this testifies to the fact that L'An 2440 is not a representation of a "saturnalia", in which the deficiencies of contemporary society were miraculously turned into a horn of plenty. Mercier's Paris of the future is not a

. . . .

27   Mercier, *L'An 2440 II* 1786, 232.
28   Mucchielli 1960, 200–201.
29   Mercier, *L'An 2440 III* 1786, 95.
30   Mercier, *L'An 2440 III* 1786, 149.
31   Mercier, *L'An 2440 III* 1786, 149.

"Land of Cockaygne"[32], where manna and quails are falling from heaven and the rivers flow with milk and honey. On the contrary: happiness is reached through very simple pleasures. The rhythm of the days is never interrupted by unrestrained orgies of food or drink. The principles of moderation and mutual sharing are glorified as the basis of production and consumption. The virtue of moderation is emphasized by the detail that in 2440 it is forbidden to use comforts such as tea, coffee or tobacco. Commercial activity is limited to trade in the home country; foreign trade is regarded as "the real father of destructive luxury".[33] Debauchery, excessive eating and drinking are vices unknown to Mercier's utopians; their nourishment consists of fruits and vegetables. Spices, liqueurs and sophisticated desserts are avoided.[34]

Against this background it is easy to subscribe to the view of Sidney Pollard that in *L'An 2440* happiness is achieved by consuming less rather than producing more.[35] Mercier's utopia follows the classic pattern of restricted needs and a simple and austere way of life,[36] which means that the problem of needs and their satisfaction is solved in a similar fashion as in the tradition inaugurated by Thomas More in his *Utopia*, in which the question of "legitimate wants", as Davis puts it, is solved in an austere and narrow fashion; both production and demand are assumed to be limited.[37]

If one applies the concepts of a "static" ("ascetic") and a "dynamic" ("want-satisfying") utopia praised by M. I Finley, *L'An 2440* is a typical representative of the former type. In Finley's classification, "static" utopia describes the ancient or early modern Utopias in which dominant themes are acceptance of the scarcity of goods, simplicity and asceticism. Finley sees the Industrial Revolution as a watershed which started a transformation towards "dynamic" or "technological" utopias, where abundance replaced scarcity.[38]

In the tradition of utopian literature, the lust for luxury has for centuries been seen as a corruptive phenomenon. In particular, in the utopias produced before the mid-nineteenth century, the tendency toward asceticism and the condemnation of luxury constitutes a rule. Most of these utopias are not only inimical to all luxury, but they challenge the prevailing concepts of

. . . .

32 "Gastronomic utopias", the common man's daydreams of a luxurious existence, date back to antiquity, and the dream of the fullest possible satisfaction of men's appetites is particularly associated with the tradition of "Land of Cockaygne". Davis 1981, 20–22; Manuels 1982, 78–81; Camporesi 1989, 78–85, especially 80. The "land of milk and honey" has throughout the centuries formed a focal theme in popular iconography. As Ernst Bloch points out, "it is one archetype with an unsatisfied tendency-latency underneath the fantastic mask that is a veiled depiction of the utopian tendencies within reality". Bloch 1989, 125. The malnutrition and wishes related to food are common themes also in the peasant tales which shaped the popular tradtion in pre-revolutionary France. Darnton 1988, 17–78, especially 39.
33 Mercier, *L'An 2440 II* 1786, 204–205.
34 Mercier, *L'An 2440 II* 1786, 235.
35 Pollard 1971, 57.
36 Kumar 1987, 38.
37 Davis 1981, 300. The view of Davis is supported by the words of More, according to which in his utopian society there is a plentiful supply of all things and no underlying fear that anyone will demand more than he needs. More, *Utopia* 1964, 77.
38 Finley 1990, 185–186. See also Kumar 1987, 31–32 and passim. See also Berneri 1951, 210.

economics.[39] Frank E. Manuel refers to these pre-nineteenth-century utopias by the term "Utopias of Calm Felicity", which seem to correspond with the "static" utopia of Finley: their dominant spirit is characterized by the demand for moderation and the exclusion of all powerful drives or passions which could upset the equilibrium. The mode of life is that of an idealized agricultural society.[40]

With some rare exceptions like Bacon's dynamic scientific utopia *Nova Atlantis*, growth and expansion were thus not yet major concerns of utopian writers in the seventeenth and eighteenth centuries. More's *Utopia*, which provided an example of a sort of "secularized monasticism", was taken as a model. Instead of being dynamic and expansive, the utopias of Enlightenment were static and a-historical, constructed on a basis of modest needs and exclusion of change.[41] Generally speaking, as for example Northrop Frye notes, the ideal of a monastic community has had a far-reaching influence on utopian thought.[42] The uniting feature in both utopias and monasticism is that the "real" world represents a temptation of luxury. Based on this, preference is given to simplicity and necessities of life.[43]

In the terminology of the eighteenth century, the emphasis on the virtue of moderation was related to the theme of "happy mediocrity". This ideal of mediocrity, or "aurea mediocritas", was simply a social transposition of the idea of repose and exclusion of passions. It was related to the eulogy of the bourgeois virtues. In that epoch the bourgeois was not yet a "capitalist", but was thought of as a man "spontaneously virtuous". His activities were thought to be limited to the domestic sphere, he found the content of his life from hard work, and in his emotional life he rejected passions and all irrational behavior.[44]

The writers and philosophers of the eighteenth century constantly repeat the idea that true happiness is synonymous with contentment with one's condition, in a spirit of moderation. For example Madame du Châtelet emphasizes in her treatise *Discours sur le bonheur* the importance of moderating one's desires. One should not want things other than those which are within reach: "...je crois qu'une des choses qui contribuent le plus au bonheur, c'est de se contenter de son état, et de songer plutôt à le rendre heureux qu'à en changer."[45] Similarly, in

. . . .

39   Ruyer 1988, 50, 95. See also Ehrard 1994, 575–577.
40   Manuel 1966b, 71–77. By and large, the agrarian suspicion of commerce and industry is of ancient origin, and it has often led to demands that men should moderate their desires rather than limitlessly satisfying them. The ideal of moderation is essential for example in the philosophy of Plato, who reasoned that the precondition of a good life is the restraint of desires. Under optimal conditions, argues Plato, man aims at satisfying only those needs which genuinely advance his well-being. See for example Pitkänen 1996, 81, 87.
41   Kumar 1987, 35–37.
42   Frye 1966, 35.
43   Manuels 1982, 50. About the connections between monasticism and utopias, see also Lapouge 1978, 73–80.
44   Mauzi 1994, 175, 272–276. For more detail on the concept of "a bourgeois" in eighteenth-century France, see Darnton 1988, 105–140.
45   Châtelet, *Discours sur le bonheur* 1997, 36, 56–57.

his treatise on happiness Fontenelle had come to a parallel conclusion some decades earlier: "Notre condition est meilleure quand nous nous y soumettons de bonne grâce, que quand nous nous révoltons inutilement contre elle."[46]

The doctrine of "contentment", founded on the idea of an optimal balance between man's desires and his capacity to satisfy them, was consistent with the general theory of the "Great Chain of Being" as it was understood in eighteenth-century France. According to Lovejoy, in the course of the century the idea of the "great chain" was turned from a cosmological generalization into a moral imperative. It could now be used as weapon against social discontent, on the assumption that the existing society is the "best of all possible worlds". Accordingly, to strive to abandon one's place in society was interpreted as an effort to "invert the laws of Order". From this perspective the inequality of conditions was not an evil, and subordination was essential.[47]

Mercier was a typical representative of his epoch in that he also assumed a skeptical attitude toward efforts at bettering one's social or economic condition. In *L'An 2440* he draws the fatalistic conclusion that a populous society can never offer the same kind of felicity for everyone; there will always exist a category of the less fortunate.[48]

As this reveals, in Mercier's view man should be content with his place in the "ladder of being", rather than nourishing his imagination with vain desires and illusions. This leads him to the conclusion that a state of rest was preferable, at least in social and economic issues, to a state of perpetual movement, restlessness and agitation. The suggestion is that in society, as in the whole of nature, where man's position was somewhere between the "two infinities", the "middle link" was always the happiest one. In *Tableau de Paris* Mercier extols the happiness of the artisans expressly on the grounds that they do not nourish their imagination with ungrounded hopes of social amelioration, but understand to remain in their place.[49]

In his *Émile* Rousseau promotes an analogous view concerning the importance of not leaving one's place in the "Great Chain of Being":

> "O homme! resserre ton existence au-dedans de toi, et tu ne seras plus misérable. Reste à la place que la nature t'assigne dans la chaîne des êtres, rien ne t'en pourra faire sortir; ne regimbe point contre la dure loi de la nécessité..."[50]

Rousseau was convinced that vain illusions and immoderate desires increase man's unhappiness, because they make him sensible to "false privations". He suggests that a man who avariciously aspires to happiness is always the most

. . . .

46   Fontenelle, *Rêveries diverses* 1994, 88.
47   Lovejoy 1950, 202–207, passim.
48   Mercier, *L'An 2440 III* 1786, 147. In *Tableau de Paris*, however, Mercier contends that a society founded on immense economic imbalance can never be the best possible: "Les deux extrêmes de la société policée ne sont pas heureux, l´un par l´ennui, et l´autre par la misère". Mercier, *Tableau de Paris I* 1994a, 650.
49   Mercier, *Tableau de Paris II* 1994a, 1062.
50   Rousseau, *Émile ou de l'éducation* 1904, 63.

miserable: "...c'est donc dans la disproportion de nos désirs et de nos facultés que consiste notre misère."[51] There thus has to be a just proportion between man's wants and his capacity to satisfy them: happiness is a state in which man has fulfilled his wants, a happy person is one whose life is free from conflict.[52]

Even though wish-fulfillment may be the necessary condition of happiness, Mercier has not totally abolished social hierarchy from his vision of 2440; despite its egalitarian features, there are still rich and poor.[53] In contrast to many other utopian writers, for example Campanella, in whose *Civitas Solis* everything is held in common,[54] Mercier did not dream of the communist distribution of goods. All he hoped for, was that there would be equal access to the basic requirements of life, in order that nobody should suffer from starvation. In Mercier's view, inequality among men was a natural fact of life, which could not be ignored: "L'homme n'est pas naturellement égal à son semblable; parce que les facultés sont naturellement inégales d'un individu à un autre."[55] In consequence, he argues, inequality is so essential for the happiness of society that if it did not exist, it would have to be created by political means: "...il seroit impossible que jamais une grande société existôt sans cette précieuse inégalité."[56]

In his thinking on property rights, Mercier differed quite sharply from Rousseau, who writes in his treatise on the origin of inequality that the establishment of private property rights was the first step in the progress of inequality.[57] Some years later, in his *Du contrat social*, however, Rousseau was willing to modify his earlier rigorous attitude regarding property rights. He no longer questioned that men had a right to their property, which was the origin of all justice.[58]

Amongst eighteenth-century French philosophers, only the most radical thinkers, such as Meslier, Morelly, and Dom Deschamps, held the opinion that the right of property had no natural basis but was a fruit of the exercise of power, an historical creation like the state itself and the primary obstacle for the organization of a happy society.[59] Even for the utopianists of the early nineteenth century who vehemently condemned revolutionary violence, such as Saint-Simon, Fourier, and even Cabet, the renunciation of a rich and prosperous civilization would have been an absurdity.[60]

. . . .

51   Ibid., 58, 308.
52   This is an ancient theme, and already for example in Aristotle's philosophy the idea of happiness is linked to the achievement of one's major goals. See for example Telfer 1980, 3–4, 113, 118, 120.
53   There seems to exist a certain contradiction when one considers that Mercier's future Paris is supposed to be a model of a perfectly egalitarian society, where the sole criteria of distinction is that based on the practise of virtue. And yet there are still rich whose duty it is to show acts of social compassion towards the poor in order that the less fortunate do not lose their human dignity altogether. This is one of the unresolved paradoxes of Mercier's utopia.
54   Campanella, *La cité du soleil* 1993, 85.
55   Mercier, *L'An 2440 III* 1786, 109, 111.
56   Mercier, *Notions claires sur les gouvernemens II* 1787, 283.
57   Rousseau, *Discours...* 1992, 249.
58   See for example Shklar 1966, 49. See also Rihs 1970, 42–54, passim.
59   Rihs 1970, 13–15, 16, 18. See also Trousson 1975, 145–160, passim.
60   Ozouf 1989, 564.

Although the radical communism of "anarchists" such as Morelly, Dom Deschamps or even Restif was alien to Mercier, his utopian society of the future breathes a kind of "sentimental communism", founded on the equal distribution of goods. *L'An 2440* is a typical moralizing utopia, which according to Mauzi formed one current in the social thinking prevalent in eighteenth-century France; the other was a cynical apologia for luxury. The moralizing utopias produced in that epoch are always based on the same features: geometry, virtue, paternalism, frugality, innocence and asceticism. What was at issue was a collective figuration of the pastoral ideal of repose. Those who spoke on behalf of luxury favoured, on the other hand, the profusion and dynamism of desires. They justified the idea that the movements of individual passions enrich the nation - *"le bonheur du mouvement"*.[61]

In Mercier's ideal society the primary duty of the state is to protect its citizens from the threat of famine. This is best ensured by establishing public corn storehouses, which are opened under the threat of famine.[62] This is a common theme in many French eighteenth-century utopias, in which images of wise patriarchs distributing grain from full granaries represent a critical comment on the famines of the Old Regime.[63] At the same time they draw their substance from the mythical stock of images related to the general availability of food and drink. Such wishful thinking has always especially flourished in epochs of crisis. As Norman Cohn points out, for example, the millenarian groups of the late Middle Ages usually emerged amidst some revolution or disaster, such as plague, famine or rising prices.[64] Mercier's image of unfailing public corn storehouses reads as one variation of the same archetypal theme which has been repeated in different historical epochs with slight modifications.

Mercier's utopian vision, focused on the general accessibility of provisions, particularly bread, directly reflects the precarious circumstances of its epoch. Owing to the agrarian structure of the economy, in this period an adequate food supply was in many cases doomed to remain mere wishful thinking, and the scarcity of bread was an everyday reality. Despite the fact that the overall nutritional and demographic situation improved over the course of the eighteenth century, starvation, under-nutrition and epidemics were still, at least in some parts of the country, common factors contributing to mortality.[65] As a consequence of bad harvests, the price of bread was one of the standard themes molded by general opinion.[66] The fear of hunger, which Georges LeFebvre terms *"la grande peur"*, easily turned into agrarian revolt.[67] It was hunger, and

. . . .

61   Mauzi 1994, 656.
62   Mercier, *L'An 2440 I* 1786, 201.
63   Manuels 1982, 24.
64   Cohn 1993, 283–284, and passim.
65   Delumeau 1978, 218; Favre 1978, 48. About demographic crisis and its relation to hunger, undernourishment and mortality in eighteenth-century France, see Goubert & Roche 1984 I, 41–47.
66   Farge 1994, 78 ja 89.
67   LeFebvre 1930, 36–37.

the fear of hunger, much more extensively than political ideas, which set the populace in motion.[68]

At the end of the *ancien régime* bread was still the principal source of nourishment for the poorer social strata,[69] which explains why bad harvests had such catastrophic consequences. When the prices of agricultural products declined, or when, in years of scarcity, they rose to heights which brought suffering to the masses, there followed a collapse in trade and industry which increased the general misery. The whole eighteenth century was characterized by continuous fluctuations and economic uncertainties due specifically to the fact that the prices of corn and bread were sensitive to supply and demand.[70]

After a relatively stable period in the first part of the century (1730–1770), there followed a less prosperous period in the 1770s, which was caused by a series of exceptionally bad harvests. The result of the most catastrophic harvest of 1788 was a steady rise in the price of corn. The Revolution broke out at a moment of severe economic crisis. As a consequence, in 1789 the price of bread was higher than ever before in the century.[71] Mercier's pamphlet *Lettre au Roi, contenant un Projet pour liquider en peu d'années toutes les dettes de l'Etat, en soulageant, dès a présent, le Peuple du fardeau des Impositions* (1789), published in the middle of great social and political convulsion, refers directly to this situation; Mercier dedicates his words to the King of France, criticizing the high price of bread and attacking those responsible for it.[72]

In the course of the eighteenth century it became more and more evident that the French economy was in need of drastic reform. As a consequence of this, many projects of reform were proposed. In challenge to the paternalistic tradition of mercantilism, there emerged the new physiocratic doctrine. Like Adam Smith[73] slightly later, the leading Physiocrats, such as François Quesnay (1694–1774), were economic philosophers who trusted in the beneficence of the laws of nature, which were thought to regulate the entire economic process. Due to the fact that the physiocrats idealized the land and agriculture as the ultimate source of all wealth, they were opposed to luxury. In opposition to the mercantilist view, they denounced all government interference in economic matters, in the name of liberal "*laissez faire*" policies.[74] Turgot's economic ideas closely resembled those of the Physiocrats; his goal was to dismantle all

. . . .

68 Bosher 1988, 33.
69 Cobban 1957, 135–136.
70 Lough 1961, 7. For more detail on the food shortages and fluctuations in the price of bread in eighteenth-century France, see Lough 1961, 14–63, passim.
71 Cobban 1957, 136; Doyle 1988, 31–32. See also LeFebvre 1930, 10; Lough 1961, 9, 73; Mandrou 1977, 311.
72 Mercier, *Lettre au Roi, contenant un Projet pour liquider en peu d'années toutes les dettes de l'État* 1789, 27, 123.
73 Adam Smith (1723–1790), the writer of *An Inquiry into the Nature and Causes of the Wealth of Nations* (1776) was a Scottish philosopher, who shared the hostility of the physiocrats to the mercantilist system of privileges, restraints and monopolies, endorsing their slogan, "*laissez-faire*". See for example Woloch 1982, 252–253.
74 Woloch 1982, 251–252; Charlton 1984, 184–187. See also Sagnac 1946, 86–88; Lough 1961, 7; Mandrou 1977, 312; Frängsmyr 1981, 88–89; Hampson 1981, 118; Bosher 1988, 50.

obstacles to the flow of free trade,[75] and in the last part of the eighteenth century (from the 1740s to the 1770s) the state began a progressive withdrawal from the economic sphere. Repeated attempts were now made to lift regulations hampering the free movement of corn.[76]

A few revealing pages are devoted to the physiocratic doctrines in *L'An 2440*. Mercier presents arguments both for and against their possible benefits and drawbacks. In the footnotes of his novel he addresses his words directly to contemporary readers, analyzing both the reform projects already put into practise under the *ancien régime* and schemes still under preparation. Mercier's comments reveal a rather sceptical attitude towards the proposals of the economic reformers and their potential impact on the course of events. This scepticism seems to have been prompted by a fear that the new doctrines might create even wider economic disequilibrium. For this reason, Mercier was not willing to accept *"laissez faire"* policies without certain reservations. It is characteristic that in his vision the price of bread remains always the same: "...nous ne vendons pas imprudemment notre bled à l'étranger, pour le racheter deux fois plus cher trois mois après."[77]

Since in Mercier's opinion the most urgent thing was that the availability of the basic food supply should not depend on chance, he criticized the foreign trade of his own time, which in his view had contributed to the famines and wrenched the access to the corn storehouses from the poor. The imprudent exportation of corn, claims Mercier, had caused death and sufferings for thousands.[78] For example, in the following passage from *L'An 2440* Mercier clearly expresses his scepticism as regards the imprudent commerce in corn:

> "Le nom de ces économistes, qui ont donné aux monopoleurs le signal et les moyens de s'enrichir et d'amener la disette, doit être flétri dans la postérité la plus reculée. Les insensés! ils parloient d'un bled superflu au milieu des récoltes incertaines; et sans avoir seulement calculé s'il y avoit une quantité suffisante de bled, ils éloignoient une denrée nécessaire... "Leurs détestables raisonnemens mirent la France à deux doigts de la famine."[79]

Mercier's words reveal that despite the fact that he believed that the world was governed by the providential laws of nature, and that everything that happened to man had been pre-ordained for his supreme happiness, when it came to more earth-bound matters like corn policies, he did not wish to be identified with the physiocrats and their *"laissez faire"* attitudes. In contrast to the physiocratic camp, Mercier did not believe that natural processes should be left intact from

. . . .

75 See for example Schama 1989, 83; Outram 1995, 132.
76 Gossman 1972, 57.
77 Mercier, *L'An 2440 I* 1786, 201–202. In *Notions claires sur les gouvernemens* Mercier restates the same idea as follows: "Je crois encore qu'on ne doit jamais fixer le prix du bled." Mercier, *Notions claires sur les gouvernemens II* 1787, 330.
78 Mercier, *L'An 2440 I* 1786, 204–205. See also Mercier, *Notions claires sur les gouvernemens II* 1787, 317–330: "Doit-on permettre ou non la liberté du commerce des bled?"
79 Mercier, *L'An 2440 II* 1786, 214–215.

human intervention. Rather, he was convinced that a general catastrophe would ensue if nothing was undertaken to regulate the situation from above.

Despite the increased popularity of the physiocratic doctrines, Mercier's warnings concerning the impact of liberalization of corn policies did not go unheeded. After all, he was not the only anti-liberal spokesman in the latter eighteenth century. As historians specializing in the economic fluctuations characterizing that epoch have pointed out, a sceptical mood was gradually increasing. Its immediate cause was Turgot's attempt to implement free trade in corn, which coincided with a period of scarcity, the result of which was misery and widespread food riots. This was the worst possible time for the reform, and it soon became evident that the liberalization of corn prices (1774) had been premature. As a consequence, the government reimposed controls and practically abolished free trade in corn at the end of 1770. Turgot was dismissed in 1776.[80] By and large, the final years of the *ancien régime* witnessed an aggravation of the financial crisis, prompted by the extravagance of the court and the cost of the American War of Independence.[81]

Gold has in utopias frequently been an object of contempt, functioning as the symbol for an attack against the principle of private property and a vision of its replacement by communal ownership.[82] Mercier's aversion toward luxury also reaches its apotheosis in his vision that in 2440 diamonds and other luxury items have been thrown into the sea. He explains that in the eighteenth century the desire for these made it impossible to enjoy "real needs". People were ignorant of genuine happiness, regarding images as reality.[83] This seems to be borrowed directly from More's *Utopia*; in More's imaginary island, gold and silver are used for the manufacture of chamber pots and "all the humblest vessels", and for the chains and fetters which they put on their slaves. Little children are decorated with pearls, diamonds and rubies, or play with them as toys.[84]

Mercier had, perhaps, also drawn his inspiration from Fénelon's fictional wonderland of Bétique. This fertile land is said to possess gold and silver mines, but the people, "happy in their simplicity", do not value anything but that which really serves man's needs. Gold is used, accordingly, in the fabrication of plows. Since no foreign trade is practiced in Bétique, money is not needed. Almost everybody is a shepherd or a laborer. Nor is oversupply in Bétique, for overproduction makes men unhappy and "slaves of false needs".[85]

Economic development was closely linked with the import of precious metals from America,[86] and Mercier's devaluation of gold can be interpreted as a

. . . .

80 Cobban 1957, 100–105; Lough 1961, 40; Woloch 1982, 252; Bosher 1988, 34; Furet 1988, 34–39; Schama 1989, 81–87; Le Roy Ladurie 1996, 427–429.
81 Cobban 1957, 55, 87, 120, 136.
82 Polak 1961, 255.
83 Mercier, *L'An 2440 II* 1786, 213–214.
84 More, *Utopia* 1964, 86.
85 Fénelon, *Les aventures de Télémaque* [1864], 187–190.
86 Meyer 1985, 448.

deliberate protest against these imperialistic policies. Both internal and overseas trade expanded considerably in France in the course of the eighteenth century, and during the period 1716–1788 France's trade with other European countries almost quadrupled. Moreover, from the mid-century until 1775 colonial trade increased fivefold.[87] There was growth in the imports of West Indian sugar, cotton, indigo, coffee and the trade in West African slaves.[88] This meant a gradual breakthrough of a "bourgeois" way of life and of new habits of consumption which this brought in its wake.[89]

For example, in the following extract from *L'An 2440* Mercier clearly expresses his hostility toward colonial exploitation, dreaming that in the far future it will have passed into history:

> "Nos vaisseux ne font plus le tour du globe pour rapporter de la cochenille et de l'indigo. Savez-vous quelles sont nos mines? C'est le travail et l'industrie... "Tout ce qui se tient au faste, à l'ostentation, à la vanité, à ce désir puéril de posséder exclusivement une chose de pure fantaisie, est sévèrement proscrit."[90]

One of the main reasons why Mercier condemned the desire for luxury items was the fact that this had given birth to the slave trade.[91] As an appeal on behalf of the abolition of slavery, Mercier projects a statue representing a triumphant black man. On its pedestal is engraved the words: "Au vengeur du nouveau monde!"[92] With these words he reflects the general anti-slavery sentiment, which had grown by the turn of the century. The enslavement of black Africans, which had formed the core of eighteenth-century maritime commerce, was abolished in the French colonial world by the revolutionaries.[93]

With his abolitionist views, Mercier joins ranks with Guillaume Thomas Raynal, whose voluminous treatise *Histoire philosophique et politique. Des*

. . . .

87 Lough 1961, 71; Gossman 1972, 53; Bosher 1988, 23.
88 Woloch 1982, 125; Bosher 1988, 24. See also Duby & Mandrou 1958, 86–87.
89 Roche 1987, 83 and passim. See also Campbell 1987, passim. In his study *The Romantic Ethic and the Spirit of Modern Consumerism* (1987), the sociologist Colin Campbell reverses the thesis of Max Weber concerning the association between the rise of capitalism and the protestant ethic by explaining that the consumer revolution which took place in eighteenth-century England was a direct offshoot of the cult of sentimentalism and the rise of romanticism. His main point is that the motive force of the spirit of modern consumerism should not be sought in materialistic pursuits, but from the illusions, day-dreams and fantasizing as a new form of hedonism; the rise of romantic fiction formed one response to this "bourgeois consumer ethic". Campbell thus comes to contradict the "emulation thesis", according to which the spread of luxury goods in the course of the eighteenth century was a consequence of the fact that the middle classes began to imitate the extravagant life-style of the aristocracy. As stated above, Mercier, for his part, emphasizes in his writings the emulation thesis: in his view, for example, the "arrogance" of women is a direct consequence of their desire of imitating the indulgence of their superiors. Campbell's theory helps, however, to understand Mercier's hostility towards luxury and consumption from a specific viewpoint; due to the fact that in his utopia there no longer exists any contraposition between the "spleen" and "ideal", there is no room for day-dreaming or fantasizing which could lead men astray from the path of virtue.
90 Mercier, *L'An 2440 II* 1786, 209–213.
91 Mercier, *L'An 2440 II* 1786, 207–208.
92 Mercier, *L'An 2440 I* 1786, 194. See also Tiainen-Anttila 1994, 300–302.
93 Woloch 1982, 130–134.

établissements et du commerce des Européens dans les deux Indes (1770), one of the first important histories of European colonialism and an argument for moral commerce, has been claimed to be one of the most widely read works of the eighteenth century.[94] Raynal's major concern is to weigh up the misfortunes and benefits drawn from the commercial exploitation of the New World, and he comes to the conclusion that in the final resort the contacts with the New World have entailed more mischief than advancement of happiness: "Cette soif insatiable de l'or a donné naissance au plus infâme, au plus atroce de tous les commerces, celui des esclaves."[95] Like Mercier, Raynal also thought that the desire for the gold, metals and money of the New World had engendered only *"besoins chimériques"*, which had not contributed to the amelioration of human life. They had not been worth all the cruelties and bloodshed needed for their attainment.[96]

The importation of textiles formed one branch of the commercial exploitation of the non-European world, and the textile industry was one of the great motors of economic prosperity in eighteenth-century France. Already in the previous century the conservatives, headed by the clergy, had thundered against luxury and depravation. In contrast, progressives criticized measures of prohibition as useless, the ineffectiveness of which the sumptuary laws of the sixteenth and seventeenth centuries had demonstrated.[97] Mercier, for his part, had no such reservations, since in his imaginary ideal state observance of the rule of moderation and resistance to the desire for luxury items is guaranteed by legal measures: "De bonnes loix somptuaires ont réprimé ce luxe barbare..."[98]

As a consequence, in the society of 2440 clothing follows a very simple line; all future Parisians are dressed in a modest way. Superficial decoration has lost all of its former importance, since, as noted in Chapter III above, in a "transparent society" the "all-seeing eye" sees through the surface.[99] Contrary for example to More's citizens, however, who were all clothed in a similar manner,[100] total uniformity of dress is not imposed.

The caprices of fashion can easily be considered as a sign of vanity and frivolity, which Mercier saw as typically feminine attributes.[101] It has been suggested that he criticized fashion (for example the fashion for excessive hairdos inaugurated by Marie-Antoinette), above all because of its artificial nature. In Mercier's mind cosmetics formed a part of the "social lie", favoring malice, which he identified with the power of women. Mercier's hostility toward the *"règne du paraître"* is also evidence of his antipathy towards the aristocracy and its values.[102]

. . . .

94 Manuels 1982, 428; Outram 1995, 131–132.
95 Raynal, *Histoire philosophique et politique. Des établissemens et du Commerce des Européens dans les deux Indes X* 1781, 297.
96 Ibid., 294–295.
97 Meyer 1985, 446.
98 Mercier, *L'An 2440 I* 1786, 35.
99 Mercier, *L'An 2440 I* 1786, 37.
100 More, *Utopia* 1964, 69.
101 See Chapter V, p. 140.
102 Thomas 1995, 35, 41.

Vanity and lavishness was one of Mercier's targets of criticism. A coiffure called "Belle-Poule". Bibliothèque Nationale, Paris.

This proves that whereas the purpose of the sumptuary laws had been to consolidate the hierarchy of orders and the political *status quo* by prohibiting the members of the lower social strata from imitating their social superiors' luxurious wardrobes,[103] in Mercier's model they are imposed for reverse reasons, i.e., to maintain the egalitarian social structure, based on the exclusion of visible representation of social power, and to promote the values of uniformity, permanence, and the dominance of the community over the individual, to restrain his fleeting desires and caprices.

A closer reading of Mercier's writings reveals that his attitude towards luxury and commercial activity was not, however, one-sidedly negative. There is some evidence indicating that he also accorded to material prosperity a positive value. When one compares the different versions of *L'An 2440* (the earlier version of 1770 and the later versions published in 1786 and 1799) one can scarcely fail to notice that in the course of these three decades the text undergoes modifications as regards the desirability of luxury and consumption by and large. To begin with, Mercier's interest in economic questions seems to have increased in the course of time: the 1770 version contains a chapter entitled "*Commerce*", but the chapter "*Luxe*" can be found only from the later versions.

. . . .
103 Roche 1994, 27–28, 39.

The chapter dealing with commerce is preserved intact from one version to another, with the exception of some comments on the theories of eighteenth-century economic thinkers, referred to above. In the 1770 version the tone adopted toward luxury is extremely negative, and one finds from it all the same moral accusations against the commercial exploitation of distant countries, which explains why Mercier's future Frenchmen no longer have colonies in the New World and why they have abandoned imported goods like tobacco and tea. As a consequence, Mercier's utopians practice only interior commerce and they have thrown all their precious metals into the sea.[104]

In the 1786 and 1799 editions of the novel the image has become more complex: Mercier has now added to his original text some episodes which reveal a shift of opinion in a more positive direction regarding commercial activity. The corruptive influence of luxury is no longer so loudly declaimed. On the contrary, the emphasis now shifts to the argument that the unequal distribution of well-being is a "necessity".[105] In these later versions Mercier praises, for example, the French navy and its victories around the world: in 2440 French wine, manufactures and fashion have become the common possession of many peoples.[106] This seems to be in glaring contradiction with Mercier's earlier condemnation of commerce and rejection of all material pleasures.

Mercier's abrupt shift of perspective tells much about his personal development, especially his highly "elastic" attitude to different phenomena of life. In addition, the textual evolution of *L'An 2440* mirrors the changes which occured in a relatively short time-span in French society itself in the final years of the *ancien régime*, increasing the value of the novel as an authentic document closely reflecting the conditions of the society in which it was produced. Despite Mercier´s general hostility towards excessive consumption, the very fact that the chapter dealing with luxury is included only in the later editons of *L´An 2440* reveals a great deal about Mercier´s heightened interest in economic matters and how extensive the polemic around the theme of luxury and commercial activity in general became in the course of the eighteenth century.

Moreover, in the brief text entitled "*Commerce*", contained in *Mon bonnet de nuit*, Mercier praises the good effects of commercial activity. Here, however, the essence of happiness is defined in a totally different manner than in *L'An 2440*; man is now regarded, with approval, as a pleasure-oriented creature. Mercier thus underscores man's prominence as the master over the rest of created beings; since everything which nature is capable of producing belongs to man, pleasure is his essence. Man is not made for privations: "il est plus tendre, plus humain, plus enjoué, lorsqu'il jouit d'une existence plus agréable."[107]

It should be noted that Mercier's views concerning the desirability of material prosperity seem to vary quite a lot even in the framework of one and the same

. . . .
104 Mercier, *L'An 2440* 1775, 407–415.
105 Mercier, *L'An 2440 III* 1786, 146.
106 Mercier, *L'An 2440 II* 1786, 325–326.
107 Mercier, *Mon bonnet de nuit I* 1784, 378.

version of *L'An 2440*, and he often presents opinions which are in sharp contradiction with each other. For example, in the chapter "*Commerce*" Mercier strictly condemns the desire for luxury and imported goods: "Vous pouvez calculer la misère d'une nation par le luxe de la capitale."[108] In the chapter "*Luxe*", on the other hand, he asserts that without material well-being man is not able to maximize his satisfaction: "On a beau exagérer les malheurs qui accompagnent le luxe, l'homme est plus heureux dans les sociétés où il brille."[109]

These more favorable statements seem to support the suggestion of Castiglione that in the course of the eighteenth century the general attitude toward luxury changed gradually in a more positive direction. Castiglione admits, however, that the Mandevillian argumentation was not even now accepted without reservations; moderation and the avoidance of exaggerated consumption was thought equally beneficial for the attainment of maximum material prosperity.[110]

The 1786 and 1799 versions of Mercier's utopia confirm the argument advanced by Castiglione, since although the critical tone against the viciousness of luxury has softened a great deal, the general attitude toward limitless material prosperity prevailing in the utopian society of 2440 is not, in the final resort, much more supportive, not even in the final version of the text published in 1799. The basic values remain the same in the 1770 and 1799 versions of the novel: frugality, moderation of needs and their moderate satisfaction, denial of passions, a way of life which resembles that of monasticism. From this it is to be inferred that in Mercier's utopian society the only means to achieve happiness already on earth leads through denial, thus opposing the ideal of happiness promoted in *L'An 2440* to a hedonistic conception of happiness.

Mercier's rather two-edged attitude towards the desirability of material prosperity reveals that his view of the world was simultaneously deeply rooted in the traditional world view and agrarian value structure, and proclaiming the rise of commercialism. His disapproval of economic expansion reflects how closely social and economic life was still related to the agrarian structure *de longue durée* in pre-Revolutionary France. The period was characterized by the breakdown of old social structures, and the traditional economic structures could no longer satisfy the increased consumption which was being born from new needs. This was a veritable "spiritual crisis", as Servier puts it.[111]

In conclusion, as a utopian writer Mercier redeems his place amongst the conservatives of his century, who thought, as Trousson comments, that existent

. . . .

108 Mercier, *L'An 2440 II* 1786, 220.
109 Mercier, *L'An 2440 III* 1786, 146. See also Mercier's treatise "*Indépendence*" in *Mon bonnet de nuit*, where he repeats the idea concerning the mutual relatedness of happiness and material well-being as follows: "Quand l'homme est riche, je ne dis pas opulent, il est meilleur". Mercier, *Mon bonnet de nuit I* 1784, 384.
110 Castiglione 1992, 162–163. Cf. Mauzi 1994, 77–78.
111 Servier 1991, 186.

reality needed only some correction to reach – if not an absolute ideal – at least a very supportable state. These conservatives put their confidence in patriarchal organization, absolute or constitutional monarchy, public granaries and hospices for the use of the poor. As they reasoned, there was no point in changing everything when simple reforms could lead to happiness. They were content with borrowing some "natural" elements in order to integrate them into their imaginary societies: community of goods, natural religion, an agricultural economy, and frugality.[112]

Mercier's utopian city of 2440 reveals in practise where the slavish pursuit of moderation and uniformity of dress and habits of eating can at its worst lead to: a vegetative existence, from which all enjoyments and pleasures of life are strictly forbidden. In contrast to the writers of the *Encyclopédie*, who argue that a happiness not animated by intervals of pleasure is not so much true happiness as *"triste bonheur"*,[113] Mercier does not seem to realize that ultimately the idealization of repose and refraining from pleasures of any kind can lead to the opposite of happiness, i.e., to a state of boredom and apathy caused by excessive reasonableness. In this sense his future Paris is literally a "land of the living dead", where mortification creates a form of happiness not far from sado-masochism.

Mercier's gravest error is in his definition of happiness only through negations. His major concern is to eliminate suffering and pain caused by the unequal distribution of goods, but he does not take into account that a "good life" consists of many different aspects, including pleasure. Rousseau, on the other hand, was well aware, in theory at least, that the avoidance of pain is not a sufficient criterion for happiness: "Le plus heureux est celui qui souffre le moins de peines; le plus misérable est celui qui sent le moins de plaisirs."[114]

Mercier's negative attitude towards corporeal and sensual pleasures reveals his view of the optimal human condition as a tranquility of the mind, which could be attained only through elimination of agitation of the soul. The underlying idea is that a man in whose life desires and their satisfaction are not in harmony, senses a negative restlessness and frustration. Rousseau's example, of a child who has always been used to getting everything that he wants, and who for this reason can never be happy,[115] illustrates this very well. Following this logic, it is better to be content with one's place in the scale of being, and forget dreaming about impossible enjoyments and their limitless satisfaction.

Health and Body Image

In emphasizing in his utopia the importance of moderation and healthy eating and drinking habits, Mercier comes at the same time to advance a new conception of an ideal human body. Good physical and mental health forms an

. . . .

112 Trousson 1975, 132, 143–144. See also Mauzi 1994, 656.
113 *Encyclopédie V* 1778, 260.
114 Rousseau, *Émile ou de l'éducation* 1904, 58.
115 Ibid., 68–69.

important element in this new body image: "La santé est au bonheur ce que la rosée est aux fruits de la terre."[116] Mercier continues by arguing that the perfect health is *"une grande volupté"*:

> "Heureux celui qui sait goûter le sentiment de la santé, cette paisible assiette du corps, cet équilibre, ce mélange parfait des humeurs, cette heureuse disposition des organes qui entretient leur force et leur souplesse."[117]

These words reflect the fact that in the course of the eighteenth century, for the first time, "health" was erected as an desirable ideal. The increased concern for a healthy human body reads as one element of the more positive view of man as general. Hence, health was conceived as man's own responsibility, and diseases were no longer regarded as a price to be paid for man's "fallen" nature. Control over one's body formed one aspect of the dream of dominance over nature. In this respect the ideal of happiness now became more "personalized" than in preceding centuries.[118] This new interest in a healthy life style and sobriety is also seen in the increase of hygienist treatises around 1750 in response to the extravagance of the Regency.[119]

The healthy, stoic and austere image of an ideal human body in Mercier's utopia reads as a total rejection of the "fallen" nature of man. The men of his future Paris are purified both morally and physically, the implication being that by controlling his diet and his bodily functions, man can profoundly influence the quality and duration of his own life. In practise this means that health is one of the responsibilities allotted to the individual.

The point should also be borne in mind that in Mercier's ideal society the value of the individual is directly dependent on his productive and useful capacity as a servant of the collectivity. The community constitutes a coherent body politic, and as integral and functional parts of this, the physical bodies of individual citizens eventually lose all their "human" bodily aspects. Rousseau writes in *Du contrat social* that the citizen has to fulfil all the services demanded by the sovereign,[120] and Mercier probably emphasized good physical condition for the same reason: a man saturated by limitless satisfaction of hedonistic pleasures would hardly be able to fill his duties as a citizen. Bodily vigor thus also means moral courage. In the society of 2440 the physical education of children is of great importance,[121] which reinforces the idea of a "Spartan", healthy and well-shaped human body.

Pierre Frantz suggests that Mercier was haunted by a great "obsession with hygiene", directly related to his aversion toward the popular culture of the body.[122] In Mercier's eyes the representatives of the lower strata of society

· · · · · · · ·

116 Mercier, *L'An 2440 II* 1786, 231.
117 Mercier, *L'An 2440 II* 1786, 231.
118 Outram 1989, 47–48.
119 Cuénin 1990, 68.
120 Rousseau, *Oeuvres complettes de J.J. Rousseau II* 1793, 45.
121 Mercier, *L'An 2440 II* 1786, 162.
122 Frantz 1995, 75.

might be appropriate targets for social compassion, but at the same time he found their dirtiness and lack of hygiene detestable. His "obsessive" attitude toward cleanliness illustrates the observation of Alain Corbin concerning a general lowering of the threshold of olfactory tolerance from about the middle of the eighteenth century.[123]

The obsessive attitude to hygiene also explains why Mercier does not say a word about intimate relations in the future. There seems to lie a certain paradox; he represents his ideal city as a totally transparent and public space, but there are still areas which are hidden from the voyeurist eye. The demand of chastity forbids this. Mercier's version of the "Heavenly City of Eighteenth-century philosophers" contains no room whatsoever for corporeal pleasures or bodily functions. This reveals a certain contradiction between the idea of "total transparency" and the demand of chastity. With this two-focal attitude Mercier seems at the same time to remain faithful to the conventions of the utopian tradition (transparency, publicity, openness) and to reflect the process of increased privatization and the rise of the concept of the individual. As has been commented by the historians of private life, in the course of the eighteenth century, bodily functions were considered indecent and removed from sight.[124]

This was a result of the "civilizing" turn of conduct; gradually in the course of the eighteenth century the body became the focus of new methods of social control. The "carnivalesque" (in the Bakhtinian sense of the term), shameless, and uncontrollable body of the lower social orders seemed to insult the "closed" body of their social superiors, who made strenuous efforts to impose constraints on them with the aid of medical improvements. The lower orders then took their revenge in the revolutionary massacre by violating the polished, cultivated and "closed" body of the educated men, who had dared to limit the scope of their bodily functions.[125]

It can easily be seen that the ideal body elevated as a model in *L'An 2440* is a typical "closed body" as opposed to the "carnivalesque body". The ideal human body as Mercier conceived it was decent and controlled, thus forming a glaring antithesis both to the shameless body of the "populace", and to the pleasure-oriented and hedonistic body of the idle aristocracy. It is also better protected against outer threats and physical pain than the "carnivalesque" and "carnal" body, which is constantly exposed to sudden outbursts either of pleasure or of violent confrontations.

The juxtaposition between the "carnivalesque body" and the "closed body" can equally well be deployed to describe the whole modern utopian tradition. Representations of the human body have been a practical means to indicate either virtue or vice in utopian literature throughout the centuries. Mercier's image of the ideal citizen as a personification of Stoic virtue, whose essential instrument of control over his life is a disciplined human body, has been much

. . . .

123 Corbin 1986, 56–59.
124 See for example Revel 1989, 188.
125 Outram 1989, 16.

favored by the writers of utopias. In anti-utopian literature, on the other hand, the human type most often represented is an immoral hedonist, who has corrupted his mind and body in excessive culinary and sexual pleasures; there is a direct line from Rabelais' glutton Gargantua to the vicious actors in de Sade's theater of cruelty. Through the representations of debauchery it has been easy to describe the decadent wickedness of human nature, perversity and egoism.

Not even Mercier imagined that men would have been able to achieve physical immortality by 2440, nor does he offer fantastic prospects about prolongation of the human life-span. In the twenty-fifth century the benefits from the advancement of medicine are, however, felt everywhere. Inoculation is generally practised, and many diseases have been cured (the most important of which are pulmonary disease and phthisis).[126]

Similarly, Condorcet put his confidence in the progress of medicine, which he hoped would achieve in the future near-immortality for mankind. He writes that man would probably never become immortal, but the average duration of life would be greatly extended. In the future (his "tenth epoch"), death would be a consequence of "natural" causes, i.e., of the enfeeblement of the inner forces of the organism itself:

> "Serait-il absurde... de supposer... qu'il doit arriver un temps où la mort ne serait plus que l'effet, ou d'accidents extraordinaires, ou de la destruction de plus en plus lente des forces vitales, et qu'enfin la durée de l'intervalle moyen entre la naissance et cette destruction n'a elle-même aucun terme assignable?"[127]

Such idealistic prospects did not yet constitute everyday reality in the lives of ordinary Frenchmen in the eighteenth century. As the historians of death have shown, people living in that century could not complacently expect a standard life span. Yet, despite the fact that everyday life was still far beyond human control, at the mercy of external perils, the battle against the omnipotence of death had already began thanks to the progress of medicine and the success of inoculation. Based on this, there was a gradual rise in population and in the average duration of life throughout the eighteenth century.[128]

It is not difficult to figure out that in ages characterized by a low average life span and high mortality rate, the dream of longevity formed one of the most tenacious aspirations. This also explains its popularity in utopian literature. Scholars have paid attention to the fact that utopian writers often introduce a "splendid old man" or an "honorable old man" ("*honorable viellard*"). This character type emerged in the pages of literature from the sixteenth century onward, and his task is to distribute wise advice. The imaginary voyages added

. . . .

126 Mercier, *L'An 2440 I* 1786, 100.
127 Condorcet, *Esquisse d'un tableau historique des progrès de l'esprit humain* 1795, 359.
128 McManners 1981, 40–49, 65–66, 89, 92–93. See also Gay 1970, 12–23, especially 12; Favre 1978, 221–244.

further variants of this theme.[129] For example in Lahontan's dialogue of savage life this character type occupies a prominent place,[130] and the special prestige accorded to men in advanced age is also emphasized in Mercier's *L'An 2440*; in 2440 old people are treated with particular respect, and it is characteristic that during his long sleep the time traveler of the novel has reached almost the age of Methuselah. As an expression of honor he is addressed as "*bon vieillard*" by the future Parisians.[131]

Otherwise, *L'An 2440* does not contain many allusions to old people. This may be a deliberate decision on Mercier's part; as stated above, everything that forms a deviance from the norm of uniformity, constitutes a danger for the perfection and purity of his imaginary city. The ideal citizen living in Mercier's future society is above all a social and political unit, whose value is measured through his capacity to fulfil his duties as a citizen. An aged and infirm, frail and feeble person does not easily fit into this mold. As Minois has pointed out, this is a common attitude in utopias, which start from the assumption of non-perverted and changeless human nature. For this reason the whole question of old age is often veiled under silence.[132]

The Concept of Work: The Curses of Idleness

Mercier did not envisage a world where men would spend their days in a state of continuous leisure. On the contrary, in his ideal society great importance is ascribed to work, which is valued as a factor contributing to man's terrestrial happiness. Mercier creates an idyllic image of a society of equal laborers: "Le travail n'a plus cet aspect hideux et révoltant, parce qu'il ne semble plus le partage des esclaves."[133] The tasks are said to be easy and pleasant because there are no more idle monks, priests, servants or manufacturers of luxury items. Since all participate in common works, nobody has to maintain another. The equal division of duties has made it possible to limit the burden of work to only a few hours each day.[134]

Mercier attributed the honor of recognizing the true value of work to Rousseau, who, he suggests, realized better than anyone before him the major

. . . .

129 McManners 1981, 86–87. See also Favre 1978, 206–207.
130 Lahontan, *Dialogues de Monsieur le baron de Lahontan et d'un Sauvage dans l'Amérique* 1993, 98–110.
131 Mercier, *L'An 2440 I* 1786, 22. It merits to be noted, however that in the figure of Mercier's time traveller there does not exist an exact correspondance between old age and wisdom. Despite the fact that the hero of the novel has reached almost the same age as Methuselah, he has not changed at all during his long dream. It is rather on the contrary; he remains forever as pupil, whose task it is to receive an instructive lesson of progress which has taken place during the centuries. The role of Mercier's old man is not to function as an advisor himself, but to assume teachings which are offered for him from above.
132 Minois 1989, 276.
133 Mercier, *L'An 2440 I* 1786, 209.
134 Mercier, *L'An 2440 I* 1786, 196.

significance of work for the liberty of man.[135] He considered laziness a mortal sin like luxury and greed. One of the greatest weaknesses of luxury, proclaims Mercier, is that it favors indolence.[136] By contrast, in his future city, activity is seen as a positive sort of restlessness, whereas laziness is condemned as a severe crime against the general well-being, and passivity is like death:

> "En aucun jour l'homme ne doit rester oisif: à l'exemple de la nature qui n'abandonne point ses fonctions, il doit se reprocher de quitter les siennes. Le repos n'est point l'oisivité. L'inaction est un dommage réel fait à la patrie, et la cessasion du travail est au fond un diminutif du trépas."[137]

Following the pattern "ora et labora", Mercier's utopians have embraced the precepts of the protestant work ethic as described by Max Weber. According to Weber one of the fundamental elements of the spirit of modern capitalism has been rational conduct on the basis of a calling, spurred by the spirit of Christian asceticism. His leading argument is that the spirit of capitalism was shaped by the same elements which characterized Puritan worldly asceticism, only without the religious basis: "The Puritan wanted to work in a calling... For when asceticism was carried out of monastic cells into everyday life, and began to dominate worldly morality, it did its part in building the tremendous cosmos of the modern economic order."[138]

Similarly, in Mercier's utopia labor is a calling, almost a sacred duty, since by fulfilling his daily tasks man is able to show his worthiness for God as well as his usefulness for the secular community. This can particularly clearly be seen in the fact that in his ideal city not even the most filthy tasks are depreciated. On the contrary, reversing the traditional association of work with pain and suffering, in Mercier's 2440 those citizens who carry out the most painful and unpleasant tasks are awarded the greatest respect. Volunteering to clean the streets is now regarded as a desire to serve society. Work diminishes the human dignity of the worker only if it demands cruelty. For this reason, butchering is reserved for foreigners who have been forced into exile from their home country, who are excluded from the class of citizens.[139] In this point Mercier follows More, in whose *Utopia* the killing of animals is left to slaves: citizens

. . . .

135 Mercier, *De J.J. Rousseau considéré comme l'un des premiers auteurs de la Révolution II* 1791, 330–333: "Rousseau avoit indiqué jusqu'à quel point le travail et l'indépendence peuvent élever le moindre individu, améliorer les hommes et les disposer à la fraternité universelle."
136 Mercier, *Tableau de Paris II* 1994a, 264. Mercier returns into this theme also in a brief article named as *"Paresse"*, where he complains that his century was characterized by laziness, the cause of which was luxury: the most severe crime caused by luxury in big cities is that it interrupts working and fills minds with futilities, hindering thus all useful activities. It does not take a long time before a lazy one falls into boredom. Mercier, *Notions claires sur les gouvernemens I* 1787, 362–366.
137 Mercier, *L'An 2440 I* 1786, 155.
138 Weber 1965, 180–181.
139 Mercier, *L'An 2440 I* 1786, 215.

are not allowed to accustom themselves to the butchering of animals, since it is believed that this would gradually destroy the sense of mercy.[140]

The value of work as an essential ingredient in men's well-being had also been recognized by the creators of earlier utopias, and an idealizing attitude towards work has formed one of the basic utopian themes across the centuries. In contrast to some other forms of ideal societies classified by J.C. Davis, a concern with full employment, waste and an efficient use of resources are common concerns in utopian literature.[141] Although asceticism is rejected in most utopias, their suggestion is that labor in moderation is a source of pleasure.[142] Following the same pattern as Mercier later, for example, Campanella suggests in his *Civitas Solis* that it is sufficient that everyone works only four hours in a day, owing to the fact that the work is divided between all.[143] The French eighteenth-century utopians repeat the same thesis: e.g. Morelly, who praises the joy of work in his egalitarian utopia *Naufrage des isles flottantes, ou Basiliade du célèbre Pilpaï*: "...nul ne se croyoit dispensé d'un travail que le concert & l'unanimité rendoient amusant & facile."[144]

Kumar suggests that the positive value which modern utopia accords to work reflects the initiation of a decisive re-evaluation of the significance of the whole concept of work, and is a symptom of change in basic values. In his view the sense of boundless material growth that began in the sixteenth and seventeenth centuries was one of the key features of modern utopianism, which rejected the concept of Original Sin in favor of the utopian project of perfection.[145]

Although in the eighteenth century some noblemen still considered it almost a crime to support themselves,[146] and they could lose their privileges if they let themselves participate in manual labor, the French *noblesse* was allowed to venture into more "respectable" fields like overseas trade or mining.[147] Mercier reflects this more egalitarian conception of work: in his future Paris princes and dukes who have done nothing worthy to be allowed to bear the brocaded hat are permitted to enjoy their wealth, but they are not distinguished by any mark of honor.[148]

By the beginning of the nineteenth century the old idea of work as a "curse" and as the "outcome of the Fall", or, as some Christian thinkers preached, valuable only for man's moral development, had finally been replaced by a new belief that work could generate inward fulfilment.[149] The majority of philosophers from Locke to Hume regarded restlessness as the mainspring of life and activity as essential to felicity.[150] They share wide unanimity that an idle

. . . .

140 More, *Utopia* 1964, 78.
141 Davis 1981, 300.
142 Manuel 1966b, 75–76.
143 Campenella, *La cité du soleil* 1993, 93, 125, 131.
144 [Morelly], *Naufrage des isles flottantes, ou Basiliade du célébre Pilpai I* 1753, 7.
145 Kumar 1987, 27–28. See also Plum 1975, 24.
146 Gossman 1972, 11.
147 Rudé 1985, 73.
148 Mercier, *L'An 2440 I* 1786, 39.
149 Charlton 1984, 183.
150 Gay 1970, 45–46.

person cannot be happy, because he was constantly in danger of falling into boredom and apathy.

To exemplify this new positive idea of work, it is appropriate to refer to Helvétius' treatise *De l'homme*, where it is argued that all individuals should contribute equally to the general well-being of the "beehive" of human society. In the view of Helvétius, the idle devour all the "honey" which the worker-bees bring to the hive, and the workers die of hunger because of the idle. Helvétius also suggests that the division of labor is not good because the idle would die of boredom; they would be envied without being enviable, because they would not be truly happy. All this leads only to one unquestionable conclusion: "L'homme occupé est l'homme heureux."[151] Montesquieu shares the same view in his *L'esprit des loix*, observing that man is not poor when he has nothing, but when he does not work.[152]

It is specifically manual labor which in most utopias is singled out for approval, and the rehabilitation of the idea of physical labor can be traced back at least to More. The same principle has been incorporated into all socialist systems, from Saint-Simon through Mao.[153] The utopias produced in the sixteenth to eighteenth centuries often condemn economic expansion, which can be seen in the strict distinction which they observe between agrarian and urban work, extolling the virtues of the former and despising the latter. For example in More's *Utopia* agriculture is said to be one pursuit which is common to all.[154] Similarly, the egalitarian community of Oudon in Restif de La Bretonne's novel *Le paysan perverti, ou Les dangers de la ville* (1775) provides a good example of this idealization of agrarian labor; in this *"petite Sparte"* the most hard-working members of community enjoy certain privileges, for example to choose the most pleasing wife amongst the unmarried girls. On the other hand, laziness is severely punished.[155] There can thus be traced a strand based on backward-looking attitudes and a desire to extol the bucolic conditions of agrarian labor at the expense of urban work.

Considering Mercier's pervasive admiration for the agrarian life style compared with the misery and corruption of big cities, one is not surprised to note that in his writings it is always, without exception, agricultural work which is glorified as a great source of pleasure in human life. He loathes the inhuman working conditions of the new industries emerging in the course of the eighteenth century, and in particular condemns forms of work which aim merely at satisfying unnecessary pleasures or individual vanity rather than the nation's common good. The description in the *Tableau de Paris* of the rich and idle who do not devote even a passing thought to the "infernal labor" of the

. . . .

151 Helvétius, *Collection des plus belles pages* 1909, 223–224, 234–235, especially 235.
152 Montesquieu, *De L'Esprit des loix* I 1749, 338.
153 Manuels 1982, 127. See also Kumar 1987, 27.
154 More, *Utopia* 1964, 68.
155 Restif de la Bretonne, *Le paysan perverti, ou Les dangers de la ville* IV 1776, 159–173, passim.

manufacturers of mirrors,[156] provides an illustrative example of the treatment of this theme.

Mercier's attitude illustrates the fact that work in towns and in the new urban industries was often regarded as dehumanizing and "alienating", whereas work on the land was praised as agreeable to contemplate and deeply satisfying for the spirit. The best illustrations of this attitude in late eighteenth-century French literature are provided by such works as Morelly's *Code de la nature* or Rousseau's *La Nouvelle Héloïse*, in particular the bucolic wine-harvest in the latter.[157] In his novel Rousseau juxtaposes the agrarian idyll with the viciousness of Paris. The agrarian way of life is the only one worthy of man: "La condition naturelle à l'homme est de cultiver la terre et de vivre de ses fruits."[158] Mercier follows suit by envisioning that the prosperity of his future France is founded on agriculture, and that in 2440 the cultivation of land is the common profession of almost every citizen.[159]

Mercier further prioritizes a life spent in a rural setting when he remarks that "c'est à la campagne où l'ame se rajeunit."[160] Despite the fact that he did not support the *laissez-faire* policies of the physiocrats, Mercier shared their ecological ideology, believing that the land and its cultivation was the ultimate source of man's terrestrial happiness. His choice of words, where the land is a "nourishing mother" who takes care of all man's needs,[161] is typically physiocratic.

Despite the fact that non-idleness is a major value in Mercier's utopian society, he also emphasizes that in addition to work men needed to rest. In the rhythm of work and rest, the fulfillment of duties is followed by relaxation and dancing in a rural setting.[162] Morelly uses a similar idea in his utopia *Naufrage des isles flottantes*: "A tous ces travaux succédoient les jeux, les danses, les repos champêtres."[163] As these extracts indicate, in Mercier's and Morelly's schemes recreational activities, too, are organized on a thoroughly rational basis; their utopians enjoy bucolic idyllic pleasures more than the allures of big cities. The healthy life style of Mercier's and Morelly's utopian workmen exemplifies the typical utopian theme of the "happy laborer". The Manuels trace an optimistic vision of singing workmen throughout the history of utopian thinking from Leibniz to Saint-Simon.[164]

A concluding remark is in order here. All the different aspects of Mercier's utopian society, – the idea that the subordination of passions under reason and self-constraint is essential, the image of a non-passionate and chaste ideal

. . . .

156 Mercier, *Tableau de Paris II* 1994a, 725–730.
157 Charlton 1984, 184.
158 Rousseau, *La Nouvelle Héloïse IV* 1925, 18.
159 Mercier, *L'An 2440 I* 1786, 207.
160 Mercier, *L'An 2440 II* 1786, 6.
161 Mercier, *L'An 2440 I* 1786, 108.
162 Mercier, *L'An 2440 I* 1786, 208–209.
163 [Morelly], *Naufrage des isles flottantes, ou Basiliade du célébre Pilpai I* 1753, 8.
164 Manuels 1982, 399.

woman, an aversion against luxury and excessive consumption, the purification of religious worship from all exterior decoration and liturgy, the concept of labor as a calling, – demonstrate how much Mercier's 2440 society is permeated by the spirit of Weberian rationalism and Calvinist-puritan asceticism.[165]

To achieve "the best of both worlds" – this is what Mercier purports to do in his *L'An 2440*. The novel reveals, however that it is almost impossible to fulfil one's duty as a citizen of the heavenly city already on earth without being forced to sacrifice all the worldly pleasures such as feasting, sexual gratification for pleasure and enjoyment gained through the knowledge of being envied and admired by others. All this testifies to the fact that Mercier's utopians are doomed to live their lives in an iron cage which they themselves have built.

The Myth of the Savage: The Apology of the Rural Repose

The flow of criticisms which Mercier directs in his *L'An 2440* against the exploitation of non-European peoples and the cruelties of the slave trade, led him to idealize the life style of primitive peoples, who were imagined as spending their life without any desire to consume more than they actually needed. Mercier's novel *L'Homme sauvage*, where he extolls the virtuous and innocent life style of the South American natives, provides the most typical example of a model of primitive happiness based on harmonious co-existence between man and surrounding nature.

In eighteenth-century France primitive utopias formed one manifestation of a general revival of pastoralism, and the vision of the "noble savages" that people them as a simple society, without absurd laws, near nature and God. In these utopias, in which nature and reason are ideally confounded, reigns the spirit of rational optimism.[166] The myth of the "noble savage" enjoyed great popularity in pre-Revolutionary France, in contrast to the unfavorable attitude toward "savages" in the Middle Ages. Catholic doctrine, especially the idea of original sin, was difficult to reconcile with the legend of the "noble savage". Although it was believed that a Golden Age had existed in the origins of the world, this Golden Age was thought to have disappeared with the sin of Adam.[167]

As we have seen, eighteenth-century philosophical writers no longer had such reservations. With their belief in man's inborn goodness rather than his original depravity, they welcomed the primitive peoples as modern inheritors of pre-Christian and pagan virtues, who did not need the artificial pleasures of

. . . .

165 As Weber has pointed out, the Calvinism of the sixteenth and seventeenth centuries adopted an entirely negative attitude to all sensuous and emotional elements in life, because they were seen as impediments to man's salvation. The ideal of asceticism was now transformed into activity within the world. Accordingly, no leisure or enjoyments were allowed, only activity for the service of God. Waste of time, idle talk and luxury were considered as sins and subject to moral condemnation. Weber 1965, 98–99, 105, 120, 157–158.
166 Trousson 1975, 129.
167 Gonnard 1946, 22, 71.

Western societies in order to be happy.[168] "Noble savages" challenged the values of European society, and their principal purpose was to function as a mouthpiece for social criticism.[169] Together with such stereotypes as the "child", the "good peasant" or the "loving mother", the "natural man" or "noble savage" was one of the images embodying new ideas about "the natural" in the latter eighteenth century.[170]

The geographical discoveries were one crucial factor which kept alive the "exotic" as a focus of controversy.[171] For example Diderot's idealistic image of Tahitian life in his *Supplément au voyage de Bougainville* drew its inspiration from Bougainville's travels. It is characteristic that on Bougainville's arrival in Tahiti in 1767 it was suggested that the island should be named "*Utopie*".[172]

L'Homme sauvage offered Mercier an excellent opportunity to declare war against all that he most hated – religious intolerance, the corruption prevailing in the contemporary French society, and lust for luxury. It reads, above all, as a didactic morality about the lustful and ruthless European conquerors, who force the Indians to leave their native country. By using the Indians as his mouthpiece, Mercier proclaims his aversion toward European norms and values. He shows in his novel how the natives are "poisoned" by wicked European habits, their cruelty and avarice. As a consequence of the encounter between the natives and the European conquerors, the Indians fall into the temptations of western civilization: "Nous estimions les Européens heureux, parce qu'ils possédoient milles superfluités dont l'image nous séduisoit."[173]

Mercier's negative attitude towards European intervention policies shows also in his ideas concerning the utopia of Paraguay: "On a donné une grande fête en mémoire de l'abolition de l'esclavage honteux où étoit réduite la nation sous l'empire despotique des Jésuite..."[174] The Jesuit state of Paraguay (1588–1768) was a political experiment which presumably drew its inspiration from Campanella's *Civitas Solis*.[175] By combining local institutions and religious discipline, the Jesuits established in Paraguay a "socialist theocracy", which rested on the principles of utopian symmetry, regularity and uniformity.[176] The Paraguayan community, which became the exemplar of a successful utopia in practise, was a subject of perennial controversy in the eighteenth century. Either the inhabitants were seen as living in bondage to Jesuit overlords, or the Jesuits admired for abolishing barbarism.[177]

· · · · · · · · ·

168 Coates, White & Schapiro 1966, 192–193. See also Gonnard 1946, 12–13.
169 Chinard 1913, 367; Charlton 1984, 106, 113.
170 Charlton 1984, 11.
171 See for example Outram 1995, 64.
172 Charlton 1984, 107–111. See also Delaporte 1988, 58–59. About the myth of Tahiti in the eighteenth-century fiction and travels of Bougainville, see Baczko 1997, 135–160.
173 Mercier, *L'Homme sauvage* 1767, 158.
174 Mercier, *L'An 2440 III* 1786, 41. About Mercier's hostility toward the jesuits, see also Chapter "*Noviciat des jésuites*" in *Tableau de Paris*. Mercier, *Tableau de Paris I* 1994a, 445–447.
175 Plum 1975, 38.
176 Trousson 1975, 128.
177 Manuels 1982, 426. See also Mucchielli 1960, 120–126.

In contrast to corrupt European customs, *L'Homme sauvage* conveys an highly idealized image of savage life. According to the moral lesson of the story, "real" and "original" happiness means that man should follow in his life the simple laws of nature.[178] The principal function of the novel is thus to highlight the huge cleavage between the "law of nature" and the "law of society", which in contemporary French society was in Mercier's view becoming wider and wider every day. The idealized existence of savage tribes was used only to demonstrate how so-called "civilized" man had become estranged from his "real origins" as a consequence of his fall into the temptations of gold, money and other luxuries.

Mercier's condemnation of the "false happiness" of European man in *L'Homme sauvage* is based on the same kind of argumentation as is advanced for example in Lahontan's depiction of the savage life in his treatise *Dialogue de M. le baron de Lahontan et d'un Sauvage dans l'Amérique* (1703). In this story, the role of the "noble savage" is played by a certain Adario, who criticizes the European life style on the basis of the knowledge which he has gained in his voyage to Paris. The point is the condemnation of money as the "demon of demons" and as the "tyrant over the French", which condemns them to live their lives as "slaves of their passions". Adario is amazed by their *"apparences extérieures de félicité"*, contrasting the pseudo-happiness of the Europeans with the genuine and innocent happiness of the Hurons, "qui ne connaissent d'autre félicité que la tranquilité de l'âme, et la liberté".[179]

There are many similarities also between Mercier's *L'Homme sauvage* and writings such as Diderot's *Supplément au voyage de Bougainville*, which is permeated by the same sentiment of moral indignation toward Europeans and their imperialist policies, the sole purpose of which seems to be the subordination of the natives. Using an old Tahitian as a mouthpiece, Diderot harshly condemns the European intervention policies, complaining that when the Europeans first arrived in Tahiti, this island where everything is held in common, they were welcomed by the islanders as friends, but rewarded their hospitality by stealing and killing.[180]

Despite the apparent points of intersection between Mercier's *L'Homme sauvage* and Diderot's *Supplément...*, Diderot's communist materialism, which also shaped his ideas relating to the question of sexual relations, was, however, alien to Mercier. Moreover, as has been noted above, Mercier did not subscribe to Rousseau's vituperations against the right of private property in the *Discours sur l'origine de l'inégalité*. The "Rousseau of the gutters" did not mechanically reproduce the ideas of his master even in *L'Homme sauvage*, which Mercier wrote when he was still working and thinking under strong influence of

· · · · · · · · ·

178 Mercier, *L'Homme sauvage* 1767, 284.
179 Lahontan, *Dialogues de Monsieur le baron de Lahontan et d'un Sauvage dans l'Amérique* 1993, 77–97, passim. The very term *bon sauvage* was introduced expressly by Lahontan. Hampson 1981, 27.
180 Diderot, *Oeuvres complètes de Denis Diderot I* 1818, 472.

Rousseau.[181] Already when he was still working on it, Mercier was obliged to rethink his position in relation to the cult of the "noble savage". He explains this crucial change in *Tableau de Paris* as follows:

> "...quand, familiarisé à vingt-sept ans avec les maladies, avec les hommes, et encore plus avec les livres, j'eus plusieurs sortes d'idées, de plaisirs et de douleurs... plus faible d'imagination, parce que je l'avais enrichie et amollie par les privations et les arts, je trouvai le système de Jean-Jacques moins délectable."[182]

It can be taken as the sign of a decisive turn in Mercier's psychological development that in the final pages of *L'Homme sauvage* he associates "false happiness" with ignorance: "Je prie Dieu de dissiper leur faux bonheur, & de les rendre plus éclairés, afin qu'ils ne soient pas plus longtems coupables."[183] In his *De la littérature et des littérateurs*, published ten years later, he draws a similar conclusion, affirming that the so-called "happiness" of primitive peoples is a negative sort of happiness, a "state of apathy": "Je ne veux point de ce bonheur, où l'homme concerve sa rudesse primitive, où tranquile par ignorance..."[184] Mercier returns to this theme in *Notions claires sur les gouvernemens*, where the assumption of the "happiness" of savages is questioned on the grounds that the arts, sciences and social institutions are all necessarily related to man's happiness.[185]

These examples drawn from Mercier's various writings are sufficient to prove that he was not, in the final resort, prepared to follow Rousseau in asserting that "civilized" existence had brought nothing but sorrow and misery into the world. As a native Parisian he was, after all, too much a city-dweller to be able to turn his back on the allure of Paris, this city of "monstrous wealth" and "scandalous luxury".[186] On the contrary; as Mercier states in *Tableau de Paris*, the concentration of philosophical thought in Paris was in itself sufficient justification for its existence.[187] Already in the first part of his vast panorama of Parisian life, Mercier makes his preferences clear: "Il y a moins de servitude et de misère à Paris que dans l'état sauvage, même pour les plus infortunés..."[188]

. . . .

181 Rovillain suggests that contrary to what is generally supposed, Mercier did not write *L'Homme sauvage* under the influence of Rousseau at all. He proposes that Mercier's real source of inspiration was abbé Prévost's novel *Cleveland* (1731). Rovillain 1931, 822–847, passim. In his article on this issue Rovillain gives a detailed comparison between those two novels, which reveals the existence of many similarities between *L'Homme sauvage* and *Cleveland*. Without denying the impact of Prévost on Mercier, the decisive influence of Rousseau should not, however, be ignored.

182 Mercier, *Tableau de Paris I* 1994a, 41. About Mercier's gradual estrangement from the immediate influence of Rousseau when he was writing *L'Homme sauvage* and how this change of opinion is reflected in the text itself, see also Béclard 1903, 44–51, passim.

183 Mercier, *L'Homme sauvage* 1767, 309.

184 Mercier, *De la littérature et des littérateurs* 1970, 12.

185 Mercier, *Notions claires sur les gouvernemens II* 1787, 259–268; Mercier, *Notions claires sur les gouvernemens I* 1787, 31–33.

186 See also Charlton 1984, 194–195.

187 Mercier, *Tableau de Paris II* 1994a, 223–228.

188 Mercier, *Tableau de Paris I* 1994a, 41–42.

When one bears in mind Mercier's firm belief in the power of education to liberate men from the burden of prejudice and superstition, one is not surprised to read his assertion in *Notions claires sur les gouvernemens* that nature calls man to live in society, and for this reason the concept of "perfectibility" is directly related to the advancement of knowledge: "La perfectionnement de la société... est encore dans l'état de nature le plus brute & le plus sauvage. Cette nouvelle espèce de civilization doit être l'ouvrage des livres lumineux & sublimes..."[189] Contrary to Rousseau, who saw luxury and idleness as phenomena parallel with the evolution of arts and sciences,[190] Mercier was not willing to go as far in the denial of the value of the civilizing process.

A closer survey of Mercier's major writings reveals, however, that in the final resort he did not see great differences in happiness between the primitive and civilized way of life. Already in *L'Homme sauvage*, in comparing savages and Europeans, he comes to the conclusion that even though savages live nearer to nature both in their virtues and in their vices, happiness does not belong to them more than to Europeans. Mercier explains this view, a little pessimistically perhaps, by arguing that men's needs remain everywhere alike, i.e., their desires are everywhere limitless, and the human heart is "*l'arène de toutes les passions*". From this he infers that the vice of vanity is no more rare in the solitude of the forests than in the noise of the cities, and that ignorance of European arts does not render better the condition of savage man.[191]

In the eighteenth century there existed no doctrinal unity regarding (American) savages. Some saw in them victims of fanaticism, others considered them as brutes, citing the accounts of voyagers to demonstrate to what point of bestiality peoples can descend who have no idea of progress and have remained in the same state since the beginning of the world.[192] Mercier comments that the concept "primitive state" had been used to serve contradictory purposes; on the one hand the errant life of primitive mankind had been identified with the condition of the brutes, but on other occasions corresponding statements were made about the kind of savages that could be born only in society.[193] This seems to be drawn directly from Rousseau's treatise on the origin of inequality:

> "Enfin tous, parlant sans cesse de besoin, d'avidité, d'oppression, de désirs, et d'orgueil, ont transporté à l'état de nature des idées qu'ils avaient prises dans la société. Ils parlaient de l'homme sauvage, et ils peignaient l'homme civil."[194]

. . . .

189 Mercier, *Notions claires sur les gouvernemens I* 1787, 18.
190 Rousseau, *Discours...* 1992, 43.
191 Mercier, *L'Homme sauvage* 1767, 239–241. Still in *Tableau de Paris* Mercier stands behind this view; he sees no difference between the African tribes and the Parisians when it comes to their habits of decorating themselvels and their desire of luxury. Mercier, *Tableau de Paris I* 1994a, 12–20.
192 Chinard 1913, 366.
193 Mercier, *Notions claires sur les gouvernemens II* 1787, 258.
194 Rousseau, *Discours...* 1992, 168.

Gilbert Chinard notes that "natural man" described by Rousseau and many others before him, could not exist elsewhere than in a exotic and tropical landscape,[195] and Mercier was also well aware that basically the "noble savage" was a mere illusion, an ideal type, a product of the imagination. On at least one occasion he remarks that the term "savage man" does not absolutely signify anything, since in reality no such men exist.[196] In the same way, Rousseau realized that man could not return to nature, and that the "Golden Age" was a condition which man had never known.[197] This did not hinder him from believing that if man could have remained in the state of ignorance, his condition would be happier.[198] Man's curiosity extends, however, with the increase of his needs. Therefore, there is a vast difference between a "natural man" living amidst nature, and a "natural man" who has adjusted his habits to living in a state of society. As a consequence, the hero of Rousseau's pedagogical novel *Émile* is described as "un sauvage fait pour habiter les villes".[199]

Despite their unrealistic nature, the popularity of primitive utopias like Mercier's *L'Homme sauvage* reflects the sharpening of criticism on the eve of the French Revolution. As a mouthpiece of social criticism, the "noble savage" simultaneously questions both the inequalities of the society of estates, and the process of modernization, urbanization and industrialization. By extolling "natural" pleasures and a life spent amidst a bucolic idyll at the expense of the desire for luxury, external decoration and extravagance, the myth of the "noble savage" breathed new life into the classical dichotomy of city vs countryside.

In the eighteenth century the classic juxtaposition between town and countryside was emphasized even further; whereas the town was seen as corrupting people and destroying tranquility of spirit, rural life was thought to promote happiness and virtue.[200] As we have already seen, Mercier had a clear awareness of the many problems relating to life in big cities like Paris, such as the lack of hygiene, overcrowding, and a general atmosphere of cruelty and crime. In the pages of *Tableau de Paris* eighteenth-century Paris is most often depicted as a dangerous city of temptations and false pleasures,[201] a "city of seduction", where innocent hearts newly arrived from the countryside are surrounded in all directions by debauchery.[202]

Deprun notes that for Mercier Paris was a city of restlessness, whereas "rural happiness" meant for him that one went to the country and left restlessness behind.[203] The term "restlessness" perceptively describes the hectic tempo of

. . . .

195 Chinard 1913, 2.
196 Mercier, *Notions claires sur les gouvernemens II* 1787, 270.
197 Rousseau, *Discours...* 1992, 168; Shklar 1969, 6, 10; Pollard 1972, 58.
198 This theme will be dealt with in a more detailed manner later in Chapter IX of this investigation. See especially p. 272 and p. 285.
199 Rousseau, *Émile ou de l'éducation* 1904, 229–230.
200 Charlton 1984, 178–198, especially 181–183.
201 See for example Mercier, *Tableau de Paris I* 1994a, 60.
202 Ibid., 47.
203 Deprun 1979, 119.

urban life, the atmosphere of continuous change and succession of passing impressions. "Restlessness", understood as a synonym for negative movement, forms an antithesis to the concept of repose, which in *L'Homme sauvage* is incarnated in the image of the "noble savage".

Mercier remarks in *L'An 2440* that the two main sources of inspiration for the writer are retreats into solitude and the company of friends.[204] His vision of the countryside as a place of voluntary retreat from the turmoil of a big city reads as a sign of a privatization of life style. Ever since the seventeenth century upper-class Frenchmen had occasionally withdrawn to a country retreat,[205] and between 1500 and 1800 there gradually emerged a new understanding of the significance of solitude as one aspect of increased self-knowledge. Solitude was no longer prized only for its ascetic value, but as a source of pleasure.[206] The extracommunal refuges described by Mercier and his contemporary writers amidst the undisturbed tranquility of rural landscapes read as a manifestation of nostalgia and yearning for a state of repose and happiness, which the accelerated tempo of modernization and the rapid growth of big cities was in the near future to cast into the night of oblivion.

. . . .
204 Mercier, *L'An 2440 II* 1786, 6.
205 Charlton 1984, 6.
206 See for example Chartier 1989, 163.

VII The Concept of Evil in the "Best of Possible Worlds"

The Theory of Necessity

It is striking that despite his belief in man's inborn goodness, Mercier has not created in his *L'An 2440* a "perfect" world from which all evil elements have been totally eliminated. As has been noted previously, in his view the power of men's passionate impulses should never be underestimated, and it is characteristic that one chapter of the novel is devoted to the execution of a murderer.[1] The thesis of Louis Marin, according to which utopias do not offer reversed images of reality that "mechanically invert the negative relations of reality into positive ones"[2] sustains this idea that the concepts of evil or sin are not entirely excluded even from utopian conditions.

The problem concerning the significance of original sin has caused extensive argument amongst scholars of utopianism. J.C. Davis, for example, takes the existence of sin even in utopian perfection for granted. He writes that Utopia "accepts recalcitrant nature and assumes sinful man".[3] Scholars such as Judith Shklar, on the other hand, have argued that utopia is a way of rejecting the notion of "original sin".[4] As for example Northrop Frye has noted, the latter view has been most widely accepted; it has been customary to assume that utopia is "an ideal or flawless state".[5] This comment is just: the idea of original sin is totally alien to the spirit of modern utopianism.

It is important to bear in mind, however, that as a fictional genre utopia is always closely related to the existing social and political conditions, which means that the writer of utopia cannot totally neglect the possibility of evil. In real life, wickedness can assume many different forms, and despite the fact that one of the main utopian aims has through the centuries been the desire to overcome the contradictory aspects of existence, at least some of these forms occupy a specific place also in utopias.

. . . .

1   This seems, however, to contradict Mercier's glorification of man's original goodness.
2   Marin 1978, 275–276.
3   Davis 1981, 36. Davis criticizes the unprecise use of the term "utopia", among other things, on the grounds that in modern research literature it has been often associated with the denial of original sin. He exemplifies his view by alluding to actual utopian works, for example James Harrington's *Oceana* (1656), where the presumption of men's wickedness is taken explicitly as granted. Davis 1981, 18.
4   Shklar 1965, 370; Shklar 1969, 2. For example Timothy Kenyon has criticized Shklar's identification of utopianism with optimism, which he regards as incorrect, since by thus arguing she ends up excluding many pre-Enlightenment utopias, which were in many cases inspired by Christian ideals. Kenyon 1982, 132.
5   Frye 1966, 31.

The term "horror of perfection" launched by Gilles Lapouge sheds new light on this issue. By this he means that terrestrial life cannot pretend to possess plenitude and rest, since these are reserved to the eternal life announced by Christ. If the social model was saved from error, history would be closed. If eternal life reigned already on earth, what could one do with another eternal life, that of Heaven? There cannot exist "two eternities".[6]

The problem of sin and evil is an eternal one, but in eighteenth-century France it aroused exceptional interest. Bronislaw Baczko remarks that in an age which had ceased to be branded by original sin, wickedness had no longer foundation. The persistence of wickedness was not easily reconciled with the assumption that nature formed an harmonious and orderly totality, which offered itself to human reason as a perfectly readable and coherent "book". In order to find a rational justification for the existence of happiness, eighteenth-century thinkers breathed new life to the old questions concerning the "Supreme Being", His plan and intentions: if God had not wanted a world without wickedness, He was not good or just; and if He could not have created such a world, He was not omnipotent or providential.[7]

As Delumeau has pointed out in his investigation devoted to the historical evolution of the concepts of sin and culpability in recent centuries, in a certain sense the notion of sin was easier to understand in the centuries characterized by religious value structures. Until the eighteenth century (and occasionally even then), the idea of evil had contained no mystery, because original sin was a kind of *deus ex machina* which could be utilized at every moment as an ultimate and definitive reason for everything that went wrong in the universe.[8]

Hence, with increased rationalism and secularization, when the belief in man's "fallen" nature was more and more in question, the issue gradually became more complicated. The persistence of evil forces aroused scepticism concerning the supposed benevolence of God: what was God's role as a regulator of men's lives? What if He had forgotten the world after having created it? And if - the most frightening proposition of all – He had never even existed, and the only truth was that there were no "final causes", and the world was only cold matter, without any plan or orientation for the better? This seemingly paradoxical situation – the obsessive pursuit of happiness and the undeniable presence of evil – thus led to an obsessive need to find rationally grounded legitimations for wickedness.

The contradiction between the probability of a good life and the existence of wickedness forms one of the most essential themes in Mercier's major writings, in particular in his moral allegories. Their focal issue can be formulated as follows: how can it be explained that even in the "best of possible worlds" there still exists corruption, oppression, and misery? Mercier was constantly

. . . .

6   Lapouge 1982, 22.
7   Baczko 1997, 12, 26, 30–32, 41, 52. See also Ehrard 1994, 639.
8   Delumeau 1983, 282.

tormented by the question why good people have to suffer unreasonably, and why evil people can wallow in abundance. This is the leading theme, for example, in the story "*L'Optimisme*": "J'avois réfléchi un jour entier sur le bonheur qui est le partage du méchant, & sur l'infortune qui poursuit l'homme vertueux..."[9]

It was expressly this problem related to moral values, i.e. to the potential for evil in human nature, that formed the core of the intellectual crisis of the eighteenth century. In the sentimental novels of that epoch, trials of virtue and the triumph of evil form a popular and recurrent theme.[10] Mercier's most important source of inspiration in this matter was, without doubt, Leibniz, in whose philosophy based on the "universal plan of harmony" integral role is played by the problem of evil and attempts to reconcile this with the system of rational optimism. For example, in his treatise *De l'origine radicale des choses*, Leibniz finds justification for the persistence of wickedness by arguing that wickedness would, in the final resort, render possible the final triumph of the forces of good:

> "...car très souvent c'est pour les meilleurs que les choses vont le plus mal...mais si l'on y regarde de plus près, ces raisons mêmes qu'on a apportées rendent évident a priori que c'est le contraire qui est vrai; et que c´est par la totalité des choses,et surtout des esprits, qu'on obtient la plus grande perfection qui puisse être."[11]

Leibniz was convinced that suffering could be a necessary precondition of happiness:"...le grain jeté dans la terre souffre avant de fructifier."[12] Mercier follows in the tracks of this prominent philosophical predecessor when he asserts that suffering and emulation are inborn characteristics of virtue; otherwise virtue would cease to be virtue.[13] The same message formed the core of a common eighteenth-century view concerning "persecuted virtue", or "trials of virtue"; it was argued that the reason why evil people seemed so often to succeed better than good ones was that the latter would finally be recompensed. The proponents of this idea found consolation from the assumption that an apparent injustice often preceded great happiness, and that present evil was the price which had to be paid for future felicity. Human destiny would have been absurd if faith in Redemption did not give sense to it.[14]

. . . .

9   Mercier, *Songes philosophiques* 1768, 7.
10   Crocker 1969, 25.
11   Leibniz, *Oeuvres I* 1972, 343.
12   Ibid., 344.
13   Mercier, *Songes philosophiques* 1768, 208.
14   Ehrard 1994, 626–628. Helvétius provides in his treatise "*De L'homme*" a very vivid example of how this theme relating to "persecuted virtue" was handled in philosophical writings produced in eighteenth-century France: "L'homme illustre achète donc toujours sa gloire à venir par des malheurs présents. Au reste, les malheurs mêmes et les violences qu'il éprouve promulguent plus rapidement ses découvertes." Helvétius, *Collection des plus belles pages* 1909, 246. As this passage clearly reveals, the present moment did not seem to promise any recompensation, and for this reason some future time needed to serve as the horizon of great expectations. The same argument was also, probably, one of the reasons for Mercier's decision to situate his ideal society in the remote future. A fuller treatment of this theme will be provided in Chapter VIII of this study.

The natural consequence of this affirmation that ultimately, from the viewpoint of the "totality", "everything is well", led to the argument that evil continues to exist because it is "necessary."[15] In the following extract from *L'An 2440* Mercier propagates this "philosophy of necessity" in a very characteristic manner:

> "Les ombres d'ici bas, les maux passagers qui nous affligent, les douleurs, la mort ne nous épouvantent point: tout cela, sans doute, est utile, nécessaire, et nous est même imposé pour notre plus grande félicité."[16]

According to this highly optimistic credo, founded on a rather fatalistic view of the world, everything is well and nothing could have been otherwise. Man has nothing to be afraid of, because God takes care of everything. A mortal creature like man, naturally limited in his understanding, has no right to question the intentions of God even when they appear unjust or purely hazardous:

> "Va, foible mortel, esprit audacieux & borné, va, apprends à adorer la Providence, lors même qu'elle te paroîtroit injuste. Dieu a prononcé un seul & même décret; il est éternel, il est irrévocable, il a tout vu avant que de le porter."[17]

In this passage Mercier returns to one of his most often repeated themes, i.e. the demand for humility. This implies that what for human reason seems merely a cold fact or "necessity", nonetheless formed part of the divine order. Hence, the resort to the conception of man's "limited understanding" or "mediocrity" made it possible to justify even the most unreasonable and unjust events in the world; they were all contained in the "universal plan of harmony", but because of man's position as a feeble creature he was incapable of understanding the "final causes". The conviction of God's benevolence and the belief in the final causes rescued Mercier from ultimate despair and from the fear that the world is in a state of chaos, in aimless and indifferent movement.

An analogous pattern can be traced in Leibniz' treatise *Théodicée*, where he endeavours to justify the existence of wickedness by arguing that if the least evil was absent from the world, it would no longer be the best world that God has chosen. Because God has chosen this world, it is the best possible, and therefore no other world would have been as perfect:

> "Il est vrai qu'on peut s'imaginer des mondes possibles, sans péché et sans malheur, et on en pourrait faire comme des romans, des utopies, des sévarambes; mais ces mêmes mondes seraient d'ailleurs fort inférieurs en bien au nôtre."[18]

. . . .

15   Ehrard 1994, 646.
16   Mercier, *L'An 2440 I* 1786, 188–189.
17   Mercier, *Songes philosophiques* 1768, 43.
18   Leibniz, *Extraits de la Théodicée* 1912, 38. It is noteworthy that in this passage Leibniz regards utopia as synonymous with a state without sin.

In other words, if there is wickedness and sin in the world, it is because it is God's will. Because God has created everything for the happiness of man, the existence of wickedness is totally reasonable and conceivable.[19] As in the case of Mercier's utopian visions, also in the philosophical system of Leibniz wickedness is thus explained by predeterminism and "necessity": "Tout ce qui existe, existe nécessairement pendant qu'il existe."[20] As Voltaire shows in *Candide, ou l'Optimisme*, from the viewpoint of necessitarian philosophy even sin could be justified: "...la chute de l'homme et la malédiction entraient nécessairement dans le meilleur des mondes possibles."[21]

Following this kind of logic, man could achieve peace of mind in a world so often torn apart by different conflicts, such as political convulsions, natural catastrophes and epidemics, only by remaining faithful to the Deist assumption that the will of God is manifested through the benevolent laws of nature, and despite their apparent arbitrariness the intentions of God have under all circumstances only one and undivided purpose: the advancement of man's happiness.

For Mercier the theory of necessity provided a practical tool to explain even the most devastating evils, such as death, on "reasonable" grounds. In speculating on the brevity of life in one of his essays ("*Briéveté de la vie*") he proclaims that man has no reason to regret the short duration of his terrestrial journey; if men died only after living for thousands of years, God would need to considerably enlarge the size of the earth, or men would be piled up on each other. From this it can be concluded that everything has been wisely arranged: all things, even those which horrify man most, have been arranged for man's supreme happiness. God has willed the existence of illnesses, of which men in their stupidity complain.[22]

Voltaire comes to a similar conclusion in his story *Le monde comme il va, vision de Babouc*; the hero of the story, Babouc, is sent to Persepolis in order to repair the injustices which have torn this country. He is horrified to witness the wars, the ignorance prevailing in hospitals, the way the dead are buried in the temples. Despite all the evil he confronts, Babouc decides to leave things as they are: "...les abus se présentent à vos yeux en foule, et le bien qui est caché, et qui résulte quelquefois de ces abus mêmes, vous échappe."[23]

To draw together the main lines of this chapter, it is important to emphasize that Mercier was evidently willing to assent to all different forms of wickedness, – metaphysical, moral and physical.[24] The philosophy of Leibniz and its

. . . .

19 Ibid., 107.
20 Ibid., 129.
21 Voltaire, *Oeuvres completes de Voltaire*, t. quarante-quatrième, 1787, 239.
22 Mercier, *Mon bonnet de nuit I* 1784, 340–344.
23 Voltaire, *Oeuvres completes de Voltaire*, t. quatre-quatrième 1787, 103–123, especially 117.
24 This division between different forms of wickedness refers to Bronisław Baczko's analysis devoted to Voltaire's conception of evil. By metaphysical wickedness he means wickedness which consists of the imperfection of man and all living creatures, by physical wickedness he means wickedness which consists of death and sufferings, and by moral wickedness he means sorrows that men cause voluntarily to each other. Baczko 1997, 41–57.

fundamental assumption concerning the "necessity" of wickedness offered him the certainty that nothing could ultimately come between man and his inborn right to search and find happiness already this side of the grave. Evil is not an enemy of happiness; on the contrary, it is the very condition of it. With this respect Mercier echoes a typical attitude propagated by eighteenth-century philosophers of optimism, who, to quote the view of Lovejoy on this matter, "were desirous of proving... that reality is rational through and through that every fact of existence, however unpleasant, is grounded in some reason as clear and evident as an axiom of mathematics."[25]

For some of Mercier's contemporaries, Leibnizian optimism sounded, however, both unrealistic and naïve. The current of "historical pessimism" was intensified especially after the Lisbon earthquake of 1755, after which Voltaire, for example, no longer considered the "optimism" of Leibniz tenable.[26] Even earlier, in his *Dictionnaire philosophique* (1734), Voltaire had criticized the axiom "*tout est bien*", which for him could no longer offer consolation. In his view, instead of giving proof of the existence of a benevolent God, this system represented God as a powerful and malicious ruler, who was indifferent toward men's sufferings.[27]

The ironic tone of Voltaire's *Candide* illustrates the deepening of his scepticism as regards the "best of possible systems" even further. In the course of the story the most horrible accidents happen, which are all explained from the viewpoint that "everything is well". The cynicism of Voltaire culminates in the words of Candide, the hero of the story, when he is asked about the essence of optimism: "...c'est la rage de soutenir que tout est bien quand on est mal."[28] This is a thesis to which Mercier would have scarcely have subscribed.

The Treatment of the "Abnormals"

Under the Mark of Cain: Expulsion from "Paradise"
The theory of necessity could offer consolation when man confronted evil that he could not control by himself. He could not do much to change the sudden attacks of natural disasters or the inevitability of death, for instance. He could, however, try to change his own morally corrupted nature (ignorance, superstition, lack of social compassion). It was expressly these forms of moral evil that were the most difficult to justify in the light of cold "necessity". One form of such wickedness is the mental or physical pain or suffering that man causes for another person or to the whole community of which he forms a part. In the following pages it will be analyzed how Mercier approaches wickedness

. . . .

25 Lovejoy 1950, 226.
26 See for example Charlton 1984, 87–88. A fully treatment of this theme is provided in the Chapter IX, pp. 253–265, especially p. 258.
27 Voltaire, *Dictionnaire philosophique* [s.a.], 54–61.
28 Voltaire, *Oeuvres completes de Voltaire*, t. quarante-quatrième 1787, 288.

as a concrete fact of everyday life in his utopia, and what kind of "remedies" he suggests for its treatment.

Due to the fact that the principle of all-encompassing uniformity constitutes the supreme ideal in Mercier's society of the future, everything that represents deviance from this norm is condemned as "abnormal". The common denominator of "abnormal" individuals is that they have not been willing to sacrifice their particular interests on the altar of collective well-being. In practise this means that they have either acted or spoken in a way which is not compatible with the official ideology of the state. "Sin" is now a synonym for social disorder.

The chapter of *L'An 2440* in which Mercier describes the execution of a murderer illustrates most clearly his propositions concerning the proper treatment of wickedness in his imaginary society. In this chapter the time traveller witnesses the execution of a man who has committed a homicide against another citizen. The motive is said to have been jealousy. Before the execution, the criminal is given the right to make a voluntary choice whether to live or die. To continue one's life would, however, mean living under the shadow of opprobrium. Under the blight of guilt and sin, life would be only an endless burden, which explains why death is less terrible than ignominy. In order to liberate himself from shame and to regain his lost human dignity, the accused condemns himself to death by his own decision.[29]

In the eighteenth century those who had committed their crime under the influence of passion might sometimes be pardoned,[30] but in Mercier's *L'An 2440* not even sentimental reasons are regarded as extenuating circumstances. On the contrary, it may not be a pure coincidence that the manslaughter has been caused by jealousy. It is as if Mercier was deliberately trying to demonstrate the devastating effects of passions.[31] This was, perhaps, his symbolic way of arguing that the state of original purity and perfection could be restored only through the total eradication of all passionate outbursts.

It is highly questionable whether the acceptance of death depicted in *L'An 2440* is genuinely based on a voluntary choice, since in this "transparent" society any person who has committed some violent act can immediately be recognized by everyone due to the fact that the "divine hand" has pressed a "monstrous mark" on his forehead.[32] This "mark of Cain", engraved in the forehead of the criminal, openly declares his guilt, and makes him an outcast everywhere:

> "Vous porterez par-tout le poids de vos remords et la honte éternelle d'avoir résisté à la loi juste qui vous condamne. Soyez équitable envers la société, et jugez-vous vous-même!"[33]

. . . .
29   Mercier, *L'An 2440 I* 1786, 113–126.
30   McManners 1981, 373.
31   Mercier, *L'An 2440 I* 1786, 115.
32   Mercier, *L'An 2440 I* 1786, 115, 120.
33   Mercier, *L'An 2440 I* 1786, 125.

By refusing to continue his life as an social outcast and by submitting to death, the murderer shows his capacity for stoic self-control and firmness of spirit, which in its extreme form means the denial of man's inborn instinct of self-preservation. This voluntary choice of death demonstrates that the happiness or unhappiness of man is no longer destined by coincidence, a revengeful God or despotic ruler. The calm acceptance of the dissolution of the "I" forms part of the general principle of dominance over nature as a focal dream of the eighteenth-century French philosophers.

This is reminiscent of "heroic suicide", which formed an integral part of the political culture of the French Revolution. It drew its inspiration from the general admiration of the ancient Stoics, such as Cato or Seneca, and their voluntary acceptance of death. Heroic suicide, which was often committed as a public act, was connected with the idea of republican virtue inasmuch as a crucial element was the display of Stoic self-control in the face of death. It thus implied admiration of suicide as the ultimate form of self-control. Violent death was often seen as a step toward heroization.[34] In the tradition of utopian literature the idealization of "heroic suicide" has formed a recurrent motif, and in addition to Mercier other creators of utopias have also been emphasized the stoic aspects of death by regarding it as a "necessity"; for example the inhabitants of Campanella's *Civitas Solis* are severely punished if they are afraid of death.[35]

It is however noteworthy that in Mercier's utopian society the voluntary acceptance of death is not based so much on the fact that the murderer has gained absolute control over his own life, but on the fact that he learns to adjust to the destiny which he cannot escape. As noted above, under the "mark of Cain" there were not many other options available. Ernest Gellner reminds us that the same attitude forms a philosophical current leading from the ancient Stoics to seventeenth-century rationalists like Descartes and Spinoza; it was more important to find contentment in adjustment to reality than to strive to bend reality to the human will. The assumption that the world could be transformed so that it would respond to men's aspirations and that it could be mastered by the human will did not emerge until the increase of technological power.[36]

. . . .

34   Gay 1970, 85; Vovelle 1983, 496–499; Outram 1989, 90–105. For more detail, see Minois 1999, 248–277, 304–311. About fear and its conquest amongst the Stoics, see for example Choron 1976, 65–66.
35   Campanella, *La cité du soleil* 1993, 133.
36   Gellner 1992, 172. Despite their justification of suicide as an aspect of man's dignity and as proof of his capability for sef-evaluation, self-destruction was not accepted without reservations by writers of the eighteenth century; it was proscribed in cases where it was not founded on rational reasons or when it was in contradiction with the individual's duties toward the social compact. The customary view, according to which suicide was an offence against God and a crime against society, was thus still very much alive. McManners 1981, 409–437, passim. See also Minois 1999, 210–247. A dichotomy of a similar sort between "legitimate" and "non-legitimate" suicide is also revealed in Mercier's views on the issue; even though in his utopia he sanctions voluntary death, he did not regard suicide as a real solution to human sufferings. In a brief text devoted to this theme ("*Suicide*"), Mercier proclaims the contrary view, according to which there is nothing "heroic" in suicide. In this context he calls suicide a "fever of the soul", and one who commits it a person tormented by a "greedy desire for rest". Mercier, *Mon bonnet de nuit I* 1784, 120.

Notwithstanding the fact that Mercier retains capital punishment in his ideal city, he did not support the cruel treatment of those who had been either accused or condemned for some crime. In his utopia he makes a plea on behalf of a more humanitarian criminal justice, aiming at inventing less inhumane ways for the treatment of criminals as a critical response to corporal punishment. In his society of the twenty-fifth century the unfortunate are no longer put for months into a dark dungeon, or their bones broken in a most horrible manner.[37] This reads as a direct attack upon the brutality and cruelty of the eighteenth century's criminal justice. It is a cold numerical fact that at the outbreak of the Revolution there were still over a hundred crimes which led to the execution of the death sentence. Executions were public and the painfulness of dying was adjusted to fit the crime.[38]

In Mercier's utopia, after centuries had passed, the principal function of punishments would be to prevent new crimes, not to offer entertainment for the bloodthirsty masses. He was not, however, willing to abolish the public nature of the execution of the death sentence. In Mercier's view the most important aspect in the treatment of those who had been either accused or condemned of some crime, was the public representation of detention, juridical process, and execution of the death sentence: "...c'est en plein jour qu'il offre la honte du châtiment."[39] This practise is consistent with the general principle of total transparency and openness that constitutes the norm in *L'An 2440*. The importance of the fact that everything takes place in clear daylight, is explained by utilitarian reasons: the purpose of the public treatment of the convicted is to offer visible examples for others.[40]

Ulrich Döring comments that in Mercier's utopian society the function of the entire public instruction is to touch the soul and the heart, which means the application of a kind of "soft pedagogy".[41] As an example of this "soft pedagogy", criminals are transported to solitary places, where they are spurred to repentance and "opening themselves to virtue".[42] The suggestion is that under ideal circumstances the punishment should be psychological rather than corporal; the essential is that its effects are felt in the criminal's soul, not in his body. By emphasizing profound repentance and desire for expiation on the part of the criminal,[43] Mercier illustrates the good effects of this philosophy in practise. Instead of a carnivalistic orgy of torture, his description of the execution resembles a public confession.

One special group of recalcitrant individuals are authors who have been charged with spreading heretical ideas. The time traveller is told by his guide that in order to be cured from his bad habits the "undoctrinal" author is visited

. . . .

37   Mercier, *L'An 2440 I* 1786, 117–119.
38   Hampson 1981, 156; McManners 1981, 368–369.
39   Mercier, *L'An 2440 I* 1786, 111.
40   Mercier, *L'An 2440 I* 1786, 111, 178.
41   Döring 1988, 658 and passim.
42   Mercier, *L'An 2440 I* 1786, 130.
43   Mercier, *L'An 2440 I* 1786, 123.

each day by two virtuous citizens, who try to restore him to the right way "avec les armes de la douceurs et de l'éloquence".[44] If the "softer" means of psychic manipulation do not make him confess his error and rejoin the herd of docile disciples, the consequence is the same as in the case of murderers, i.e. stigmatization with shame. Public shame and expulsion from the community are also applied to lazy persons, since working now means fulfilling one's duty as a citizen. There are censoring authorities in charge of exposing "unsocial elements".[45]

In Mercier's utopian society, which Döring justly compares to a great school, the citizens remain forever pupils. Döring criticizes the pedagogical system advocated by Mercier on the grounds that its aim is not to develop men's personality, but to reinforce the dominant ideology. Art has an ideological role to fulfil; artists and writers coerce the people to assent to the norm. There are hierarchic structures between those who are educated, and those whose task it is to put allegorical reality on the stage. Under these circumstances the norm is represented as synonymous with good, whereas dissidence is associated with the image of evil, and the major strategy of the state is to marginalize those who do not adapt. Those who deviate from the norm are made to suffer from bad consience, to feel that they are not worthy of such a moral society. The fear of moral stigmatization and psychological torture keeps the citizens in their subordinated position. The "abnormals" are regarded as ill, against whom the community of the "normals" has to be protected.[46]

Mercier's underscoring of the psychological rather than the corporal aspects of punishment illustrates the ideas advanced by Michel Foucault in his investigation *Surveiller et punir*, where he traces the rationalization of modern penal practises in the course of the last two hundred years. The main focus in Foucault's study is on the gradual disappearance of torture as a public spectacle and on a shift of emphasis in the goal of punishment from the torture of the body to the pain of the soul, heart, and will, which was a new tendency first expressed by Mably.[47]

Mercier's proposals for the reformation of the criminal justice were thus not doomed to be totally ignored. Gradually, in the course of the eighteenth century, there emerged a counter-tendency against the savage penal justice. The most striking consequence of this "softer" orientation was the progressive abolition of torture in various parts of Europe from the early 1770's onwards. The weakening of Christian pessimism and a belief in a beneficent Providence encouraged this more humanitarian outlook.[48]

A more humanitarian orientation is also revealed in a significant reduction in the use of *lettres de cachet* (documents with far-reaching authority to order detention without trial), the most visible symbol of arbitrary use of power under

. . . .

44 Mercier, *L'An 2440 I* 1786, 66.
45 Mercier, *L'An 2440 I* 1786, 217.
46 Döring 1988, 657–660.
47 Foucault 1975, 13, 21–22.
48 Hampson 1981, 155.

the *ancien régime*.[49] It does not cause great surprise to read that in Mercier's ideal Paris the *lettre de cachet* has been discontinued.[50] All this testifies to the steady increase of support toward the end of the eighteenth century for philosophical teachings concerning the importance of social compassion and humanity also as regards the reformation of the penal law and the treatment of criminals.[51]

One of the most ardent spokesmen for this more humanitarian outlook was the Italian philosopher of criminal justice, Cesare Beccaria, the writer of *Trattato dei delitti e delle bene* (1764). Beccaria's leading idea was an attempt to apply utilitarian principles to the reformation of penal law, which should be purged of all religious conceptions of evil or original sin, so that its sole purpose would be the restoration of the disturbed harmony.[52] The most important goal, as Beccaria conceived it, was to ensure a righteous proportion between the crime and the punishment. In other words, the punishment should be measured according to the damage that the crime had caused to society.[53]

The main lines of Beccaria's humanitarian philosophy are all reflected in the pages of *L'An 2440*, and it is characteristic that Mercier advises his readers to read Beccaria's treatise. There is no doubt about the fact that he had himself learned his lesson meticulously, as is shown, for example, in his insistence that there should be a right proportion between crimes and punishments; in 2440 theft, for example, is no longer punished by death.[54]

Beccaria thought that criminals could provide the maximum profit[55] for society if the death penalty was replaced by hard labour. In his view the former was an appropriate punishment only in extreme cases, when the crime constituted a threat to the security of the State.[56] Rousseau develops a similar line of argumentation in his *Du Contrat social*, where he proclaims that criminals should be treated as betrayers of the fatherland, as enemies of the state, who have insulted the sacred nature of the social contract. Because the criminal has insulted the social pact, he should no longer be considered as a member of the state: "Or, comme il s'est reconnu tel...il en doit être retranché par l'exil, comme infracteur du pacte, ou par la mort, comme ennemi public..."[57]

Mercier's preservation of the death penalty in his utopian society can be adequately explained by similar reasons. The underlying idea is that in the case

. . . .

49   See for example Rudé 1985, 119.
50   Mercier, *L'An 2440 I* 1786, 112. See also Mercier, *Tableau de Paris II* 1994a, 186–193.
51   Gay 1970, 36–38.
52   Venturi 1971, 100–116, especially 100–101; McManners 1981, 392.
53   [Beccaria], *Traité des délits et des peines* 1766, 143–152.
54   Mercier, *L'An 2440 I* 1786, 109.
55   Amongst the eighteenth-century's French philosophers, utilitarian ethics found strong support – for example from Maupertuis, who proposes in his *"Lettre sur le progres des sciences"* that instead of being killed, criminals could show their usefulness by offering themselves for use in medical experiments. According to this plan, criminals who survived in the tests should be pardoned, and the crime would be expiated through the utility that it had procured. Maupertuis, *Les oeuvres de M. de Maupertuis* 1752, 343.
56   Venturi 1971, 105–106; McManners 1981, 399, 403.
57   Rousseau, *Oeuvres complettes de Rousseau II* 1793, 52–53. See also Favre 1978, 359.

of the most severe crimes, such as murder, the death penalty is the only acceptable "remedy", because the homicide is not only a private affair between the criminal and his victim, but it forms a threat to the security of the whole community. Since murder represents a threat to the general well-being of the collectivity, the broken harmony can be restored only by eliminating the antisocial elements from the socio-political organism altogether. This explains why death is the only way in which a murderer can expiate his sins against the secular community, purify himself from shame after which he is restored to the class of citizens in order to regain his lost human dignity.[58]

The offence thus opposes an individual to the entire social body and the society therefore claims the right to oppose him in its entirety. As Foucault explains it, "the criminal designated as the enemy of all falls outside the pact, disqualifies himself as a citizen and emerges as a wild fragment of nature; he appears as a villain, a monster, a madman, perhaps, a sick and, before long, 'abnormal' individual. It is as such that, one day, he will belong to a scientific objectification and to the 'treatment' that is correlative to it."[59]

As an example of this kind of "scientific objectification" practiced in Mercier's utopia, offenders are put into an iron cage, above which is written the cause of their imprisonment.[60] This further reinforces the perception that criminals (or anyone who has individual ideas) are "monsters",[61] "sick", inhuman creatures. What, in the last resort, distinguishes Mercier's imaginary criminals from beasts in the zoo or from natural freaks on display?

This is a further example of eighteenth-century philosophers' obsession with categorization, which has made Lapouge draw parallels between the methods used by creators of utopias and natural historians. He argues that in these "radiant cities", abnormal is no better considered than in the system of Linné. If a child is not convenient, Plato[62] murders him. The suppression of monsters, poets,[63] anarchists, lunatics, the passionate, consecrates the wish to destroy the individual, which is an imperative condition if one wants to codify chaos or suspend historical impermanence.[64] In identifying innovation with evil, the utopists defeat not only decrepitude, but also progress, luxury and misery. Their passion is for equilibrium. The plan of their cities attests this as well, with their mania of order and the division of citizens into castes, *registres*, etc.[65]

. . . .

58   Mercier, *L'An 2440 I* 1786, 129.
59   Foucault 1975, 92, 104.
60   Mercier, *L'An 2440 I* 1786, 111.
61   This reminds one of Mercier's image of "ideal woman"; a woman who refuses to obey her husband is stigmatized as a kind of "monster", a "mad-woman" who is in war against her "true self", i.e. her inborn vocation to find happiness only through subordination to man.
62   In Plato's *Republic*, those that have been born deformed are hidden away in an unseen place, which is a means of maintaining the purity of the species of the guardians. Plato, *The Republic of Plato* 1991, 139.
63   In Plato's *Republic*, poets are not admitted to the city, because they are assumed to destroy men's calculating ability. Plato, *The Republic of Plato* 1991, 288–289.
64   Lapouge 1978, 223.
65   Lapouge 1982, 18.

This typically utopian pattern is repeated for example in Restif de la Bretonne's novel *La Découverte australe* (1781), where the well-being of the community is assumed to demand the exclusion, marginalization and compulsion of nonconformists. The hero of Restif's fantasy, the "bird-man" Victorin, creates an utopian society on an inaccessible mountain. In this utopian enclosure, life is restricted by rigid rules; murderers are thrown down from the top of the mountain, unfaithful wives are condemned to be slaves of their husbands for two years, disobedient children are sent to live far away from their friends.[66] In the same way, anything that could disturb the impression of esthetic and visual perfection is eliminated from Mercier's ideal city, whose sole purpose of existence is to preserve its purity from all dissident voices and opinions. Thus, the exceptional "monstrosity" of the "aberrants" stems from the awareness that they are seen to revolt against the sanctity of the social pact in a grotesque and unforgivable manner.

Mercier's or Restif's treatment of "unsocial elements" has many similar features with rites of purification practiced in archaic and primitive societies. Mircea Eliade explains that such societies have a customary habit of purging the faults of the entire community through ceremonies of expelling demons, diseases and sins. This expulsion can be practiced under the form of sending away an animal (a "scapegoat") or a man, regarded as "the material vehicle through which the faults of the community are transported beyond the limits of the territory".[67] Following the same logic, in the utopian societies criminals (or "disobedient" individuals) function as "scapegoats", forced to sacrifice their own lives in order that the community can periodically purify itself from the principle of evil.

In traditional societies the entire society had been conceived as a "magic circle", which was consecrated by the founding ancestor, renovated through sacrificial blood and destined to protect the individual from all evil and from the consequences of his own offences. As an integral part of the collectivity, the individual was afraid of nothing so much as being excluded or separated from his group.[68] Mercier's fictitious society of the future can also be conceived as a kind of "magic circle". By stigmatizing his imaginary murderer with the "mark of Cain" Mercier shows that in the same way as in archaic and primitive societies, the "purity" of the "magic circle" (the utopian community), can be restored only by certain symbolic rituals. Also in the ideal state of 2440 the individuals exist only through society and on its terms, and for this reason exclusion from the community means "civic death", the most severe punishment which can confront an "abnormal" individual. Because expulsion from "Paradise" would mean a mortal blow to their very existence, Mercier's utopian citizens are prepared to sacrifice their individual needs and passions, even their lives, in order to serve the "public good".

· · · · · · · · ·

66   Restif de la Bretonne, *La Découverte australe par un Homme-Volant ou le Dédale français* 1977, 82.
67   Eliade 1969b, 68.
68   Servier 1991, 15.

In Mercier's ideal society the demarcation line between "normals" and "abnormals" is extremely sharp, and the "contaminated" elements are very easily recognized by everyone. This is due to the fact that different exterior emblems, such as clothes and other visible symbols, have a specific role to play as indicators of belonging to a certain category of individuals; the "mark of Cain" provides one example of this. Moreover, aberrants are obliged to bear a "mask of shame", by virtue of which they can be immediately recognized as enemies of social harmony. The writer who bears a mask of shame on his face has published dangerous ideas, which "declare war to pure and universal morals".[69] The language of symbols can tell as well of honor as of shame. As we have seen, a citizen who has done services to the state is allowed to bear a "brocaded hat".[70]

Mercier's contempt for visible marks of power, such as expensive jewellery, gold and clothes, has already been discussed above.[71] More's *Utopia* provides a classical example of a similar use of symbols. In his utopian island, visible symbols are used "to punish slaves, to stigmatize evil-doers, or to amuse children". If somebody is decorated with gold or silver, it is interpreted as a mark of ill fame in every possible way: "As for those who bear the stigma of disgrace on account of some crime, they have gold ornaments hanging from their ears, gold rings encircling their fingers, gold chains thrown around their necks, and a gold crown binding their temples."[72]

The constant interplay of symbols and emblems designating either normality or abnormality, vices or virtues, transforms Mercier's utopian world into a book open for anyone to read. The entire public space of the city is set as a stage for moral and pedagogical allegory, which has a specific function to perform. The exterior symbols have a power to reveal immediately if the person is guilty or not. As Döring explains it, the citizens, surrounded by different emblems, marks and symbols, live in an allegorical universe as in the middle of a theater, in which they are simultaneously both spectators and actors.[73]

The episode devoted to the death sentence provides the most illustrative example of this symbolic use of exterior symbols in Mercier's moral allegory. Once a murderer has sentenced himself to death, his shirt, which has been soiled with the blood of his victim, is changed into a white one as a symbol of forgiveness.[74] The white color of the shirt functions as a symbol of regained purity, the rebirth of the convicted into a new life which awaits him in the other-worldly existence. By this means, he also expiates his offences against the

· · · · · · · · · ·

69   Mercier, *L'An 2440 I* 1786, 66.
70   Mercier, *L'An 2440 I* 1786, 37–42.
71   See Chapter VI, pp. 166–169.
72   More, *Utopia* 1964, 86. The fascination of the utopian writers to stigmatize wrong-doers with some visible symbol of disgrace finds its counterpoint in the real world. In the Middle Ages, for example, certain groups of social margins, such as prostitutes, homosexuals and some types of criminals, were obliged to bear in their clothes a mark or to wear specific garments.
73   Döring 1988, 656–657.
74   Mercier, *L'An 2440 I* 1786, 126.

secular community, regaining his citizenship. This symbolic rebirth to another, more perfect and worthy form of existence provides yet a further example of the significance of initiation in Mercier's utopian vision.

As Servier has pointed out, a similar pattern can be traced in many utopias: simplicity of clothes invokes purity, and the importance given to clothes in utopias underlines the will to renaissance, the beginning of a new life. The utopia refinds the theme of initiation through a new cloth. It marks the ascendance of the individual to a new purified life. It is for this reason that for example Campanella dresses in white his inhabitants of the *Civitas Solis*.[75]

Despite Mercier's fascination with the allegorical language of symbols, the invention of the "yellow star" which Jews were forced to bear in the Third Reich, would have fallen beyond the scope of his imagination. Nonetheless, in his vision of the future, too, Jews are treated with special suspicion and hostility. Mercier even refers to a kind of "Zionist conspiracy", which would have threatened the whole of Europe if the utopians had not taken measures of revenge against the Jews, who are described as fanatic and greedy hunters of money.[76]

Mercier's allusions to a Jewish "conspiracy" and to persecution of the Jews create a threatening prophecy about the racist policies practiced in Nazi Germany during the Second World War. It has been aptly remarked that Mercier develops in his utopia ideas which belong to the writer of *Mein Kampf*.[77] Open hostility toward the Jews is rather surprising in a utopia, which otherwise purports to support toleration. It reveals clearly how the Jews have always been seen as convenient scapegoats when things have gone wrong in society and when people have wanted to direct their collective malaise and fears to some group of strangers as an incarnation of the vicious "other".

Mercier's proposals for the "purification of the race" can, perhaps, also be explained by his rather obsessive concern for hygiene, which also encompasses the conception of different races. In point of fact, this is not rare in the tradition of utopian literature, where it has been a commonplace to treat sexuality as an object of civil experiment, at least since Plato, More and Campanella.[78] Moreover, the theme of eugenic controls is also frequently met in modern antiutopias. Selective breeding as a form of "modern perfectibilism" is often associated with authoritarian societies.[79]

Against this background it is easy to understand why so many studies of utopias have emphasized their authoritarian aspects. Mercier reveals in his utopia, perhaps unwittingly, how a "magic circle" can easily turn into a "vicious circle". The methods of psychic manipulation, indoctrination and brain-washing, which Mercier proposes as "remedies" for the treatment of the "abnormals", led for example Döring to question the humanitarian nature of

. . . .

75 Servier 1991, 336–338.
76 Mercier, *L'An 2440 III* 1786, 177–183.
77 Vissière 1977, 326.
78 Holstun 1987, 70.
79 Passmore 1972, 186–188.

L'An 2440. He sees it as a precursor of modern antiutopian literature, arguing that the methods of punishment which Mercier applies in his utopia are "nothing but cruel torture of the soul".[80] Minois joins ranks with Döring, characterizing Mercier's utopian society as a "dictatorship of virtue", with an atmosphere no less suffocating than that prevailing in Orwell's *1984* under the permanent surveillance of "Big Brother".[81] For Hermann Hofer, too, *L'An 2440* invokes a terrifying vision of a world whose sterile perfection has become a synonym for nightmare, and where freedom signifies nothing but the blind following of public opinion. Under such circumstances the illusion of liberty turns out to be a new form of omnipotent tyranny in which everyone is a slave of public opinion, the incarnation of an illusory liberty.[82]

After the holocaust of two world wars and the global catastrophes of the twentieth century it is, however, much too easy to commit an error of anachronism and of being wise after the event. Surveyed from the perspective of the twenty-first century, Mercier's society of 2440 reads as a warning example of the destructive impact of exaggerated rationalization and of an obsessive desire to eliminate the organic and non-calculable. It is an image of a society based on a purely instrumental use of reason, in which all things are measured and evaluated solely by their public utility. It forms a prophecy of the increasingly rationalized, bureaucratized, and threatening world, revealing in action the same self-destructive elements of the whole "project of the Enlightenment", which Adorno and Horkheimer have found so alarming. In their opinion its desire to free the world from animism and superstition has led to a new mythology based on the omnipotence of unity. The ideal of the Enlightenment was a throughly coherent and rational system, but it could not work because it was based on domination over nature. The Enlightenment behaved toward men as a manipulative director.[83]

The social utopias produced in late eighteenth-century France represented a culminating point of that tendency toward rationalization which has characterized the entire tradition of utopian thinking ever since Plato. Admittedly, the ideal of happiness promoted by the creators of utopian societies has always contained the seeds of authoritarianism. Holstun, for example, sees no difference in this respect between the utopias of the Age of Enlightenment or post-Enlightenment and the utopias produced before that epoch. The leading point of his argumentation is that the program of domination is already embedded in the utopian schema of rationality in for example More's *Utopia*; the initial "*promesse de bonheur*" begins to fade as soon as the distinction between reason and domination blurs, and the reader of the work realizes that the world he encounters is actually founded on an imperialist ideology. This

. . . .

80   Döring 1988, 663–666.
81   Minois 1996, 442–443.
82   Hofer 1975, 250. See also Denoit 1989a, 1628.
83   Adorno & Horkheimer 1979, 7, 9. See also Niiniluoto 1994, 60–62.

shows in action how Enlightenment reason "produces not freedom but rational domination".[84]

Is it possible that Mercier was himself aware of the dangers contained in extreme forms of rationality? Would it be justified to suggest that he invented his imaginary society of the far future as an warning image of a world which has been transformed into a nightmarish landscape of over-rationalized surveillance, classification and organization? Did Mercier, perhaps, want to warn his contemporaries on the threshold of irrevocable social and political convulsions? This alternative cannot be totally excluded; one should not forget Mercier's "irrational" and "mystical" side, which made him, at least occasionally, question the value of the whole concept of rationality and exclaim with desperation: "Quel siècle malheureux que celui où on le raisonne!"[85]

However fascinating, playful speculations on Mercier's "antiutopian" intentions do not belong to the framework of the present study. Suffice it to note that this is not very plausible. It is more probable that he believed he had created an image of an ameliorated world, rather than a nightmare. Nevertheless, without himself fully realizing it, Mercier came to highlight how closely linked utopia and antiutopia actually are. The positive predictions of the eighteenth century have been transformed into the counter-utopias of the twentieth century, and dreams which have become reality are revealed to be nightmares.[86]

To a certain extent, at least, the whole rise of antiutopianism can be interpreted as a manifestation of hostility to the aspirations of the French Enlightenment and the French Revolution. This reading is put forward for example by George Kateb, who writes in his study *Utopia and its Enemies* (1963) that "the attack on the French Enlightenment and the French Revolution is, at some points, an attack on utopianism."[87] Where does this hostility basically stem from? One could argue that the essence of the rise of antiutopian reaction was grounded on the recognition that the constructors of earlier utopias had defined the relation between reason and domination in an untenable manner. Contrary to their eighteenth-century precursors, the writers of antiutopian literature in the nineteenth and twentieth centuries have been well aware that nobody can be "forced" to be free or happy, that individual happiness does not ensue automatically as a by-product of public felicity, and that the compatibility of virtue and nature constitutes the exception more often than the rule. The great antiutopian discovery lies precisely in the realization that without the possibility of free choice there can be no happiness either.

Sanctions beyond the Grave: The Idea of Hell
In addition to punishments on earth, in *L'An 2440*, as in many of his moral allegories, Mercier envisages that vicious people will pay for their evil deeds

. . . .

84   Holstun 1987, passim., especially 58.
85   Mercier, *L'An 2440 I* 1786, 202.
86   See for example Minois 1996, 443.
87   Kateb 1963, 2.

also beyond the grave. As noted above, in his moral allegories he often treats different sort of vices, such as egoism, avarice and low-mindedness, and a recurrent theme in these visionary fantasies is the final distribution of reward and punishment. It has been suggested that almost all religious thinkers in eighteenth-century France agreed on a similar understanding of the afterlife: there had to be a system of rewards and punishments to redress the abuses that the virtuous were forced to suffer on earth. This argument in itself was considered sufficient proof of the necessary existence of a land beyond the grave where injustices would be rectified. What was of special importance was to invoke the sanctions of the afterlife for sins such as pride and luxury which were left without punishment this side of the grave.[88]

Mercier's educative allegory entitled "*Cupidité*" gives a striking illustration of this kind of argumentation. The narrator finds himself in a dark forest, and after having found his way out he arrives hungry and exhausted in vast plains where the trees are full of fruit; but he is permitted to satisfy his hunger only if he submits to be chained to the greedy owner of the land and follow him to a high mountain. In the middle of the rocks there is an abundant well, full of money, and the valleys are peopled by chained men striving to recover some drops of the mercury floating from the well. The main priest of avarice, a black phantom, bears on his face a "mask of justice". The mercury has been stolen from the feeble women and children, old men, cultivators of land and the poor. The greediness of the oppressors is insatiable, and it will not end until the appearance of three figures white marble – Religion, Humanity, Chastity. This apocalyptic-infernal moral allegory ends in the triumph of the forces of good when the narrator breaks the chain which binds him to the "monster", and the greedy are crushed into rocks in their blind avarice.[89]

Mercier returns to this theme in "*L'Optimisme*", where he declares that "la vérité est terrible au méchant". In order to demonstrate this apocalyptic thesis, he sets up a juxtaposition between the land of the unfortunate, where virtue is constantly persecuted, and the empire of a lustful tyrant, which is built by crimes and oppression. The narrator sees through a magic mirror that the latter will collapse and turn to dust, and the punishment which awaits the evil is eternal oblivion.[90]

Similarly, in a solemn religious allegory entitled "*Songe terrible*",[91] the day of the Final Judgement has arrived, and the narrator finds himself surrounded by

. . . .

88 McManners 1981, 125, 134, 146, 176, 186.
89 Mercier, *Mon bonnet de nuit II* 1784, 159–171. "*Cupidité*" provides a typical example of what Majewski refers to by the term "persecution dream". He uses it to refer to Mercier's stories, in which the narrator is transported into the land of the dead or to the "island of blood". In these dreams, haunted by sepulchers, cadavers and mummies, images of blood and horror related to crime, vice and black magic are associated with Hell. Majewski 1971, 50–51. Mercier's story "*L'île du Sang*", which has been discussed in the chapter devoted to the material aspects of happiness in his utopian society, provides one of the most illustrative examples of Mercier's inclination to antiutopian imagination.
90 Mercier, *Songes philosophiques* 1768, 25–26.
91 The same story is also contained in the collection *Songes et visions philosophiques* ("*Le dernier jour*").

eternal Silence. He hears the voice of "a universal trumpet", which crushes the tombstones and awakens humanity from the night of Death. An Angel appears, and division is made between the good and the wicked (malicious kings and their ministers, those "bloodthirsty monsters"). Whereas the virtuous rise to Heaven, the lot of the vicious is damnation to a night that never ends:

> "...ceux qui avoient demandé la vie, monterent vers les voûtes radieuses...les autres, s'enfoncerent dans les gouffres ténébreux, d'ou j"entendis sortir des gémissemens qui ressembloient aux accens prolongés du désespoir."[92]

This extract reveals that Mercier's conception of the system of rewards and punishments is closely related to the theory of the "Great Chain of Being". He presents life after death either as a progression of souls through different worlds toward greater and greater happiness or, conversely, their retrogression according to their crimes committed and degrees of evil. Hell is thus synonymous with descent to a lower and lower status on the scale of existence. This is a similar idea of Hell to that held by the people of Mercier's utopian future: they believe that those who are guilty of crimes have to descend in the scale of being to the same point from which they have left. These criminals are forced to remain in a tenebrous darkness where hardly a pale ray of existence shows. In contrast, "generous souls" rise up toward the divine light.[93]

One of Mercier's allegorical visions, entitled *"Le méchant sera seul"*, provides the most revealing picture of his conception of Hell. Its narrator is travelling through Creation, pushed forward by a secret power. Finally, he arrives at the outer borders of Nature, a tenebrous abyss, a region of Silence and darkness, where eternal night begins. The Angel of Darkness tells the traveller that this place is Hell – a place where the wicked have to be alone, which is their Punishment. As a state of eternal loneliness, Hell is the total absence of happiness and light; in Hell man has no other company but his own thoughts. The heart of those doomed to solitude has become stone, it cannot feel compassion, they do not recognize other men as their brothers, they have been abandoned by the whole universe, they can no longer see the sun, they do not exist for creation, but live alone with their hard and perverted souls; this is Hell.[94]

Instead of a fiery empire of the Devil, Mercier thus describes Hell rather as a synonym for solitude, expulsion from the magic circle of light, which is the worst punishment which a human being can ever suffer. Whereas on earth Hell is a synonym for a state of marginalization from the collectivity, the Hell beyond the grave is total estrangement from God. It is a synonym for a state of existence in which man has lost all contact with surrounding society, other men

. . . .

92   Mercier, *Mon bonnet de nuit III* 1786a, 27–29.
93   Mercier, *L'An 2440 I* 1786, 164.
94   Mercier, *Mon bonnet de nuit IV* 1786a, 77.

and God. It has been suggested that this representation of Hell was typical of the Romantics, and it is met for example in Byron's *"Darkness"*.[95]

The idea of eternal loneliness as the price of sin is far from the idea of solitude as a voluntary retreat to the wilderness from the turmoil of big cities. In this framework, to be left alone means shame, the antithesis of happiness. It is not difficult to understand that enforced solitude was the worst possible sanction that eighteenth-century writers and philosophers, committed to the idea of man's natural sociability, could imagine.

Mercier's vision of Hell as a state of mental suffering was, nevertheless, intended to be more humane than the traditional conception of Hell that it replaced. The underlying idea is that liberated from the fear of physical pain and the threatening image of Hell, man can live a more happy life already on earth.[96] In *L'An 2440* Merrcier comments that the traditional image of Hell was a "monstrous system" with its idea of eternal punishments, a revenge invented by priests against their unfortunate victims. The idea of eternal physical torture would have been too glaringly in a contradiction with the supposed benevolence of God: "L'enfer des chrétiens est sans contredit le blasphême le plus injurieux fait à la bonté & à la justice divine."[97]

Most eighteenth-century "enlightened" writers shared the same view. In their minds the empire of Satan was unworthy of God's goodness, and was good enough only as an absurd subject for ridicule. In contrast to previous centuries, when the terrors of Hell were paralleled in a savage penal code, by the second part of the century the traditional conception of Hell had come more and more under attack. The general trend was toward softer and more humane values, and attempts were now made to pass from haunting visions of the torture of the flesh to emphasizing the sufferings of the soul. The secularization of the religious notion of Hell thus followed a more humanitarian orientation of penal law. In particular, the idea of eternal duration of punishment was now seen as incompatible with the idea of the love of God and with optimism concerning the progress of happiness. Amongst the elites, it now became customary to replace Hell by Purgatory, or, alternatively, to exclude the perspective beyond the grave altogether and to transpose the notion of Hell to life on earth.[98]

. . . .

95   Bousquet 1964, 259.
96   It does not seem to have occured to Mercier that the pain of the soul can, occasionally at least, be equally devastating as the suffering of the body. Or perhaps he understood this even too well.
97   Mercier, *L'An 2440 I* 1786, 188, 309.
98   McManners 1981, 133, 176, 178, 181; Minois 1991, 319–321. This shows how the religious images of Paradise and Hell have been progressively secularized since the late eighteenth century. For Swedenborg, for example, whose visions of Heaven and Hell (*De cielo et inferno ex auditis et visis*) were published in 1758, both Heaven and Hell were contained in the human soul itself. Swedenborg no longer accepted that men were sent after their death either to Heaven or Hell; in his mind, Hell was a place of low-minded people. Bousquet 1964, 18, 62.

VIII Happiness and Time: The Path to Utopia

The Philosophy of Change

The first section of this investigation was devoted to a comprehensive survey of nature of Mercier's ideal society of 2440. In Mercier's vision, the citizens follow their "inner voice" in all their thoughts and actions. France is ruled in the twenty-fifth century by an enlightened despot, Rousseau's doctrine of social contract has been implemented, and the magnificence of the Supreme Being is adored through the telescope. Moderation has replaced abundance and extravagance. The treatment of criminals is no longer based on torture of the body. One crucial factor, however, still remains unanswered: How has this marvelous society of harmony and happiness come into being in the first place? How does Mercier explain the temporal process which has produced the shift from the unhappy conditions prevailing in late eighteenth-century France to the urban paradise of 2440? Who or what bears responsibility for this change, i.e., is it regulated by man himself, the Law of Nature, or divine Providence?

To begin with, it is important to bear in mind that unlike Thomas More and his disciples in the two intervening centuries, Mercier decides to situate his image of an ideal condition in a concretely existing city, Paris. For the first time in the tradition of modern utopian thinking, the utopian society is not located in the present on some exotic island, but in the remote future. Compared with "magic island" utopias, characterized by a total discontinuity between "real time" and the "time of utopia", in Mercier's model there is continuity between those two temporal categories. Despite the fact that Mercier's two cities – in the 1770s and in 2440 – are separated by a temporal hiatus of almost seven hundred years, they nevertheless form two points in the same historical process. From now on, it is only the passage of time which separates the "*spleen*" and the "*ideal*", the time of unhappiness and the time of happiness.[1]

Mercier's utopian vision is no longer a mere platonic ideal without contact points with everyday reality. For the first time in the history of modern utopian literature, the hope is proposed that some day utopia could become living reality. Mercier believed in time as the realizer of utopian dreams, and never tired of asserting that it was only the passage of time which separated the present misery of the human race from its happiness in some future epoch. For example in *Notions claires sur les gouvernemens* Mercier deplores the common habit of conceiving the passage of time in pessimistic terms, rather than as a positive force of change:

. . . .
1   See also Baczko 1974, 485.

"Jamais nous n'avons voulu nous peindre le Tems que comme un viellard destructeur... "Pourquoi, sous ce rapport ne pas le considérer aussi comme un Etre bienfaisant? N'est-ce pas lui d'ailleurs qui édifie tout, qui pose la première pierre de tous les Royaumes? J'aime à le voir donnant la naissance à tout, élaborant toutes choses, à menant tout par des gradations insensibles... "C'est au Tems seul qu'il est réservé d'annoncer d'abord, & d'effectuer ensuite des réformes sur les nations."[2]

The implication is that if humankind had not an immensely long future ahead, no beneficent transformations could be implemented. Mercier rejects pessimistic theories foretelling decadence, destruction and the end of the world, and accepts that in the course of time even the most fantastic projects concerning the advancement of human well-being could be put into effect. An essential criterion for the belief in infinite progress, i.e. the assumption that there is plenty of time ahead, is thus fulfilled. To invoke the authority of J.B. Bury: "As time is the very condition of the possibility of Progress, it is obvious that the idea would be valueless if there were any cogent reasons for supposing that the time at the disposal of humanity is likely to reach a limit in the near future."[3]

Mercier's vision of the passage of time as a productive, not a destructive, force, reads as the sign of a new kind of temporal orientation. It has been argued that in the course of the eighteenth century it became common to see even the most familiar phenomena as being in a state of continual change.[4] From now on, perpetual change was elevated as a positive force, and regarded as a better state than changeless repetition. "Restlessness" was now harnessed to serve the purposes of happiness. Jean Deprun talks about the sublimation of restlessness in the form of progress; restlessness became a providential preservative against stagnation and inaction, the very motor of history.[5] The conception of change thus underlies the possibility of improvement. If nothing ever changed under the sun, the anticipation of the future would serve no purpose.[6]

With his belief in the passage of time as a positive source of change, Mercier joined ranks with the most progressive French eighteenth-century philosophers, who had began to conceive of time as a possible factor of betterment. Turgot was the first to frame all the differences between cultures in progressive terms. In his view the idea of progress constituted an all-powerful motive force in history. For Turgot the earth, a place of change, was no longer doomed to death.[7] The progressive vision which he formulated was grounded on two basic arguments: 1) Progress had occurred in the past from the primitive stages of humanity's origins through the enlightened present; 2) Since retrogression was

. . . .

2   Mercier, *Notions claires sur les gouvernemens II* 1787, 390–391.
3   Bury 1920, 5.
4   Hampson 1981, 221. See also Wallgren 1993, 4–6.
5   Deprun 1979, 111.
6   Cazes 1986, 11.
7   Clarke 1979, 24–25; Delon, Mauzi, Menant 1998, 80.

no longer possible, future progress was inevitable.[8] From now on, the linear march of historical change was clearly distinguished from change in natural phenomena. In his second discourse on the successive progress of human spirit (December 1750) Turgot expresses this clearly:

> "Les phénomènes de la nature, soumis à des lois constantes, sont renfermés dans un cercle de révolutions toujours les mêmes. Tout renaît, tout périt; et dans ces générations successives... le temps ne fait que ramener à chaque instant l'image de ce qu'il a fait disparaître. La succession des hommes, au contraire, offre de siècle en siècle un spectacle toujours varié. La raison, les passions, la liberté, produisent sans cesse de nouveaux événements."[9]

In the course of the eighteenth century this new consciousness of time began to develop in the shadow of absolutist politics. The German scholar Reinhart Koselleck describes this process over a relatively long time span, reaching from the beginning of the sixteenth century until the beginning of the nineteenth, as a progressive exposure of the asymmetry prevailing in the mutual relation of experience and expectation. By this he refers to the fact that the gradual breakthrough of a secular, progressive outlook brought a decisive change in the traditional conception of time, based on the Christian vision. The new temporal horizon introduced by the modern notion of progress, by contrast, laid the ground for a new idea of time as a transnatural, long-lasting and even limitless process. It was no longer haunted by the expectation of the world's end and the apocalyptic idea of time in the form of a sudden and violent catastrophe. The relation between the categories of experience and expectation thus changed, in the sense that the modern prognosis saw the passage of time as a productive process, whereas the apocalyptic expectation had accorded to it exclusively negative, destructive, signification.[10]

Images of the future thus have a direct impact on the actual course of events. Those periods which have held positive images of the future will never die, but periods which have no constructive images of the future (for example the Middle Ages), are doomed to perish.[11] In addition to Mercier, Félix Bodin, one of his followers in future-oriented utopian thinking, was acutely aware of this. In his *Le roman de l'avenir* he writes:

> "L'idée de la perfectibilité fondée sur l'histoire, a au moins le mérite d'encourager l'espèce humaine à bien faire, puisqu'elle entretient l'espérance d'arriver à un meilleur résultat; tandis que la doctrine du mal progressif, ou même seulement du mal permanent, telle que l'enseignent certaines personnes, n'aboutit qu'à comprimer tout ressort, qu'à entretenir l'apathie, l'insouciance..."[12]

. . . .

8   Manuels 1982, 479. See also Nisbet 1980, 183.
9   Turgot, *Oeuvres de Turgot II* 1844, 597.
10 Koselleck 1985, 13–14, 16–17, 241, 288. See also Rifkin 1987, 156–157.
11 Polak 1961, 233; Rifkin 1989, 154.
12 Bodin, *Le roman de l'avenir* 1834, 18–19.

According to the official line of the Church, heavenly pursuits were glorified and secular endeavors were denounced.[13] Whereas believers in secular progress emphasized the gradual march of humanity toward happiness, Christians conceived the passage to the final state of peace only through violent, planetary convulsions, the announcement of which they read in the Apocalypse.[14] It, however, would be exaggerated to argue that the idea of temporal development was totally exluced from the Christian vision of the future; one aspect of the Christian millennium was the conviction that over time there would be increasing revelation, i.e., spiritual advancement, and this sense of cumulative truth resembles the optimistic belief in progress.[15]

Despite their mutual differences, the Christian vision of the future and the modern progressive outlook thus have many similarities, and the eschatological aspects of the Christian conception of history – the idea that the history has a goal, towards which the whole humankind is marching –, led Karl Löwith and his followers to claim that the historical philosophical thinking that started in the eighteenth century is merely a secularized variation of the Christian story of salvation.[16] One of the most ardent proponents of this view has been Carl L. Becker, who suggests that the philosophers of the eighteenth century secularized the Christian drama, by toning down the picture of salvation in the Heavenly City to an image of a "future state".[17]

Holding this similarity in mind, some Mercier scholars have traced an analogous pattern between *L'An 2440* and the biblical Apocalypse. It has been suggested that when Mercier extols 2440 in the "*épitre dédicatoire*" of his novel as "a year that will bring felicity on earth",[18] he invokes the image of a "secular last judgement".[19] There is thus some justification for the argument that Mercier represents in his utopia a secularized version of the ancient Judeo-Christian millenarist prophecy. In Trousson's view this can clearly be seen in the fact that the utopian condition is projected into the future, in which it differs radically from the model set by More, which has no understanding of the meaning of historical development. Whereas the traditional utopian world had been static, Mercier anticipated Wells in imagining a kinetic utopia in the state of perpetual becoming. He conceived time as a factor of continual progress, but his progressive vision differed from millenarism in the sense that the progress has no end.[20]

The temporal structure of Mercier´s utopian schema crucially differs from millenarianism, however, in that the shift to a happier world is not foreseen as

. . . .

13   For example, in Saint Augustine's view, men's progress towards perfection was totally dependent on God's will, and there was no suggestion of improvement in secular society. See for example Passmore 1972, 196–197.
14   Delumeau 1995, 316, 326. See also Keohane 1982, 27; Cazes 1986, 48.
15   Keohane 1982, 27; Cazes 1986, 56. See also Tuveson 1972, 6–7.
16   Viikari 1995, 358. See also Keohane 1982, 25. Cf. Bury 1920, 6–7, 20–22.
17   Becker 1965, 48.
18   Mercier, *L'An 2440 I* 1786, ix.
19   Hoffmann La Torre 1986, 101.
20   Trousson 1982, 275–279. See also Lequenne 1992, 34.

being achieved through violent confrontation, but through a gradual process of amelioration. In Alkon´s view, *L´An 2440* offers a perfect illustration of the absence of any real connection between the emergence of secular future-oriented fiction and apocalyptic visions of the future. He states: "Mercier provides no apocalyptic model of transition to a better world of 2440."[21]

As Alkon has remarked, *L´An 2440* also drastically differs from apocalyptic visions of the future in that Mercier´s vision is not based on predictive purposes. He is convinced that regardless of the fact that in the post-Revolution edition of his utopia Mercier elevates himself as a prophet of the French Revolution,[22] his intention was to investigate a possible future rather than to foretell it with confidence. In practise, this means that Mercier explores the future starting from the premise that future is open, and has many different potential outcomes. Those who set out to provide predictions of the future, by contrast, do not offer alternate futures, but represent what is to come as perfectly fixed and inevitable.[23]

The most conspicuous aspect in which the utopian vision of *L´An 2440* differs from religious millenarism is precisely the fact that whereas the creators of apocalyptic visions presume the future as totally fixed (even if the exact moment of the world´s end cannot be known for sure), in Mercier´s model no such fixed end of temporal evolution is postulated. Accordingly, *L´An 2440* provides a classical example of what Karl Mannheim has termed a liberal-humanitarian utopia. He sees this concept as characterizing the utopias of the Enlightenment, which incarnated the hopes of the rising bourgeoisie. They were projections of an unlimited future, which means that henceforward utopianism became bound up with a process of gradual improvement. The liberal-humanitarian utopia thus constituted an opposite to the chiliastic mentality of the Middle Ages,[24] which had no sense of the process of becoming.[25]

A standard account of this change in temporal exprience in the second half of the eighteenth century is grounded in the dynamics of bourgeois society, advanced urbanization, mechanization, rationalization and the development of transportation and communication networks.[26] In addition to the rise of the bourgeois class and the advanced tempo of modernization, the gradual replacement of the traditional Christian vision of the future by a modern secular evolutionary time scale was a result of the advances made in the field of natural sciences and increased secularization as its consequence. The scientific revolution of the seventeenth and eighteenth centuries entailed enlargement not

. . . .

21 Alkon 1987, 119, 162, 306. As we have seen, however, Mercier´s ideal city retains many features from the biblical image of a "Heavenly Jerusalem". Despite the fact that Mercier foresees a non-apocalyptic manner of transition to a better existence, on a thematic level it is perfectly justified to read his future Paris as a secular version of the heavenly city.
22 This theme will be dealt with in more detail in Chapter VIII, pp. 241–242 of this study.
23 Alkon 1987, 125–126.
24 See Chapter II, p. 45.
25 Mannheim 1972, 197–206.
26 See for example Lowe 1982, 35–39. See also Rifkin 1989, 156–170.

only in conceptions of space, but also in time. From the doctrine that the world was infinitely extended in space it was only a step to the assumption that it was equally unbounded in time.[27] Lovejoy suggests that the temporalization of the Great Chain of Being was one of the most important intellectual dramas of the eighteenth century.[28]

The biblical conception of the creation of the world was thus increasingly challenged by the discoveries made in geology and astronomy. The path was opened to a new view according to which the earth was formed in the course of many thousands of years and that it was a result of a very slow evolution.[29] Already in the beginning of the eighteenth century Voltaire had made fun of the biblical timespan, according to which the world was only six thousand years old,[30] and gradually it became more and more evident that the physical form of the earth had experienced many radical transformations in the course of time. In scientific circles the hostility towards the conception of a static universe, regulated by divine intervention, was steadily increasing.[31] In his *Époques de la nature* (1778) Buffon discards the Bible-based chronology of nature and suggests that the universe may be hundreds of millions years old.[32]

With the recognition of the ancient origins of the earth, the older conception of the earthly paradise also underwent a decisive transformation. The belief that a place close to paradise still existed in some remote part of the earth had survived in the Middle Ages and even through the Reformation, but in the course of the eighteenth century it was finally abandoned as it was recognized that the true age of the earth was not compatible with the biblical chronology.[33]

A few revealing pages are devoted to these new evolutionary doctrines in Mercier's utopia. Mercier, obviously, no longer believed in the literal truth of the biblical chronology. His future Parisians are said to believe in natural evolution, which has lasted immense periods of time. The following excerpt from the novel illustrates this clearly:

> "Tandis que nous passons comme l'ombre sur cette terre, tout a sa marche autour de nous: la nature épuise les siècles pour l'accomplisse- ment de ses lois; il faut des milliers d'années à ce torrent pour percer ce rocher et cette montagne... nous dormons sur des volcans qui jadis vomissoient la flamme."[34]

. . . .

27   Toulmin & Goodfield 1965, 86.
28   Lovejoy 1950, 244–245.
29   Sagnac 1946, 80; Delon, Mauzi & Menant 1998, 80–81.
30   Pollard 1971, 25.
31   Brumfitt 1972, 115; Hampson 1981, 91.
32   Whitrow 1988, 154.
33   Delumeau 1992, 18–19, 153, 277, 280. Despite this gradual change in attitudes towards the idea of terrestrial paradise, for example the *Encyclopédie*, usually distinguished by its fresh and innovative opinions, assumes in this respect a very traditional position. The article *"Paradis"* represents all old views on this matter, leaning on the traditional Christian interpretation. *Encyclopédie XXIV*, 21–23. This prudent attitude can be explained by the fact that the encyclopedists were not willing to irritate the religious authorities.
34   Mercier, *L'An 2440 III* 1786, 32.

The chapter in Mercier's novel entitled "*Le Cabinet du roi*" gives further evidence that he believed in the successive phases of natural history and the transformation of species. In this chapter the time traveler pays a visit to the royal cabinet of animals and plants, receiving from his guide an instructive lesson about natural history. He observes that all the different species are carefully classified and provided with a brief explanation of their natural history.[35]

In this context Mercier refers explicitly to the theory of the Great Chain of Being, using the expression "*l'échelle des êtres*" intertwining all different species together from the smallest to the greatest. In 2440, it is known that similar causes determine their growth, life span and ultimate destruction.[36] The future Frenchmen assume that the chain of species forms an uninterrupted continuity through the centuries, and it has demanded co-operative efforts of many generations to reveal all the hidden links constituting it:

> "La chaine n'est jamais interrompue; chaque anneau s'unit fortement à l'anneau voisin; c'est ainsi qu'elle plonge dans l'étendue de plusieurs siècles; et cette chaine d'idées et de travaux successifs doit un jour environner, embrasser l'univers."[37]

Lovejoy suggests that in the eighteenth century the theory of the Great Chain of Being still provided an absolutely static scheme of things, which was inconsistent with any belief in progress or any significant change.[38] Similarly, Mercier cannot be called an evolutionary thinker in the proper sense of the term. He believed, for example, that man's biological structure was entirely pre-destined, and that all men derive their origin from one and the same female ancestor:

> "...tout foetus, soit animal, soit végétal, étoit un être organisé... mais en miniature, qu'il existoit dans son ensemble avant sa naissance, c'est-à-dire avant son plus grand développement..."[39]

In this passage Mercier presents the organizing principle of "preformationism". In eighteenth-century terminology this meant a theory according to which all creatures developed from a pre-formed embryo contained in their mother's egg or father's semen. Some scientists, for example Charles Bonnet (1720–1793), added to this the idea of "*emboîtement*", a suggestion that the "germs" of all future generations were already contained within the egg or sperm. The future creature would thus be what was already contained in the embryo, and nature was merely thought to develop what had been there since the act of creation.[40]

. . . .

35   Mercier, *L'An 2440 II* 1786, 31.
36   Mercier, *L'An 2440 II* 1786, 31.
37   Mercier, *L'An 2440 II* 1786, 37.
38   Lovejoy 1950, 242–243.
39   Mercier, *L'An 2440 II* 1786, 267.
40   Charlton 1984, 73. See also Coates, White & Schapiro 1966, 244; Chaunu 1982, 206; Hankins 1985, 140–145.

In his utopia Mercier creates his own version of the birth of the human species based on this theory of "*emboîtement*":

> Ainsi, nous existons depuis des milliers d'années. Nous dormions tous dans les flancs de la première femme... "L'Etre des êtres et leur législateur a crée, par un seul acte de sa volonté, toutes les générations des êtres organisés pendant la durée de la planète où ils doivent habiter. Les générations aujourd'hui vivantes, c'est-à- dire, développées sur le théâtre du monde, étoient pressées dans ce que nous appelons un petitesse infinie..."[41]

Mercier's rather naive theory of the origins of humankind and its subsequent evolution, in which the accomplishments of modern science are intertwined with fantastic mythology, is consistent with the idea that if there is evolution, it can only mean development towards a pre-ordained form of existence: a movement which does not create anything new or unexpected. There is no room for innovations or chance elements: the passage of time does not mean a movement toward totally new vistas, but the gradual realization of a rigorously pre-ordained plan of creation. Such an interpretation reinforces the idea dealt with above, in the chapter on the spiritual side of Mercier's utopian vision: Mercier follows in the traces of Leibniz, believing that the Universal Plan of Harmony had remained immutable since the moment of creation. Thus everything that exists, will exist or has ever existed, was pre-ordained in the universal cosmic scheme in the moment of creation. To accept the possibility of subsequent changes would mean suspecting the omnipotence and wisdom of God. The following extract from *L'An 2440* explicitly illustrates this focal idea: "Dieu que gouverne l'univers par les lois durables, ne crée rien de nouveau. Le développement successif est conforme au plan initial..."[42]

From this it is to be concluded that despite its "evolutionary" aspects, Mercier's utopian vision is actually as static and deterministic as the traditional Christian vision of the future. As a deeply religious mind, he could not imagine a world without God. Moreover, in a certain sense Mercier's vision is no less mechanistic than the Newtonian universe which he so vigorously criticized. It is consistent with the idea of a mechanical universe formulated by philosophers living in the sixteenth and eighteenth centuries, which was a completed and immutable system, determined in all its operations and generating no novelties: fixed stars, fixed plant and animal species, a respect for the eternally same perfect order.[43]

L'An 2440 mirrors the same ambivalence towards evolutionary thinking which Michel Foucault argues was typical of the whole eighteenth century. Foucault points out how thinkers in the school of Maupertuis, Diderot, Robinet or Benoît de Mallet were all equally convinced of the transformation of species,

. . . .

41 Mercier, *L'An 2440 II* 1786, 269–270.
42 Mercier, *L'An 2440 II* 1786, 274.
43 Charlton 1984, 68.

but this was not yet "evolutionism" in the modern sense of the term. In the same way as Leibniz had established the law of continuity, their argumentation was still based on the belief in hierarchical order, in which time was merely one of the pre-established factors of *taxonomia*. This did not mean rejection of the dogma of fixism; what was at issue was a *taxonomia* which included time as a supplementary aspect.[44]

This reveals that the hold on people's thinking exercised by the static conception of the Great Chain of Being was too tenacious to be easily rejected. In the course of the eighteenth century the predictable *order* of nature was, however, gradually being replaced by the unpredictable, dynamic *power* of nature, capable of producing novelties not fixed in advance.[45]

One of Mercier's most remarkable essays, "*Globe*", expresses the sentiments prompted by the shift from a static order of things towards a modern, dynamic conception of nature in a state of constant flux:

> "Il ne faut point regarder la masse de la terre comme un morceu de boue inanimé, un entassement grossier de parties stagnantes; il y regne une véritable circulation; tout est animé dans ce grand corps."[46]

In his imagination Mercier creates an analogy between the circulation of blood and the movements of natural phenomena: "...c'est un véritable corps animé, où les mers, par leur mouvement, représentent assez bien le sang qui circule dans le corps humain."[47]

In "*Globe*" Mercier announces the rise of the Romantic notion of "wild nature" which is no longer domesticated and tamed, but a kind of "unbound Prometheus". The account of the unpredictable convulsions of nature in Mercier's essay anticipates the suggestion of Merchant that "in their desire to act against the Scientific Revolution and the Enlightenment, the Romantics of the early nineteenth century turned back to the organic idea of a vital animating principle binding together the whole created world".[48]

Béclard believes that Mercier had taken some of his ideas concerning natural evolution from Diderot's *Rêve de d'Alembert* (1769).[49] This can easily be confirmed by comparing Mercier's ideas on the evolution of species with Diderot's doctrine of transformation. As Diderot conceived it, the principle that dominates all natural phenomena was continuous change: "Tous les êtres circulent les uns dans les autres, par conséquent tout les espèces... tout est en fluc perpétuel..."[50] Diderot's general scepticism towards all static explanations of the world also led him to attack the idea of biological preformationism and

. . . .

44 Foucault 1966, 163–165.
45 Charlton 1984, 77–78.
46 Mercier, *Mon bonnet de nuit I* 1784, 34.
47 Ibid., 34–35.
48 Merchant 1983, 100.
49 Béclard 1903, 135.
50 Diderot, *Oeuvres complètes de Diderot* 1875, 138; Charlton 1984, 77.

the pre-existence of the germs, as a theory in contradiction with "experiment and reason", in his *Entretiens entre d'Alembert et Diderot*.[51]

In the course of the eighteenth century there emerged a sharpened contrast between those who believed in the immobility of nature (above all Linné) and those, such as Bonnet and Diderot, who already had a presentiment of life's creative power of transformation.[52] Mercier's vision of the future provides an illustrative example of this conflict between a static and a more dynamic view of the world, which was characteristic for the entire period in transition. *L'An 2440* reads as a representation of a society which had not yet liberated itself from the static view of the world in order to embrace a totally secular, constantly changing universe. Around 1800, however, the biblical timescale and story of creation was finally overthrown.[53]

A Never Ending Journey: The Theory of Indefinite Progress

The discoveries made in the field of the natural sciences in the course of the eighteenth century had far-reaching impacts on men's general views concerning the prospects of time and future. It has been suggested that already in the course of the seventeenth century the doctrine of universal decline was gradually put into question, and the older belief that nature was "exhausted" and run its course, was put under severe re-examination. The difference was considerable compared with the preceding centuries, during which the belief that nature was approaching its final dissolution had blinded many from seeing anything praiseworthy in their own times. In the sixteenth and early seventeenth centuries it was still commonly supposed that everything in the past had been superior to anything in the present.[54] For example the Renaissance humanists had worshipped the classics of antiquity to the point that it was doubted if the human race would ever again be able to reach the same heights.[55]

In terms of the formation of a more positive view on temporal evolution and man's future destiny on earth, the philosophical debate known as the quarrel between the Ancients and Moderns formed an important watershed, for from this battle the modern idea of progress emerged. In its simplicity the whole dispute, which had started as a literary controversy in the course of the seventeenth century, was waged around the following question: which were superior, the literary, philosophical, and scientific works of the classical Greece and Rome, or instead, the works of the modern world; that is, the sixteenth and seventeenth centuries? The chief partisans were Boileau for the Ancients and

. . . .

51   Diderot, *Oeuvres* 1951, 876–877.
52   Foucault 1966, 139.
53   Asplund 1981, 180.
54   Tuveson 1972, 71; Lowenthal 1986, 87; Frängsmyr 1989, 190–191.
55   Toulmin & Goodfield 1965, 113.

Perrault and Fontenelle for the Moderns. The quarrel lasted throughout the eighteenth century and ended with the rise of Romanticism.[56]

The proponents of the Modern outlook, such as Fontenelle, went to great effort to demonstrate that nature was not exhausted but was equally capable of producing great talents as ever before. For him the human spirit appeared to march towards higher rationality and knowledge, and time constituted a creative force.[57] In his treatise *Digressions sur les anciens et les modernes* (1688), Fontenelle advances the idea that different centuries do not entail any natural differences between men; all differences were caused by exterior circumstances. He admits that the Ancients had invented everything, but if his contemporaries would have been put into their place, they would have accomplished the same. It is for this reason that Fontenelle was inclined to support the superiority of the Moderns: "Ainsi étant éclairés par les vues des anciens, et par leurs fautes mêmes, il n'est pas surprenant que nous les surpassons."[58]

The juxtaposition between the Ancients and Moderns forms an important thread in Mercier's major writings. As an ardent apostle of progress and man's perfectibility, he joined ranks with the adherents of the Moderns. Despite the fact that his view of the world had also a more somber side, which will be explored in Chapter IX of this study, the pessimistic idea that the end of the world was near at hand and that the way forward would be only a way toward destruction and death, was largely alien to him. In many occasions Mercier deliberates on the advantages and disadvantages of different epochs, comparing the conditions of his own century with the historical periods of the past. For example in an article contained in *Mon bonnet de nuit* he follows in the footsteps of the Moderns when he argues that even if no new great inventions took place, the art of printing had already massively contributed to the superiority of his own age compared to the past. It makes possible the conservation of prior achievements.[59] As will be shown with more detail below,[60] Mercier accorded to the art of printing a great innovative value, which he constantly praises in his various writings.

By extolling printing as evidence of the superiority of his contemporaries in relation to the Ancients, Mercier promotes an attitude typical for his age. The advent of print popularized the metaphor of the Moderns standing on the

. . . .

56   Nisbet 1980, 151; Männikkö 1986, 31–32; Le Goff 1992, 30–32. This is not a proper place to provide a penetrating analysis on the often amusing twists and turns of the controversy. For a more detailed analysis, see Nisbet 1970, 107–114; Nisbet 1980, 151–156. See also Bury 1920, 78–97; Passmore 1972, 198–201; Lowenthal 1986, 74–124.
57   Delumeau 1995, 313. For more detail, see Bury 1920, 98– 126. See also Passmore 1972, 199; Cazes 1986, 57–59.
58   Fontenelle, *Rêveries diverses* 1994, 33–47, passim.
59   Mercier, *Mon bonnet de nuit I* 1784, 121–127. See also Mercier's writing "*Des prôneurs de l'antiquité*" on the same theme; in it he explains the superiority of the men living in the Modern epoch by arguing that they are more benevolent and more sensitive to the sufferings of the lower social classes than their ancient predecessors. Mercier, *Mon bonnet de nuit IV* 1786a, 7. See also Mercier, *De la littérature et des littérateurs* 1970, 86.
60   See Chapter VIII, pp. 230–238.

shoulders of ancient giants: "Even if individually dwarfed, Moderns grasped secrets that Ancients lacked because they came after them."[61] The superiority of the Moderns was thus not thought to be based on their higher intellect or reason, but on the mere accident that they had happened to have appeared on earth at a later stage than their predecessors, which allowed them to draw benefit from the accumulated accomplishments of arts and sciences. This view was shared by many of Mercier's contemporaries, and for example in Gabriel Bonnot de Mably's (1709–1785) treatise *Progrès et des Bornes de la Raison* the privileged position of the Moderns compared with their ancestors is explained as follows: "...ils n'avoient pas les mêmes secours, il falloit qu'ils trouvassent eux-mêmes les vérités qui ne m'ont rien couté et qu'on m'a données."[62]

Marquis de Chastellux draws a similar conclusion in his *De la Félicité publique, ou Considérations sur le sort des hommes dans les différentes époques de l'histoire* (1772),[63] where no doubt is left about the superiority of the Moderns vis-à-vis the Ancients:

> "Qu'il y a donc tout à espérer du progrès des lumières; qu'elles ont amélioré et qu'elles améliorent journellement le sort des hommes; enfin, que loin d'avoir à envier les siècles passés, nous devons nous regarder comme beaucoup plus heureux que les anciens..."[64]

Chastellux' comment indicates that for enlightened philosophers of the eighteenth century the question of their own superiority no longer posed a problem; the struggle between the Ancients and the Moderns had been won. For them it was self-evident that they stood higher than any previous epoch in the history of humankind.[65] The most important change thus occurred in men's attitudes towards the value of their *own time*. Educated men of the eighteenth century were convinced that they were themselves living in a *siècle de lumières*. In their eyes humanity was at last visibly freeing itself from the prejudices and superstitions of the past.[66] The following words of Turgot give a good picture of this new self-confidence: "Enfin toutes les ombres sont dissipées. Quelles lumière brille de toutes parts! Quelle perfection de la raison humaine."[67]

Despite the fact that Mercier did not conform to his century, he too was happy and proud for being privileged to witness a unique epoch.[68] He was acutely aware of the great importance of his century in the historical continuity leading

. . . .

61 Lowenthal 1986, 89. See also Delumeau 1995, 317.
62 Mably, *Collection complète des oeuvres de l'abbé de Mably XV* 1794–1795, 21.
63 The originality of Chastellux lay in his way to concentrate attention on the eudaemonic issue and to examine each historical period for the purpose of discovering whether people on the whole were happy. In contrast to Turgot or Voltaire, who had traced the growth of civilisation, he took it as his task to find out if there had been a time in which public felicity was greater than in his own time, and to which it would be desirable to return. Bury 1920, 186–191.
64 Chastellux, *De la Félicité publique II* 1822, 286.
65 Toulmin & Goodfield 1965, 115; Pollard 1971, 50; Frängsmyr 1989, 193.
66 Hampson 1981, 150–151. See also Bury 1920, 165; Mortier 1969, 114.
67 Turgot, *Oeuvres de Turgot II* 1844, 610.
68 Rufi 1995, 4.

from the past through the present to the future: "Notre siècle peut donc être considéré moins comme le siècle des vérités, que comme le siècle de transition aux plus importantes vérités".[69] The message contained in these words is that even if the forces of darkness, superstition and prejudices, had already been forced to retreat, the high point of perfection had not yet been attained.

Like Mercier some decades later, Charles Pinot Duclos (1704–1772), the writer of a penetrating analysis on French manners and human character entitled *"Considérations sur les moeurs de ce siècle"* (1750), also had a vivid sentiment of living on the threshold of important social and political changes:

> "Je ne sais si j'ai trop bonne opinion de mon siècle, mais il me semble qu'il a une certaine fermentation de la raison universelle qui tend à se développer... et dont on pourrait assurer, diriger, et hâter les progrès par une éducation bien entendue."[70]

It would be, however, excessive to claim that the eighteenth-century French philosophers admired their own age at the expense of the ancient past without reservations. Their attitude towards the past was rather two-dimensional,[71] and for example Luc Capiers de Vauvenargues, (1715–1747), one of the most perceptive critics of the century, illustrates this double position in his treatise *"Réflexions sur le caractère des différents siècles"*, where he admits that his century had inherited the inventions of all centuries, but that did not justify indulgence towards the precedent epochs. He was convinced that despite the fact that the ancient peoples were deprived of modern inventions and philosophy, they had not had much to complain about. For this reason he demands: "Détrompons-nous donc de cette grande supériorité que nous accordons sur tous les siècles".[72]

Even the most progressive thinkers of the epoch like Mercier preserved the ancient inheritance. It is noteworthy that most of the ideals put into practise in his future Paris are founded on ancient models, in particular on the stoic conception of virtue. Moreover, the "ideal king" of 2440 reigns following the teachings of the philosophers in the same fashion as the mythical "philosopher-king" in Plato's *Republic*. To continue the list further, Mercier's image of an ideal woman is a reincarnation of the Roman matriarchs, and the costumes of future Parisians are reminiscent of the floating togas of antiquity. *L'An 2440* thus provides plenty of testimony that Mercier's relation to the ancient past was far from one-sidedly pejorative.

All this testifies to the fact that the eighteenth century was an epoch characterized by a profound tension between tradition and innovation. Without totally rejecting the admiration of ancient models, the human mind now started,

. . . .

69 Mercier, *Eloges et discours philosophiques* 1776a, XIV.
70 Duclos, *Moralistes français* 1864, 679.
71 A fuller treatment of this theme will be provided in Chapter IX, pp. 266–271, passim.
72 Vauvenargues, *Moralistes français* 1864, 663–666.

however, to be more preoccupied with the prospects of the future than with a nostalgic yearning for the past. In contrast to the period stretching from the fourteenth century to the late eighteenth century, when the mentality was, for the major part, directed to the past, and antiquity served as the counterpoint and opposite to the past, in the second half of the eighteenth century men became more concerned about the future. Comparisons with the past lose now their central position. The new understanding of the nature of time which was established around 1800 meant a radicalization of our awareness of history.[73] Generally speaking, the temporal perspective of the eighteenth century extended much further both into the mythical past and into the future than that of previous centuries.[74]

We have already noted that this modern notion of time as an extended evolutionary process is directly reflected by Mercier's vision of the future. The most conspicuous aspect that characterizes the temporal structure of *L'An 2440* is the idea that despite the improvements which have occurred in all domains of life, even the Parisians of the twenty-fifth century have not yet reached the ultimate point of perfection. The time traveler, who is marveling at all the signs of progress which he sees around him, hears from his guide that there is actually still a lot to accomplish. The society of 2440 is a representation of only one phase in the continuous process of amelioration, which has no limits in space or time:

> "Il nous reste encore bien des choses à perfectionner. Nous sommes sortis de la barbarie où vous étiez plongés; quelques têtes furent d'abord éclairées, mais la nation en gros étoit inconséquente et puérile. Peu-à-peu les esprits se sont formés. Il nous reste à faire plus que nous n'avons fait; nous ne sommes quère qu'à la moitié de l'échelle: patience et résignation font tout. *Mais j'ai bien peur que le mieux absolu ne soit pas de ce monde.*"[75] (my emphasis)

Mercier was convinced that future generations would be able to enjoy a happiness which had not yet been possible: "Tout se fait à la longue. Les secrets qu'on croyoit exactement renfermés, vont se rendre au public, comme les rivières vont à la mer: nos neveux sauront tout."[76] He dreamed that in the future men would be privileged to enjoy the achievements of arts and sciences accumulated in the course of the centuries, and for this reason they would surpass in happiness their eighteenth-century predecessors. The time traveler of *L'An 2440* congratulates the men of the twenty-fiftieth century for their good fortune: "Tout a son temps. Le nôtre étoit celui des innombrables projets; le vôtre est celui de l'exécution. Je vous en félicite."[77]

. . . .
73   Wallgren 1989, 36–37.
74   Polak 1961, 240.
75   Mercier, *L'An 2440 I* 1786, 292–293.
76   Mercier, *L'An 2440 I* 1786, 367.
77   Mercier, *L'An 2440 I* 1786, 45.

All these excerpts drawn from *L'An 2440* contain the same message: the establishment of a better world would be the end result of a long and even painful process. This explains why Mercier has situated his utopia in a far future century; it is his way of showing that no profound changes could be executed on a brief time scale.[78] The underlying idea is consistent with the classical definition, described in the introductory Chapter above, which J.B. Bury and Robert Nisbet have given to the modern idea of progress as a "theory of a slow, gradual, but continuous and necessary ascent to some given end".[79] Even if the end result is taken for granted, the theory always contains the assumption that progress will continue to advance indefinitely in the future.[80] According to this idea, as it was formulated by thinkers like Condorcet, Comte or Spencer, civilization has progressed, is now progressing, and *will continue to progress forever* into the illimitable future, which makes it different both from the Christian story of salvation and from the classical theories.[81]

The intellectual origins of this modern idea of infinite progress can be traced to the philosophy of Leibniz, who proclaims in his treatise *De l'origine radicale des choses* that "progress would never come to its term".[82] The leading thesis of Leibniz was that the whole universe is marching toward greater and greater happiness:

> "Et même, pour ajouter à la beauté et à la perfection universelle des oeuvres divines, il faut reconnaître un certain progrès perpétuel et absolument illimité de tout l'univers, de sorte qu'il marche toujours vers une plus grande civilisation."[83]

The argument of Leibniz, according to which the Universe displays "perpetual and limitless progress", is based on the idea of temporal evolution as a great store of potentiality towards higher and more perfected forms of existence. In his view the whole universe, man included, was in a state of constant, gradual, irreversible and indefinite change.[84] As we have already seen, for Leibniz the universe was no longer a static, Newtonian "machine", but a great cosmic organism. In his treatise *Principes de la philosophie (Monadologie)* Leibniz formulates this constituent principle of the vitalist universe as follows: "Je prends aussi pour accordé, que tout être crée est sujet au changement, et par conséquent la Monade crée aussi, et même que ce changement est continuel dans chacune."[85] The principle of perfect continuity between all forms of existence in the universe is a focal idea in his theory of the "universal plan of

. . . .

78   It is not exactly knowable why Mercier has chosen the specific year 2440 as the temporal location of his ideal state. A possible reason is that he counted the year from his own year of birth, 1740.
79   Bury 1920, 5; Nisbet 1980, 171.
80   Bury 1920, 7.
81   Nisbet 1970, 47, 105.
82   Leibniz, *Oeuvres I* 1972, 345.
83   Leibniz, *Oeuvres I* 1972, 344–345; Delumeau 1995, 313.
84   Passmore 1972, 215. See also Manuels 1982, 404–405.
85   Leibniz, *Principes de la Nature et de la Grâce/Monadologie* 1996, 244.

harmony": "Tout va par degrés dans la nature, et rien par sauts; et cette règle, à l'égard des changements, est une partie de ma loi de continuité."[86]

With his law of continuity Leibniz introduced a new predictive model of the future,[87] and it may not be mere coincidence that Mercier has chosen as the motto of his utopia the famous phrase of Leibniz: "Le tems présent est gros de l'avenir." The title of Mercier's novel and the reference to Leibniz reveal how the notion of time is introduced into utopia.[88] In its entirety the textual point to which Mercier refers can be found in Leibniz' *Principes de la nature et de la grâce*:

> "... le présent est gros de l'avenir, le futur se pourrait lire dans le passé, l'éloigné est exprimé dans le prochain. On pourrait connaître la beauté de l'univers dans chaque âme, si l'on pouvait déplier tous ses replis, qui ne se développent sensiblement qu'avec le temps."[89]

The Leibnizian metaphor of "pregnancy" and his formula that "the present is big with the future" can be used to describe the suggestion of F.L. Polak, according to which the image of the future is a "womb, fertilized by past and future".[90] This refers to the fact that the challenge of the times need not only be based on the past. It can also be based on the future, which draws the present to itself: "The future challenges us to examine and prepare in advance to solve the problems which it has in store for us... It is the not-yet-existent future, or certain special possibilities out of a numberless infinity of possible futures, which throws light or shadow on the present... Past and future come together with a... clash in the present, and out of the reverberations of this clash the images of the future emerge."[91]

In his *L'An 2440* Mercier receives the challenge of the future as a "womb" of limitless possibilities, when he recognizes that the future may produce new scientific discoveries which are still beyond the scope of human imagination: "... car où s'arrête la perfectibilité de l'homme armé de la géométrie et des arts mécaniques, instruit de la chimie?"[92] In *Mon Bonnet de nuit* he reshapes this idea as follows:

> "...nulle connoissance complette n'est donnée à l'homme, il marche sans la carrière des sciences, il ignore jusqu'où elle s'étend, & plus il avance, plus il voit s'augmenter l'espace qui lui reste franchis..."[93]

The message is that regardless of how much man tries to complete his knowledge of the world, this is not within his reach. As a creature endowed with

. . . .
86 Leibniz, *Extraits de la Théodicée* 1912, 273.
87 Nisbet 1970, 116. See also Delumeau 1995, 313.
88 Pons 1977, 15; Lapouge 1978, 235–236; Manuels 1982, 459; Kumar 1987, 38.
89 Leibniz, *Principes de la Nature et de la Grâce/Monadologie* 1996, 230.
90 Polak 1961, 53.
91 Ibid., 51.
92 Mercier, *L'An 2440 II* 1786, 369.
93 Mercier, *Mon bonnet de nuit III* 1786a, 23.

an inborn capacity of perfectibility, however, he bears within himself a world of limitless possibilities. It is just this same desire which forms the core of all utopian longing. To quote the words of Ernst Bloch, "utopian is set to man, who is a creature wanting for change". Bloch writes that the world has been given as a *potentiality*, as a great possibility of *dynameion*. The category "not-yet" is possible in the world, which is still in an open, imperfect and processual state.[94]

Despite their mutual dissidences all eighteenth-century philosophers of progress shared the same certainty that historical process produces *irrevocable changes*. This meant that in the course of history phenomena will emerge which have never been met before. They perceived the future in largely open terms.[95] In his *Esquisse d'un tableau historique des progrès de l'esprit humain* Condorcet formulates this credo of the modern age as follows:

> "Il est également impossible de prononcer pour ou contre la réalité future d'un événement qui ne se réaliserait qu'à une époque où l'espèce humaine aurait nécessairement acquis des lumières dont nous pouvons à peine nous faire une idée."[96]

Upon what premises was this self-confident faith in indefinite progress basically founded? How could Mercier and other progressive philosophers of his age be so sure that the progress was advancing in a desirable direction and would continue to do so forever? Was it not possible, even more probable, that the future would bring only hazardous and unpredictable events and eventually a Fall back to the misery and barbarism of past centuries?

One of the cornerstones of this new optimistic faith in progress was the idea that the future could be controlled by laws of probability. In the course of the eighteenth century it came be thought that not only nature, but also the future was subject to laws. Knowing these laws would make possible without risk of error to know what tomorrow would bring. Progress was now seen as inevitable, and for this reason it could be predicted for sure. In its final form this conviction is contained in Laplace's *Essai sur le calcul des probabilités*.[97]

The assumption that society operated in accordance with fixed causal laws now gradually began to replace the doctrine of universal decay.[98] The theory of history regulated by mathematically exact and calculable laws, governed by human action, seemed to offer more consolation than the intervention of divine Providence, which had appeared totally arbitrary, without any certainty about the time of Redemption.[99] One of the most ardent propagators of this idea that the future could be predicted by mathematically exact laws, was Condorcet, who proposes in his treatise on the theory of human progress that prediction of

. . . .

94 Bloch 1985, 27.
95 Viikari 1995, 358.
96 Condorcet, *Esquisse d'un tableau historique des progrès de l'esprit humain* 1795, 338.
97 Minois 1996, 427, 453.
98 Toulmin & Goodfield 1965, 113.
99 Polak 1971, 88. See also Lowe 1982, 46.

the future course of the political, social, and economic history would be a relatively simple matter:[100]

> "Si l'homme peut prédire, avec une assurance presque entière, les phénomenes dont il connaît les lois; si lors même qu'elles lui sont inconnues, il peut, d'après l'expérience du passé, prévoir avec une grande probabilité les événements de l'avenir."[101]

Another factor that offered a bulwark against the insecurity of the future was the conviction about the general validity of "enlightened" values. This was one of the main features that eighteenth-century French philosophers inherited as their legacy from the quarrel of the Ancients and Moderns. One could scarcely find a more appropriate example than *L'An 2440* to demonstrate this self-confident attitude as regards the value of the focal ideals of one's own century. Mercier was not able to recognize that men's basic ideals of life might change as the centuries pass. The following examples are sufficient to illustrate this thesis: when the time traveler of the novel pays a visit to the royal library of 2440, he finds there in the place of honor the works of the writers and philosophers of his *own* age; for example the work of Rousseau has been preserved in its entirety. Also Montesquieu's *L'esprit des lois*, Buffon's *l'Histoire naturelle* and the works of Linguet are taken seriously in the twenty-fifth century.[102] Moreover, when Mercier's *alter ego* goes to a theater, he notes to his surprise that the play tells about eighteenth-century heroes.[103] These examples are sufficient to illustrate that Mercier projects into the remote future the basic ideals of the philosophical thinkers of his proper age. His ideas are those of Voltaire, Rousseau, Diderot, Montesquieu, Raynal, the abbé de Saint-Pierre, and Beccaria.[104] In reality Mercier projects in this work his faith in progress,[105] and *L'An 2440* is a realization of the projects of the eighteenth century.[106] To use the expression of Cioranescu, Mercier's inventions "make us smile"; Mercier had no capacity to see into the future; indeed, it is justified to ask if it even interested him. *L'An 2440* is, perhaps, a representation of an ameliorated but still French eighteenth-century world.[107]

Mercier's undeveloped view of the nature of temporal evolution already aroused criticism at an fairly early stage. In his *Le Roman de l'avenir* Bodin expresses his contempt for Mercier's lack of innovative capacity as follows:

> " ... et sa monarchie philantropique, qui n'est qu'une modification du pouvoir absolu, ne paraît quère plus avancé que les têtes de ces citoyens futurs sur lesquelles il croit innover audacieusement en se bornant à les

. . . .

100 Nisbet 1980, 209. See also Pollard 1971, 88.
101 Condorcet, *Esquisse d'un tableau historique des progrès de l'esprit humain* 1795, 309.
102 Mercier, *L'An 2440 I* 1786, 320–367.
103 Mercier, *L'An 2440 I* 1786, 277–293.
104 Trousson 1982, 271–272.
105 Baczko 1974, 486, 489.
106 Denoit 1989a, 1625.
107 Cioranescu 1972, 194–196. See also Ruyer 1988, 205–206; Lequenne 1992, 35.

blanchir d'un soupcon de poudre, et en relevant les cheveux en chignon."[108]

The lack of predictive talent does not, however, diminish the value of Mercier's utopian vision as an authentic document; rather the contrary, since with his short-sighted view of the future he turns out to be a very typical representative of the general outlook of his time. The French eighteenth-century writers, being convinced that they were themselves living at the high point in the history of Western civilization, could envisage future change merely in terms of degeneration. Their failure to imagine the positive developmental curve of history made them believe that even at best the future could bring merely an ameliorated stage of the present conditions.[109] In other words, their belief in progress actually meant progress until the present time, not to the future.[110] "Over-civilization" was even considered to be a threat, and some philosophers believed that technical progress should remain in some *"moyen term"* in which the maximum amount of happiness would be best ensured.[111] Thinkers such as Rousseau, Voltaire and Diderot were equally persuaded that society had a point of perfection which could not be surpassed.[112]

Mercier's incapacity to understand the nature of historical changes over the course of long periods of time reflects the general fact that in the eighteenth century there was not yet a clear understanding about the mechanisms by which historical phases develop out of the preceding ones.[113] In this specific sense the philosophers of progress had more in common with their ancestors than with the modern man of the following centuries. Though they aimed at emancipating themselves from the past by rejecting old myths, their loyalty to some fundamental assumptions about certain universals, such as nature or reason, still survived.[114]

In the final resort, the fact that Mercier has situated his ideal city in a remote future is not founded on any innovative concept of the passage of time. There seems to be a certain paradox; while Mercier refers to continuous change as the source of happiness, his progressive vision is simultaneously teleological, in the sense that he has no doubt about the desirable end-result of amelioration: it is the gradual dissemination of Enlightenment values. There exists a profound tension between tradition and innovation, ancient and modern. From this it can be concluded that in Mercier's vision the linearity of time does not mean a processual development towards the new and unforeseen. Even if the present may be "pregnant with the future", the challenge offered by the future is not a new one.

. . . .

108 Bodin, *Le roman de l'avenir* 1834, 54–55.
109 Hampson 1981, 149–150. See also Ehrard 1994, 783.
110 Frängsmyr 1989, 193. See also Männikkö 1986, 33.
111 Crocker 1969, 14.
112 Ehrard 1994, 781; Minois 1996, 421.
113 Toulmin & Goodfield 1965, 113, 118.
114 Gossman 1972, 125.

Moreover, Mercier's optimistic view of the future was based on an assumption about simultaneous progress in different domains of life, revealed in his habit of speaking in his utopia of "reforms" in plural.[115] He put his confidence in the co-operative efforts of different branches of sciences and arts, envisaging, for example, that in the remote future theology and philosophy would no longer be rivals but would contribute together for man's perfection.[116]

This was one of the commonplaces amongst the eighteenth-century French philosophers of progress: they supposed that the increase in knowledge, the establishment of control over nature, and the perfecting of the moral excellences would reinforce one another and thus increase the amount of human happiness.[117] This view concerning simultaneous progress was also typical for example of Turgot: "... ainsi, malgré la diversité de leur marche, toutes les sciences se donnent l'une à l'autre un secours mutuel."[118] Marquis de Chastellux follows the same path when he remarks that legislation, commerce, agriculture and navigation "*marche d'un pas égal*".[119]

Mercier did not believe, however, that progress would proceed exactly contemporaneously in all domains of life. In his twenty-fifth century society the progress of experimental sciences has been the motor of all positive change, which has gradually contributed also to the advancement of men's moral and spiritual perfectibility. It appears that the development of political sciences has been more slow; this can be inferred from the fact that Mercier is rather hesitant as regards the optimal governmental rearrangement.[120] Speculations of a similar sort can be easily traced from the treatises elaborated in eighteenth-century France; for example Helvétius shared the same idea of unequal march of progress, but as a harsh materialist he had no rosy illusions about man's capacity of moral perfectibility. In *De l'Esprit* he remarks that whereas poetry, geometry, astronomy and all sciences in general tend more or less rapidly towards perfection, human morals seem "hardly to have risen from the cradle".[121]

A distinction can be made also between the progress of the sciences and the progress of the arts. In an article "*Progrès des arts*" contained in *Tableau de Paris*, Mercier praises the books written in his century as more important and profound than those produced in previous centuries. He observes, also, that there are visible signs of progress in music, comedy, dance, habits etc. There is no doubt, however, that the future generation would be even more advanced.[122] Similarly, the time traveller of *L'An 2440* is informed by his guide that in 2440

. . . .

115 Ruyer 1988, 206. It is characteristic that the expression frequently used by French philosophers from Fontenelle to Voltaire and Condorcet was "*les progrès de l'esprit humain*" in contrast to the German term "*cultur*". See for example Burke 1997, 20.
116 Mercier, *L'An 2440 I* 1786, 91.
117 Keohane 1982, 26.
118 Turgot, *Oeuvres de Turgot II* 1844, 601.
119 Chastellux, *De la Félicité publique II* 1822, 227.
120 See Chapter V, p. 103.
121 Helvétius, *Oeuvres complètes d'Helvétius II* 1793, 338–339.
122 Mercier, *Tableau de Paris I* 1994a, 243–244.

the progress of different arts is much more advanced than in the eighteenth century.[123] Generally speaking, it is much more difficult to measure the "progress" of art than that of the sciences, since so much depends on taste and personal preference. There is thus no sense in applying the idea of progress to art.[124] The underlying idea is compatible with Turgot's comment: "Le temps fait sans cesse éclore de nouvelles découvertes dans les sciences; mais la poésie, la peinture, la musique, ont un point fixe..."[125]

The Agents of Change: The Power of the Printed Word

One argument advanced by the adherents of the secular idea of progress was the idea that the process must not be at the mercy of any external will.[126] Man's active role as the prime mover of history was strongly emphasized, or, alternatively, it was believed that history unfolds according to its own inner logic.[127] The most extreme proponents of rationalism, such as Condorcet, were eager to eliminate the whole idea of God as totally useless from their progressive schemes. As Condorcet conceived it, the sole obstacles for happiness were prejudice, intolerance, and superstition, and in order to end the public misery it was sufficient to instruct the people and to develop reason.[128]

It was in this crucial respect that the modern theory of progress differed from the religious story of salvation; whereas in Christian thinking the end of history is realized regardless of what men do as members of their community, in the secular vision the emphasis is on the free and creative role of man himself. It is especially this aspect which the proponents of the "thesis of secularization" failed to take sufficiently into consideration in their argument that the linear conception of time shaped in the eighteenth century was merely a secularized version of Christian thinking.[129] Trousson suggests that Mercier's utopian vision differs from the Judeo-Christian image of the future expressly in this specific sense, i.e. that the utopian state is a product of man himself, not that of providential grace.[130] In other words, in Mercier's mind man was himself responsible for his own terrestrial happiness or unhappiness instead of being merely a puppet at the mercy of powers which were not under his control.

As an introduction to the theme it is appropriate to refer to one of Mercier's pedagogical allegories, entitled "L'homme de fer"[131], in which the narrator is wandering in a dream state in the Swiss mountains, where he meets a Giant. The Giant demands that he should plunge into the stream, and after this the whole

. . . .

123 Mercier, *L'An 2440 II* 1786, 77–84.
124 See also Krieger 1982, 449–469, especially 449.
125 Turgot, *Oeuvres de Turgot II* 1844, 605.
126 Tuveson 1972, 6–7.
127 Keohane 1982, 26–27.
128 Badinters 1988, 84.
129 Viikari 1995, 358–359. See also Poggi 1982, 337–338.
130 Trousson 1982, 276, 278.
131 "*L'homme de fer*" is contained in the later versions of *L'An 2440*.

body of the narrator changes into iron. The newly born "man of iron" is then given the high task to remedy the deplorable state of affairs in the world. He opens, among other things, the doors of prisons, passes death sentences on murderers, sends thieves to forced labor, eliminates antiquated laws and abolishes frivolous luxury: "Comme mon haleine devenoit dévorante lorsque je voulois la faire servir au bien de l'humanité..."[132]

Mercier's story of the "man of iron" is his grandiloquent apotheosis for man's power to liberate himself from the tutelage of oppressive authority. Majewski sees in Mercier's superhuman man of iron "a precursor of romantic-Faustian man who revolts against the restrictive yokes of reason and the static order of things".[133] Prometheus has always symbolized the human spirit that rises to oppose the established law, and who has been understood as a benefactor, a defender or savior of humankind, who reclaims for men another condition than that under which they are reduced.[134] Similarly, Mercier's "l'homme de fer" is a kind of a "new Prometheus", who has stolen the fire of gods. He is no longer merely a faithful transcriber of the will of the gods, but the creator of his own future.

An enthusiasm for various kinds of gigantic human figures was one of the many features that united Mercier with other pre-Romantic and Romantic writers, for example Restif de la Bretonne. Mercier´s "man of iron" is a kindred soul with the superman Multipliandre in Restif´s peculiar novel Les Posthumes (1802); Multipliandre has a fantastic talent to fly from place to place, he can make himself invisible, detach his soul from his body, perform good deeds or prepare revolutions by slipping into the bodies of statesmen with the aid of "metempsychosis".[135]

Polak suggests that eighteenth-century philosophers were not blind to the fact that man was himself responsible for the destruction of the harmony of the social order, and they were equally aware that broken harmony could be restored in the future. He distinguishes two divergent approaches through which they attempted to solve this problem: 1) It was contended that the evil would ultimately turn to good of itself in the course of history, and an optimal social order would be eventually realized as a result of that process; 2) According to the second view man should himself recreate the social order. Polak calls these two different images of the future *essence-optimism* and *influence-optimism* respectively.[136]

Religious optimism based on *essence-optimism* forms the foundation in a line of thought which reaches through Descartes to Leibniz, Spinoza and later to Hegel. A feature common to all their philosophical systems was the view that

. . . .

132 Mercier, *L'An 2440 III* 1786, 218–312, especially 264.
133 Majewski 1971, 56.
134 Mucchielli 1960, 173, 250.
135 Restif de la Bretonne, *Les Posthumes II* 72 and *III* 31, 78, 1802.
136 Polak 1961, 236–237.

man should not intervene in the divinely rational order. By attacking the tradition of *essence-optimism*, the belief in the best of possible worlds, in his *Candide*, Voltaire set a new trend shared by rationalists and Romantics alike, who were both opposed to *influence-pessimism*, the passive acceptance of man's "fallen" nature and the feeling that man had no power over his own life.[137]

In his dissertation on Mercier's utopian vision Dennis Wiseman argues that Mercier breaks with the general philosophy of essence-optimism: "Man must act as if the realization of this kingdom (of God on earth) were to depend solely on him, as if the categorical imperative of moral law for his own behaviour were to become a universally valid natural law through his act of will. Social peace and harmony become the object and possible result of human action, independent of an intervening divine agent. The categorical imperative, the core of moral law, comes to man through the voice of his super-rational conscience."[138]

Wiseman draws a justifiable conclusion in emphasizing the active role of man himself as the harbinger of his own salvation as it is represented in Mercier's model; as we have seen, Mercier had a firm belief in the existence of men's "super-rational conscience", which as a categorical imperative told them automatically how to behave in a virtuous and righteous manner. This reads as a sign of a decisive shift from superhuman to human power: man is now responsible for his own actions. Despite the fact that Mercier had a fatalistic belief in the "best of possible worlds", God is no more the prime mover.[139] As Polak puts it: "This joyfully certain progress is to come through *man*. Whether it is thought to come through purposive action or unconscious activity, the emphasis is always on *man*..."[140]

In Merciers' view not all human groups, however, were capable of bearing responsibility for their own lives (people of low social origin, women, savages). Therefore, they were in need of teachers, whose task it was to help them to know right from wrong. Mercier gave high respect to exceptional individuals, geniuses, as bearers of progressive change. He envisaged the idealistic image of a writer-philosopher whose almost sacred duty would be to liberate suffering humankind from the burden of superstition, ignorance and prejudices:

> "; qu'un seul homme influe également sur l'univers et sur les siècles; qu'il détermine le bonheur ou le malheur des peuples; qu'il est l'origine des révolutions les plus extraordinaires et les plus éloignées."[141]

. . . .

137 Ibid., 237–239.
138 Wiseman 1979, 121–122.
139 Mercier's suggestion seems to be that if man really is a microcosmos of the whole universe, he may use the divine potential within him to bring his own salvation. This does not, however, mean full mastership over nature; Mercier's future men rule nature by understanding her laws, not by striving to bend reality to the human control. From this it is to be inferred that the intellectual attitude promoted in *L'An 2440* is based on a simultaneous *essence-optimism* and *influence-optimism*. In Mercier's moral allegories, by contrast, the emphasis is almost onesidedly on *essence-optimism*.
140 Polak 1961, 319.
141 Mercier, *L'An 2440 II* 1786, 288.

In one of his moral stories ("*Le philosophe soi-disant*"), Marmontel creates a satirical portrait of a cold-minded philosopher, through which he ironizes the view that the task of the philosopher is "to be happy through making other men happy".[142] For Mercier, however, the figure of a philosopher is far from being a subject of ridicule, since in his fictitious society of 2440 the philosophers occupy an important role as educators of the princes and as molders of general opinion. He calls them "suns", who launch ideas into circulation and who will eventually undermine despotism.[143]

With his belief that exceptional talents are a gift of God, Mercier repudiates theories propagated by such philosophers as Helvétius, according to which man is nothing but a result of education and environment: "Comment peut-on avancer que les hommes ont tous les mêmes dispositions, que l'inégalité extrême des talens ne dépend que des circonstances, lorsque l'on voit les influences les plus extraordinaires sortir d'une seule tête..."[144]

As a pre-Romantic Mercier proclaimed the cult of misunderstood genius: "... deux ou trois hommes entrent dans ses idées, & le reste méprise ce qu'il n'est pas en état de comprendre."[145] In thus emphasizing the insurmountable gulf separating writers from the "vulgar" (common people, the lustful and the rich), he was advancing the view of writers as a voice crying in the midst of silence, corruption and stupidity: "Le génit subit le destin du despotisme; on s'humilie devant lui, mais en même-tems on cherche à le détrôner."[146] These extracts illustrate how those who thought themselves "enlightened" in the eighteenth century believed that they were "a small band of crusaders fighting against ignorance, prejudice, and superstition, which it was their vocation to eradicate".[147]

Mercier's elevated view of the role of the men of letters as molders of opinion reveals how in his mind the idea of progressive change was always closely related to the belief in the power of education and literature: "Les ennemis de livres le sont des lumières, et par conséquent des hommes."[148] Feeling constantly persecuted and isolated from society, he found in literature a form to express his creative energy. He saw his work as liturgy and mission by developing the idea of the poet-prophet, "mage" and "*bienfaiteur*", guide for

. . . .

142 Marmontel, *Contes moraux II* 1787, 2 and passim.
143 Mercier, *L'An 2440 I* 1786, 74.
144 Mercier, *L'An 2440 II* 1786, 285; Mercier, *Tableau de Paris I* 1994a, 361–362.
145 Mercier, *De la littérature et des littérateurs* 1970, 58.
146 Ibid., 28.
147 Doyle 1988, 83.
148 Mercier, *Tableau de Paris I* 1994a, 757. By and large, books had an enormous impact both in Mercier's personal life and in his literary production. He did not conceive the book merely as a concrete object to be studied, read and finally abandoned; it had also more "metaphysical" and metaphorical significations. It is the metaphor of the book which binds together the complex web of symbols constituting Mercier's utopian world founded on total transparency. In his vision of the future he represents the whole of nature as an enormous book, full of God's imprint. Similarly, the ideal society of 2440 reads like an open book in the sense that all the streets and statues have the function to teach moral lessons. Moreover, the offenses which criminals have committed are engraved on their foreheads, so that their evil deeds can be read like an open book (a kind of "public confession").

humanity.[149] For Mercier the writer was thus not only a seer but also a prophet, because the writer has a capacity to see further than the others, and also because the vision of the writer "denounces and destroys". In other words, the writer is an instructor, who sees and makes other men see, and who by this means ameliorates the human condition. For Mercier the act of writing always involves a demand for participation.[150]

All important periods of transition have had their "charismatic leaders", and Mercier liked to see the writer as a new Moses leading his chosen people to a promised land of the future. It is characteristic that he calls the writers by such terms as *"peintres de la vertu"*, commenting that it is necessary to love men, if one wants to write for them.[151] For Mercier a writer was *"le vengeur de la cause publique"*, whose duty it was to be the bearer of justice: "L'infraction de la justice est une injure faite au genre humain; voilà pourquoi tout Auteur digne de ce nom, sent vivement le tort que l'on fait à son semblable; il ne peut le tolérer."[152]

In Mercier's writings the men of letters are typical personifications of what Koselleck has termed *"prophète philosophique"*, a figure who has escaped from authoritarian rule.[153] In the same way Mercier defines the role of the "philosophical prophet" through his oppositional position in relation to the official ideology:

> "J'ai connu cette haine vertueuse que l'être sensible doit à l'oppresseur; j'ai détesté la tyrannie, je l'ai flétrie, je l'ai combattue avec les forces qui étoient en mon pouvoir."[154]

As a voice of social consciousness the man of letters should thus function as the mouthpiece of the "suffering poor". Mercier, who spent most of his life on the margins of the social elites, was convinced that only someone who had personal experience of misery could have a genuine capacity to identify himself with those living at the bottom of the social hierarchy. He believed that it was precisely for this reason that rich and happy men so rarely felt a desire to write; they had no reason to raise their voice against the tyrants.[155]

Mercier believed that a writer who wished to be an instructor of his people was obliged to sacrifice his personal happiness (at least the material side of it) on the altar of collective well-being.[156] As a figure born on earth for the sole purpose of suffering on behalf of his fellow creatures, the writer, for Mercier, is a kind of "substitute-Christ". One scholar has drawn attention to the fact that Mercier's writings do not contain many mentions of Christ, and in contrast to nineteenth-century utopian writers their predecessors in the eighteenth century

. . . .
149 Majewski 1971, 16–17. See also Hofer 1977a, 29.
150 Bollème 1978, 45, 71–72.
151 Mercier, *De la littérature et des littérateurs* 1970, 78, 82.
152 Ibid., 3.
153 Koselleck 1985, 17.
154 Mercier, *L'An 2440 I* 1786, xj–xij.
155 Mercier, *De la littérature et des littérateurs* 1970, 83.
156 See also Majewski 1971, 5.

had no tendency to elevate Christ as their hero,[157] which explains, in part, the prominent role accorded to writers in Mercier's utopian vision.

The belief that a writer-philosopher might have genuine power as an agent of progress can be seen as a reflection of the increasing social importance of writers in the second half of the eighteenth century. As a critic and judge of the institutions and principles of his times, the writer becomes a "transmitter of values" and a "legislator". In Enlightened opinion it is now men of letters, no longer the priests, who consititute the first estate in the social pyramid, the most important function of which is to consecrate the entire order of society.[158] From now on, "spirit" became a principle of distinction in the same way as rank and fortune. In their new role as "citizens", men of letters came to possess intermediary power between the state and civil society. The promotion of an intellectual was followed by proclamation of irrevocable symbolic power.[159] As possessors of symbolic power, men of letters were now to occupy the leading position as moral leaders of society in a way like that described by Mercier in many of his writings.

This belief in the exceptional "mission" of the man of letters had even mythical or magic undertones. The "power of the word" was one of the themes favored by the eighteenth-century illuminists. They were convinced that primitive language was a gift of God, and that the word was equivalent to Creation. The mission of "*l'homme de parole*" was conceived to be the recreation of the purity of language out of the Babel of languages.[160]

As an adherent of illuminist doctrines, Mercier proclaimed the rise of Romanticism by elevating writers as a kind of substitute God, who had a secret power to create new worlds through their imagination. In one of his most peculiar literary contributions, *Néologie ou Vocabulaire de mots nouveux* (1801), he rejects the idea that a writer should be content to lean on classical norms and conventions, and asserts the need to invent new words and expressions instead: "... mais l'homme pensant ne connaît point d'autre autorité que son propre génie; c'est lui qui fait la parole..."[161]

All this points to the conclusion that Mercier believed that it was the power of the printed word that would eventually bring about the miraculous transformation from the unhappiness of the eighteenth century into the glorious year 2440. As Darnton has pointed out, Mercier returns to this topic in several different contexts: "Enlightenment is spreading everywhere; writers are the unacknowledged legislators of the world; the printing press is the most powerful engine of progress; and public opinion is the force that will sweep despotism away."[162]

. . . .

157 Bowman 1975, 433, 439.
158 Delon, Mauzi & Menant 1998, 30.
159 Roche 1988, 220.
160 Delon, Mauzi & Menant 1998, 159–160.
161 Mercier, *Néologie ou Vocabulaire de mots nouveaux* 1801, xvii.
162 Darnton 1997, 229.

Mercier accorded great significance to the power of the printed word as an accelerator of progress. Luigi Sebastiano Mercier, drawing by Mme Sergent Marceau, engraving by Torchiana, Vizille, Museum of the French Revolution.

For Mercier the press meant an agent of communication with the future, which implies that *"books are our true time machines"*.[163] He never tires of praising the art of printing as a tool for the distribution of efficient instruction: "Elle ébranle les préjugés; elle démolit le vieux temple de l'erreur; elle abat les masures des siècles, leurs lois usées et impertinentes."[164] In this respect Mercier joins ranks with many other progressive writers of his age, for example Volney, who in his *Ruines* glorifies the art of printing as a "sacred gift", which has provided a means to communicate simultaneously the same idea to millions of men.[165]

Yet it is difficult to know for sure how far Mercier believed that books had genuine power to transform present misery into future happiness. For example in his brief text "*Apologie des gens de lettres*", Mercier argues that if despotism had become less powerful in his lifetime, this was thanks to the writers. This claim is followed, however, by a comment that the power of the writer in eighteenth-century France was still more an illusion than a reality: "Il est obscur est sans puissance; mais il met en mouvement le cri de la raison universelle."[166] In the final resort, the role of the writer is reduced to that of a kind of catalyst,

. . . .

163 Alkon 1990, 61.
164 Mercier, *Tableau de Paris II* 1994a, 739. See also for example Mercier, *Notions claires sur les gouvernemens II* 1787, 414.
165 Volney, *Oeuvres choisies de Volney* 1836, 82.
166 Mercier, *Tableau de Paris I* 1994a, 961–962.

whose task it is to stimulate social imagination susceptible to new ideas. Mercier's message seems to be that even if men of letters may be the moral leaders of their society, they have at present no say in the domain of political decision making. Consequently, there prevails a far-reaching contradiction between the ideal of happiness and the coercive structure of society, which still in eighteenth-century France prevented the expression of "enlightened" ideas except in the guise of utopias. As Koselleck comments, "if the critique could be justified at all, it had to become utopian".[167] Since the members of the rising bourgeoisie still had no access to the sphere of political decision making, their interests were promoted behind the scenes.[168] This view is compatible with the conclusion in Chapter V above: absolutist politics was not public politics, and there existed no other public instance than the king to which or whom petitions could be addressed.[169]

Hence, there is no doubt that Mercier recognized the impotence of the writers and philosophers of his own age to genuinely influence the course of events or planning of the (political) future of their country. On the other hand, he argues in *Notions claires sur les gouvernemens* that a man who writes, is today (in the late eighteenth century) "*un Orateur public*", who speaks at the same time to all men throughout Europe; in the course of the preceding century books had changed the ideas and moral system of Europe.[170] Similarly, in *Eloges et discours philosophiques* Mercier suggests that the triumphant march of progress can no longer be held back:

> "C'est en vain que l'on voudroit éteindre aujourd'hui le flambeau de la Philosophie. Le fanal est allumé & domine l'Europe: le vent du despotisme, en courbant la flamme, ne peut que l'attiser, & lui donner un éclat plus vif & plus brillant."[171]

It is thus justified to say that although Mercier had no illusions about the extent of the power of men of letters in his contemporary society, at the same time he was aware of their increased influence. Regardless of tyrants, persecutors or the "vulgar", the torch of philosophy could no longer be extinguished. There is no doubt that Mercier saw in the formation of public opinion a powerful counter-force which might have genuine power to resist the abuses of absolutism. The following passage from *De la littérature et des littérateurs* illustrates this idea:

> "Depuis trente ans seulement, il s'est fait une grande & importante révolution dans nos idées; l'opinion publique a aujourd'hui en Europe une force prépondérante, à laquelle on ne résiste pas."[172]

. . . .

167 Koselleck 1988, 10.
168 Gossman 1972, 56–57.
169 See for example Baker 1987, 42.
170 Mercier, *Notions claires sur les gouvernemens II* 1787, 413–414.
171 [Mercier], *Eloges et discours philosophiques* 1776a, xv; *L'An 2440 I* 1786, xiij.
172 Mercier, *De la littérature et des littérateurs* 1970, 8.

According to Keith Michael Baker, the "important revolution" to which Mercier refers in this passage was to be accomplished by men of letters who raised their voice against political vices. In his view Mercier was one of the first eighteenth-century writers to be acutely aware of the emergence of enlightened public opinion and its political significance.[173]

Mercier placed his trust in the emergence of a free press as the forum of public opinion. He formulates this idea with particular firmness in an article published in 1796 in *Annales patriotiques*; public opinion is suggested to be "the first punishment for the tyrants" and "a necessary forerunner of the Revolutions that will restore liberty for those who have lost it". It is the press that creates public opinion, and a free press is the germ of all freedom. The first and most sacred right of all human societies is to communicate one's ideas, opinions, and sentiments, and the sole purpose of this communication is the restoration of social felicity.[174]

In *L'An 2440*, Mercier had already elevated freedom of thought and the liberty of the press as the constitutive elements of his ideal society.[175] One of his most ambitious visions projected into the future related to the hope that the generations not-yet-born would have access to all the benefits from the advancement of learning and the betterment of communication networks. As an illustration of this, the time traveler of *L'An 2440* reads in a journal that in 2440 it is possible to transmit information simultaneously from all the different parts of the world – from China to Paraguay, from Tahiti to Paris.[176] This wishful image mirrors the course of actual development in the latter eighteenth century, for in 1777 a daily newspaper made its appearance in Paris.[177]

By emphasizing in his utopia the importance of a free press, the increased significance of public opinion, and writers as its molders, Mercier creates within and above the state itself an autonomous public domain, a construction similar to what Jürgen Habermas has termed "the sphere of private people coming together as a public". By this he means the increased power of public opinion, based on the open use of critical reason, which in Habermas's view had genuine power to challenge authoritarian rule already in late eighteenth-century France.[178] Many later scholars have criticized Habermas for locating this public sphere narrowly in such institutions of sociability as clubs, cafés, salons and academies, which he suggests provided a forum for the bourgeoisie excluded

. . . .

173 Baker 1987, 56. See also Koselleck 1988, 95; Habermas 1989, 95–96.
174 Mercier's article *"Sur la liberté de la presse"*, published 27.2. 1796 in *Annales patriotiques*, contained in the new edition of *Le Nouveau Paris*. Mercier, *Le Nouveau Paris* 1994b, 1569–1573.
175 Mercier, *L'An 2440 III* 1786, 116–120. A certain paradox emerges here: despite the fact that Mercier emphasizes the importance of freedom of speech, in his utopian society all dissidences of opinion are severely punished.
176 Mercier, *L'An 2440 III* 1786, 30–83.
177 Doyle 1988, 78. For more detail on the evolution of the press as a political force in eighteenth-century France, see Censer 1994. It merits to be noted also that the chapter *"Gazettes"* is contained already in the 1770 edition of *L'An 2440*.
178 Habermas 1989, 27, 67–71.

from state politics.[179] As Arlette Farge, for example, has pointed out, pre-Revolutionary Paris was filled with public noises, the significance of which the authorities pretended not to acknowledge, feeling simultaneously threatened by them.[180]

Without wishing to deny the deficiencies of Habermas' argument, one cannot overlook the fact that the new social institutions which he lists had a certain function to perform in the constitution of the autonomous sphere of public debate in pre-Revolutionary France. Moreover, under the prevailing political situation secret underground societies like the republic of letters and masonic lodges had a decisive role to perform. They provided a nurturing ground for the emergence of "enlightened" opinion. They formed an autonomous forum for voices which were otherwise suppressed by the monologic discourse of the absolutist state. Mercier was acutely aware of their importance for the formation of public opinion, which can be traced for example from the article *"Clubs"* in *Le Nouveau Paris*:

> "On peut trouver dans l'etablissement des journaux, des sociétés littéraires, de ces clubs, où l'on parlait avec beaucoup de liberté, et surtout dans les loges de franc-macons, où l'on s'exercait à l'art de parler, où l'on obtenait la parole à peu près dans les mêmes formes usitées dans le corps législatif; on peut, dis-je, reconnaître les différents foyers de cet esprit insurrecteur, dont l'explosion ne pouvait guère tarder."[181]

Despite Mercier's optimism concerning the increased importance of public opinion already within his own lifetime, in the beginning of *L'An 2440* his voice is resigned to the inevitable conditions. He describes the situation prevailing in French society of his time as follows: "Déjà même la voix de la philosophie, lasse et découragée, a perdu sa force; elle crie au milieu des hommes, comme au sein d'un immense désert."[182] According to Koselleck's interpretation, Mercier's words express sentiments typical for a situation of crisis when critical polemic against the State had turned into conscious political demands. In other words, the antagonistic dualism between the domain of morals and the domain of politics had matured to a point "in which the bourgeoisie came to realize that the power of the spirit, the power of morality, had grown so greatly that it could now seek to assert itself in the political arena".[183]

In this context Mercier sees the voice of philosophy as suffocated, doomed to solitude; the desert metaphor reinforces this impression even further. Moreover, he compares the silence prevailing in his country to the "silence of the tombs",

. . . .

179 See for example Goodman 1992, 6; Graham 1997, 80, 102–103. For more details, see Farge 1995. Moreover, Habermas oversimplifies the whole question of public opinion in identifying the interest of the bourgeois class with the general interest. Habermas 1989, 87.
180 Farge 1994, passim.
181 Mercier, *Le Nouveau Paris* 1994b, 63.
182 Mercier, *L'An 2440 I* 1786, xii.
183 Koselleck 1988, 158.

calling his contemporaries "painted and walking corpses".[184] What is thus at issue here, is the expression of a deep sense of hopelessness and despair, caused by awareness of the unresolved conflict between the "ideal" and the "real". As Mercier's dramatic allusion to the "voice of philosophy doomed to echo in the desert" testifies, in his view there still existed a deep cleavage between the domain of morals and the domain of politics. Under existing circumstances, characterized by the political *status quo*, the conflict between utopia and reform had no practical solution. There was no direct way the private initiatives could be channeled as projects of public actions.

By virtue of the extracts from Mercier's different texts one can see that his view concerning the question whether books had genuine power to impact on the actual course of events or not, remained rather ambivalent. He certainly sincerely wished to believe in the transforming power of the printed word, even when harsh contemporary realities so often reduced it to a mere wishful image. Mercier had no doubts that in the course of time it would be the power of the word which would eventually liberate men from the chains of oppression; the "voice of the philosophy" could no longer be suffocated. There remained, however, a knotty problem: how could the bridge from ugly reality to future happiness be constructed in practise?

In order to answer this question, it is necessary to remind ourselves of Mercier's interest in secret societies like the Freemason lodges and their activities. It has been suggested that the popularity and significance of the Masonic lodges on the eve of the French Revolution can be properly understood only by the political exclusion of the bourgeoisie and their resulting frustration. According to Servier the same sentiment of being excluded also explains the proliferation of utopias in that epoch; they express the sentiments of an economically powerful class, which was nonetheless excluded from power. In revenge they created dreams of a wise society governed by enlightened bourgeois, the spiritual inheritors of Plato's philosopher-princes.[185]

Within their walls the members of the lodges or the "*Illuminati*" could create their own schema of the course of history. The ultimate goal of their activity was a secret plan to abolish the state. Because they realized that absolutism could not be eliminated directly, the course of this plan to achieve the peaceful victory of morality, freedom and equality was projected temporally into the future. The philosophy of progress offered them the certainty that in the course of time the

. . . .

184 Mercier, *L'An 2440 I* 1786, xii..
185 Servier 1969, 409–411. In reducing the dualism between utopia and reform as a struggle of the bourgeoisie, Servier's interpretation oversimplifies the complexity of the actual realities. In this respect he echoes Habermas. As Darnton has pointed out, this has, however, constituted a common practise in particular in Marxist historiography; it has been customary to stress the clash between the economic power of the rising bourgeoisie and their political exclusion, and the ensuing class consciousness which was to smoothe the path towards revolution as its consequence. Closer inspection, however, reveals that as a matter of fact the "bourgeoisie" did not yet exist at that epoch in the sense of modern "economic man". Darnton 1988, 105–140, especially 107–108, 123.

indirect political plan would be realized. This long-term prognosis reveals that the bourgeoisie did not understand that the decision demanded by the growth of tension between morality and politics (the cleft between State and society) had sooner or later be a political decision. All aspirations toward revolutionary change were suppressed, since it was assumed that the absolutist regime would collapse anyway. Consequently, rational-critical public debate on absolutist rule interpreted itself as unpolitical: public opinion aimed at rationalizing politics in the name of morality. At the same time the practical situation became more difficult to deal with, because the intensification of the dialectic of morality and politics exacerbated the tension.[186]

The solution set forth by Mercier in *L'An 2440* resembles in its main lines this secret plan of the *Illuminati*. The implicit message embedded in the structure of the novel is that the absolutist state will collapse in due course from its own "impossibility" without the need of violent intervention. This sheds more light on Mercier's decision to project his vision into a remote future and his trust in the idea of indefinite and endless progress; the suggestion is that without patience no optimal condition can be attained, and all that man needs is the certainty that time is not going to end.

As has been explained above,[187] Mercier creates in his utopia an idealistic image of harmonious alliance between the rulers and the philosophers. The scholars lead public opinion, and the governors convert their advisors' ideas into practise. Public opinion does not rule, but the enlightened monarch follows its insights.[188] The same attitude is met in many eighteenth-century French philosophers, who regarded it as their responsibility to keep a distance from political intrigues and yet to consider themselves as "the true governors of the people".[189] In their minds the belief in progress was associated with an implicit or explicit unwillingness to be involved in practical politics.[190]

Mercier's highly idealistic vision of an egalitarian, cosmopolitan and universal republic of letters, formed by exceptional personalities, illustrates the basically utopian undertones in this kind of reasoning: it is based on the assumption already advanced in *Le Bonheur des gens de lettres* that despite their marginal status in society, misunderstood by the tyrants and the "vulgar", writers are the moral leaders of their society, living far above harsh everyday realities in the spheres of perfect beauty and harmony. This explains the priority accorded to the progress of morality over that of politics. This provides a new explanation for the vagueness in Mercier's treatment of political issues in his utopia, where he avoids giving an explicit answer to the question concerning the exact form of government in his ideal state. A more probable explanation, however, is that there were no concrete solutions available to the impossible conflict between utopia and reform, i.e., "spleen" and "ideal".

. . . .

186 Koselleck 1988, 127–137, passim.
187 See Chapter V, p. 107.
188 Habermas 1989, 95–96; Darnton 1997, 231.
189 Passmore 1972, 192.
190 Poggi 1982, 339.

"Une heureuse révolution" – Do Books make Revolutions?

In emphasizing the important role of the printed word, education, and the writer-philosopher as the agent of progress, Mercier promotes the view that the only acceptable way to pass from present misery to future happiness is a gradual, peaceful and long-lasting evolutionary process, not an abrupt or violent change. His idealistic hope for the gradual spread of enlightened ideas is focused on his concept of a "happy revolution" generated by literature and philosophy: "Tout est révolution dans ce monde: la plus heureuse de toutes a eu son point de maturité, et nous en recueillons les fruits".[191] Similarly, in the following passage he emphasizes the specific "happiness" of the revolution which has led to the future world of 2440: "... cette révolution, dites-vous, s'est faite de la manière la plus paisible et la plus heureuse? ... Elle a été l'ouvrage de la philosophie: elle agit sans bruit..."[192]

This concept of a revolution accomplished in a non-violent manner was typical of the political terminology in eighteenth-century French philosophy. The "Glorious Revolution" of 1688 served as a model to be idealized, with its demonstration that a vicious government could be discarded through parliamentary reform, avoiding bloody confrontations. The major importance of the "Glorious Revolution" was in the fact that it contributed to the linking of revolutions with the idea of progress.[193]

The linking of the concepts of progress and revolution was symptomatic of a decisive transformation in the course of the seventeenth and eighteenth centuries in the ways the concept of revolution was conceived. The concept was now detached from its original signification of "circulation". A brief look at the etymological origins of the term "revolution" reveals that its earliest usage was marked by the notion of a return to some anterior condition; in the same way as natural processes remained the same from year to year, so men´s lives were thought to forever imitate the same changeless pattern.[194]

Despite the fact that the theme of revolution as a *return* is of great importance in Mercier´s utopian thinking,[195] he had at the same time a clear awareness of the modern connotations of revolutionary change. The following extract from *L´An 2440* illustrates that Mercier conceived revolution as a change toward a totally different order, which owes nothing to the pattern of cyclical repetition or to the ebb and flow of events:

> "Tous est révolution sur ce globe: l'esprit des hommes varie à l'infini; le caractère national change les livres et les rend méconnaissables... "Ne nous moquons- nous pas de nos devanciers? Savons-nous les progrès que feront nos enfans? Avons nous une idée de secrets qui tout-à-coup peuvent sortir du sein de la nature?"[196]

. . . .

191 Mercier, *L'An 2440 II* 1786, 105; Mercier, *Notions claires sur les gouvernemens II* 1787, 412.
192 Mercier, *L'An 2440 I* 1786, 141.
193 Cohen 1985, 69–73; Koselleck 1985, 45.
194 Koselleck 1985, 41–42. See also LeFlamanc 1934, 74; Cohen 1985, 63–64; Jarrett 1989, 8–9.
195 See Chapter IX, pp. 271–286, passim.
196 Mercier, *L'An 2440 I* 1786, 329.

Koselleck, who has focused his attention on Mercier´s expression quoted above, "*tous est révolution sur ce globe*", remarks that for the "enlighteners" of the eighteenth century, the whole world appeared to be in a state of a constant and permanent revolution. In their eyes revolution was global by nature, and all the different domains of human endeavor, from religion to economic matters, law to moral conduct, could now be conceived in terms of a revolution.[197]

In this context, the idea of revolution was welcomed with approval as a natural and desirable event. It was inconceivable to imagine revolution in the form that it was going to assume in the near future, i.e., as a carnivalistic upheaval of existing power relations. It was only after 1789 that this new significance for the notion of revolutionary turn asserted itself, and henceforward revolution became a synonym for an irretrievable and radical change in the form of government.[198] For example in the *Encyclopédie* the term "*révolution*" is defined in this modern sense: "Un changement considérable arrivé dans le gouvernement d'un état".[199]

In the "*Nouveau Discours préliminaire*", which Mercier added to the final edition (1799) of his utopia, published after the Revolution, he represents his views concerning the influence of philosophical writings on the explosion of revolutionary turmoil. Despite the fact that he is praising the benefits of revolutionary change, which has overthrown vicious institutions, he at the same time accuses the Jacobin leaders Danton and Marat of barbarism. Mercier emphatically distances himself from the executors of the Revolution's bloody actions, and discharges himself of all responsibility: men whose sole motive was the thirst for power and blood have distorted the philosophical writings and turned them to serve their own, morally wrong purposes. Mercier states that especially the massacres of September had destroyed everything that he had predicted.[200]

Mercier's anger when he was forced to testify to the violent turn of events, which had started in 1789 as a relatively peaceful process, reveals that he had not imagined revolution in the sense of an abrupt, violent turnover of the existing political system. As Denoit has also noted, Mercier had no understanding of the popular subversion which was under preparation, and even if the Bastille is destroyed in his utopia, this has happened through the wisdom of the King and not because of the revenge of the people. Mercier could not see how the reality would brusquely overtake the imagination.[201]

Against this background it is easy to see that Mercier exaggerates his role as a prophet of the French Revolution at the beginning of the post-Revolutionary edition (1799) of *L'An 2440*: "Jamais prédiction, j'ose de dire, ne fut plus

. . . .

197 Koselleck 1985, 44–45. See also Cohen 1985, 53.
198 Cohen 1985, 63–64, 205. See also Lowe 1982, 39. See also LeFlamanc 1945, 74.
199 *Encyclopédie XXIX* 1780, 87.
200 Mercier, *L'An 2440 I* 1799, v–vij.
201 Denoit 1989a, 2033–2034.

voisine de l'évenement... Je suis donc le véritable prophète de la révolution..."[202] In point of fact, contrary to what Mercier himself wanted to believe, he was far from being the only one who claimed to have predicted or prophesied the Revolution in the eighteenth century; similar "prophecies" circulated quite widely in Paris on the eve of the Revolution.[203]

Mercier's conviction that the Revolutionaries had falsified and misinterpreted the writings of the philosophers provides one answer on the issue which has been a focal concern in many scholarly disputes: How far-reaching was the impact of the eighteenth-century French philosophers for the outburst of the Revolution in 1789? Did the various utopias and projects of reform have any power to catalyze social discontentment? Do books make revolutions? Were the writers of utopias hoping for a total change in their society in the form of a sudden and violent turnover of the existing relations of power?

It is not possible, in the scope of this investigation, to attempt a comprehensive assessment of the influence of the philosophical ideas as the intellectual roots of the French Revolution. Some comments of a more general nature are, however, in order here. To begin with, it is necessary to bear in mind the point discussed above that the philosophical writers of the French Enlightenment were not especially concerned with political issues. They were not "revolutionaries" in the modern sense of the term, and the same nonpolitical attitude to life also characterizes Mercier.[204] This has been the common view at least since the classical thesis of Daniel Mornet, according to which none of the philosophers could be considered a revolutionary, and they all distrusted popular government. Unquestionably, the Revolution was in one respect a protest against misery and a spontaneous revolt against suffering. Yet, the philosophers did not teach democracy or revolution.[205]

Most scholars have echoed Mornet in this issue: utopias and other projects of reform did not anticipate the Revolution, e.g. by offering a program of social or political convulsion. Even the writings of such more radical philosophers as Rousseau, Mably, or Morelly were generally moral dissertations rather than social demands; the theory of socialism still operated on a purely theoretical level, without practical implications. There is little sign in these philosophers of profound indignation or the voice of real suffering. All the evidence confirms that there was no socialist movement in the eighteenth century.[206]

Mornet argues, however, that even without a revolutionary tendency, eighteenth-century philosophy had a very definitive role to play in transforming men's minds by undermining respect for tradition and by preparing people to reflect upon revolution and democracy. In a word, "it cleared the soil in which the seeds of new harvests could germinate".[207]

. . . .

202 Mercier, *L'An 2440 I* 1799, ij.
203 Koselleck 1985, 19; Minois 1996, 443–444.
204 See Chapter V, p. 110.
205 Mornet 1969, 205–206.
206 Lichtenberger 1899, 15–17; Trousson 1975, 131; Baczko 1978, 413. See also Pingaud & Mantéro 1992, 34–40.
207 Mornet 1969, 206.

In Darnton's view the whole question of the connection between the Enlightenment and the French Revolution, or what were the intellectual roots of the French Revolution, is much more complex. He criticizes straightforward cause-and-effect models of diffusion advanced by Mornet and his followers, on the ground that they miss their target because by assuming the existence of a unilinear movement from the Enlightenment to the Revolution, they fail to take into account independent factors such as nonliterary sources that contribute to the formation of public opinion, and the fact that the act of reading is not merely a passive reception[208] but an active process. He also points out that there still is no clear consensus about who composed the general public in pre-Revolutionary France and how their opinions were actually molded. It cannot be known for sure whether banned literature had any affect upon public opinion whatsoever, or, alternatively, if the literature in fact merely reflected prevailing attitudes. At any event, the desacralization of attitudes and the process of delegitimation had already started before the success of the *livres philosophiques*, and despite the hardening of their tone towards public figures, not even the *libelles* urged the French to rise against the monarchy or to overthrow the social order.[209]

Darnton is probably right in suggesting that the reading public should not be treated as soft wax. The diffusion of ideas should be seen as part of a wider social-cultural setting. In the same way, it is important to subject the traditional view of the "Enlightenment" as a monolithic and homogeneous movement to critical re-examination. This leads to the conclusion that the intellectual origins of 1789 cannot be found in the philosophical thinking of Voltaire or Rousseau. In reality there existed no causal connection: the writings of contestation did not contribute on the level of praxis to the fermentation of social imagination in the pre-Revolutionary period.

Yet even if it is reasonable to assume a rather sceptical attitude to the thesis that the intellectual roots of the French Revolution can be found from the treatises of writers such as Mercier, Morelly, Restif de la Bretonne or Rousseau, it is not, however, legitimate to deny any connection between the spreading of the Enlightenment and the outbreak of the Revolution. For their own part, – how minor that part may have been –, utopias such as *L'An 2440* functioned as a catalysis which accelerated the process towards revolution. The main function of Mercier's utopia and other writings of a similar sort was to enlarge men's scope of understanding better to see that the society was not the best possible, that there was something terribly wrong and that something should be done to repair the situation. By creating a utopian vision of a happier society, liberated from the vicious burdens of the past, Mercier revisualizes the worst abuses of

. . . .

208 This view is also strongly emphasized by Roger Chartier, who lays great stress on the fact that cultural consumption is not a passive process: a text does not contain one unique "truth" imposed by the author; its meaning is constructed only through the strategies of interpretation. Chartier 1988, 40–42.
209 Darnton 1997, 169–181, 188, 214, 231–233.

his contemporary society in monstrous proportions. As a technique this is much more effective than a lengthy moralizing project of reform.

The same concerns all visions of the future: they are, above all, a catalysis of the collective imagination. As Polak puts it, "positive images of the future... have foreshadowed the outlines of the oncoming course of general events; through their imaginative representations of the future they have helped to push events in this direction".[210] Negative images of the future have, correspondingly, been visible signs of cultural pessimism, the sense of malaise and desperation.

The general tone of moral indignation in Mercier's *L'An 2440* demonstrates that despite his non-revolutionary discourse, his philosophical propaganda struck, nonetheless, at the foundations of the *ancien régime* by exposing the unjust basis of privilege and the outrageous scandal of the famines. Unwittingly, perhaps, the philosophers thus smoothed the path for the Revolution: the project to create a society of well-being already here on earth increased the impatience of nonprivileged groups by undermining the faith in a life after death which had formerly made bearable the sojourn in the vale of tears.[211]

In other words, it was the very idea of terrestrial happiness and progress which legitimized and prepared the ground for the road which was finally to lead into Revolution. There was no other possible way: sooner or later the voice of morality had to be transformed into openly expressed demands for change. The scope which this change was going to assume fell, however, beyond the comprehension of Mercier and that of many of his educated contemporaries. Their beautiful vision of a "happy revolution" was doomed to be overwhelmed by Revolutionary terror.

The Scope of Education

Mercier's idealistic vision, that in the course of time the good effects of philosophical teachings (religious toleration, the gospel of social compassion and sharing, moderation) would start to transform the abuses of absolutist politics, reveals his trust in the power of education. Previously in this study the future society he created has been compared with a large pedagogical institution,[212] and amongst eighteenth-century thinkers it was common to argue that it would be possible by education to considerably accelerate the progress of reason.[213] Most philosophers were unanimous that it was education, rather than revolution, which would be the key to a better, rational society.[214] This order of preferences united political reformers from More to Kant and Marx. Thomas More preferred utopia to revolution, and Kant believed that mankind's progress would proceed only gradually, not by revolution but by evolution.[215]

. . . .
210 Polak 1961, 379.
211 Peyre 1974, 170–172.
212 See Chapter V, p. 197.
213 Polak 1971, 89.
214 Pollard 1971, 51. See also Manuels 1982, 463–464.
215 Lasky 1976, 591–595.

When one considers the theme of education from the perspective of time as it is represented in *L'An 2440*, the following questions arise: What was Mercier's conception of the time span which the process of spreading Enlightenment ideas would take? Who would profit from this educational process? Was Mercier's goal to enlighten the whole nation, or to limit the supreme knowledge within a restricted circle of "*savants*"?

To begin with, it is appropriate to refer to the Chapter on the "two infinities" of *L'An 2440*, in which Mercier tells about the rites of initiation to the mysteries of the universe. What is of concern in the present context is the fact that the young men of 2440 are told not to reveal to others what they have learned during their initiation:

> "Dès ce jour il est initié avec les êtres pensans; mais il garde scrupuleusement le secret, afin de ménager le même degré de plaisir et de surprise à ceux qui n'ont point atteint l'âge où l'on sent de tels prodiges."[216]

This allusion to the "secret" nature of superior knowledge implies an esoteric idea of science. In practise this means that in Mercier's ideal state supreme wisdom and happiness are reserved only for the few and chosen, i.e., for those who have advanced to higher levels in the ladder of spiritual and moral growth. Science is transformed into a religion based on initiation, a mystery cult.[217] In addition to many other features discussed above, this esoteric conception of knowledge links Mercier's utopia with the Freemason rituals; the requirement that the initiated "hold the secret scrupulously" is characteristic of Freemasonry.[218] Moreover, it leads one back to a great intellectual ancestor, Francis Bacon, and his mechanistic utopia, *Nova Atlantis*. In Bacon's scientific research institute, called Salomon's House, decisions are made for the good of all by the scientists, who alone possess the secrets of nature. They decide which secrets are to be revealed to all and which remain the private property of the institute.[219]

The pedagogical system of Mercier's utopia, based on an invisible hierarchy of the elite and the mass of the population which has not yet shared in the gospel of the Enlightenment, is thus no more egalitarian than that elaborated for example by Plato. In Plato's *Republic* a clear distinction is made between a perfectible *élite* and the non-perfectible multitude.[220] In the first part of the seventeenth century this esoteric idea of knowledge was advanced in particular by the *libertins*. Their point of departure was contempt for the "vulgar", founded on the assumption that the common people were incapable of understanding the truth.[221] This is a familiar theme in Mercier, starting from his

. . . .

216 Mercier, *L'An 2440 I* 1786, 178.
217 Vissière 1977, 317. Cf. Rufi 1995, 14.
218 Labbé 1978, 43.
219 Bacon, *The Advancement of Learning and The New Atlantis* 1906, 274; Merchant 1983, 180–181.
220 See for example Passmore 1972, 44.
221 Mortier 1969, 61–62.

treatise *Le Bonheur des gens de lettres*, where he extols the happiness of men of letters because of their exceptional capacity to feel and sense. It is expressly this capacity which in his view separates them from the "vulgar".[222]

Mercier believed that education had a decisive impact on man's perfectibility, but it had to be a slow and gradual process. From this it ensues that enlightened ideas should not be spread amongst the whole nation in too brief a time span: "Le vrai est sous nos yeux; mais nous n'avons pas encore le courage de l'adopter; la masse des esprits reste inactive, incertaine, pendant des années entiéres..."[223] As this reveals, Mercier was rather sceptical when he weighed the possible consequences of the rapid education of the masses. In *L'An 2440* he reinforces this view through the mouthpiece of a future Parisian who suggests that even in 2440 not all inventions are equally accessible for the whole nation:

> "... que plusieurs secrets singuliers, merveilleux, n'étoient remis qu'entre les mains d'un petit nombre de sages; qu'il étoit des choses bonnes par elles-mêmes, mais dont on pourroit abuser par la suite: l'esprit humain, selon eux, n'étoit pas encore au terme où il devoit monter, pour faire usage sans risque des plus rares ou des plus puissantes découvertes."[224]

The suggestion that underlies this statement is that in the "wrong hands" the misapplication of new ideas might have fatal consequences. Mercier returns to this theme in *Tableau de Paris*, where he states that the public good demands, at times, that some truths be kept hidden, for if they are revealed, without preparation, to the people, they may cause an explosion.[225]

Mercier's negative attitude toward the education of the whole nation in a brief time span reflects his general scepticism regarding the members of the lower social orders and his fear of the unpredictable movements of the masses. With this respect he joined ranks with the majority of his contemporary philosophers, who were fearful of the uneducated masses, whose behavior was seen as alien and threatening. At best they envisaged a very long-term evolution in which education would eventually filter down to the masses and modify their behavior. Presently, they regarded the masses as ignorant, violent and irresponsible.[226]

Supporting the idea of the gradual spreading of enlightened ideas, Voltaire for example made a clear distinction between those truths which should be divulged urgently, and those which it would be wisest to reserve for the élite. Amongst the eighteenth-century French philosophers only Helvétius, Turgot and Condorcet propagated the opposite view, refusing to make the Enlightenment the private property of any one class. Condorcet, in particular, was an adversary of all kinds of esotericism.[227]

. . . .

222 Mercier, *Le Bonheur des gens de lettres* 1766, passim., especially 36.
223 Mercier, *De la littérature et des littérateurs* 1970, 26.
224 Mercier, *L'An 2440 II* 1786, 58.
225 Mercier, *Tableau de Paris II* 1994a, 158.
226 Woloch 1982, 240.
227 Mortier 1969, 73–79, 100–101. See Condorcet, *Esquisse d'un tableau historique des progrès de l'esprit humain* 1795, 326: "... par un choix heureux... et des méthodes de les enseigner, *on peut instruire la masse entière d'un peuple...*" (my emphasis)

Mercier's general hostility towards the education of the masses seems to be in contradiction with the fact that as a member of the Convention he was one of the twenty-four members of the Committee of Public Instruction created in 1792, which was charged with preparing for the National Assembly a new plan of instruction intended for all Frenchmen without exception.[228] This shows that despite his fear concerning the violence of the uneducated masses, Mercier did not, in principle, resist the idea that the gospel of the Enlightenment would gradually penetrate also amongst the members of the lower social classes. Also in *Tableau de Paris* he presents a wish that all men should have equal access to books: "Il en faut pour toutes les conditions, qui ont un droit égal à sortir de l'ignorance".[229]

Mercier's recognition of the need for the gradual spreading of enlightened ideas was not limited merely within national boundaries. As has been pointed out frequently in the preceding Chapters of this study, in his utopian vision the idea of uniformity is one of the key principles. Consistently with this view, Mercier presents in his novel the hope that in the course of time the entire globe will be brought under the same uniform structure of values. In his view progress should always be universal and global by nature, and for example in *Mon bonnet de nuit* he emphasizes the importance of disseminating enlightened ideas over national frontiers as follows:

> "Les lumières qui nous sont utiles aujourd'hui, ne se borneront pas à nous seulement; elles se répandront de proche en proche par la communication; elles iront éteindre le fanatisme, l'ignorance & la misère, chez des peuples de brigands qui nous connaissent à peine; elles tourneront autour du globe."[230]

This passage confirms the point already discussed above that Mercier had no doubts that the essential ideas of his own age, those propagated by Enlightenment philosophers and disseminated from the intellectual circles of Paris, would be equally acceptable all over the world. One of the features in his utopian dream is the point that even in the far future France has preserved its status as a leader of nations and the master of the whole world in every sense of the term. In 2440, for example, Egypt has been subordinated under the rule of King Louis XXXIV.[231] Also the fact that in 2440 French has become the universal language, which is known even in China, reflects the leading status of French civilization and culture in Mercier's imaginary future world.[232]

Mercier's cosmopolitan vision of an ideal future based on harmonious coexistence between nations and on the leading position of France illustrates the "ecumenical" character of his utopian thinking. To paraphrase Mucchielli,

. . . .
228 L'Aminot 1995, 288–289.
229 Mercier, *Tableau de Paris I* 1994a, 351.
230 Mercier, *Mon bonnet de nuit IV* 1786a, 8.
231 Mercier, *L'An 2440 III* 1786, 352–354.
232 Mercier, *L'An 2440 III* 1786, 34.

the creators of ideal cities have preferred to describe mankind as a secularized version of Christendom, in the sense that it is *in its entirety* destined to become a new society, in which men would be united with each other through a mystical bond. In the myth of the ideal city, humanity is conceived as a totality, as a unique collective being, constituted by the dead as well as the living, marching and progressing constantly toward perfection which it approaches little by little.[233] In *Notions claires sur les gouvernemens* Mercier expresses this idea as follows:

> "Jamais un peuple n'a récu à la fois toutes ces idées; il faut des développemens successifs, & avant que la raison publique ait fait en quelque sorte d'une nation entiere *un seul individu*, il faut une marche graduée."[234] (my emphasis)

To illuminate this issue further, it is appropriate to refer to the beginning of *L'An 2440*, where Mercier creates an analogy between the life span of one individual and the history of the entire humankind: "Pourquoi le genre humain ne seroit-il pas semblable à l'individu? Emporté, violent, étourdi dans son jeune âge, sage, doux, modéré dans sa vieillesse."[235] Set in the general intellectual framework of its age, this statement contains nothing unusual. The philosophers of the eighteenth century had a predilection for such antique metaphors and they liked to picture civilizations as individuals, with a distinct life cycle.[236] Mercier's model may well have been Fontenelle, who uses the same metaphorical language in his treatise *Digressions sur les anciens et les modernes* in juxtaposing all those who have lived across the centuries with one sole human individual. He compares his own time with a human who has reached the age of virility and is more enlightened than ever before.[237] Following this same logic, Bacon, Pascal and the abbé Saint-Pierre had suggested that civilization had reached the "age of virility". For example Saint-Pierre proposed that whilst individuals lose their happiness in their advanced age, humanity as a whole will become happier and wiser from century to century.[238]

Moreover, with its dream of European hegemony, *L'An 2440* has many points of contacts with the "pansophic utopias"[239] and their dream of a universal Christian republic. Following this same globalizing tendency, the utopias of the late eighteenth century broke the limitations of specific place, addressing themselves directly to the reformation of the entire species. Utopian philosophers conceived of themselves as "universal lawgivers", proclaiming

. . . .

233 Mucchielli 1960, 177, 195–196, 204–205.
234 Mercier, *Notions claires sur les gouvernemens I* 1787, 106.
235 Mercier, *L'An 2440 I* 1786, 2.
236 Gay 1970, 100.
237 Fontenelle, *Rêveries diverses* 1994, 43.
238 Bury 1920, 136–137. It is noteworthy that in contrast to Fontenelle or Perrault, who had not yet addressed the future prospects for humanity (Bury 1920, 137), Mercier modifies in his utopia the ancient metaphor based on the human body analogy. He makes no allusions to the inevitable enfeeblement of bodily forces as a consequence of aging.
239 See Chapter II, p. 48.

that they were laying down laws not merely for France but for the entire universe.[240] Restif de la Bretonne's treatise *Le Thesmographe* (1789), which is a project for legal reform, offers a good image of this attitude. Its author assumes the role of an educator and a legislator:

> "Que je m'estimerais heureux si je pouvais contribuer au bonheur de mes concitoyens..."Je crois avoir parlé raison; j'ai dit la vérité, j'ai averti les Hommes de leurs véritables intérêts..."[241]

Many eighteenth-century philosophers of progress, e.g. Condorcet and Turgot, shared the same cosmopolitan dream; they thought that men could use their reason to gradually discard irrational superstitions in order that the world would become "a truly cosmopolitan whole".[242] The philosophers projected this ideal vision of the unity of the human race into the future, and thought it could be realized in historical time.[243] The Enlightenment was permeated by an understanding of reason as a universal force, which provided a program of action.[244] This was a rather deterministic view of human progress, however, for it implied the possibility of deducing generalizations which would remain valid for a considerable time into the future.[245]

It was Condorcet, in whose thinking the deep-rooted preconception of Eurocentrism found its purest manifestation.[246] He had a tenacious belief in a program of universal education, in which the leading position would be occupied by the members of the altruistic, white European race:

> "Si nous jetons un coup d'oeil sur l'état actuel du globe, nous verrons d'abord que, dans l'Europe, les principes de la constitution française sont déjà ceux de tous les hommes éclairés."[247]

The feature uniting many philosophical writers of the late eighteeth century was a very monolithic view of the world. The differences between the nations were explained away by claiming that they were at different points along the same path.[248] For example in Turgot's scheme, represented in his *Second discours, sur les progrès successifs de l'esprit humain* (1750), the human species is conceived as an immense totality, which is compared with one individual with its "childhood and its progress": "...la masse totale du genre humain... marche toujours, quoiqu'à pas lents, à une perfection plus grande."[249] The differences in the level of progress are said to be caused by environmental factors:

. . . .

240 Manules 1982, 3; Whitrow 1988, 151.
241 Restif de la Bretonne, *Idées singuliers V* 1789, 61.
242 Outram 1995, 78.
243 White 1987, 61–62.
244 Coates, White & Schapiro 1966, 183.
245 Pollard 1971, 9–10.
246 Manuels 1982, 504.
247 Condorcet, *Esquisse d'un tableau historique des progrès de l'esprit humain* 1795, 313.
248 Pollard 1971, 10.
249 Turgot, *Oeuvres de Turgot II* 1844, 598.

"Sans doute l'esprit humain renferme partout le principe des même progrès; mais la nature, inégale en ses bienfaits, a donné à certains esprits une abondance de talents qu'elle a refusée à d'autres: les circonstances développent ces talents ou les laissent enfouis dans l'obscurité; et de la variété infinie de ces circonstances naît l'inégalité des progrès des nations."[250]

In his utopia Mercier develops the same theme concerning the unequal march of progress in different parts of the world. In order to ensure that the temporal limit of the dissemination of enlightened ideas would never reach its final end, he proposes that when the spirit of the "leading nation" would some day be exhausted, other nations would take its place, so that they could draw benefit from the inventions of their predecessors.[251] The focal idea that underlies this statement is the same as that advanced by the supporters of the Moderns in the controversy between the Ancients and Moderns: those who come after, are not more fortunate than their predecessors due to the fact that they are more talented, but for the sole reason that they can draw benefit from the scientific inventions of their ancestors. Similar reasons led Turgot to suggest that "les régions qui ont été les premières éclairées, ne sont pas celles où elles ont fait le plus de progrès".[252]

Mercier hoped that after the whole world had gradually been restored under a single undivided structure of values, all differences in opinion would automatically disappear. As a consequence of this, in 2440 there are no more wars, because the rulers have opened their minds to the voice of philosophy.[253] Despite the fact that Mercier's utopian men admit that the possibility of war can never totally be excluded,[254] the dream of eternal peace put forward by the abbé Saint-Pierre in *Abrege du projet de paix perpetuelle* (1729) has become a reality. In this project of reform, dedicated to the monarchs, five propositions are presented for the establishment of eternal peace in Europe.[255]

Following the path set by Saint-Pierre, Mercier dreamed of a kind of union between the European nations: if the whole Europe formed only one political body, it would obviously enjoy greater liberty, peace and happiness.[256] He saw in the peaceful coexistence of nations an important factor contributing to the restoration of "universal happiness". This idea can also be traced in Mercier's allegorical story *"De la Guerre"*, in which he speculates on the arbitrariness of wars in an apocalyptic tone. In this story, filled with macabre horror and anti-utopian elements, the narrator is metamorphosed into a white skeleton, and a

. . . .
250 Ibid., 598–599.
251 Mercier, *L'An 2440 III* 1786, 12. As this passage hints, Mercier did not nourish an over-optimistic belief that the torch of the Enlightenment could never be exhausted; the suggestion is that eventually everything was doomed to degeneration. The issue related to the more pessimistic side of Mercier's thinking will be explored in Chapter IX, pp. 253–265.
252 Turgot, *Oeuvres de Turgot III* 1844, 601–602.
253 Mercier, *L'An 2440 I* 1786, 297.
254 Mercier, *L'An 2440* 1786 *III*, 184–201, passim.
255 Saint-Pierre, *Abrege du projet de paix perpetuelle* 1729, 21.
256 Mercier, *L'An 2440 III* 1786, 131.

rain of blood falls upon those who have thirsted for war. In this story, the events of which take place, once again, in a state of dream, Mercier meets Saint-Pierre, whose universal plan of happiness of nations used to be nothing but "*la chimere des belles ames*".[257]

Helvétius advances the same idea in his treatise *De l'homme*, proposing that once individual interests have been brought to serve the general interest in the name of universal love, different nations would support each other in their march towards higher and higher levels of progress:

> "L'horizon de nos idées s'étend de jour en jour; et si la législation, comme les autres sciences, participe au progrès de l'esprit humain, pourquoi désespérer du bonheur futur de l'humanité? Pourquoi les nations, s'éclairant de siècle en siècle, ne parviendraient-elles pas un jour à toute la plénitude du bonheur dont elles sont susceptibles?"[258]

Volney, referring to an alliance between nations, provides yet another example of this kind of reasoning:

> "... et l'espèce entière deviendra une grande société, une même famille, gouvernée par un même esprit, par de communes lois, et jouissant de toute la félicité dont la nature humaine est capable."[259]

Against this background it is not difficult to see that in the minds of eighteenth-century philosophical thinkers, universal history was identified with the history of Western civilization. This included an implicit assumption about the civilizing mission of the European nations.[260] In the background of this Eurocentric view can be traced a static conception of human nature, based on the universal validity of the structure of values in all eras and countries. With rare exceptions such as the Italian Gianbattista Vico (1668–1744),[261] the philosophers were incapable of recognizing any authentic value to anything which was not consistent with their own ideals. This led to a consolidation of the *status quo* and to a very limited understanding of the nature of historical change.[262] The eighteenth century could understand only itself and judged all others after itself.[263]

This one-dimensional view of human nature and the incapacity to deal with difference leads to an imperialistic and patronizing attitude in regard to different cultures and people, and the annihilation of the non-European world.[264] In

. . . .

257 Mercier, *Songes philosophiques* 1768, 246–247.
258 Helvétius, *Collection des plus belles pages* 1909, 244–245.
259 Volney, *Oeuvres choisies de Volney* 1836, 84.
260 Iggers 1982, 44; Viikari 1995, 357.
261 Contrary to most of his contemporaries Vico realized that in order to understand earlier stages of human history, the historian has to project himself back to that age, to "see the problems of those days through the eyes of the men then living". Toulmin & Goodfield 1965, 127.
262 Hampson 1981, 109–110. See also Coates, White & Schapiro 1966, 196.
263 Renan 1922, 27. See also Gossman 1972, 121.
264 Outram 1995, 78–79.

Mercier's case this is especially true; he had no capacity to understand cultural or racial diversity. This shows clearly in his vision that in 2440 the enslavement of African peoples has ended, and that the apostles of reason and arts have transported their inventions and enlightenment amongst these peoples, corrupted by the "most terrible despotism". He calls this process a "*belle conquête*",[265] reflecting the well-meaning intentions of the European conquerors in their relation to the native peoples.

Mercier thus believed that the natives had to be "saved" from the obscurity of ignorance, superstition and barbarism. According to this patronizing attitude, without the contribution of European civilization, science and philosophy, they would have remained forever beyond the scope of reason. The suggestion is that natives are like children (or women) who have to be restored under rational (masculine) control. This patronizing view of the natives is compatible with the conclusions drawn in Chapter VI, pp. 182–187 above: despite the fact that Mercier echoes, in particular in *L'Homme sauvage*, the fashionable cult of the "noble savage", in his case the admiration of the primitive life was restricted, in the final resort, within rather narrow limits.

There are good grounds to believe that the "beautiful conquest" which Mercier speaks about, was, for the most part at least, an ideal construction. It is to be presumed that in reality the motives of the white conquerors would not be as disinterested as Mercier wished them to be. The term "beautiful conquest" is reminiscent of what Mary Louise Pratt refers to by the term *anti-conquest*: an innocent vision of European global authority created in the eighteenth and nineteenth centuries, basically utopian by nature. In this framework the systematizing of nature represented "not only a European discourse about non-European worlds, but an urban discourse about non-urban worlds, and a lettered, bourgeois discourse about non-lettered, peasant worlds".[266]

. . . .
265 Mercier, *L'An 2440 III* 1786, 7.
266 Pratt 1992, 34–35, 39.

IX Between Optimism and Pessimism

The Cycles of Life and Death: Progress through Destruction

Mercier's thinking also had a more pessimistic side, which seems to contradict his belief in the "best of possible worlds". It would be a grave misunderstanding to suppose that he was a naïve supporter of progress and continuous amelioration, with no sense of the tragic aspects of life. The pessimistic tones are not entirely absent even from *L'An 2440*. In the first pages of the novel Mercier alludes to man's transitory journey on earth, speaking about the successive chain of generations, which forms an uninterrupted continuity from the past through the present into the far future. He argues that the world has not been made solely for the small number of people who currently occupy the earth:

> "D'autres générations viendront occuper la place que nous occupons, elles paroîtront sur le même théâtre; elles verront le même soleil, et nous pousseront si avant dans l'antiquité qu'il ne restera de nous ni trace, ni vestige, ni mémoire."[1]

The above quoted words reflect the fact that Mercier was acutely aware of the fragility of human achievement and the less pleasant aspects of existence. The message is that time is a destructive force, which sweeps over mankind, changes them to a pile of dust and throws them into an eternal night of death.

In the chapter *"Histoire universelle"* of *L'An 2440* Mercier creates his own version of occidental history from ancient times to the potential future. Also in this context his view on the course of history emerges as basically pessimistic. Mercier relates how the ancient prospering empires were destroyed, wars and plague have sown death, America was subordinated by a handful of cruel and destructive people. It was not until Luther that the first sparks of philosophy were born. Without the progress of sciences, arts, and legislation mankind would not have been saved from total oblivion. He laments the rapidity of the passage of time, regretting how the memory of the empires vanishes like mankind; how often in its history mankind has been on the verge of total destruction, and not even science and printing can ensure the ultimate survival of the human race. Even the slightest physical convulsion can cut the file of knowledge and push the human mind back into obscurity. There exists even a possibility that the whole of Europe is annihilated from the surface of the earth

. . . .
1   Mercier, *L'An 2440 I* 1786, 3.

in some future time: "... tout est tombé, tout est englouti dans l'abîme du temps!"[2]

These are unexpected statements in a novel in which the basic philosophical thrust is to promote unlimited faith in Progress. Mercier's warning message seems to be that there could be setbacks in the march of progress at any moment, and the powers of darkness (ignorance, superstition, despotism) could await behind any corner, lurking in the shadows to destroy innocent victims.

It has been justly argued that in his utopia Mercier lays the foundations for the great battle between optimism and pessimism, and for example the introductory chapter ("*epitre dédicatoire*") of the novel gives the impression of restlessness.[3] One can scarcely deny this; despite the fact that Mercier imagines that he can divide his life into two, i.e., the unhappy contemporary reality and a future characterized by happiness and virtue,[4] he doubts if this optimistic wish can be realized except in dreams: "... je crains plutôt que ton soleil ne vienne un jour à luire tristement sur un informe amas de cendres et de ruines."[5]

As Mercier's words reveal, the tragic, "*romantique*" tension between the "ideal" and "real" is always present in his work; he was acutely aware about the fact that even if the power of imagination made it possible to reach the worlds of absolute beauty and perfection, the simultaneous recognition of the unrealistic nature of this dream of happiness could all too easily lead to frustration and melancholy. As Alkon has pointed out, Mercier's allusions to ruins, like his images of corpses and deserts, function as symbols of the desolation in the real world, thus underscoring the purely fictitious nature of his future Paris. He argues that the images of possible destruction in *L'An 2440* suggest that Mercier's optimistic dream should not be taken as a prediction, since the "destruction of civilization seems more likely to Mercier than its perfection".[6]

Mercier was not the sole thinker who experienced an inclination to melancholy and frustration in late eighteenth-century France. To claim that the eighteenth century was one-sidedly an optimistic age is only an tenacious myth, the fallacy of which has been pointed out for example by Peter Gay, who has aimed at demonstrating that the French philosophers were often pessimists with limited expectations. He criticizes the common image of them as "naïve optimists" or "cold rationalists", utopians without any sense of ambiguity or tragic aspects of life.[7] As a matter of fact, many philosophers of that epoch remained sceptical about the possibility of progress, estimating that one can not put confidence into evolution alone to ameliorate the human condition; in addition to this, the destiny of the world needed a serious push in order to be maintained in a right direction. The optimism was often modified by cyclical models.[8]

. . . .

2   Mercier, *L'An 2440 I* 1786, 221–266, especially 248.
3   Hudde 1978, 253.
4   Mercier, *L'An 2440 I* 1786, xij.
5   Mercier, *L'An 2440 I* 1786, xvj.
6   Alkon 1987, 124.
7   Gay 1964, 262–263, 270–271. For more detail, see Vyverberg 1958; Hawthorn 1976, 8–27.
8   Minois 1996, 427; Delon, Mauzi & Menant 1998, 81.

Lester Crocker reinforces this interpretation in arguing that the eighteenth-century Enlightenment knew also "the labyrinth of evil and disorder in man". It opened the consciousness of modern man to the fact that he was "lost among the stars, with no meaning to his existence except the meaning he creates."[9] The Scottish moral philosophers, such as David Hume and Adam Ferguson, assumed a skeptical attitude to progress,[10] and even the most optimistic thinkers, such as Condorcet[11], had their moments of doubt. As the Finnish scholar Matti Männikkö has observed, the identification of eighteenth-century thought exclusively with a strong belief in progress overlooks another essential strand of Western future-oriented thinking: the belief or fear that history is leading toward the end of the world, total destruction or a catastrophe. In other words, alongside the dream of future happiness there always lurks a simultaneous "fear of future evil" or a threatening image of a total destruction.[12]

Montesquieu's *Lettres persanes* provides a typical example of this pessimism of the century of light. Its author speculates on the reasons for the fact that the world is no more as peopled as it used to be. Is it so that the world is already reached its old age? How is it possible that nature has lost the prodigious fecundity of its first times? If this trend continues, Montesquieu argues, after the centuries the world would be reduced as a desert. Even the laws of movement, will eventually lose their force: "... que savons-nous si la terre entière n'a pas des causes générales, lentes et imperceptibles, de lassitude?"[13]

Similarly, Diderot's *Lettre sur les aveugles* (1749) breathes the same sentiment of frustration and the melancholy sentiment that the world is only a composite of revolutions, which have a continual tendency toward destruction:

> "Quelle suite prodigieuse de générations d'éphémères atteste votre éternité? quelle tradition immense? Cependant nous passerons tous, sans qu'on puisse assigner ni l'étendue réelle que nous occupions, ni le temps précis que nous aurons duré. Le temps, la matière et l'espace ne sont peut-être qu'un point."[14]

This pessimistic current which can be traced from Mercier's *L'An 2440*, from Montesquieu's *Lettres persanes* and from the above quoted treatise of Diderot, supports the suggestion of Hayden White that many among the eighteenth-century thinkers were contaminated by Rousseauist pessimism based on the sentiment of immediate decay and destruction.[15]

It is characteristic, also that the French literature of the eighteenth and nineteenth centuries is filled with anticipations related to the Apocalypse. This reads as a sign of a shift in the general atmosphere in a more pessimistic

. . . .

9   Crocker 1969, 30.
10   Nisbet 1970, 126–127.
11   Although Condorcet hoped for relief in the future, in the Tenth Epoch, even in the present, Ninth Epoch, he saw little to cheer him. See for example Gay 1964, 272.
12   Männikkö 1996, 145.
13   Montesquieu, *Lettres persanes II* 1894–1895, 81–87.
14   Diderot, *Oeuvres* 1951, 842.
15   White 1987, 56.

direction: there aroused a fear that modern cities might be threatened by a similar catastrophe which had confronted Pompeii. Works such as Mercier's *L'An 2440* or Cousin de Grainville's *Dernier Homme* offer prophetic images of the disappearance of the human race.[16] It is thus to be presumed that the historical pessimism of the age was spurred by the recognition of evil human actions, but also by natural catastrophes, such as volcanic eruptions and earthquakes. The Herculaneum and Pompeii were excavated in the mid-eighteenth century, and the traumatic memory of the Lisbon earthquake (1755) was still much alive.[17]

The pessimistic under-current of Mercier's view of the world finds its most grandiloquent manifestation in his visions of different kind of catastrophes. In particular the idea of the destruction of big cities like Paris fascinated him. Simon Schama, who calls Mercier a "connoisseur of catastrophe", observes that Paris was for Mercier at one and the same time "a rotting, oozing place of ordure, blood, cosmetics and death, and a kind of irrepressible, omnivorous organism". It was on this metropolis of money and death that Mercier declared war by imagining a vast, cosmic convulsion, a second Lisbon earthquake.[18]

Mercier develops further this fantastic theme concerning the possible destruction of Paris as well in *Tableau de Paris* as in one version of *L'An 2440* (the one published in 1785) under the rubric "*Que deviendra Paris*".[19] In it he refers, probably inspired by the contemporary archeological excavations, to the destruction of ancient powerful cities, suggesting that "les grands villes modernes éprouveront un jour la même révolution". He speculates on many possible causes for this potential destruction as follows:

> "Est-ce la guerre, est-ce la peste, est-ce la famine, est-ce un tremblement de terre, est-ce un inondation, est-ce un incendie, est-ce une révolution politique qui anéantira cette superbe ville? Ou plutôt plusieurs causes réunies opéreront-elles cette vaste destruction?"[20]

In the issue of "*Paris mort*", Mercier was the first to envision diverse possibilities for the disappearance of Paris. The sole alternative which he did not treat, was the divine punishment.[21] This was probably due to the reason that the vindicative idea of God would have been difficult to adjust with the theory of the "best of possible worlds", where everything was pre-ordained by a benevolent God for the supreme happiness of man.

. . . .

16   Roudaut 1990, 58–68, especially 66.
17   See for example Charlton 1984, 87.
18   Schama 1989, 198.
19   Despite the fact that Mercier himself denied vigorously the authentic value of this edition of his utopia, some parts of it, at least, can thus be attributed to him. The same text is comprised also in *Tableau de Paris*. Mercier, *Tableau de Paris I* 1994a, 979–985: Chapter CXXLV, "*Que deviendra Paris?*"
20   Mercier, *L'An 2440* 1785, 341; Mercier, *Tableau de Paris I* 1994a, 980.
21   Citron 1961, 123.

In the centuries characterized by general pessimism it had been a customary thing to regard the modern immorality as responsible for continuing decline,[22] and Mercier's social pessimism derived from this same source, i.e., from the sentiment of moral indignation. This made him to conclude that the greatest cause of destruction would, probably, be of human origin; Mercier was ensured that if the "repulsive opulence" continued to be channeled only to few hands, the situation would eventually become unsupportable. He thought that in addition to economic inequality the destruction might be exploded by "la poudre infernale, dont les magasins se sont multipliés sur-tout en Europe, & auxquelles une étincelle suffit pour tout dévorer".[23]

As Mercier's above quoted words reveal, he suspected, already, the dangers contained in the existence of artificial and scientific tools of extermination. He was convinced that in "ambitious and vengeful hands" the "infernal gunpowder" could become a thousand times more dangerous than the fire of volcanoes. Despite the fact that Mercier was not able to anticipate the misuse of technology in a large scale, he saw man as the severest threat for the future of the earth. He sensed that the scourges of nature could not support comparison with those that man had imagined for the destruction of cities.[24]

These statements testify clearly to the fact that Mercier was not prepared to give his unreserved support to the assumption that technological progress was solely a beneficial and good thing; progress and happiness were not necessarily one and the same thing, after all. The "new Prometheus" of technological power had to be kept in chains.

As it has already been observed many times in this study, Mercier saw in Paris of the *ancien régime* many things worth hating, to name the social and economic imbalance and the lack of social compassion toward the "suffering poor". Against this background it is easy to assume that he did not conceive the possible destruction of Paris as a purely negative and unfortunate event. Schama's notion that Mercier welcomed positively the doom of Paris and France as a catharsis, "terrible but necessary to cleanse the metropolis of the excesses of both riches and poverty", supports this kind of interpretation.[25]

Burton Pike draws a similar conclusion in examining the fantasies of destruction related to the cities: "The fascination people have always felt at the destruction of a city may be partly an expression of satisfaction at the destruction of an emblem of irresolvable conflict."[26] The same concerns also the conceptions related to the cosmic imaginary of the world's end, which has not been understood merely as a negative thing. It has often been associated with the belief that after the catastrophe a specific era of happiness would dawn

. . . .

22   Lowenthal 1986, 87.
23   Mercier, *L'An 2440* 1785, 432, 344; Mercier, *Tableau de Paris I* 1994a, 981, 983.
24   Mercier, *L'An 2440* 1785, 344–345; Mercier, *Tableau de Paris I* 1994a, 983; Macchia 1988, 371. See also Mercier's article *"Poudre a canon"* in *Mon bonnet de nuit*. In it he refers to gunpowder as a weapon of collective massacre, which has a power to destroy entire cities in one single moment. Mercier, *Mon bonnet de nuit II* 1784, 46.
25   Schama 1989, 198.
26   Pike 1981, 8.

for mankind. The fear of coming evil and the expectation of good have, thus, been interrelated from the beginning.[27]

The final scene of Mercier's utopia reveals better than anything else this thought that destruction may function as a catalysis, or a catharsis, for a better condition. As we have seen,[28] in it the time traveler arrives at Versailles, the ancient glory of which has turned into a mass of ruins. Sitting on a pile of ruins he meets the phantom of Louis XIV, who tells him that the place has collapsed by itself: .''..Que les monumens de l'orgueil sont fragiles!...''[29]

There is no doubt about the fact that Mercier felt, – to some extent perverse, perhaps, – pleasure from the thought of seeing the "modern Babylons", those "cities of seduction" , or the visible symbols of luxury and idleness like Versailles, turn to a pile of ruins. The images of horror, death and destruction, the *"beau horrible"*, as Majewski calls it, fascinated his pre-romantic imagination.[30] In Mercier's eyes the ruins were more beautiful than the monuments, and in this sense he anticipated the theories of the romantics.[31] The ruins were a visible symbol of the final disappearance of the emblems of rotten institutions invented by avaricious and selfish mind. This proves the general fact that instead of being satisfied by the ideal of "calm felicity", the romantic ideal of happiness can be equally well satisfied by pain and suffering.[32]

This tragic tension forms an important theme in Mercier's visionary thinking. Michel Delon remarks that as well in Mercier's as in Restif de la Bretonne's descriptions of Paris, the dialectics of shadow and light is at the same time dialectics of renovation and destruction. They were reclaiming a city, which would be open to sun and air, hoping for that the archaic houses and Bastille would collapse. At the same time they felt shiverings in thinking that one day Paris may, perhaps, be nothing but a pile of ruins. They were haunted by ruins as reminiscence of the fact that all is nothing but dust and that progress takes place through death. The idea of progress was still only feebly distinguished from the cycles of history devoted to repetition.[33]

Even the most devastating catastrophes, such as the earthquake of Lisbon, which made for example Voltaire to re-examine his famous axiom *"Tous est bien"* in his poem on the disaster of Lisbon,[34] did not change Mercier's confidence in great revolutions which modify the sense of history; he did not hesitate to admit the political, physical and social advantages which the earthquake had provoked in the life of the capital of Portugal. In his opinion it

. . . .

27 Männikkö 1996, 149.
28 See Chapter V, p. 109.
29 Mercier, *L'An 2440 III* 1786, 206.
30 Majewski 1971, 39–40.
31 Citron 1961, 128.
32 Telfer 1980, 97.
33 Delon 1990, XVI.
34 The earthquake of Lisbon of 1755, which demanded thousands of human lives (for a more detailed analysis, see for example Salmi 1996, 26–30) gave a severe blow to the optimistic idea that everything in nature was pre-ordained for the sole purpose of terrestrial happiness. It is a well known fact that for example in Voltaire the disaster of Lisbon started a philosophical and moral crisis: his perception of wickedness changed. Baczko 1997, 20.

was just the disaster which set the country into the way of reforms. Mercier was not concerned about the victims but about those who came after.[35]

This testifies in its part to the fact that Mercier was willing to see even death as a positive source of change. It is easy to argue that this sort of forced optimism lacked, occasionally, reasonable grounds; did Mercier sincerely believe that the death of thousands of innocent people would be a positive thing? It is to be presumed that for Mercier, who wanted to see world through the lenses of Leibnizian optimism, even this kind of reasoning caused no difficulties. In the "best of possible worlds" even the worst things contributed in the last resort to man's supreme happiness and everything found eventually its justification.

Visions of different kinds of catastrophes have been characteristic for all important periods of crisis. As breakers of the course of life, the catastrophes have been experienced both as natural and historical turning points, as watersheds between past and future. They have given birth to fantasies of fear; the end of history and death are themes which inevitably emerge. Catastrophes, such as earthquakes or volcanic eruptions, have through human history been interpreted as metaphysical signs, as supernatural punishments, even as omens of the final destruction. Yet in the eighteenth century it was generally thought that the calamities are not merely accidental occurrences prompted by nature, which come and go, but that they have a secret logic of their own. They were seen as reminiscences of the perishableness of all things and of the fact that in the final resort, everything was solved by God.[36]

Also Mercier's catastrophic visions mirror the sentiments of a period of transition characterized by a simultaneous sentiment of fear and hope. Pierre Citron remarks that during the French Revolution, when the Parisians felt themselves to be in constant danger, it was a very common thing to imagine the destruction of Paris.[37] The years preceding the revolution were a period of great revival of catastrophic thinking in general, and it became customary to create fantasies of the death of the whole universe. Despair was as fashionable as optimism.[38] Also the revival of the pre-romantic myth of the end of the world reflected the sentiments of decadence and political disorder.[39]

According to Mircea Eliade the myths of the end of the world express the archaic idea that the progressive "degradation" of the Cosmos makes necessary its periodical recreation.[40] This pattern of destruction and renovation, characteristic in particular for mythical thinking, is compatible with the cyclical conception of time.[41] In archaic mentality the great catastrophes have often

. . . .
35   Macchia 1988, 372–373.
36   Salmi 1996, 24–26.
37   Citron 1961, 145.
38   Sambrook 1966, 26.
39   Majewski 1971, 29.
40   Eliade 1963, 78.
41   See for example Männikkö 1996, 147.

been conceived as obligatory consequences of great sins, often collective. The religious signification of the deluge follows this pattern; the disappearance of the world into water was a sort of return to chaos, and a necessary condition for the renewal of the world. The sins have, thus, a purifying character.[42] This reminds also of the important role which water has in Mercier's utopian city as a symbol of purity.

In its purest form the view of a cyclical return of catastrophes is met in the stoic philosophy, maintained by the idea of a repetitive end of the world. The stoics believed that the population would periodically disappear through a cataclysm – deluge or general conflagration –, from the surface of the earth. According to stoicism, the whole universe was in a constant circulation and consisted of successive and long-lasting cycles, distinguished by a cosmic catastrophe. After the disaster the universe would be reborn and go through similar phases of history as the previous cycle. It was also generally believed that the end phase of the cycle would be a time of moral degeneration, whereas the beginning was a time of virtue and happiness. The intermediary catastrophe would thus function as a purifying force, a kind of catharsis.[43]

In one of his unpublished manuscripts, entitled "*Reflexions antiques et philosophiques sur les six premiers chapitres de la Génèse et sur le Déluge universel*", Mercier revives this ancient theme of deluge. Also in this context he invokes the possible destruction of nations and the disappearance of arts and sciences. The image of disaster is associated with the passage of time, which is totally indifferent in regard to human aspirations: "Le temps effacera, jusqu'à leurs moindres traces, les monumens que les hommes de génie élevent."[44]

Even in this peculiar manuscript Mercier does not, however, totally exclude the possibility that after the corrupted nations have disappeared from the surface of the earth, there remains a little group of people, which has survived general destruction; it may be that these individuals gather a small community around themselves.[45] The final impression is not entirely pessimistic, because the catastrophe helps the human species in its battle of survival. There is a certain sort of utopia rising from the ashes of cosmic convulsion, and once again progress takes place through destruction.

In Mercier's catastrophic visions the destruction is not always based on the idea of cyclical repetition. At least equally often it is final, totally "infernal" and exterminatory. Berthier has paid attention to the fact that Mercier was haunted

. . . .

42 Neyton 1984, 80–84.
43 Cazes 1986, 42; Männikkö 1996, 148–149.
44 Bibliothèque de l'Arsenal, Fonds Mercier, Ms. 15086(b), ff. 53–55.
45 Bibliothèque de l'Arsenal, Fonds Mercier, Ms. 15086(b), ff. 57–60. The survivors constituting a new "micro-society" in Mercier's manuscript recall the romantic theme centred around the notion of a "last man." Jean-Baptiste Grainville's novel *Le Dernier Homme* (1805) was the masterpiece of this "school of death." In Grainville's story the "last man", Omégare, arrives in Paris which has changed to a desert, "the place of silence and death". See for example Macchia 1988, 375. Grainville's novel completes the eighteenth-Century romantic myth of total annihilation. The same theme is repeated also for example in Byron's poem "*Darkness*" and in Mary Shelley's novel *The Last Man* (1826). Sambrook 1966, 28, 31. For more details, see Alkon 1987, 158–191.

by the theme of the Last Judgment,[46] and in the story named as "*Songe 35*" of *Songes d'un Hermite* Mercier asserts this himself:

> "Je venois de lire attentivement les visions mystérieuses de Saint Jean, connues sous le nom d'Apocalypse & ces étonnantes révélations m'avoient vivement frappé... & je crus vois en songe la destruction du genre humain."[47]

Many of Mercier's images related to different sort of catastrophes owe a lot to the biblical prophecies, in particular those of the Revelation to St. John. His vision of the world's end and of the final destruction of humanity is expressed in an exemplary manner in an allegory telling of a giant, which is enslaving the whole universe under its demonic power. The hands of this promethean figure, spitting fire from its nostrils, are said to be made of bronze, its arms are pillars of fire, its feet form the basis of volcanoes, its heart is of steel and eyes of lead: " ... il jette un cri, ce cri menace le monde d'une prochaine destruction."[48] In Mercier's vision of a giant throwing flames from its nostrils can be seen hidden symbolism; the flames function as a symbol of cosmic fire, which will eradicate the evil from the world in order that a new order of things could dawn. It is easy to note that Mercier's allegory has many points of contact with the Old Testament's story of the dream of Nebuchadnezzar, which Daniel explains to the emperor.[49]

The convulsions of nature form a dramatic stage in Mercier's nightmarish visions of the world's end and of the universal destruction of humanity. In his allegorical fantasy-world and doomsday prophecies the tombs open not to receive the dead but the living, the sun is darkening, the stars are falling and extinguished, the planets are losing their positions, a comet sends a storm of fire on the earth. The following long extract from *Songes et visions philosophiques* gives a good image of the treatment of this issue:

> "... le bouleversement s'étend jusqu'aux confins de l'univers; la mort, aux aîles ténebreuses, plane dans l'immensité des airs; les ossemens de la race humaine sont blanchis, les corps célestes percés à jour, n'offrent plus qu'une pierre dure, & calcinée: le fantôme despotique, tenant le sceptre de la violence, élève sa tête par-dessus les nuages: que je lise le nom de cet être redoutable, il est gravé sur son front, les caractères en sont ineffacables; je m'approche en tremblant, je baisse la tête & je lis: La Nécéssité!"[50]

. . . .

46 Berthier 1977, 304.
47 Mercier, *Les Songes d'un hermite* 1788b, 392.
48 Mercier, *Songes et visions philosophiques* 1788a, 291.
49 The Book of Daniel has through the centuries been tirelessly commented in particular by the millenarian thinkers. In this story it is told about a great statue with a golden head, arms and breast made of silver, feet of iron. See for example Delumeau 1995, 19–20. The theme of a great purifying destruction is represented in many texts of the Old Testament. The Apocalypse gives a detailed description of the destruction of a satanic world through celestial fire. After a great cosmic revolution the heavenly Jerusalem appears, Babylon the great is fallen and is utterly burned with fire. *The Holy Bible*, The Revelation to St. John, 17: 22. On the mutual relation between apocalyptic and revolutionary thinking, see Mucchielli 1960, 147–159.
50 Mercier, *Songes et visions philosophiques* 1788a, 291–292.

Mercier's allegory of "necessity", incarnated in the figure of a giant, reflects a desperate sentiment that the "laws of nature" were not, perhaps, so "benevolent" as the most optimistic thinkers of this "century of light" were willing to presume. As a vision of a final and irrevocable catastrophe it mirrors the total disappearance of hope. There was nothing man could do in order to regulate this process, however disastrous its effects on his happiness or future destiny may be.

A. J. Sambrook suggests that pessimistically necessitarian philosophical notions formed the basis of Mercier's "suicidal mood".[51] In Mercier's mind the concept of Necessity, – or Fatality –, was associated with a belief in historical determinism. He applied it to different sort of phenomena from nature's "revolutions" to the inevitable march of historical events.[52]

In Mercier's writings the fatalistic attitude is not always expressed as violent and passionate outbursts of total hopelessness and desperation. It can equally well assume the form of a kind of "soft melancholy", silent frustration or mournful contentment with one's lot. Especially one of Mercier's essays, named "*Mélancolie*", provides a perfect example of this sentiment of vanity and fragility of human life, the merciless flow of time, after which nothing remains to be remembered by the future generations:

> "Qu'est-ce que le monde? il flotte au milieu de l'abime muet de l'éternité rien n'existe, car tout passe: la vie n'est que la mort sous un autre nom: la destruction est à côté de tout ce qui se meut, une consomption lente, mais toujours agissante, mine le grand Tout de la nature: tout s'efface, tout meurt."[53]

According to Mauzi the "*mal de vivre*" was not unknown in the eighteenth century, and the illnesses of the soul assumed two major symptoms, boredom and restlessness. Also death began to fascinate imagination. Mauzi regards these different forms of malaise of the soul as a sign of a profound crisis.[54] Mercier's "*Mélancolie*" has been named as an important text announcing romanticism, and it has been claimed to contain all the basic symptoms which are typically related to the "*mal de vivre*".[55] It is saturated with the sentiment of profound frustration and rootlessness, prompted by the breaking down of the traditional value structures. The narrator experiences restlessness, the origin of which remains obscure even to himself: "... mais le mal inconnu qui mine mon existence, détruit aussi les facultés de mon ame..."[56] As so often with the more somber visions of Mercier, also in "*Mélancolie*" the only certain thing in the precarious world is the passage of time and oblivion as its consequence: "... que verront les générations futures quand ils n'existera plus rien de nous: pourquoi,

. . . .

51   Sambrook 1966, 28.
52   Patterson 1960, 106, 108.
53   Mercier, *Mon bonnet de nuit III* 1786a, 157.
54   Mauzi 1994, 22–28, passim.
55   Eggli 1922, 258–267.
56   Mercier, *Mon bonnet de nuit III* 1786a, 157.

ai-je poursuivi la renommée, lorsque, j'étois né pour passer si rapidement sur la terre?"[57]

One of the best examples of the eighteenth-century's "*mal de vivre*" is provided in Bernardin de Saint-Pierre's novel *Paul et Virginie* (1788), in which the wilderness of the natural landscape supports the unhappy lot of the main characters. It exemplifies the mournful sentimentality on the eve of the revolution in a most sweeping manner:

> "Nul depuis vous n'a osé cultivé cette terre désolée... "Vos chèvres sont devenues sauvages; vos vergers sont détruits; vos oiseaux sont enfuis, et on n'entend plus que les cris des éperviers qui volent en rond au haut de ce bassin de rochers."[58]

After the French Revolution the pessimistic mood started to prevail even further. The general sentiment of destruction led to a certainty that the end of the world would occur in 1800. Belief in benevolent Providence was now replaced by the awareness of the unpredictable precariousness of the universe, influenced by Diderot's materialistic theories concerning the dynamic and organic view of nature's flux.[59] Major values seemed now to be in process of corruption, and after the Revolution opinions diverged greatly on the significance of the social and political convulsion; whereas for some it had meant a beginning of a new and better life, for the others it was totally unacceptable and beyond human comprehension.[60] Many, who had laid optimistically their confidence on the hope that the revolution would have had a power to change the unjust social and political structures as a condition of general happiness and prosperity, faced a profound disappointment when they were forced to admit that instead of justifying their belief in the perfectibility of the human race, it turned out to be a blind force of destruction that seemed to threaten the very existence of European civilization.[61]

Does this change of mentality have any effect whatsoever on Mercier's conception of happiness? Was he equally confident of man's glorious future after 1789 as before it? The edition of *L'An 2440* published after the revolution does not give an explicit answer to this question. This can quite naturally be explained by the fact that the basic text has remained the same from the edition of 1786 to that of 1799, as Mercier himself asserts in the "new preliminary discourse" of his work. This important addition reveals, however, Mercier's eagerness to withdraw from all responsibility for the massacre.[62]

Before the revolutionary action had turned into spectacles of unchecked massacre, Mercier had been willing to praise the year 1789 as a "unique and honorable year". In a brief treatise of only some pages, entitled "*Adieu à*

. . . .

57   Ibid., 159.
58   Saint-Pierre, *Paul et Virginie* 1996, 123.
59   Majewski 1971, 31–32.
60   Hampson 1989, 239. See also Nisbet 1970, 130–131.
61   Dawson 1929, 195–196.
62   See Chapter VIII, p. 241.

l'année 1789" he is pleased to remark that the accumulated miseries had been repaired in only some months. In his view the Declaration of Man and Citizen had "abolished the veil, which had until then hidden the truth".[63]

Le Nouveau Paris (1799), written after the outburst of Revolution, provides the most detailed picture of the growth of Mercier's personal anger and frustration after the sanguinary actions. Even the more moderate wing of the revolutionaries that constituted by the Girondists, which Mercier had previously supported himself, are no more spared from the flow of accusations. Mercier vituperates that the Republic is surrounded by "worms", and many crimes have been committed in the name of the Revolution. He complains also that after the Revolution luxury is prospering as ever; nothing has really changed for the better.[64]

Thus then, as Rufi also remarks, after the Revolution Mercier's confidence in Reason was no more as strong as "before the Apocalypse". He began to feel more and more attraction toward the mysteries, reacting against the rationalism, the *"philosophisme"*, which had "engendered the monster".[65] Denoit draws a similar conclusion in observing that a certain change of opinion can be traced already when one compares the different versions of *L'An 2440*; Mercier's view on progress has changed into a more pessimistic direction from the edition of 1770 to that published in 1786, and the edition of 1786 contains criticism directed against the idea of progress. This is to say that whereas in the first edition of the novel Mercier speaks on behalf of patience, in the edition of 1786 more emphasis is put on the dangers of waiting; the suggestion is that unpredicted, the revolution would be uncontrollable.[66]

The increase of Mercier's personal disillusionment reflects a general disbelief in the omnipotence of reason. In the Revolutionary period the concept of reason itself entered a state of crisis. The immediate cause was recognition of the impotence of reason, which had been elevated as an autonomous, authoritarian "court of appeal", in the face of violent revolution. Those who had put their faith in the omnipotency of immutable reason were now forced to admit that it could not provide any valid justification for the massacre. The "Goddess of Reason" had changed into an arbitrary distributor of faceless destruction.[67]

Despite the increase of pessimism, in Mercier's case the idea of historical determinism seemed, nevertheless, to offer the ultimate justification for the Revolution, which of all revolutions, to use his own expression, was "the most legitimate".[68] He returns to these necessitarian notions in the last pages of his utopia; after have awakened back to his own time, the narrator of the novel speculates on the issue, if the public felicity was only a vain name, if wishes had

. . . .

63   Mercier, *Adieux à l'année 1789* [s.a.], 1–3.
64   Mercier, *Le Nouveau Paris* 1994b, 9–27, *"Avant-propos"*.
65   Rufi 1995, 6.
66   Denoit 1989b, 2032–2033.
67   Windsor 1990, 27.
68   Mercier, *Le Nouveau Paris* 1994b, 36.

any power. The final conclusion seems not to be totally pessimistic, because "il faut brûler les vieilles forêts pour épurer l'atmosphère".[69] By thus saying Mercier seems to give a certain justification for the revolutionary violence. The suggestion is that only a total destruction would be efficient enough to thoroughly annihilate the vicious customs, laws and practises from the surface of the earth.

There is a continuous antagonistic tension between optimism and pessimism, which can be traced throughout Mercier's major texts. As Majewski sees it, it is just this romantic tension, which exists in the heart of Mercier's life and work and makes him the "fascinating man of paradoxes incomprehensible to his contemporaries."[70] This dual character of Mercier was noted already by Béclard, who writes that Mercier gave often an impression of being in contradiction with himself, because he reconciled in his consciousness two faculties which seemed to exclude one another.[71] This "paradox" was not, however, peculiar for Mercier alone. The simultaneous sentiments of optimism and pessimism characterize the whole eighteenth century. The observation of Hermann Hofer that Mercier helps us better to understand the nature of an "epoch of transition",[72] illustrates this clearly.

The simultaneous existence of darkness and light even in Mercier's most optimistic works like *L'An 2440* reveals how misleading it would be to claim that the first half of the eighteenth century was a period dominated one-sidedly by reason, the latter one by sentiment. Despite the fact that there are visible signs of the increase of frustration and melancholy in Mercier's writings produced toward the end of the century, the antagonism between the belief in the power of cold reason and sentimental awareness of the precariousness and vanity of existence is not totally absent even from the first edition of *L'An 2440*.

Past – A Time of Happiness or Corruption?

The Burden of the Past

One thread of Mercier's pessimism was founded on his devaluation of the past.[73] In particular, in *L'An 2440* he assumes an extremely pejorative attitude toward the historical past, and because for Mercier's imaginary future Frenchmen history is described as a "shame for humanity", the schools of 2440 reserve little place for the teaching of history. Every page of history is full of crimes and madness,[74] sounds Mercier's verdict.

Mercier did not believe that one could learn from history:

. . . .

69   Mercier, *L'An 2440 III* 1786, 210.
70   Majewski 1971, 17–18.
71   Béclard 1903, 27.
72   Hofer 1977b, 8–9. See also Denoit 1989a, 1626.
73   Lapouge 1978, 236; Elliott 1982, 475.
74   Mercier, *L'An 2440 I* 1786, 84.

"En vain dira-t-on que l'histoire fournit des exemples qui peuvent instruire les siècles suivans; exemples pernicieux et pervers, qui ne servent qu'à enseigner le despotisme..."[75]

He repeats this view in his *Portraits des rois de France*, which is a five-volume description of the barbarian conquests and massacres executed in the course of the centuries, arguing that the history of our ancestors can help to understand what the passions of the great can bring about.[76] The sole purpose that Mercier accords to history is the fact that it can instruct by providing warning examples:

"Ainsi l'exemple du passé doit effrayer sur le présent, et inspirer aux administrateurs des Etats une crainte salutaire qui les engage à former des citoyens au lieu de marionettes disciplinées."[77]

Mercier's pessimism that the past could no more offer positive examples to be imitated, illustrates Koselleck's argument that until the eighteenth century it was customary to believe that there existed a close symmetry between past and future, and that one could, from the history of the past, learn lessons for the future. The past could only be experienced insofar as it contained an element of that which was to come, and the temporal structure was understood as a kind of "static movement". The new temporal horizon, on the contrary, was no more construed on the basis of analogy, since the singularity of events knew no iterability: "Progress opened up a future that transcended the hitherto predictable, natural space of time and experience and provoked new, transnatural, and long-term prognosis. This being the case, conclusions drawn from the past about the future not only seemed out of place but also appeared impossible. One could no more learn from history."[78]

Mercier's repudiation of the value of the past reads as a symbolic attack against the traditional centers of power. By denying the past he at the same time denies the legitimacy of absolutism and the tradition which was incorporated in the image of the ruling monarch. This attitude can be described by the term "death of the past", launched by J.B. Plumb, which characterizes, above all, industrial societies, which no longer need the past owing to the fact that they are mentally oriented toward change rather than conservation. The past becomes, therefore, a matter of nostalgia. In previous times the past was needed to strengthen the position of those who possessed power; it was a "huge catalogue of examples", which people used as a guide, believing that by studying the past they could predict the future.[79]

In the chapter "*La Bibliothèque du Roi*" of *L'An 2440*, Mercier develops further his idea that the past is merely a shame and burden to subsequent

. . . .

75   Mercier, *L'An 2440 I* 1786, 85–86.
76   Mercier, *Portraits des rois de France* 1783, "*Avertissement*".
77   Mercier, *L'An 2440 I* 1786, 258. This statement contains a certain irony; Mercier does not seem to realize that the attribute "disciplined marionettes" describes, as a matter of fact, his utopians living in Paris of the twenty-fifth century.
78   Koselleck 1985, 17, 56–57, 114. See also Viikari 1995, 357.
79   Plumb 1969, 14–15, 27, 31, 45, 60–62.

generations. Here the time traveler pays a visit to the royal library of the twenty-fifth century, and is surprised to find that it contains only a small cabinet. He is told that most books have been burnt by voluntary decision. This is explained by reasons which could easily be interpreted as an aversion toward literature itself:[80]

> "Le temps n'a voituré jusqu'à nous que les choses légères et brillantes qui ont eu l'approbation de la multitude, tandis qu'il a englouti les pensées mâles et fortes qui étoient trop simples ou trop élevées pour plaire au vulgaire."[81]

Despite the fact that eighteenth-century France witnessed a great interest in history in the sense that extensive efforts were made to understand the "sense" of historical development, it is commonly labeled as a typically "anti-historical" century.[82] Many of Mercier's contemporary writers shared his pejorative attitude toward the value of the past and everything that it had to offer. Norman Hampson writes that from the viewpoint of the Enlightenment the story of the past was an educative manual, in which reason struggled with ignorance and superstition.[83] The philosophers were united by the common practise of turning history into propaganda; Leopold von Ranke's (1795–1886) dictum, that "all epochs are equally close to God", was still beyond their comprehension.[84]

For many eighteenth-century philosophers history was either "entertainment or an ugly spectacle of human vice", as Fritzie P. Manuel puts it. As they viewed it, it was difficult to discern any philosophical sense in acts whose motivation was either bestial passion or cruel necessity.[85] Even if the classical past was regarded as a storehouse of glorious achievements, the historical past was seen as a "tragic pile of error and crime, to be studied for mistakes to avoid and injustices to repair, not for models to imitate".[86] Turgot expresses this typically pessimistic view, shared by Mercier and many of his contemporaries, as

· · · · · · · · ·

80 In his analysis devoted to this chapter of Mercier's utopia Enrico Rufi suggests that Mercier did not mean the burning of books to be taken seriously (for a closer analysis, see Rufi 1995, 119–129). Rufi's view is acceptable when one holds in mind the great value that Mercier conferred to literature and its producers. Against this background it is hardly probable that he would have been pleased to see this kind of destructive operation executed in practise. Also in this context fire has, above all, a purifying function to play as a metaphor referring to a destruction of the principle of evil. On the other hand, as it has been pointed out previously in this study, Mercier had a rather limited conception of what is "good", i.e., morally righteous, literature; from this it can be concluded that it would not have been such a great surprise, if he had wished to see his proposition to turn from a theoretical possibility into a practical solution.
81 Mercier, *L'An 2440 I* 1786, 324. See also Chapter CXCIV, "*Bibliothèque du roi*" in *Tableau de Paris*, where Mercier promotes a view, that only few useful books have been written in the world. Mercier, *Tableau de Paris I* 1994a, 479–482. This line of argumentation is consistent with Mercier's above mentioned opinion that in order to be enlightened mankind needs only a few luminous ideas. See Chapter V, p. 118.
82 Cassirer 1966, 263–303, passim. On the eighteenth- century French philosophers' attitudes toward the past, see also for example Plumb 1969, 126–145.
83 Hampson 1981, 236.
84 Gay 1964, 274.
85 Manuel 1959, 152–153.
86 Gay 1970, 92. See also Le Goff 1992, 161.

follows: "J'y cherche le progrès de l'esprit humain, et je n'y vois presque autre chose que l'histoire de ses erreurs."[87]

Most creators of utopian societies have shared a similar hostility toward the historical past. To paraphrase the ideas of Lapouge, this negative attitude stems from the same desire of rationalization and categorization as the natural historian's desire to classify, to abolish natural categories in order that artificial categories could be created. The aim of the utopianists is to repair the miseries of history.[88] The same chain of reasoning can also be traced from the background of Mercier's rejection of the past; by emphasizing in his utopia all the mischiefs and abuses accumulated during the centuries of the past, he seems to imply that the hazardous and unpredictable course of historical evolution cannot be controlled except by totally denying it authentic value.

Owing to their hostility toward historical evolution, utopianists have always confronted the same dilemma: how to explain in a convincing way the process which has produced the transformation from imperfect historical reality to their imaginary ideal, i.e., from unhappiness to happiness? The most common way has been to ignore the description of the intermediary phases and analyze only cursorily – if at all – the process which has led to the utopian situation. Utopia has no history.[89]

The utopian fashion to repudiate the value of the historical past constitutes one element of the basically static character of most utopias. They are born to resist change. As Bronislaw Baczko formulates it, the time of utopian societies, even when they are not situated on islands, is insular time, withdrawn within itself. This reads as an attempt to liberate the ideal society from its past. Within a new society the utopias aim at inaugurating *another history*.[90] To be more precise, utopias are not anti-historical but *meta-historical*, which is the term used by Mucchielli. By this he refers to the fact that utopias exist in the "heaven of platonic ideas", beyond time because they do not alter.[91] The ideal of a kind of "timeless time" can be found in the background of all constructions of ideal worlds.[92]

In classical utopias such as Plato's *Republic* or More's *Utopia*, the contradiction between historical time and insular time is extremely sharp. In these utopias a topographic rupture marks equally a rupture in time, since the imaginary land has not known "our" history. Thus the narrator often has great difficulties to explain to the utopians the march of his own history, for example religious wars and their causes. In the structure of the story, time assumes a double function of assuring both the continuity and the rupture between "the time in utopia" and "the time of real history". Spatial utopias are not, however, devoid of all references to history. The "real" history – that of the narrator and

. . . .

87   Turgot, *Oeuvres de Turgot II* 1844, 600.
88   Lapouge 1978, 213–221, passim.
89   Cioranescu 1972, 35.
90   Baczko 1974, 478, 483.
91   Mucchielli 1960, 100.
92   Rifkin 1989, 146.

readers – is present in a negative manner, through its absence. Utopians have succeeded to escape this history, and it is for precisely this reason that they have not known our evils, vices, and injustices.[93]

One is rather surprised to note that despite the fact that in Mercier's utopia the "time of utopia" and the "real time" form two successive points in one and the same historical continuum, no higher value is accorded to the historical past than in the classical "magic island" utopias. It appears rather paradoxical that a novel which pretends to draw its supreme inspiration from the theory of progress almost totally lacks references to its historical evolution, and the rare mentions are almost one-sidedly pejorative. As an utopian writer Mercier is no exception to the general rule; he does not seem to be at all interested in the successive phases which have led to his ideal city of the future. Instead of giving a detailed description about the nature of the evolutionary stages that have finally led to the ideal conditions of 2440, Mercier contents himself with telling – in a rather vague and uncertain manner – that this "happy revolution" is the result of successful co-operation between monarchs and philosophers.[94]

Amongst utopian writers Etienne Cabet (1788–1856) was the first who did not use the direct approach, like Mercier, but attempts to sketch a possible course of development for the future indirectly, in his communist utopia *Le Voyage en Icarie* (1840). Cabet's novelty lies in the fact that he takes full account, for the first time in the history of utopian planning, of the transition in time, from present to future.[95] In practise this means that Cabet explains that Icarie, this land of prodigies and marvels which has remained unknown until recent times, was for a long time oppressed by tyrannical kings and aristocrats, and during many centuries it had been a battleground of conflicting interests between the poor and the rich. After the last despot was killed about sixty years previously and his son banished, the people chose a new ruler, the good and courageous Icarie, and their time of happiness began.[96]

As indicated above, *L'An 2440* provides ample evidence that Mercier was not able to realize that people's basic ideals of life might change as the centuries pass. In his vision of the future the processual nature of history does not yet hint at the possibility that there could occur a profound change in the level of mental structures. This is due to the fact that for Mercier such concepts as "reason" or the "law of nature" still constituted *a priori* categories, immutable in all cultures and epochs.

The rather one-dimensional worldview prevailing amongst the majority of Enlightenment thinkers, based on their quest for eternally valid truths about society, led them to judge all previous ages by the standards of eighteenth-century French civilization. It was far from simple, however, to insist that the

. . . .

93 Baczko 1974, 474–475.
94 See also Collier 1990, 98.
95 Polak 1961, 302–304.
96 Cabet, *Voyage en Icarie* 1842, 2–3, 39–40.

world was governed by a few immutable and generally applicable rules, and at the same time to recognize that everything was in a state of constant flux. Cassirer notes that for example Voltaire, an enthusiastic prophet of progress, was acutely aware of this dilemma: How could one reconcile the belief in the progress of humanity with the conviction that humanity has always remained fundamentally the same; that its "real" nature has not been changed?[97]

Against this background it is easy to subscribe to the thesis of George G. Iggers that "from the historical perspective the idea of progress represented a distortion of the past. Instead of comprehending the past in its own terms, the idea of progress viewed the past philosophically as a stepping stone to an end result. It thus reduced history as a scheme which violated the individuality and diversity of the past."[98]

The temporal structure of *L'An 2440* provides an illustrative example of this paradox still characterizing historical thought in the final years of the eighteenth century. The novel reveals the inner conflict caused by Mercier's strictly teleological idea of progress, founded on the assumption of the immutability of reason, combined with a simultaneous belief in a continuous change for the better. In the framework of the utopia, everything which does not fit easily into the pre-determined vision of progress is rejected. For this reason there exists an irretrievable conflict between two different views of the world: a collision between a static and a dynamic vision.

Mercier's repudiation of the authenticity of the past falsifies the progressive vision of *L'An 2440*, since it creates insurmountable difficulties in convincingly explaining the nature of the intermediary phases from the unhappiness of the past to the prosperity and general well-being in the future; it is a painful task to illuminate the gradual ascent from misery to perfection when nothing honorable is credited to the past.

Mercier does not seem to realize that the passage of time forms an uninterrupted continuum, and the expectations of the future always arise from premises posed by the present moment, which, correspondingly, is molded by its own past. As argued in the introductory chapter of this study, this assumption about the processual nature of progress "from the past through the present toward the future" is contained in the classical definitions of the modern idea of progress, for example in that formulated by Nisbet, who names belief in the value of the past as one of the major premises when one speaks about progress.[99] Strictly speaking, therefore, Mercier's vision does not fulfil the criteria of progress at all.

Hayden White has drawn attention to a similar contradiction embedded in the thinking of most eighteenth-century philosophers. He traces a certain paradox in the fact that they readily rejected everything inherited from the past as shameful and irrational, simultaneously, however, believing in the existence of a

. . . .

97   Cassirer 1966, 287.
98   Iggers 1982, 41
99   Nisbet 1980, 317. Cf. Kenyon 1982, 150–151.

rational order of nature. The latter idea was founded on a premise that there had once existed "natural", "primordial" man, who had been as rational as the whole of nature. From this viewpoint, it was difficult to understand how men's rational capacity had increased in the course of times from the "irrational" flow of history; and how could it be convincingly explained that the historical past had nothing to offer but manifestations of passions, ignorance and irrationality, considering that man, as a part of nature, was considered to be basically equally rational as the order of nature itself? The escape from this dilemma was provided by the argument that men had lost their original rationality because of their ignorance, caused by society with its "unreasonal" practises. In consequence, progress was now identified with a gradual revelation of the original rationality which lay behind rotten social arrangements. In other words, the logic of history should not be sought so much from the increase of reason out of unreason, but from the reason which had once existed before the passions, ignorance and superstitions had made their entrance into the world.[100]

A certain uninterrupted and logical continuum could thus be discerned through the apparent "insanity" of history, after all. The idea of a primitive condition when people were as rational as nature itself, but which had since been broken because of man's Fall, did not disturb the assumption of man's original goodness. In relation to this, one of the common ideas among eighteenth-century philosophers was to refer to the "subterranean" nature of progress in certain historical epochs. Nisbet suggests that they were fascinated by the idea that beneath the crimes and follies of history there was a deep current of "natural progress", which had only to be freed of superstition and tyranny. The idea that progress was a natural tendency in human history was compatible with the belief that there existed a "natural order".[101] Especially the Middle Ages were now condemned as a period characterized by despotism and barbarism, which had temporarily hindered the "natural march" of progress.[102]

Similar pattern can also be traced from *L'An 2440*. Mercier's belief in man's original goodness formed the basis of his conviction that if there were miseries and corruption in the world, it was not man's own fault. Man was not "unreasonable" by nature, since he was born with an inner moral instinct which told him what is right and what is wrong. In other words, it was the vicious and corrupted political and religious institutions which were responsible for all that had gone wrong. This did not, however, necessarily exclude the vague possibility that man could some day return into his original state of mythical happiness, where the "ideal" and "spleen", utopia and reality, had presumably once been merged in one harmonious whole.

. . . .

100 White 1987, 63.
101 Nisbet 1970, 116–117.
102 Passmore 1972, 200; Cazes 1986, 57–58; Le Goff 1992, 149; Delon, Mauzi & Menant 1998, 100.

A Return to the Dream Time

The hope that in some remote future people could live happily has throughout the centuries been closely linked with the conviction that this blissful state could be achieved if people were able to return to some previous condition, some Golden Age. The idea of a return has been always closely related to the assumption that the world is in a state of inevitable decline and corruption, caused by Original Sin. The dream of a return to happier conditions before the Fall has been conceived in terms of a "revolution", as an arrival in a renovated "new Jerusalem".[103]

The assumption of some mythical state of original happiness, which people have since lost, was prevalent in particular in pre-modern ways of thought. According to the Greek myth of the "Golden Age" the world was in a state of inevitable degeneration: or, as the Stoics conceived it, human history was cyclical in character, progressing to a point at which it reaches its climax only in order to start again. This led to the idealization of the immutable as possessing a higher value than that which varies, and the prejudice against change excluded belief in future progress. Belief was placed in the ideal of an absolute order of society, from which any deviation must be for the worse.[104]

The belief that ancient mankind had lived a happier life has been called "chronological primitivism".[105] The memory of the "Golden Age" has never totally disappeared, and it has been thought to have been miraculously conserved amongst the American savages.[106] It often occurred that the myth of the "Golden Age" and the idea of the "state of nature" were confounded. For example Rousseau describes in his discourse on the origin of inequality the supposed first phases of the human race, creating a picture of some very distant, mythic, "natural state", where mankind had lived in mutual happiness and harmony:

> "Les temps dont je vais parler sont bien éloignés. Combien tu as changé de ce que tu étais!.... "Il y a, je le sens, un âge auquel l'homme individuel voudrait s'arrêter; tu chercheras l'âge auquel tu désererais que ton espèce se fût arrêtée. Mécontent de ton état présent... peut-être voudrais-tu pouvoir rétrograder..."[107]

The idea of a return also forms one of the leading themes in Mercier's utopian thinking. For example in the moral allegory "*D'un monde heureux*" he tries to provide evidence that there had existed some previous, very distant time, when people had lived in mutual happiness and harmony amidst benevolent nature. In this story Mercier describes the arrival in a rediscovered earthly paradise, which

. . . .

103 Cohen 1985, 64.
104 Bury 1920, 7–20; Passmore 1972, 195. See also Cazes 1986, 35–48; Whitrow 1988, 158. Nisbet criticizes Bury's habit of limiting the idea of progress only to the modern times, i.e., to the seventeenth and eighteenth centuries. He makes a relevant point by suggesting that the idea of progress should be conceived in a very large historical framework. In his view the Greeks were not suspicious of change; the sense of a decline from an original "Golden Age" did not exclude a simultaneous awareness of the advance of knowledge and culture. Nisbet 1970, 46–47.
105 Frängsmyr 1981, 22.
106 Chinard 1913, 219.
107 Rousseau, *Discours...* 1992, 169–170.

means a return in a time before the Fall. The glorification of this state of perfect happiness is followed by a mournful lamentation of its loss in a tone that recalls Rousseau's historical pessimism: "O combien tu es déchue de ta beauté primitive, terre autrefois bénie & fortunée! aujourd'hui livrée à la colere d'un Dieu vengeur, tu as perdu tous tes attraits..."[108]

The message conveyed by Mercier's story of a happier world is thus that in the course of history mankind has lost its primordial sense of completeness and perfection. What, then, caused this dramatic fall from the original state of happiness? According to Mercier responsibility for the Fall rests foremost with those who have "blinded their reason" and "hardened their hearts".[109] As a consequence, instead of being a microcosm reflecting the macrocosm, man has been expelled from the original paradise, or "Cosmopolis". This idea of the Fall, Mircea Eliade suggests, constitutes a crucial theme in myths of paradise produced in many different parts of the world. It is followed by a dream of returning to the mythical days of a "Lost Paradise".[110]

From the background of this archetypal aspiration centered around the rediscovery of a lost paradise can be traced the dream of original purity. To paraphrase Servier, just as the navigators searching for the terrestrial paradise hoped to find a state of uncorrupted virginity, the utopianists of all centuries have been looking for a state prior to original sin. This desire is related to the dream of starting the passage of time from the zero point. Utopia resembles in many aspects the immutable land which the myths of all civilizations place after the death.[111]

Mercier's primitive myth *L'Homme sauvage* provides a typical representation of a mythical and archaic state of paradisal happiness. The corruptive Europeans with their evil habits have, however, destroyed it and deported the natives from their terrestrial paradise.[112] Following the same pattern as in *"D'un monde heureux"*, in *L'Homme sauvage* linear time is revealed as the source of all mankind's miseries. It is the time of sin, which started to flow at the moment of expulsion from the original paradise. Once the floodgates of historical time have been opened, nothing can any more hinder the process of gradual destruction and ultimate death. In opposition to this, cyclical and repetitious time is the time of happiness, because despotic governments, avarice and egoism had not yet destroyed the harmonious coexistence between man and the nature. Using a native indian as a mouthpiece Mercier writes as follows: "J'ai été plus éclairé; mais j'ai perdu le bonheur."[113]

L'Homme sauvage thus repeats the ancient formula that in knowledge lies the beginning of the fall from felicity; from this it can be concluded that at least in this specific textual context Mercier's purpose is to preach the virtue of

. . . .
108 Mercier, *Songes philosophiques* 1768, 196 and passim.
109 Ibid., 201.
110 Eliade 1969a, 61–74, passim.
111 Servier 1991, 338, 354.
112 See Chapter VI, p. 182.
113 Mercier, *L'Homme sauvage* 1767, 130.

ignorance, rather than a Baconian belief in the close mutual link between knowledge and the increase of general well-being. In this respect Mercier seems to imitate Rousseau, in whose *Discours sur l'origine de l'inégalité* the critical attitude toward the presumed benefits of "perfectibility" reaches its point of culmination. Like Mercier, Rousseau also regarded perfectibility as a specifically human faculty, which separated man from the rest of the animals. In his view it made of man an even inferior creature compared to the brutes: "... que c'est elle, qui faisant éclore avec les siècles ses lumières et ses erreurs, ses vices et ses vertus, le rend à la longue le tyran de lui-même et de la nature."[114]

Set into a philosophical-religious framework, Mercier's and Rousseau's reasoning follows the mythical pattern of the story of Abel and Cain; the crime of Cain has led to the fall from original purity, which means the flow of historical time. By murdering his brother, Cain puts the burden of guilt on the shoulders of humanity. From now on, historical time is the time of sin, corruption and death. In the great drama of universal history, the role of the villain is given to Western civilization, which "murders" its brother Abel, the non-European world, by poisoning it with its dangerous idea of illusory happiness, which in reality is synonymous with misery – the flow of history.

Despite the fact that the temporal structure of *L'An 2440* is founded on a progressive conception of time, here too the passage of linear time means, in the final resort, a Fall into a state of sin and corruption. For example, in speculating on the reasons which have contributed to the creation of language, mechanics, agriculture, the art of navigation, physics, astronomy, music and painting, Mercier asserts that the genius which has produced all these inventions could only have existed in the first days of the world – "car la nature humaine pouvoit avoir alors une énergie, une force créatrice, une pénétration qu'elle a pu perdre depuis".[115]

This pattern of the Fall is based on the assumption that there once existed an original pact between man and nature, which man has since broken (compare with the argumentation of Hayden White, above). In consequence, he has lost the original paradise and is forced to submit to the degenerative effects of linear time. The underlying idea is compatible with the distinction which Northrop Frye has made between two social myths: one is the contract, which is an account of the origins of society; the other is utopia, which represents an imaginative vision of the end of social life. In Christianity the myth of contract is the myth of Creation, and the fall from the garden of Eden is the result of a breach of the contract. Frye claims that "any serious utopia has to assume some kind of contract theory to explain what is wrong with the state of things the utopia is going to improve. But the vision of something better has to appeal to some contract behind the contract, something which the existing society has lost... or violated, and which the utopia...is to restore."[116]

. . . .

114 Rousseau, *Discours...* 1992, 183–184.
115 Mercier, *L'An 2440 I* 1786, 251–253.
116 Frye 1966, 25, 34, 38–39; Bowman 1975, 428.

Basically all efforts made by eighteenth-century French constructors of social pact theories can be interpreted as attempts at reviving that original state of perfection which man is assumed to have lost in the course of history. The underlying idea is to cleanse history from the burden of the past, in order that the fundamental contract, purified and simple, could be restored. Once this has been done, the cycle can return to its origins, and the circle completed.

The eighteenth-century philosophers believed that with the support of the discoveries of modern science they had rediscovered the ancient secret wisdom.[117] Mercier illustrates this idea in *L'An 2440* when he tells that the Frenchmen of the future are privileged to benefit from the inventions of their primitive ancestors. He thus suggests that they have found a kind of "philosophers' stone", which had for many dark centuries been buried under the double tyranny of ignorance and prejudice. In the following extract Mercier refers to the mythical primitive origins of the human race, when mankind had once possessed the sacred gift of rationality and happiness:

> "Ces arts familiers et nombreux qui font le charme de la vie domestique, nous viennent... de quelque peuple ancien, qui n'aura laissé aucun trace de son existence,et dont nous recueillons les bienfaits sans en connoître la source."[118]

As this passage reveals, instead of explaining the nature of the historical phases that have led from the past through the present to the future in a "scientific" manner, Mercier contents himself with the statement that the Parisians of 2440 are not exactly sure to whom they owe their superiority. This illustrates the observation of Jean-Louis Vissière that like alchemists and witches, Mercier too preferred to talk about "secrets", "mysteries", "treasures", "*métempsychose*", and so on. Mercier's thinking contains traces from medieval theology, and his belief in the unanimity of science[119] leads to mystical scientism. His conception of science has an occult, esoteric character like that typical of obscurantist regimes.[120]

According to Vissière the "non-progressive" character of Mercier's future society is clearly revealed in the following aspects: It is 1) retrograde: the return to the earth, patriarchy, women as housewives; 2) obscurantist: esoteric science, elite monopoly; 3) totalitarian: indoctrination of young people and adults through education and the arts, censorship, elimination of non-conformists such as "immoral writers" and atheists. The feature that Vissière finds the most curious in Mercier's utopia is the replacement of the deism of Voltaire by an oriental doctrine inspired by Zoroastra and Pythagoras: "*métempsychose*" flourishing on the ruins of Catholicism.[121]

. . . .

117 LeFlamanc 1934, 27.
118 Mercier, *L'An 2440 I* 1786, 250.
119 Mercier expresses this idea as follows: "La science, comme on le soupçonne, est sans doute une, et n'a point de branches isolées et séparées..." Mercier, *L'An 2440 I* 1786, 252.
120 Vissière 1977, 316–317.
121 Ibid., 326.

All this reinforces the impression that in *L'An 2440* progress is understood, above all, as a return to an original "Golden Age".[122] This is not a scientific or progressive conception of progress. Denoit comes to a similar conclusion when she suggests that in Mercier's utopia, cyclical time has the same regenerative function as the catalysis imagined by Mercier for the destruction of the perverted Paris. Progress thus means the same thing as the rediscovery of the past.[123]

As the excerpts from Mercier's utopian writings clearly demonstrate, utopia does not necessarily mean belief in progress in the sense of movement toward something totally new and unprecedented. Scientific-technological progress is thus not a necessary precondition of a utopia projected in a remote future. It would be difficult to find a more illustrative example than *L'An 2440* to demonstrate that future-oriented thinking may mean a return to an anterior condition as easily as movement forward. As a literary genre, utopia may be either progressive or retrogressive. The same is true with the concept of "progress", for much depends on how it is conceived. Jacques Le Goff, for example, sees the combat between the "antique" and "modern", which has been discussed above, less as a combat between past and present (tradition and innovation) than between two forms of progress: either progress can be bound to the pattern of Eternal Return in the form of a cyclical progress, when the antiquity is situated at the beginning of the circular movement, or, alternatively, there is the theory of linear progress, which is evaluated through its distance from antiquity.[124]

In his studies of the historical evolution of the myth of paradise, Jean Delumeau illuminates this seeming paradox between tradition and innovation by tracing the relations which bind together millenarian thinking and utopias with the modern ideology of progress. One of his essential points is that millenarianism and modernity do not necessarily exclude one another. One of his main concerns has been to explore how the passage from nostalgia to the garden of Eden has changed into the hope for a new terrestrial paradise and how this hope has been secularized in order to be incarnated as a concept of progress. Taking as his point of departure the formula "*la nostalgie du futur*" launched by Raymond Ruyer, he promotes a thesis that there has been an enduring hope of re-finding in the future the terrestrial paradise of our origins.[125]

The famous words of the utopian socialist Saint-Simon (1760–1825) that "the Golden Age lies before us and not behind us",[126] clearly illustrate the changed mentality of the age: instead of conferring their unreserved admiration on some mythical "Golden Age", the loss of which was greeted with mournful

. . . .

122 See also Rufi 1995, 73.
123 Denoit 1983, 94, 121.
124 Le Goff 1992, 25.
125 Delumeau 1995, 9–12 and passim.
126 See for example Delumeau 1995, 353–354. For example Charles Rihs reminds, however that already a long time before Saint-Simon the utopianists had declared that the "Golden Age is not behind us but ahead of us". Rihs 1970, 10.

regrets, the new period of unforeseen happiness was now seen as dawning in the remote future. The statement of Saint-Simon mirrors the captive power that the idea of a future paradise in the meaning of a "return" held on the social imagination in the later eighteenth and early nineteenth centuries. The time of happiness was no more sought from some mythical past, but the memory of primordial happiness was now intermingled with the hope that the lost paradise could be re-established in the future. As one scholar explains it, whereas the seventeenth-century writers preferred Jerusalem, Rousseau pastoralized utopia, and the pre-Romantics and Romantics finally merged the garden of Eden and the city of Jerusalem.[127] In this process the two social myths distinguished by Frye, the myth of origins and the myth of the *telos*, are fused together.

Many scholars of utopian thinking have emphasized the fact that the cyclical conception of progress still represents the general attitude to time in most ideal constructions in the eighteenth century. They are largely in agreement that utopian writers of that epoch had in mind mystic ancient communities or exotic populations, and were aiming to reconstruct the "Golden Age" from a totally new starting point, i.e., in the future. "Progress" was now understood as a cataclysmic and revolutionary return toward a "Golden Age" through future regeneration. According to this view, after the complete cycle of human history the world would return to its first status, and henceforward virtue and abundance would reign on earth. Man would have no more needs, and disease would be unknown. Mankind would live in peace and nature would satisfy everybody's desires.[128]

Mercier's fascination with mysticism, occultism and Freemasonry further illuminates his nostalgia for the mythical origins of mankind, i.e., his vision of the past as ideal, and his quest for refuge in mystical communion with this ennobling heritage. As Jean Servier points out, for example, in eighteenth-century France this backward-looking attitude was particularly widespread within Freemason ideology. The Freemasons were searching for a mythic primitive world, which was supposed to possess some mysterious wisdom and science. The Freemasons wished for a total physical regeneration which would restore the Golden Age on earth.[129]

All this testifies to the fact that in pre-Revolutionary France no clear separation had yet been made between rational science and occultist practises. As Darnton has reminded us, in the first phases of the Enlightenment, mesmerism and magnetism expressed a faith in reason. Pseudo-science took the Parisians into the occultism which had existed on the margins of science since the Middle Ages. The Italian adventurer Cagliostro (1743–1795) was only one of many alchemists whom Mercier met in Paris. Alchemists, witches and fortune-tellers were firmly established in Parisian society, and the interest in

. . . .
127 Bowman 1975, 428.
128 LeFlamanc 1934, 74–75, 80; Rihs 1970, 27 and passim; Dupront 1996, 55; Delon, Mauzi & Menant 1998, 87–88. About the myth of the Golden Age, see also Neyton 1984, especially Chapters I, V and XIII.
129 Servier 1969, 412.

mesmerism far exceeded the interest in political theories. Science seemed to open limitless possibilities for human progress, and pre-Revolutionary France was a golden age of popular science.[130]

This admixture of rational thinking with esotericism is particularly clearly revealed in the nature of the scientific achievements in Mercier's future Paris. He describes, for example, how mankind has been able with the help of machines to explore the oceans, and the subterranean world has been brought under human control by establishing subterranean contacts between the volcanoes; and in 2440 dangerous animals (lions, bears, etc.) have been tamed and trained to pull carriages.[131]

Moreover, the time traveler is informed that the future Frenchmen have also rediscovered other miraculous secrets which the eighteenth century had lost: like the ancients, they possess malleable glass, spectacular stones, the mirror of Archimedes, the ancient Egyptian art of embalming and the machine which elevated their obeliskes, the art of melting stones, and inextinguishable lamps. In addition, they know the composition of water and fire. Mercier also projects that by the twenty-fifth century men will have found new species of animals and cross-bred them, with amazing results.[132]

As an interesting detail, Mercier refers in his utopia to a kind of telephone. He describes how the future Parisians can communicate with each other through *"une trompette parlante"*:

> "Cétoit le bruit du canon qu'on avoit assujetti à une orgue volumineuse qui alloit frapper un écho lointain; et comme la progression du son a un rapport avec la progression de la lumière, rien n'empêchoit qu'on ne se parlât d'une ville à l'autre."[133]

As a matter of fact, a prototype of the phonograph had already been invented by Cyrano de Bergerac, in whose "extraordinary journey" novel *Voyage dans la lune et aux etats du soleil* (1657) there is a reference to "speaking books": "... enfin, c'est un Livre où, pour apprendre, les yeux sont inutiles: on n'a besoin que des oreilles."[134]

All in all, the scientific inventions of Mercier's utopians do not impress by their innovative power. Rather than reflecting the accelerated tempo of technological advance, many of Mercier's proposals for scientific and technological improvement differ little from those that the scientists of

· · · · · · · · ·

130 Darnton 1995, 33, 39, 41–49. In *Le Nouveau Paris* Mercier accuses, however, Cagliostro and Mesmer of charlatanism. He complains also of the fact that in disastrous times the revolutionaries have been able to allure people to consult oracles and witches. Mercier, *Le Nouveau Paris* 1994b, 267–277 (Ch. LXIII, *"Le tireur de cartes"*). This reveals that in his mind it was an immoral thing to take advantage of mankind's sentiments of insecurity when they were forced to face the uncertainty of the future in a world, which had undergone a total transformation in a brief time span.
131 Mercier, *L'An 2440 II* 1786, 368–369.
132 Mercier, *L'An 2440 II* 1786, 42–43.
133 Mercier, *L'An 2440 II* 1786, 238. The first "telephone", invented by a certain Dom Gauthey, was represented to the Academy of Sciences in 1782. Dupront 1996, 53.
134 Bergerac, *Voyage dans la lune et aux etats du soleil* [s.a.], 117.

"Salomon's House" in Bacon's utopia *Nova Atlantis* were already supposed to have discovered in the early seventeenth century.[135]

Mercier´s ignoring of the achievements of the industrial revolution, including the technological inventions of his own age, appears somewhat paradoxical if one considers that a future-oriented utopia could be expected to provide the best opportunity for the treatment of the benefits of technological progress.[136] One possible explanation for this paradox is suggested by Braudel, for example: that Mercier´s argumentation was simply too totally rooted in the mental structures of his own society for him to have any capacity to foresee the shape that future change was going to assume.[137]

Mercier's indifference in regard to technological progress illustrates the point noted by Kumar that the utopianists of the seventeenth and eighteenth centuries showed great respect for the new science, but believed that the "new Prometheus" had to be kept in chains. The sole purpose of science was to serve religious or ethical ends.[138] Cioranescu, for his part, speaks about different phases of progress. As he sees it, the desacralization of the idea of progress has been slow, and the function of progress has changed in the course of time. Whereas in the eighteenth century this function was a moral one, by the following century it had become scientific and technical. This justifies the claim that even "progress progresses".[139]

Mercier's *L'An 2440* provides the most typical example of a utopia in which technology is subordinated to moral purposes.[140] As we have seen, in his depiction of the society of the twenty-fifth century, experimental inventions like the telescope are useful only to the extent that they help man in his process of spiritual perfectibility by revealing the hidden mysteries of the universe. Correspondingly, the pursuit of material prosperity occupies only a secondary place in the hierarchy of the ideals of the good life, after moral values such as the principle of mutual sharing and the expression of social compassion.

Apart from Mercier´s glorification of the art of printing and references to the progress of medecine, one of the most ambitious of his "modern" scientific visions was related to the conquest of the air. In the chapter "*L'Aréostat*" the time traveler observes an immense machine which is flying at a prodigious height above the city. He is told that it is arriving from Peking, and is manned by "*aéronautes*", or "man-birds." The name of the "inventor of the air" is stated as Montgolfier.[141] This refers to a contemporary event; on the fifth of June, 1783,

. . . .

135 Bacon, *The Advancement of Learning and the New Atlantis* 1906, 268–272.
136 Alkon 1990, 45; Collier 1990, 97; Minois 1996, 441.
137 Braudel 1981, 557.
138 Kumar 1987, 36.
139 Cioranescu 1972, 192–193.
140 See also Alkon 1990, 54.
141 Mercier, *L'An 2440 II* 1786, 304–307. This chapter is not, quite naturally, included in the first version of *L'An 2440* (1770 or 1771). Allusion to Montgolfier's invention reveals that Mercier was following keenly his time, adding new chapters into the basic text always when there appeared new signs of progress or changes of any kind in his contemporary society. See also Mercier's article "*Le ballon-Montgolfier*" in *Mon bonnet de nuit*, where he writes: "L'année 1783 a été l'année des merveilles..." Mercier, *Mon bonnet de nuit I* 1784, 386–410, especially 406.

The ascent of a hot-air balloon, in 1783, flown by the brothers Montgolfier, was a great event. For Mercier, 1783 was "a year of marvels". Bibliothèque Nationale, Paris.

the brothers Montgolfier succeeded in launching the first balloon filled with hot air, and this was one of the first steps in the evolution of aviation.[142]

I.F. Clarke suggests that there may have been some connection between the first balloon ascents and the growth of the literature of anticipation; the period after 1783 witnessed a rapid increase in tales of the future.[143] Restif de la Bretonne had, however, already invented a kind of "airplane" in his *La Découverte australe par un Homme-Volant ou le Dédale français*[144] in 1781, probably inspired by the drawings of Leonardo da Vinci.[145]

Except for this dream of the conquest of the air, the traffic in Mercier's future society is organized on a very traditional basis. Paris in 2440 evokes the image of a rural village rather than that of a large city with passing impressions, smells and voices. Instead of the hectic tempo of big cities, the society of 2440 seems to be petrified in a changeless eternal present moment. The best illustration of this slow tempo of life is provided by the fact that Mercier's future Parisians prefer moving from place to place by foot.[146] He also describes how the sea is traversed with rowboats, following in the traces of the ancient Phoenicians.[147] There is no coal dust, factories or locomotives. Mercier was incapable of predicting the development of machines or the revolution in transportation. It is

. . . .

142 Pomeau 1991, 16. On the first balloon ascents, see also Schama 1989, 123–131; Darnton 1995, 31–34.
143 Clarke 1979, 31.
144 Restif de la Bretonne, *La Découverte australe par un Homme-Volant ou le Dédale français* 1977, 35–56 and passim.
145 Chadourne 1958, 204.
146 Mercier, *L'An 2440 I* 1786, 32–37.
147 Mercier, *L'An 2440 II* 1786, 239–243.

also possible that he has consciously excluded industrial work from his ideal city. This point again indicates how the prediction of the future can serve a reactionary ideology.[148] It illustrates my previous thesis that Mercier's utopia has to be understood, above all, as a critique directed against the accelerated tempo of urbanization and modernization.[149]

Yet another retrogressive feature of Mercier's vision of the future is that little concern is devoted to time as a regulator of the everyday life of the citizens. This does not mean, however, lack of discipline; the absence of artificial measures of time is not by any means a synonym for the lack of self-constraints and self-discipline. Just as the entire existence of Mercier's utopian citizens is ordered from above, so also their use of time is de-personalized. No time is left for purely personal activities. In practise this means that the use of time is objectified and emptied of all subjective or psychological connotations. The underlying principle is the same as Foucault attributes to monastic communities, within which a strict timetable was first introduced. Their methods – rhythms, particular occupations, the cycles of regulation – were the same which were later to be found from schools, workshops and hospitals. For centuries, suggests Foucault, the religious orders have been masters of discipline, and the principle that underlay the timetable in this traditional form was negative. It was the principle of non-idleness: it was forbidden to waste time, and the purpose of the timetable was to eliminate the danger of wasting it.[150]

As Alkon has remarked, it is rather ironic that despite the fact that time plays such an important role in Mercier´s utopian schema, the text does not mention watches or clocks.[151] Not all references to time, however, are excluded. As an interesting detail, the 1786 and 1799 versions include two illustrations which remind us that Mercier was preoccupied by the notion of time. In the first of these, reproduced on the cover of the present study, the time traveler of the novel has just arrived in twenty-fifth-century Paris after his long sleep through the centuries. He is surrounded by a crowd of future Parisians, who are amazed by his ancient costume. In one of the monuments there is engraved the date 2440, from which the narrator realizes that he is in the remote future. It is noteworthy that this illustration does not contain anything suggestive of a modern, dynamic idea of time. As Alkon has reminded us, the picture has, however, a specific value despite the fact that it does not include references to technological development. This is due to the fact that it represents the first effort, if the images of religious apocalypses are not included, at depicting a scene set in future time.[152]

The other illustration, entitled "*La France et le Temps*" ("France and Time"), is also fascinating. It offers, however, no images of interplanetary journeys, time

. . . .
148 Vissière 1977, 311–312.
149 Forsström 1995, 23.
150 Foucault 1975, 151–155.
151 Alkon 1990, 51.
152 Ibid., 50.

The illustration of Mercier's utopia, entitled "La France et le Temps".

machines or references to any form of future technology. Quite the opposite, since the picture represents figures in an antique setting: an old man with wings holds in his hand a scythe, a feminine figure bears in her hands a horn of plenty, another woman has on her knees a scroll.[153]

The hope for a new reconciliation between the "law of society" and the "law of nature" was Mercier's focal utopian dream. The absence of clocks from his society of 2440 can be read as a symptom of this desire to abolish all differences between the "law of nature" and the "law of society". It is an deliberate statement that "genuine" time is static, agrarian or cyclical, and should not be subordinated to the nerve-racking tempo of urban life. It is as if by eliminating the artificial measurement of time from his ideal city Mercier had wanted to express his longing for a return to a kind of "dream time", a pre-industrial and organic time when the "law of nature" and the "law of society" were asserted to have existed in total harmony. It forms one aspect in his vision of the rediscovery of the lost paradise.

The rejection of the artificial measurement of time in Mercier's ideal city thus reveals a secret wish to return to the society dominated by the temporal structure of "*longue durée*", to a past when the rate of acquisition of new knowledge had been so slow that the possibility of progress could scarcely be conceived. It can be interpreted as a conscious reaction against the accelerated tempo of societies dominated by linear time.

The new, dynamic, bourgeois world, by contrast, needed a mechanically measurable time, which was a symptom of a new conception of time and of the change in the tempo of life. In the process of urbanization and industrialization time gradually lost its subjective meaning and became objective "clock time".[154] The political and social space of action became radically denaturalized as a consequence of technological expansion in the sense that its periodicity became less strongly dictated by nature.[155] In replacing the organic and cyclical movements of nature, the mechanical clock is characteristic of societies dominated by the linearity and countability of temporal experience.[156]

The same tendency to annihilate all divisions between the categories of "natural time" and "social time" also characterizes other eighteenth-century French novels which emphasize rural happiness as the supreme ideal. In Rousseau's *Nouvelle Héloïse*, for example, the cyclical conception of time

. . . .

153 This illustration is open to various interpretations. The old man with the scythe represents an angel of death, the inevitable passage of time, which finally effaces all mankind in the night of oblivion. The horn of plenty alludes to the abundant and glorious future which has succeeded in abolishing famine and shortages of food; this is compatible with Mercier's vision of public grain storehouses and a constant supply of bread.
154 Virtanen 1986, 40.
155 Koselleck 1985, 95. It should be noted, however, that all differences between the spheres of "physical time" and "social time" can never be totally obliterated. Referring to this fact Elias writes that "with the development of human-made time-meters, the relative autonomy of social timing in relation to the timing of non-human physical events increased; their connection became more indirect but it was never broken – it is, in fact, unbreakable." Elias 1993, 44–45.
156 Shallis 1983, 16.

organizes the repetitive pattern of daily events; the sense of security is based on the fact that the passage of time cannot produce any novelties:

> "Ici le fruit du labeur passé soutient l'abondance présente, et le fruit du labeur présent annonce l'abondance à venir; on jouit à la fois de ce qu'on dépense et de ce qu'on recueille, et les divers tems se ressemblent pour affermir la sécurité du présent."[157]

The message conveyed by this passage is that in agrarian society, characterized by a perfect symmetry between the past and the future, i.e., the categories of experience and expectation, life is happier, due to the fact that the future is totally predictable. The element of fear does not spoil the happiness, because the future cannot bring totally unpredictable or hazardous elements. In *L'Homme sauvage* Mercier expresses an analogous idea when he writes, using an Indian native as his mouthpiece: "L'espérance m'étoit étrangere, je ne prévoyois point l'avenir. Borné au présent, rien ne m'allarmoit."[158]

This extract demonstrates that Mercier was not convinced that pre-knowledge of the future would, in the final resort, increase the sum of human happiness. The suggestion is that living in the present moment is better than being preoccupied by what the future may bring; when all days are identical, there is no room for coincidence or for fears prompted by an unknown future. Similarly, in *Notions claires sur les gouvernemens*, under the rubric "*Du bien éloigné, ou du vain prétexte*", Mercier criticizes the way of thinking according to which the well-being of the present generation should be sacrificed on the altar of the felicity of future generations. He demands that the benefit of the "suffering generation" has to be given prioroty over speculations and "*chimères*".[159]

Mercier's reasoning seems, once again, to follow the path set by Rousseau. As the following quotation illustrates, in his *Émile* Rousseau also condemns predictive activity as the source of all human misery:

> "La prévoyance! la prévoyance qui nous porte sans cesse au dela de nous, et souvent nous place où nous n'arriverons point, voilà la véritable source de toutes nos misères. Quelle manie à un être aussi passager que l'homme de regarder toujours au loin dans un avenir qui vient si rarement, et de négliger le présent dont il est sûr?"[160]

Rousseau draws an analogy between ignorance and happiness, arguing that someone unable to predict the future will not be afraid of losing his life, either.[161] In other words, savages neither regret the past nor bother their minds by thinking about the future, since they live in an absolute present moment. This illustrates the fact that in societies dominated by a cyclical perception of time

. . . .

157 Rousseau, *La Nouvelle Héloïse IV* 1925, 45.
158 Mercier, *L'Homme sauvage* 1767, 68.
159 Mercier, *Notions claires sur les gouvernemens I* 1787, 73–74.
160 Rousseau, *Émile ou de l'éducation* 1904, 62.

there is no place for nostalgia, because "eventually time lost will be instituted again".[162]

The idea of exceptional happiness, innocence and virginity is often associated with childhood. Similarly, Mercier's and Rousseau's habit of idealizing a mythical, primitive, and "primordial" condition as a resort of exceptional happiness invokes the metaphor of the "childhood" of the human race. This is particularly clearly expressed in *L'Homme sauvage*, where the innocence of the natives is said to represent the "childhood of the world".[163]

The conception of the "childhood" of mankind as a period of innocence and happiness always contains, at least implicitly, the idea that ultimately so-called "progress" signifies moral corruption, destruction and unhappiness. In this primordial state, where savages are presumed to have lived without any benefits of progress, the repetitive passage of time remains always the same. The underlying suggestion is that due to this basically static structure of time, man never loses his initial innocence by falling into the temptations of historical time, which, as it is represented both by Mercier and Rousseau, can bring nothing but crime and misery. Rousseau formulates this idea of the "youth" of mankind as follows:

> "L'exemple des sauvages...semble confirmer que le genre humain était fait pour y rester toujours, que cet état est la véritable jeunesse du monde, et que tous les progrès ultérieurs ont été en apparence autant de pas vers la perfection de l'individu, et en effet vers la décrépitude de l'espèce."[164]

A similar line of thought can also be traced for example from Diderot's *Supplément au voyage de Bougainville*, where metaphors are applied to aging and different stages of life as follows: "L'Otaïtien touche à l'origine du monde, et l'Européen touche à sa viellesse."[165] Diderot's allusion to the "oldness" of European man revives the classical metaphor of the "aging world" and the idea that the present is also a time of advanced degeneration. This shows how in the course of the eighteenth century increased scepticism with regard to the benefits of linear progress produced a gradual return to older theories of decay. One scholar has even suggested that Mercier elaborated a static view of history without allusions to the real historical process expressly due to the fact that his generation had already began to lose its faith in progress.[166]

The idea of the "childhood" of mankind, as it is treated by Mercier, Rousseau and Diderot, confirms a pattern which has shaped collective mentalities for many centuries. Mucchielli suggests that the idea of a "Golden Age", which is one of the archetypal forms of humankind's collective unconsciousness,

· · · · · · · · ·
161 Ibid., 60–61.
162 Chase & Shaw 1989, 2–3.
163 Mercier, *L'Homme sauvage* 1767, 291.
164 Rousseau, *Discours...* 1992, 231.
165 Diderot, *Oeuvres complètes de Denis Diderot* 1818, 469.
166 Hudde 1978, 252.

presents the world emptied from all frustrations and limits on adult existence. In Jungian psychology, the "Golden Age" would be an extrapolation of a return to the bosom of the mother.[167] The quests of paradise thus stem from the same source as the yearning for the mother's arms: the Western images of paradise recollect life in the womb or the early months of life, dreaming of re-establishing the union of mother and child.[168]

In the context of utopian thinking, this maternal symbolism underscores the basically cyclical and mythical structure of most utopias. What is at issue is a desire to revive a state before the Fall, i.e., a state before chaos, and to rebuild the broken bond between man and nature, in other words between the "law of nature" and the "law of society", – mother and child, if you like.

Maternal symbols lead one back to the "Cosmopolis", which is a representation of the purest form of human existence. It is a model of a closed circle as a manifestation of ultimate repose, from which all restlessness is excluded. It is a representation of a return to an original "dream time", when man had not yet awakened to confront the corrupt world. This reminds one of the theory of "Great Time" which Eliade sees as a temporal structure especially typifying primitive societies. He suggests that "almost all theories of "Great Time" are found in conjunction with the myth of successive ages, the "Age of Gold" always occurring at the beginning of the cycle, close to the paradigmatic *illud tempus*".[169]

On the basis of all this evidence, one comes to a conclusion that despite the fact that Mercier viewed the historical past as nothing but a collection of human misery, barbarism and wickedness, he was nonetheless deeply nostalgic for a primordial state that blends childhood memory with the religious ritual of rebirth to a new and more dignified existence. All of Mercier's writings which are of any importance, from *L'Homme sauvage* and *L'An 2440* to many of his "*songes*", reinforce the same impression that for Mercier progress did not mean so much the increase of scientific-technological inventions or a rush forward into a totally new future, but rather a return to an original, mythical state of purity. The implication contained in all these diverse writings is that it is only in the beginning of the world or in the first phases of the human consciousness that ultimate purity can reign; it is a condition where the child is not yet separated from its mother, and where the world has just been created, waiting only to be discovered.

. . . .

167 Mucchielli 1960, 286. There is no doubt about the fact that along with the other utopian visions, also Mercier's *L'An 2440* would, probably, provide substance for psychoanalytical approaches. As fascinating as this perspective may sound, in this context it has to be contented with these rather general observations.

168 Manuels 1982, 62. About maternal symbols in utopias, see also Servier 1991, 329–352, passim.

169 Eliade 1969b, 131.

X Death – The Ultimate Utopia

In his efforts to maximize his happiness already on earth, man always confronts the same dilemma: How is it possible to attain tranquility of mind under the oppressive shadow of the inevitability of death? Even if belief in limitless terrestrial progress seems to promise a golden future for humankind as a whole, this does not entail much consolation for the individual; as a mortal creature he is subject, even under the best of circumstances, to the curses of old age, sickness, the enfeeblement of bodily forces and ultimately death. As McManners notes, even if the doctrine of man's innate perversity had been abolished, the necessity of dying could not be denied. There was a "curse" on man, after all.[1]

It is natural to end this investigation with a brief survey focused on the theme of death and its relation to the idea of happiness as it is manifested in Mercier's utopian vision. As has been noted frequently in the preceding pages, death in its various forms is one of the themes to which Mercier constantly returns. In *Tableau de Paris* death is represented most often in a threatening and repulsive guise, but in the ideal state of the twenty-fifth century the inevitability of death is received with stoic resignation. Or, alternatively, the places which remind people of its existence, such as slaughterhouses and hospitals, have been deported from the center of the city to the margins, out of sight. All in all, the idea of death as it is dealt with in Mercier's diverse writings constitutes a field of study which would deserve a comprehensive analysis of its own. Despite the fact that this is not the proper place for an extensive treatment of this theme, some statements are necessary in order to complete the image of happiness as it is conveyed through Mercier's utopian vision.

Michel Vovelle notes that few periods have left more utopias on death than the eighteenth century, and in Mercier's *L'An 2440* four entire chapters (a sixth of the whole work)[2] are devoted to this theme.[3] In the course of the novel the time traveler takes part in the execution of a death sentence and in the funeral ceremonies of an old peasant (Ch. "*Oraison funèbre d'un Paysan*", t. III, 84–94), follows the funeral processions and receives a lesson about the prevailing attitudes toward death (Ch. "*Le Convoi*", t. I, 303–310). He is also lectured on the ideas of posterity and immortality (Ch. "*Les Nouveaux Testamens*", t. I, 71–76).

. . . .
1   McManners 1981, 123.
2   This is not exactly true when one considers the later editions of *L'An 2440*; Vovelle refers to the edition of 1770 (or 1771) of the novel.
3   Vovelle 1983, 500. See also Vovelle 1974, 178–180.

Irrespective of its omnipresent nature, in Mercier's utopian society the thought of death does not fill minds with images of fear and horror. For example in the chapter "*Le Convoi*" the following words are put into the mouth of the commentator, as the funeral processions are rolling through the streets of Paris: "C'est le char de la victoire".[4] To give up one's life is no longer seen as a loss but as a gain, because after having triumphed over human misery the dead will join the Supreme Being, "the source of all happiness". For this reason death has nothing worth mourning for. To leave this world behind means an increase of human happiness, and death is depicted as "a peaceful state which can only ameliorate man's existence".[5]

Amongst the eighteenth-century French utopian writers, Morelly also softens the harsher aspects of death in his communist utopia *Naufrage des isles flottantes, ou Basiliade du célèbre Pilpai*. As in Mercier's writings, with Morelly too death is seen as a liberator from sufferings: "Oui, mon Ami, vous allez dans un Pays encore plus heureux, où nous nous trouverons tous réunis."[6]

Mercier sees death in positive terms also owing to the fact that it makes possible total equality between men. In the future Paris the deceased are laid in ashes outside the city, and princes and dukes receive their last resting place in the same urn with simple citizens: "A la mort toute distinction cesse..."[7] This was one of the often repeated "*clichés*" in the eighteenth century: virtue did not ask for "pompous éloges, nor monuments of brass or marble".[8]

In Mercier's moral allegories, death is almost always a synonym for liberation and ascendance to a better condition. For example in the "vision number four" contained in *Songes et visions philosophiques*, entitled "*Je suis mort*", he dreams that he has died and been released from the prison of bodily restraints:

> "Je rêvois que j'étois mort, & je considérois le corps d'où mon ame venoit de sortir, étendu sur mon lit: qu'il me fit pitié! & j'étois bien aise de n'être plus lié à ce vêtement charnel qui me clouoit à la terre, devoltiger dans les airs avec la rapidité de la pensée".[9]

As this quotation reveals, in the experience of death, as Mercier conceived it, the feeling of happiness attains its highest level, because the soul, liberated from its bodily chains, can follow its free will, float amongst the planets of the universe, pay visits to totally new places, conquer the limits of time and space. It is in death that the eternal dream of mankind, that of flying, finds its supreme apotheosis. This is reminiscent of the philosophical-religious systems of thinkers like Plato or St. Augustine. Deprun states that according to Platonic

---

4   Mercier, *L'An 2440 I* 1786, 304.
5   Mercier, *L'An 2440 I* 1786, 304.
6   [Morelly], *Naufrage des isles flottantes, ou Basiliade du célébre Pilpai I* 1753, 12.
7   Mercier, *L'An 2440 I* 1786, 305.
8   McManners 1981, 171.
9   Mercier, *Songes et visions philosophiques* 1788a, 309.

philosophy the soul suffers in the body of incarceration, and according to Augustinian philosophy spirituality is defined through restlessness.[10]

The idealization of death forms the leading theme again in Mercier's allegory *"Nouvelles de la lune"* ("vision III"). It describes the narrator wandering in the garden, remembering his dead friend, whose present habitation is in the moon. Using as his mouthpiece this dead friend Mercier expresses his conviction that the horrors of death have been very much exaggerated. Also in this context death is a synonym with ultimate liberation, flying, and a step toward a more perfect existence:

> "Non, la mort n'est pas ce que l'on s'imagine, les vivans se font d'elle une image épouvantable & fausse... "Lorsque je sentis le mouvement de mon coeur se briser, je me trouvai doué de la faculté de pénétrer des corps les plus durs, aucune épaisseur ne pouvait arrêter mon élévation...je me transportois aux lieux où je voulois, traversant sans peine & sans crainte un espace immense, plus je m'élancois, plus je sentois la flamme de la vie augmenter en moi de force & d'activité...".[11]

In a peculiar chapter of *L'An 2440*, seemingly without any internal connection with the rest of the novel, entitled *"L'éclipse de lune. C'est un Solitaire qui parle"*, the narrator is wandering during the night in a cemetery, where he finds consolation and a place of retreat from the tumult of the cities. Also in this story, filled with Romantic elements, Mercier reiterates his conviction that it is vain to be horrified at the sight of human remains, which the soul has inhabited, because they offer nothing but "l'image heureuse de sa délivrance". The idealization of death makes Mercier assert: "...mais tout crie au fond de mon ame que la vie future est préférable à cette vie présente."[12]

All the quoted passages drawn from Mercier's diverse writings support the general conclusion that the most integral element in his visions of death is the belief that death does not mean the end of everything but a transformation towards a better condition, the beginning of genuine and ultimate happiness. The suggestion is that compared with the supreme felicity which awaits man beyond the grave, the happiness accorded to him on earth can even at its best be only a pale shadow:

> "Qu'est-ce que la mort? un repos absolu, ou le commencement du bonheur...et pourquoi craindre la mort, comme si notre félicité... sur la terre étoit réelle, comme si nos maux étoient incertains? La raison veut qu'on regarde la mort comme une suite nécessaire de la vie."[13]

With his beautiful vision of a direct continuity between terrestrial and other-worldly happiness, Mercier lays the ground for a new reconciliation between a religious vision and a more secular outlook. Mauzi has shown that this view

· · · · · · · · ·

10   Deprun 1979, 133.
11   Mercier, *Songes et visions philosophiques* 1788a, 302–303.
12   Mercier, *L'An 2440 I* 1786, 314–316.
13   Mercier, *L'An 2440 I* 1786, 308.

began to gain ground in people's minds in the course of the eighteenth century; it was based on an assumption that there no longer existed any contradiction between happiness according to the world and the religious ideal. All opposition between Nature and Grace had lost its sense. By the end of the century, man no more needed to choose between terrestrial happiness and the beyond, which were now seen as two successive moments in the miraculous adventure. Now, when the idea of God's goodness was no more put into question and when salvation was thought to be possible for all without exception with the abolition of the traditional image of hell, terrestrial happiness was seen as preceding without discontinuity eternal happiness. Paradise was merely the final achievement of terrestrial happiness, and terrestrial happiness was an anticipated image of Paradise.[14]

In advancing the idea of death as the most beautiful experience of human life and the final stage of man's moral and spiritual perfectibility, Mercier rejects the older notion of death as a "curse", a consequence of man's disobedience. Although the inevitability of death had to be accepted even in an ideal city (since utopias always draw their substance from the real conditions of life, which means that the creators of utopias cannot posit physical immortality), the experience of death could be transformed into a positive source of extreme pleasure.

Mercier's wish to veil the harsh material reality of death in the guise of solemn visions of happy souls transmigrating through the universe towards absolute perfection and wisdom reveals his aversion towards the purely material, physical and carnal aspects of death. As a contrast to eighteenth-century Paris, that city of rotting corpses and smells of putrefaction, in the "Heavenly City" of 2440 no oppressive shadow hangs over the city of ultimate purity. The image of death is now sublimated and transformed from the worst obstacle of happiness into its ultimate fulfillment. It is expressly in conjunction with the theme of death that the contradiction between the "spleen" and "ideal" emerges most sharply.

Mercier's positive image of death prefigures the rise of Romanticism, which has been argued to have given a kinder face to death. By thus doing the Romantics joined ranks with the philosophers of the classical tradition, who promoted the idea of gentle and beautiful Death, of Thanatos, "the brother of Sleep and the friend of mankind".[15] They sometimes conceived of death as a return to the Wholeness of Nature, or the beginning of a new life, a truer and higher existence.[16] In the same way, death and dream are revealed in Mercier's utopian visions like twin brothers; they are two sides of the same coin, opening the gate to the irrational, fanciful worlds beyond everyday realities.

As these excerpts from Mercier's visions indicate, in his writings the themes of death and happiness are keenly intertwined, due above all to the fact that by

. . . .

14   Mauzi 1994, 182, 509–512.
15   Guthke 1999, 121, 128–172, especially 131.
16   Choron 1976, 156–161.

dying man is assumed to attain immortality. A treatment focused on the purely religious side of immortality has already been provided previously in this study. In 2440 belief in the immortality of the personal soul constitutes a dogma. Mercier's utopian men are said to believe in a transmigration of the souls, "metempsychosis".[17]

The idea of immortality can also assume more secular forms. In Mercier's ideal society the most certain way to reach personal immortality is through literature. This is possible owing to the fact that in 2440 every man is a writer; the duty of each and every citizen is to write down the most important events which he has experienced in his life. Before dying he collects them as a book, which is read aloud at his funeral. By this means posterity can gain a vivid image of the life of the deceased.[18]

This hope of the establishment of an universal and egalitarian republic of letters, which would constitute an uninterrupted chain through the generations, is consistent with the high value which Mercier gave to the power of the printed word and to the idea that books form the collective memory of the human race. As this reveals, in his mind there existed a close mutual link between literature and the dream of immortality. Mercier dreams on many occasions that after everything else had turned into ruins and dust, the spirit of exceptional individuals continued its existence in the memory of posterity:

> "La pensée survit à l'homme; et voilà son plus glorieux apanage! La pensée s'élève de son tombeau, prend un corps durable, immortel; et tandis que les tonnerres du despotisme tombent et s'éteignent, la plume d'un écrivain franchit l'intervalle des temps, absout ou punit les maîtres de l'univers."[19]

The immortality gained through the power of the printed word was the sole form of glory that Mercier was prepared to accept. Also for example in an essay entitled *"Imprimerie"* he proclaims that a writer, who regardless of his oppressors produces works which make glory for humankind, deserves to be remembered by the future generations.[20]

Many of Mercier's educated contemporaries argued in a similar fashion. It has been suggested that the idea of immortality was crucial for the majority of eighteenth-century philosophers, who replaced the hope of immortality in another world by the hope of living in the memory of future generations.[21] For example Diderot believed that man's true immortality and glory consisted in the survival of the memory of his deeds in the minds of those who came after.[22]

. . . .

17   See Chapter IV, pp. 94–95.
18   Mercier, *L'An 2440 I* 1786, 73.
19   Mercier, *L'An 2440 I* 1786, x–xi.
20   Mercier, *Mon bonnet de nuit I* 1784, 121–127, passim.
21   Becker 1965, 119–168, passim.
22   McManners 1981, 167–168; Mauzi 1994, 492–495.

Basically this secular conception of immortality did not differ considerably from the Christian hope of salvation: both were directed toward the future.[23]

Mercier's and many of his contemporaries' belief that through his heroic deeds man would be able to redeem his place of immortality among posterity predicates that there actually will be a posterity who will keep the memory of their ancestors alive. This shows how the eighteenth-century cult of secular immortality was encouraged by the new way to envisage time as continuing endlessly into the future; it was by this means that the conception of immortality was related to the theory of limitless and indefinite progress. Compared with previous centuries, it was not nature, but man himself, who was now thought to confer this form of survival in the memory of his descendants. It was born from the recognition that time had ceased to be finite and soon to be terminated by the end of the world and the Day of Judgement. Now, it was time itself which became endless, or "timeless".[24]

Mercier also approaches the idea of immortality at least in one text, entitled "*Anatomie*", from a purely biological point of view. He writes that immortality can be found from the transubstantiation of matter; nature destroys with one hand, repairs with another. Focusing his analysis on a dead human body he recognizes death as a part of the order of nature, noting that through the cycle of death and rebirth matter incessantly changes its form: "La vie & la mort forment les deux bouts de la chaîne dont tu embrasses tous les êtres. L'individu meurt, dit ton historien, & l'espece subsiste immortelle."[25]

The message conveyed by "*Anatomie*" is that the idea of transubstantiation makes death a necessity in order that life in its entirety could be maintained. Following the cycle of death and rebirth, from the viewpoint of the total order of things, death has a purifying effect. The suggestion that underlies this line of thought is that it is only through death that death can be conquered. This reflects yet another customary reading of immortality that took shape in the course of the eighteenth century. It was now argued, D.G. Charlton suggests, that death was biologically useful. It was a process within organic and dynamic nature: what died was not lost but was essential for the sustaining of future life. Because matter was according to this view thought to be indestructible, man would survive eternally.[26]

It is appropriate to conclude this chapter by noting that in Mercier's utopian visions death is without exception regarded as synonymous with absolute rest and the final stage of man's journey toward supreme perfectibility and light. It is in the experience of death that the individual "I" dissolves and assimilates with Divinity, which is the manifestation of the absolute truth. In practise this means that the principle of movement (the idea of continuous progress as synonym for man's terrestrial journey) is replaced by the principle of eternal rest. From this it

. . . .

23   Gay 1970, 90; McManners 1981, 172.
24   Charlton 1984, 100–104.
25   Mercier, *Notions claires sur les gouvernemens I* 1784 263–264.
26   Charlton 1984, 101–102.

is to be concluded that in Mercier's mind the supreme form of happiness is found from the state of rest, not from the state of perpetual movement. As he conceived it, death is the condition of absolute rest, because it is a state in which there is no more restlessness, in which all time ends. It is the end of time, the end of suffering, the ultimate utopia.

Conclusions

Mercier had a dream. It was a dream of a regenerated world in every sense of the term, – religious, political, social and economic. In his *L'An 2440* he projects into the far future a vision of a society where men could live in mutual respect and understanding, in total harmony both with their inner selves and with surrounding nature. It is a representation of the imaginary Paris and of the world of the twenty-fifth century, when the powers of darkness and obscurity have been dissipated, when the tyranny of despotic rulers and their avaricious ministers as well as that of the intolerant doctrines of the catholic priests has turned to dust and fallen into the eternal night of oblivion. Even the memory of these monstrous figures of the "gothic" past has vanished from the minds of the future generations, and the sole function accorded to them is to provide warning examples. For Mercier this was the worst conceivable punishment which could confront a reasonable being, because in his view the vision of a secular immortality through being remembered by posterity was the most consoling bulwark against the haunting vision of death.

Mercier's grandiloquent vision of the remote future was born from a sentiment of moral indignation, acute anger and frustration, as a critical antithesis against the inequalities and abuses of the French society in the final years of the *ancien régime*, which he thought to be in a state of total chaos and disorder. Wherever he turned his eyes, he saw only cruelties, stupidity, low-mindedness and vestiges of barbarism. What most aroused Mercier's concern was the widening of the social and economic gulf between the richest and poorest layers of society. His anger was particularly inflamed by the selfish lust for luxury, which made people forget the gospel precept, according to which without the practise of virtue, moderation and modesty, the gates would be closed to the pleasures of an earthly paradise. Mercier's preoccupation with the weakening of morals was also related to his misogynist conviction that the increased arrogance of women and their special lust for luxury items had began to constitute a danger threatening masculine power in the public sector of life.

With his two masterpieces, *L'An 2440* and *Tableau de Paris*, Mercier left to posterity an image of two cities, one destined to happiness and light, the other dominated by the omnipotence of death, the oppressing shadow of which makes its repulsive presence felt in the smell of rotting corpses, in the merciless reality of slaughterhouses, and in a general atmosphere of violence, prostitution, crime and executions. As a chronicle of horror Mercier depicts in his *Tableau de Paris* the capital of France, on the eve of the French Revolution, as an abode of blood and terror, above which the angel of the Apocalypse seems to be floating. As the opposite to this, Paris in 2440 appears as a city of utmost purity, chastity, cleanliness and virginity in both its physical and moral aspects. To use feminine metaphors, whilst the former of these two cities is veiled in mourning, the latter rises as a bride in her wedding clothes far above all unhappiness and sorrow. By this means Mercier breathes new life into the ancient dichotomy between the "Vicious Babylon" and the "Heavenly Jerusalem", which has not lost anything of its magnetic allure.

Mercier, himself an outsider from the elitist academic circles focused around the great philosophers, and who for this reason felt unjustly ignored, represented a voice from the margins. It is above all in this marginal position where his strength lay. As Mercier himself asserted, only a writer living in a marginal social position can have a genuine capacity to identify himself with the heartbreaking lot of the "suffering poor". Seen from this perspective, mental and physical pain and suffering is the great catalyzing force, which makes man create visions of a better and more beautiful world. In Mercier's literary production the happy Other is most often represented under the guise of a dream. It can also be a land beyond the grave, as in many of his "*songes*", an escape to some exotic and mythic primitive condition as in *L'Homme sauvage*, or a journey to a not-yet-existent temporal projection as in *L'An 2440*,

Throughout his life Mercier was spurred by a strictly two-focused attitude to the world. The seemingly unresolved antagonism between "spleen" and "ideal" runs like a *leitmotiv* throughout his voluminous literary production. Mercier was profoundly aware that man's terrestrial journey was too often paved with tears, and that the most virtuous ones were often those who had to suffer most, whereas the rich and selfish could wallow in abundance. Yet Mercier never lost his faith in man's ultimate goodness and his inborn capacity for perfectibility. The underlying idea in all his major writings is that evil institutions had led man away from his original destination, and if the vicious political and religious systems were abolished, humankind would have the possibility to return to its primordial state of happiness.

Mercier conceptualized life through juxtapositions and contrasts, such as light – darkness, knowledge – ignorance, public – private. This was his way to bring organization and rationality to the seeming chaos of life, into the polyphony of dissident and often conflicting voices. If one approaches Mercier's utopian vision from the viewpoint of different kinds of polarization, one can draw the following conclusions: 1) Light is synonymous with happiness, whereas darkness refers to the principle of evil (ignorance, superstition, prejudice); 2) The accumulation of scientific knowledge increases the sum of human happiness, because it contributes to the enlargement of spatial and temporal horizons. This is not, however, a totally uncomplicated matter. Sometimes, Mercier seems to suggest, man is happier in ignorance than when he is educated. For example, the savages are happier by this means, owing to the fact that foreknowledge of the future may increase the sense of unhappiness instead of decreasing it; 3) In Mercier's utopian society total transparency, openness and publicity constitute the rule, which is based on an assumption that secrecy and privacy can do damage to "public felicity". For this reason there is no room for private intentions, passions or interests, which are seen as a threat against the general well-being of the community.

Like the majority of his educated contemporaries, Mercier put his faith in the power of reason. In his utopian society of 2440 it is a magic word, which, it is believed, will finally unlock all the mysteries of the universe. To put it metaphorically, the "Goddess of Reason" sits on her majestic throne, ensuring that the bright new day shines above men liberated from all authorities except that of their own reason. The message of Mercier's novel is that with the help of experimental science man would be able, by rather simple means, to learn the intentions of God which are manifested through the laws of nature. The lens of the telescope discloses for the young men of 2440 a channel of initiation towards wisdom and divinity, because it makes them feel a sentiment of cosmic joy prompted by the recognition that they are related to a much larger totality than themselves.

Mercier did not, however, believe that man's reason could ever be "complete" in the sense that the human brain could develop a totally coherent intellectual system, which would be able to explain everything that exists. In his writings he urges men to accept the limitations of their understanding compared with absolute wisdom and perfection, which is reserved for God alone. Since, in Mercier's view, man formed the "middle link" in the scale of creatures, man should always recognize his human weaknesses and admit that in the final resort he was living amidst a mysterious universe which could never be known in its entirety. This double-position with regard to man and his relation to God and the whole cosmos forms one integral aspect of Mercier's contradictory attitude to the world; on the one hand he stresses the fact that man can, with the aid of the rational part of his soul, learn to master nature, while on the other he emphasizes that ultimately God's plan remains under the veil of obscurity, and contains many irrational and mystical elements.

In Mercier's case the awareness that not all God's intentions were exposed to man's eye did not, however, lead to sentiments of desperation or frustration. Following in the footsteps of Leibniz, he laid his confidence in the existence of a "universal plan of harmony", in which everything had been planned in advance for man's supreme happiness. He believed in God's benevolence and that the whole of nature, including man himself, was animated by this same benevolence. Accordingly, because "everything is well", man had nothing to be afraid of, and even the most frightening and devastating events had been preordained by God.

Mercier's firm belief in man's inborn goodness and benevolence led him to argue that man has a natural inclination for virtue. One of the leading tenors of L'An 2440 is that without virtue no man can find happiness, and only a man who uses his reason can be virtuous. In practise this means that those who follow their inborn instinct to do good things in the spirit of social compassion will be able to find tranquility of mind, which is the necessary precondition for happiness. Following this logic, the sum of man's happiness increases from the knowledge that he has contributed to the happiness of his fellow creatures.

This fundamental thesis concerning man's inborn capacity for virtue forms the basis of Mercier's focal idea that the necessary condition of happy life is sociability. This explains why the utopians that he created let themselves be bound by a Rousseauist social pact which imposes on them mutual rights and duties. Their most important duty is to follow the precepts of "righteous" morals in all their thoughts and actions, in order that they never commit an infraction against the collective well-being. Mercier believed that this would not be an impossible task, since if men were assumed to be good by nature, an evil man would be naturally at war against his own inner self.

Since in Mercier's utopian society the social pact, the legitimacy of which is founded on the "law of nature", constitutes the supreme norm and the ultimate court of appeal, no dissidence of opinion is permitted. The highest ideal in all domains of life is uniformity, which resembles the art of the fugue; everything has to play in perfect harmony, in the same way as the "universal music of the spheres" plays in the heavens above. The thesis is that when there exists harmonious reconciliation between the "law of nature" and the "law of society", an optimal ground is laid for the principle of total uniformity and unity in man's relations to society, nature and the entire universe.

In order to follow the norm of uniformity Mercier's utopians are constantly forced to develop their skills in the art of becoming obedient and disciplined citizens. Because the society of 2440 resembles in its entirety a great pedagogical institution, a prominent role is accorded to education. The process of perfectibility consists of practicing virtue through useful works and contemplation. In men's contemplative life the telescope is of supreme importance, as suggested above.

In the lives of Mercier's utopian citizens the highest level of moral and spiritual perfection on earth is attained when man has been able to purify himself from all egoistic passions (excessive eating and drinking, exterior decoration and other luxury items, uncontrolled outbursts of sexual desire). *L'An 2440* breathes a profound aversion toward all passions, or "particular interests", which aim at satisfying only passing and personal caprices. The only legitimate passions are purely spiritual or intellectual by nature. The pleasure reached through this kind of passions rises from the elevated sentiment caused by an experience of the magnificence of the universe or from the knowledge that one has contributed to the general well-being of the whole community, for example by helping those in need or by offering voluntarily to do filthy works. In the hierarchy of passions, carnal passions thus occupy only a secondary place. Consequently Mercier represents in his utopia, in total antithesis to a hedonistic and pleasure-oriented conception of happiness, a worldly and puritan asceticism.

This rigorous attitude can particularly clearly be seen in Mercier's ideas about luxury and consumption. As Mercier hoped, in the twenty-fifth century frugality and moderation would constitute the rule, whilst "conspicuous consumption" in the form of abundance and the unlimited satisfaction of desires would be strictly banned. As a utopian writer Mercier preaches the virtue of contentment, asserting that under optimal conditions there exists a justly balanced proportion between man's desires and his possibility to satisfy them. The implication is that if there is a contradiction between desires and their satisfaction, man falls, eventually, into a state of frustration, melancholy and desperation.

By emphasizing the importance of moderation and the equal distribution of goods, Mercier focuses his criticism against the cruelty and lack of social compassion characterizing France on the eve of the Revolution. With his utopian image of an ever-full and inexhaustible grain store house he directs his attack against the monstrous disproportion between wealth and poverty in eighteenth-century society as well as against the shortage of bread ensuing from devastating harvests, which in Mercier's view made all advancement of happiness impossible in late eighteenth-century France, at least for the poorer social strata.

There can be seen, however, some changes between the different versions of *L'An 2440* considering the problem of production and consumption. Whereas in the edition of 1770 (or 1771) great stress is laid on the denial of all earthly pleasures, in the versions of 1786 and 1799 Mercier's attitude is less rigorous and more ambivalent, which means that not all enjoyments are simply condemned. In the later versions of the novel he includes comments supporting the desirability of economic progress and the possibility that luxury might also increase the amount of human happiness instead of solely decreasing it. The ambiguities in Mercier's text reveal his status as a writer living and working amidst the turmoils of economic, social and political convulsions.

Despite its secular tendency Mercier's future society is, in many respects, deeply indebted to the religious ideals of monasticism. Religion forms the cornerstone of life, never interrupted by "carnival" pleasures or unexpected outbursts of either sorrow or joy. The passage of days forms a monotonous chain of repetitious events, following the rhythm of work and leisure. Also recreational activities are organized on a rational basis, devoted to healthy and moral pursuits such as the cultivation of one's mind and amusements in a rural setting, which is preferred to the temptations of big cities. The suggestion is that only when all seductions are eschewed, thus man has the opportunity to concentrate on what is most important in life: the improvement of one's moral character. It is thus spiritual and moral perfectibility that counts most. Progress in other domains of life occupies only a secondary place in the scale of values.

All this sustains the same conclusion: In Mercier's utopia man can attain genuine happiness only when reason controls the passions. The basic demand is that there should exist no discord or conflict in man's inner self. Following this logic, immutability and rest is a better condition than continual movement; man should not be a slave of the caprices of the passions and of the negative sort of restlessness prompted by them. In Mercier's utopia, calm felicity is the ideal human condition.

Mercier's ideal citizens of the future are a combination of a Christian saint and a Cartesian-Stoic hero, who display considerable courage when confronted by dangers and who are always ready to sacrifice their personal interests when the advantage of the whole community demands it. The more fortunate ones keep their tables open for those in need, and luxury is put into general circulation from the upper social strata to the lower. Men do not hesitate to publicly protest when some calamity threatens to put the social equilibrium in jeopardy, because they know that when one man is forced to suffer, the whole society is doomed to suffer. This proves that cold rational reflection is not, in the final resort, the only path to happiness. In order to find tranquility of the mind, one also has listen to the voice of one's own heart. This is the uniting idea in Mercier's utopia: when man helps those in pain, virtue is rewarded in the form of deep inner satisfaction and a good conscience.

In Mercier's new terrestrial paradise there are also mansions reserved for "fallen angels", which means that not all evil elements have automatically been eliminated even from the "best of all possible worlds". They form dissident voices in the polyphonic chorus praising the glory of God and the holiness of the social pact. Since uniformity forms the basis of life, instead of being a consequence of the "Fall" of Adam, sin is now a synonym for social disorder. All manifestations of Otherness, which could form a threat for the all-encompassing norm of uniformity, are treated with fear and condemned as "abnormality". In order to protect itself from the danger of collapsing back into a state of social chaos, Mercier's imaginary community protects itself with secrecy and exclusion. The worst sanction which can confront a disobedient citizen is to be marginalized and excluded from the magic circle of social life. Expulsion from the community means a kind of civic death, since Mercier's utopians have no life beyond their social role which they are predestined to perform as functional units of the human "beehive".

The section of Mercier's utopia devoted to the treatment of the "abnormal" or antisocial elements illustrates in extreme doctrinal form the argument advanced by Adorno and Horkheimer according to which in the Enlightenment's attempt to purify itself from the fear of the unknown through demythologization, the mythology entered into the profane. In this process the fear of uncomprehended, threatening nature, the consequence of its objectification, was reduced to animistic superstition: "Myth turns into enlightenment, and nature into mere objectivity."[1]

Mercier's utopia shows in practise how myth and the Enlightenment were intertwined in the eighteenth-century project of emancipation itself. The main focus of the novel is an attempt to find ways through which man would be able to liberate himself from the burden of superstitions and prejudices by using his own reason. Eventually, however, this ambitious dream of all-encompassing rationalization, based on the condemnation of all mythical, barbaric, or "gothic" vestiges of men's life, returns to those same "pre-modern", "pre-rational" and "pre-logical" practises that it aims at eradicating. In Mercier's utopian society the obsessive fear of everything which deviates from the criteria of normality and abnormality is exposed to the same kind of "magic" or ritual practises used in archaic societies: the "abnormals" are stigmatized with the

. . . .
1   Adorno & Horkheimer 1979, 9, 27–32.

"mark of Cain" in the forehead, the scapegoats are deported from the community. Their situation is desperate in the sense that under the visible mark of shame they have no place to hide. Because life spent under the shadow of opprobrium is more burdensome to bear than death, Mercier's imaginary murderer chooses voluntary death, which illustrates the formula that man is "forced to be free".

In Mercier's utopia the "mark of Cain" or the "mask of shame" function as visible symbols hinting that the principle of evil has entered paradise. By stigmatizing the "abnormals" with visible symbols indicating shameful and marginalized status, the community protects itself against all dissident elements which could disturb its intact virginity. Through various purifying rituals the utopians of 2440 aim at tearing out the roots of evil from the life of the collectivity.

The cycle is the symbol of utmost purity. Similarly, the utopian city of 2440 is not merely one concrete geographical location, but "the city", a meta-empirical and immutable idea of a beautiful urban environment. It forms a "magic circle", which exists for the sole purpose of preserving its immutability against all foreign intrusions. In its desire to maintain the condition of *status quo* at any cost, Mercier's model does not eventually differ much from the classical "magic island" utopias, where isolation is thought to be a necessary precondition of happiness.

The "magic circle" turns, however, to be a "vicious circle". The way Mercier treats the "abnormals", – psychic manipulation, indoctrination, stigmatization, – is reminiscent of authoritarian societies. In the final resort, the bright light which is supposed to penetrate Mercier's city of all-encompassing purity and transparency by day and night, rather resembles the cold light of the interrogation chamber. This leads to the conclusion that Mercier's so-called paradise is actually a living hell. It is a zombie-land, peopled by impersonal and anonymous automata, without any individuality, privacy or capacity to influence on the conduct of their own lives. The atmosphere prevailing in Mercier's future Paris is equally oppressive as in Huxley's or Orwell's nightmarish visions of the future. This reveals the self-destructive elements of the philosophy of the Enlightenment, its annihilation of its own ideals. *L'An 2440* shows in practise how a well-intentioned movement aiming at the liberation of man from his self-imposed tutelage becomes transformed into its opposite, an iron cage of excessive rationalization.

What Mercier was incapable of realizing was that in its ultimate form the idealization of uniformity becomes the opposite of happiness, a monotonous state of boredom. As so often occurs with utopian experiments, so also in Mercier's model the utopia changes into the antithesis of happiness, a "land of the living dead", or a "necropolis", from which all pleasure is excluded. The paradox lies in Mercier's assumption that virtue and nature are automatically compatible, and that individual happiness follows as a natural by-product of collective well-being. As a consequence, his utopians are not free men in the modern sense of the term, but slaves of a universal norm, which makes them prisoners of illusory freedom.

Mercier's gravest deficit is precisely his blindness to the fact that basically happiness is a feeling, an inner sentiment, which cannot be imposed on the individual from above. Eventually, "happiness" grounded on a strict educational program and on the imposition of a common and invariable normative yardstick for all, does not lead to happiness but tragedy.

The organization of man and his relation to society in Mercier's year 2440 demonstrates that the concept "collective well-being" is in itself highly problematic. If one takes it for granted that all men automatically want the same things, the entire concept of individual happiness is severely compromised, since, even if men's primary needs remain everywhere approximately the same (in order to survive, they need drink, food and sleep), there are many individual variations between men as regards the scale of secondary needs. In the category of these secondary needs can be classified, for example, the desire to be distinguished from the others. The scale of these secondary needs allowed for Mercier's "ideal citizens" is extremely limited; in his future Paris the sole criteria of social distinction is that based on the practise of virtue, which is rewarded with a "brocaded hat". Because the leading ideals are humility, moderation and scarcity, all pursuits aiming at the attainment of personal glory or the satisfaction of "self-interest" are condemned.

The authoritarian nature of Mercier's utopia shows in its clearest form in the treatment of the "women question". The social, political, economic and sexual *status quo* is maintained by the rigorous exclusion of women from all possibilities to influence public affairs. The society of 2440 is profoundly patriarchal; women are regarded as naturally subordinated to men. Because of their presumably precarious nature they cannot live as autonomous human beings; the "happiness" of women is directly dependent on their capacity to please their husbands, who have become "sovereign masters" in their homes. The end result is a kind of "dictatorship of virtue", which means that a "passionate" or independent woman is labeled as "unnatural" or "monstrous".

Despite the fact that in Mercier's "paradise" women have not reached the status of "*citoyennes*" even in 2440, he was one of the first writers living in late eighteenth-century France who had a clear awareness of the increased significance of "public opinion". Mercier's message in all his major writings is that there should be no secrets, the word should have its full power, an alliance between government and education should be established. Despite this progressive attitude he was sceptical as regards the scope of education and the rights of political participation. Mercier did not believe that the members of the lower social orders had sufficient intellectual capacity to participate in the common affairs, any more than he believed in women's active role in the public sphere. He believed that since both the masses and women were easily misled by their "violent passions", they should be constantly supervised and guided under the paternalistic protection of the "father's eye".

This is one of the aspects in which the contradictory nature of Mercier's utopia appears most striking: at the same time as he criticizes the authoritarian censorship practiced in eighteenth-century France, Mercier makes the writers and artists of 2440 function as mouthpieces of the official ideology of the state.

Discordant opinions are silenced, and undoctrinal writers are forced to bear on their face the "mask of shame". Similarly, Mercier preaches on behalf of religious toleration, yet at the same time suggests that in 2440 a "Jewish conspiracy" has been revealed and led to measures of revenge by the French.

One section of this examination was devoted to the concept of time and its significance in Mercier's utopian vision. A crucial aspect in which *L'An 2440* differs from previous utopian models, such as those created for example by Plato and More, is that the ideal state is no longer projected beyond mysterious sea journeys in some "magical island", or in a mythical past, but in the future. In contrast to the earlier utopian tradition, in Mercier's vision of the twenty-fifth century the imaginary time of utopia and the "real" time of historical duration are no longer separated by an insurmountable gulf. The categories of "spleen" and "ideal" ("is" and "ought") no longer form two totally autonomous categories of experience, which, like east and west, can never meet. Instead, they form two separate points in one and the same linear process of continuous progress. From now on, the ideal can become reality, a platonic ideal can be transformed into a living utopia.

This reveals a decisive change in the temporal horizon, i.e., in the mutual relation of experience and expectation; time is no longer man's enemy, but the realizer of all good things on earth. The dream of terrestrial happiness is no longer haunted by the oppressive prospect that the end of the world may come at any moment. The passage of time is now the very precondition of happiness, a necessary factor which will eventually ensure indefinite and endless amelioration in all domains of life.

As a mechanism of transformation from the miseries of eighteenth-century France to the ideal state of 2440 Mercier relies on the theory of gradual and slow, but uninterrupted, indefinite and irrevocable progress. The underlying idea is that the shift from "is" to "ought" cannot occur miraculously in a moment or even in a brief time span. Only a long-lasting and possibly painful evolutionary process can achieve the optimal end result. Mercier did not support abrupt or violent changes, and his extremely hostile attitude toward the massacres of the French Revolution, together with his denial of any causal connection between philosophical ideas and revolutionary action, gives ample evidence of this. Instead of a revolution in terms of the sudden violent turnover of existing power relations, he believed in a "happy revolution" which would be executed through the power of education and the spreading of enlightenment.

As a harbinger of this positive and gradual change, Mercier accords a prominent place to the "*prophète philosophique*", whose quasi-sacred duty it is to be responsible for the dissemination of enlightened thinking. This writer-philosopher is a promethean figure, a kind of "substitute-Christ", whose task is to accelerate the tempo of progress and ensure that men do not regress back to a state of ignorance, superstition and prejudice. His mission is to awaken men from their state of blindness caused by evil political, social and religious institutions, and to recognize their "real interests".

In *L'An 2440* it is thus man himself whose task it is to achieve the shift to an ameliorated state in the future. As we have seen, the role of God in the conduct of men's lives is not, however, ruled out. Vehemently rejecting the idea of a vengeful God, Mercier believed in a benevolent Creator, who could never have intended unhappiness for mankind. And, since everything has been preordained by God in the moment of creation, nothing can hinder the gradual realization of God's secret plan. Accordingly, Mercier's utopians dominate the natural order by discovering its laws.

As regards the treatment of this theme in Mercier's various texts, however, slight differences emerge: whereas in *L'An 2440* the main emphasis is on man's own role as the prime agent of his happiness or unhappiness, in his mystical and religious "*songes*" more stress is laid on the assumption of God's pre-ordered plan and man's duty to accept his lot.

Mercier's belief in a preordained and providential plan laid the foundation for his basically deterministic view of the nature of historical processes and the future destiny of man. This deterministic attitude is focused on a fatalistic concept of "necessity", which means that both the good and the bad things which happen to man are inevitable. According to this logic, it is "necessary" that man has been born on earth in order to search for happiness, because by thus doing he acts according to his nature, which distinguishes him from the rest of created beings. The theory of necessity also provides an answer to the haunting problem how to explain all the wickedness in the world: evil exists because it is God's will. Even the worst of evils, natural disasters, suffering and death, can be explained by following the philosophical notion of "necessity".

This necessitarian philosophy seems to be in contradiction to Mercier's promethean view of man as the prime mover of progress. It eliminates man's active role as a free agent, the master of his own life. On the one hand great emphasis is put on man's omnipotence and dominant position over the rest of created beings, on the other hand Mercier refers constantly to the limited nature of man's understanding and his merely relative and mediocre happiness compared with the supreme wisdom and perfection reserved only for beings more spiritual than himself. In this sense man is a split creature, with his feet in the mud and his head reaching the skies.

This leads to the conclusion that despite his good intentions, Mercier was ultimately not able to resolve the problem of man's basically tragic nature. In his view it was man's lot to be engaged on a never-ending journey towards higher and higher spheres of happiness, but as a limited creature he was doomed to chase an illusion. The tragic nature of man is born expressly from the knowledge that absolute happiness cannot be from this world. Because of man's inborn capacity for perfectibility and his unique inclination to create elevated visions of a better existence without being ever totally capable of reaching them, the state of absolute rest can never be achieved on earth.

Mercier's faith in a Leibnizian God who had created the world through the sole act of His will, after which no further interventions from His part had been needed, also laid the ground for his belief in the theory of biological "preformationism". He had no doubt that if there is natural evolution, it can only be towards a preordained goal. Although Mercier believed in the transformation of species, this does not lead to an innovative idea of natural evolution. In his vision the factor of time constitutes merely one element in a basically static taxonomy, which irrespective of the passsage of time cannot produce anything fundamentally new. Mercier still held to a rather static idea of the Great Chain of Being, which also encompasses his ideas concerning social and economic advancement; as he suggests in his utopia, the best thing is for man to be content with his position in the scale of created beings, without striving at bettering his social or economic status. The ideal position exists somewhere between the extremes, reinforcing the idea of a "happy middle way".

All this testifies to the fact that Mercier did not yet have a full apprehension of the nature of evolutionary change. This is particularly clearly to be seen in his projection into the far future of the focal philosophical ideals of his own time. Mercier put his confidence in the hegemony of Enlightenment values even in the far future. This leads him to believe that in the course of time the whole of humankind will become like one collective being, and differences in the level of progress between different nations merely reflect different stages on the same progressive journey. With the exception of Mercier's eulogy of the primitive and "natural" life style of the noble savages in *L'Homme sauvage*, the idea of cultural diversity was alien to him, and he believed that over the centuries the whole globe would be liberated from "false happiness" and brought under a single (European) structure of values. In practise this assigns the members of the white, European race the mission of the "beautiful conquest", as Mercier calls it, to ensure that all peoples and races would sooner or later benefit from the gospel of progress.

Obviously, despite Mercier´s intention to provide a vista of possible futures, his thought was thus too keenly rooted in the mental structures of his own age for him to imagine a future world founded on ideals different than those of the late eighteenth-century world. In this respect Mercier emerges as a typical representative of the common attitude of his century, which still held to a static and a-historical conception of progress, founded on the premise that if progress did occur, it could only lead to an ameliorated version of the present conditions.

The linear, forward-looking structure of Mercier's utopian vision does not, however, exclude cyclical and mythical elements. There are several points in the text which demonstrate that Mercier's dream of the future was not so much a totally new horizon of expectations but also to some extent a return to a primordial condition. This nostalgic element can particularly clearly be seen in the agrarian way of life of the society depicted in Mercier's utopia. There are no major signs of scientific-technical advance. Science is esoteric in character, and rational means to study nature exist side by side with mysticism.

This retrogressive aspect of Mercier's vision can be interpreted in two different ways. It is possible to argue that he had not sufficient prophetic capacity to foresee the breakthrough of the industrial revolution and the accelerating tempo of modernization and urbanization. Another solution is that Mercier was all too acutely aware of the dangers contained in scientific-technological progress, and that he felt anxiety in the face of the inevitable disappearance of the traditional life style dominated more strongly by the cyclical movement of time.

In this study it has been shown that a proper understanding of Mercier's utopia necessitates that it is read, above all, as a nostalgic apologia on behalf of a rural world and an agrarian life-style, which the rapid tempo of industrialization was in the near future to cast into oblivion. This interpretation finds support from the fact that in Mercier's imaginary Paris men prefer walking to using carriages, and they traverse the oceans with rowboats. There is no mention of factories, industrial work or steam machinery.

In addition to this, there are also many other elements which reveal the reactionary nature of Mercier's vision of the future. To begin with, in the important chapter of *L'An 2440* on the "two infinities", the secrets of the universe seen through the lens of the telescope are reserved only for the few and chosen, which implies an esoteric conception of supreme knowledge. Women are not admitted to these initiation rites, which reinforces the patriarchal structure of Mercier's utopian society. Against this background it is justified to argue that the observatory of Mercier's twenty-fifth century resembles the "Salomon's House" in Bacon's *Nova Atlantis* more than modern research institutions based on public access to the fruits of scientific progress.

Moreover, the focal ideals of Mercier's utopia are drawn from a stock of mythical and a-historical images. The most important of these is the social contract, which, based on the theory of natural law, is basically static. By elevating it as the foundation of the social and political life of his future citizens, Mercier pays homage to Rousseau, and, by implication, to ancient Sparta and to the Stoic conception of virtue. The admiration of ancient models shows in many details, such as the similarities of the ideal women of 2440 to Roman matriarchs, the modeling of the clothing of Mercier's utopians on the floating togas of antiquity, and the description of the ruler as a descendant of the "philosopher-king" of Plato, who rules according to the philosophical teachings of his advisers.

It is also striking that *L'An 2440* contains no mention of clocks or the artificial measurement of time. This too reads as a symbolic appeal on behalf of a pre-modern way of life, when the passage of days was determined by the cyclical processes of nature. This does not, however, mean a lack of discipline or laziness. By contrast, Mercier's utopians follow rigorous puritan morals, which tells them not to waste time, since work is a calling, a special duty to serve God. All of these features reinforce the reading that a return back to a Golden Age, original paradise or Dreamtime formed the inner core of Mercier's utopian longing.

A cyclical view of the world also dominates many of Mercier's exterminatory visions, where a periodical natural disaster or convulsion is destined to purify the world from moral and physical evil. In these visions various different elements, such as water and fire, often function as symbolic instruments of purification. In addition to being based on a cyclical pattern of repetition, the destruction may be totally final, infernal and apocalyptic. In the same way as the utopian community depicted by Mercier resists intrusion by foreign elements with rites of purification (e.g, the excommunication of the "non-believers"), natural disasters have a cathartic function to restore the ruptured harmony of the world. Following this pattern, it sometimes occurs that the existing chaos can be solved only by abolishing everything inherited from the past and starting everything from the beginning: a new utopia rises from the ashes of the old world, progress takes place through destruction.

The most striking aspect of Mercier's utopian vision is his complex and often contradictory view of the different phenomena of life. His work reveals a constant and unresolved tension between a static and a more dynamic view of the world. On the one hand Mercier was an ardent supporter of progress and the "civilizing process"; on the other he dreamed of a return to some primordial condition of happiness, where all days were similar and were time was petrified in an eternal present moment. The same man who saw continuous change as the main source of human happiness also expressed sceptical views of the possibility of the destruction of Paris and the whole universe as a consequence of some devastating disaster, bursting into mournful and melancholic lamentations on the precariousness of human existence amidst a mysterious and irrational universe.

The supreme value of Mercier's utopian vision as an object of cultural historical study lies expressly in its status as a document of a period in transition. It mirrors the sentiments of an epoch not yet emancipated from the traditional structure of values attached to the mentality of *longue durée*, but already beginning to grasp the idea of accelerated change. *L'An 2440* thus also reflects the changes which had begun to transform utopian discourse itself. Mercier's novel constitutes an intermediary stage between static and closed classical spatial utopias focused on "calm felicity", at the same time anticipating the innovative and dynamic "uchronias" of the nineteenth and twentieth centuries.

All in all, Mercier's inexhaustible productivity and his wide range of subjects, from contemporary philosophical debate to the everyday life of the common people of Paris in the years immediately preceding the great explosion, offers immeasurable new, fresh perspectives for the cultural historian of the *ancien régime*. Mercier's habit of constantly modifying and reshaping his writings, without caring to correct his former views, even further increases their documentary value.

Mercier's utopia of 2440 opens a vista to the eighteenth-century mind with a profundity not equaled by many novels, essays or treatises produced in late eighteenth-century France. With its wider scope than many recognized and canonized works of the elite culture, Mercier's utopia succeeds in reanimating the often cacophonous voices of the French *ancien régime*. Through the jungle of these voices Mercier traces one voice above all the others: the conquering voice of philosophy, which would eventually triumph over the tyranny of the persecutors, break the omnipresence of death and ensure the status of immortality for the "despised" and "forgotten" – for "voices from the margins" like Mercier himself.

It would be much too easy to criticize Mercier for the lack of predictive power, which has been the common charge directed against him in scholarly discussion. There is no point in denying this: in his writings Mercier does not present strikingly original ideas, but is content to echo views first put forward by more prominent literary and philosophical talents than himself. From this perspective, one has to admit some justification for labels such as "ape of Rousseau" or "ape of Diderot". Admittedly, Mercier distinguished himself as a critical descendant of the preceding philosophical tradition, but this did not mean any increase of radicalism. By contrast, as a utopian writer he belonged to the camp of the conservatives. Mercier was a reformist, not a revolutionary. He believed that no pervasive turnover of the existing order of things was needed in order to ameliorate the world, and all the reforms suggested by him in *L'An 2440* were basically rooted in the structures of the *ancien régime*.

This does not, however, diminish the value of Mercier's utopian vision as an authentic document of its time; rather the contrary: Mercier managed, with inexhaustible skill, to weave into the texture of his diverse writings a critical examination of all things that the majority of his contemporaries, from the wealthy members of the cultural elites to the despised writers of *libelles*, wished to condemn – tyranny, superstition, prejudice. As such it functions as a kind of a magic mirror through which the entire life of an epoch of the past is filtered with all its shades and colors. As Simon Collier puts it, *L'An 2440* "gives us an unusual portrayal of Enlightenment social ideals as adumbrated in this fantasized form."[2]

The utopian novels of the eighteenth century express a critical attitude towards various aspects of life more vividly than any scientific essay or moral treatise could have been capable of. They thus capture the potentiality for change in a society on the threshold of vast social, economic and political convulsions. The French eighteenth-century utopias functioned as precursors of all important ideologies which have molded the formation of modern societies. To quote F.L. Polak in this issue, "the utopia of the Enlightenment was not only seeking the answer to the challenge of its own time, but the answer for our time as well."[3]

One can only imagine how distant the twenty-fifth century must have appeared over two hundred years ago, when Mercier saw it as a horizon of a new "golden age" in the history of mankind. For us living in the first years of the twenty-first century, optimistic faith in the omnipotence of progress has, by contrast, for the most part lost its magnetic appeal. The belief in a paradise on earth has vanished like a mirage in the desert. It has been suggested that in the literature of our time everything but happiness seems to be possible. It does not interest writers anymore. The very term happiness has become despised in the same manner as "virtue", "innocence" or "virginity". From the perspective of

. . . .
2   Collier 1990, 89.
3   Polak 1961, 317.

the new philosophy, happiness has no place, because existence is dominated by angst.[4]

Although Mercier was not totally unaware of the potential dangers contained in excessive scientific-technological progress, he as yet had no such reservations. He had no doubt that despite possible setbacks and obstacles, in the final resort the continuous march of progress could no longer be hindered. Joining ranks with the most optimistic of his contemporaries, such as Condorcet or Turgot, Mercier was convinced that the world could be changed into a place of general prosperity and well-being by relatively simple means. The gulf between "spleen" and "ideal" would not be insurmountable, after all. For him man was still a sojourner in the best of all possible worlds; the magic spell of the universal music of the spheres had not yet been broken.

. . . .

4   Cioranescu 1995, 28.

Bibliography

MERCIER'S WRITINGS

Printed sources

Mercier, Louis-Sébastien: *L'An deux mille quatre cent quarante. Rêve s'il en fut jamais; suivi de l'Homme de fer: songe.* Nouvelle édition. Avec figures. 3 vol. [s.l.] 1786.

Mercier, [Louis-Sébastien]: *Le Bonheur des gens de lettres.* Cailleau: A Londres, & se trouve à Paris 1766.

Mercier, [Louis-Sébastien]: *L'Homme sauvage.* Histoire traduite de... La Veuve Duchesne: Paris 1767.

Mercier, [Louis-Sébastien]: *Des malheurs de la guerre et des avantages de la paix.* Discours proposé par l'Académie Françoise en 1766. L. Cellot: A La Haye et se trouve à Paris 1767a

Mercier, [Louis-Sébastien]: *Songes philosophiques.* Lejay: A Londres, et se trouve à Paris 1768.

Mercier, Louis-Sébastien: *L'An deux mille quatre cent quarante. Rêve s'il en fut jamais.* Londres 1775.

[Mercier, Louis-Sébastien]: *Éloges et discours philosophiques,* Qui ont concouru pour les Prix de l'Académie Française & de plusieurs autres Académies. Par l'Auteur de l'Ouvrage intitulé L'an deux mille quatre cent quarante. E. van Harrevelt: Amsterdam 1776a.

[Mercier, Louis-Sébastien]: *Les Hommes comme il y a en a peu, et les génies comme il n'y en a point. Contes Moraux, Orientaux, Persans, Arabes, Turcs, Anglois, Francois, & etc., les uns pour rire, les autres à dormir debout.* Nouvelle édition. 3 vol. Société typographique: Bouillon 1776b.

Mercier, Louis-Sébastien: *Portraits des rois de France,* tome premier. Société Typographique: Neuchâtel 1783.

Mercier, [Louis-Sébastien]: *Mon bonnet de nuit.* Vol. I–II. Société typographique: Neufchâtel 1784.

[Mercier, Louis-Sébastien]: *L'An deux mille quatre cent quarante.* Nouvelle édition, exactement corrigée et augmentée d´un volume. Tome second. Londres 1785.

Mercier, [Louis-Sébastien]: *Mon bonnet de nuit.* Vol. III–IV. J. P. Heubach: Lausanne 1786a.

[Mercier, Louis-Sébastien]: *Les entretiens du Palais-Royal.* Vol. I–II. Buisson: A Utrecht et se trouve à Paris 1786b.

Mercier, [Louis-Sébastien]: *Notions claires sur les gouvernemens.* Tomes I–II. Amsterdam 1787.

Mercier, [Louis-Sébastien]: *Songes et visions philosophiques.* Voyages imaginaires, songes, visions, et romans cabalistiques. Tome trente-deuxième. A Amsterdam, et se trouve à Paris 1788a.

Mercier, [Louis-Sébastien] : *Les Songes d'un hermite* (1770). Voyages imaginaires, romanesques, merveilleux, allégoriques, amusans, comiques et critiques. Suivis des songes et visions, et des romans cabalistiques. Tome trente-unième. A Amsterdam, et se trouve à Paris 1788b.

Mercier, [Louis-Sébastien]: *Lettre au Roi, contenant un projet pour liquider en peu d'années toutes les dettes de l'État, en soulageant, dès-à- présent, le Peuple du fardeau des Impositions.* Les marchands de nouveautés: A Amsterdam, et se trouve à Paris 1789.

Mercier, [Louis-Sébastien]: *De Jean-Jacques Rousseau, considéré comme l'un des premiers auteurs de la Révolution.* 2 vol. Buisson: Paris 1791.

Mercier, [Louis-Sébastien]: *Fictions morales.* 3 vol. Cercle social: Paris 1792.

Mercier, L.-S.: *L'An deux mille quatre cent quarante. Rêve s'il en fut jamais; suivi de L'Homme de fer, songe.* 3 vol. Nouvelle édition. Brosson et Carteret & Dugour et Durand: Paris An VII [1799].

Mercier, [Louis-Sébastien]: *Adieux à l'année 1789.* [s.l.] [s.a.].

Mercier, [Louis-Sébastien]: *Néologie ou Vocabulaire de mots nouveaux, à renouveler ou pris dans des acceptions nouvelles.* 2 vol. Moussard: Paris 1801.

Mercier, L[ouis]-S[ébastien]: *De l'impossibilité du système astronomique de Copernic et de Newton.* Dentu: Paris 1806.

Mercier, L.-S.: *De la littérature et des littérateurs. Suivi d'un nouvel examen de la tragédie francoise.* Réimpression de l'édition d'Yverdon, 1778. Slatkine Reprints: Genève 1970.

Mercier, Louis-Sébastien: *Parallèle de Paris et de Londres.* Un inédit de Louis-Sébastien Mercier (c. 1780). Introduction et Notes par Claude Bruneteau et Bernard Cottret. Didier Érudition: Paris 1982.

Mercier, Louis Sébastien: *Tableau de Paris* (1782–1788, 12 vol.). Tomes I–II. Édition établie sous la direction de Jean-Claude Bonnet. Mercure de France: Paris 1994a.

Mercier, Louis Sébastien: *Le Nouveau Paris* (1798 ou début 1799, 6 vol.). Édition établie sous la direction de Jean-Claude Bonnet. Mercure de France: Paris 1994b.

Manuscript sources:

Bibliothèque de l'Arsenal, Fonds Mercier, Ms. 15078(2), f.4. Mercier's undated letter.

Bibliothèque de l'Arsenal, Fonds Mercier, Ms. 15078(2)b, f. 48. Mercier's letter to Thomas 22 juin 1768.

Bibliothèque de l'Arsenal, Fonds Mercier, Ms. 15086(b), ff. 1–254. "Refléxions critiques et philosophiques sur les six premiers chapitres de la Génèse et sur le Déluge universel".

Other primary sources:

Aristotle: *The Nicomachean Ethics*. Translated with an analysis and critical notes by J.E.C. Welldon. (First Edition in 1891). The MacMillan Company: London 1897.

Bacon, Francis: *The Advancement of Learning and the New Atlantis* . With a preface by Thomas Case, M.A. ("The Advancement of Learning" was first published in 1605, and the "New Atlantis" in 1627). Oxford University Press: London 1906.

[Beccaria, Cesare Bonesana de]: *Traité des délits et des peines* (1764). Traduit de l'italien, D'après la troisième édition, revue, corrigée et augmentée par l'Auteur: Avec des Additions, de l'Auteur, qui n'ont pas encore paru en Italien. Lausanne 1766.

Bergerac, Cyrano de: *Voyage dans la lune et aux etats du soleil* (1657). Editions Nilsson: Paris [s.a.]

Bibliothèque des sciences et des beaux arts. Juillet-décembre 1771. Tome trente et sixième.

Bodin, Félix: *Le roman de l'avenir*. Lecointe et Pougin: Paris 1834.

Cabet, Etienne: *Voyage en Icarie*, roman philosophique et social (1839). Deuxième édition. J. Mallet: Paris 1842.

Campanella, Tommaso: *La cité du soleil* [1623]. Texte latin de l'édition de Paris, 1637 établi, traduit et commenté par Roland Crahay. Classe des lettres. Académie royale de Belgique: Bruxelles 1993.

Chastellux [Francois Jean, marquis de]: *De la Félicité publique, ou Considérations sur le sort des hommes, dans le différentes époques de l'histoire*, tomes I– II. Nouvelle édition, augmentée de notes inédites de Voltaire. (Parut pour la première fois en 1772). Antoine-Augustin Renouard: Paris 1822.

Châtelet, [Gabrielle-Émilie Le Tonnelier de Breteuil], Mme du: *Discours sur le bonheur* (1746 ou 1747). Préface d'Elisabeth Badinter. Rivages poche: Paris 1997.

Condorcet, [Maria Jean Antoine Nicolas de Caritat, marquis de]: *Esquisse d'un tableau historique des progrès de l'esprit humain*. Ouvrage posthume de Condorcet. [s.l.] 1795.

Correspondance littéraire, philosophique et critique, adressée a un souverain d'Allemagne, depuis 1770 jusqu'en 1782. Par le baron de Grimm et par Diderot. Seconde Édition, revue et corrigée. Tome second. Paris 1812.

Descartes, René: *Discours de la méthode pour bien conduire sa raison et chercher la vérité dans les sciences*. Librairie de la Bibliothèque Nationale: Paris 1898.

Diderot, Denis: Supplément au voyage de Bougainville, ou Dialogue entre A. et B (1772). *Oeuvres complètes de Denis Diderot*. Tome premier. A. Belin: Paris 1818.

Diderot, [Denis]: Rêve de d'Alembert (1769). *Oeuvres complètes de Diderot*. Revues sur les éditions originals comprenant ce qui a été publié a diverses époques et les manuscrits inédits conservés à la bibliothèque de l'Ermitage. Tome deuxième. Paris 1875.

Diderot, Denis: *Oeuvres*. Édition établie et annotée par André Billy. Bibliothèque de la Pléiade, Gallimard: Paris 1951.

Duclos, [Charles Pinos]: Considérations sur les moeurs de ce siècle. *Moralistes français*. Firmin Didot Frères: Paris 1864.

Encyclopédie, ou dictionnaire raisonné des sciences, des arts et des métiers. Publié par Diderot – d'Alembert. Tomes II, V, XIII, XXII, XXIV, XXIX. Les Sociétés Typographiques: Lausanne & Berne 1778– 1781.

Fénelon, [François de Salignac de la Motte]: *Les aventures de Télémaque* (1699). Suivies des aventures d'Aristonoüs. Accompagnée de notes philosophiques et littéraires. Nouvelle édition. Garnier Frères: Paris [1864].

Fontenelle, [Bernard le Bovier de]: Entretiens sur la pluralité des mondes habités (1686). *Oeuvres complètes*, tome II. Fayard: Paris 1991.

Fontenelle, [Bernard le Bovier de]: *Rêveries diverses*. Édition préfacée, établie et annotée par Alain Niderst. Les éditions Desjonquères: Paris 1994.

Helvétius: Claude Adrien: Le Bonheur, poëme allégorique (1772). *Oeuvres complètes*. Tome XIII. Georg Olms Verlagsbuchhandlung: Hildesheim 1967.

Helvetius, [Claude Adrien]: De l'esprit (1758). *Oeuvres complettes D'Helvetius*. Tomes I– II. Paris 1793.

Helvétius, [Claude Adrien]: De l'esprit. – De l'homme. – Notes, maximes et pensées. – Le bonheur. – Lettres. Troisième édition. *Collection des plus belles pages*. Mercure de France: Paris 1909.

[d'Holbach, Paul Henri Thierry]: *Système de la nature, ou Des loix du monde Physique & du monde moral* (1770). Premiere partie. Par M. Mirabaud. Nouvelle Edition à laquelle on a joint plusieurs pièces des meilleurs Auteurs relatives aux mêmes objets. Londres 1771.

The *Holy Bible*. Revised Standard Version. Containing the Old and New Testaments. Thomas Nelson & Sons: Toronto, New York, and Edinburgh 1952.

Hume, David: *An Enquiry concerning the Human Understanding, and an Enquiry concerning the Principles of Morals*. Reprinted from the posthumous edition of 1777 and edited, with an introduction, comparative tables of contents, and an analytical index, by L. A. Selby-Bigge. The Clarendon Press: Oxford 1894.

Johnson, Samuel, *The Rambler*. Ed. by W.J. Bate and Albrecht B. Strauss (the third of three volumes). Yale University Press: New Haven and London 1969.

Kant, Immanuel: *Critique of Practical Reason*. Trans. by T.K. Abbott. Prometheus Books: New York 1996.

Lahontan, [Louis-Armand de Lom d´Arce, Baron de]: *Dialogues de Monsieur le baron de Lahontan et d'un Sauvage dans l'Amérique* (1703). Édition présentée, établie et annotée par Henri Coulet. Les éditions Desjonquères: Paris 1993.

La Mettrie, Julien Offray: *L'Homme machine suivi de l'art de jouir* (1747). Le texte reproduit dans ce volume est, pour l'Homme machine, celui de 1748, et pour l'Art de jouir, celui de 1753. Introduction et notes de Maurice Solovine. Éditions Bossard: Paris 1921.

Leibniz, [Gottfried Wilhelm von]: De l'origine radicale des choses (1697). *Oeuvres*, tome I. Aubier-Montaigne: Paris 1972.

Leibniz, [Gottfried Wilhelm von]: *Extraits de la Théodicée* (1710). *Essais sur la bonté de Dieu, la liberté de l'homme et l'origine du mal*. Publiés avec une introduction et des notes par Paul Janet. Quatrième édition. Hachette: Paris 1912.

Leibniz, [Gottfried Wilhelm von]: *Principes de la Nature et de la Grâce/Monadologie et autres textes 1703–1716*. Flammarion: Paris 1996.

Locke, John: *An Essay concerning Human Understanding* (1690). Edited with a foreword by Peter H. Nidditch. (First published in 1975). Clarendon Press: Oxford 1979.

Mably, [Gabriel Bonnot de]: "Du Développement des progrès et des bornes de la raison". *Collection complète des oeuvres de l'abbé de Mably*. Oeuvres posthumes, tome quinzième. A Paris, L'An III de la République (1794 à 1795).

[Mandeville, Bernard de]: *Pensées libres sur la religion, l'eglise, et le bonheur de la nation*. Traduites de l'Anglois du Docteur B.M., tome premier. La Haye 1722.

Marmontel, [Jean François]: *Contes moraux*. Nouvelle édition, corrigée et augmentée. Tome second. Jean Christ. Holmberg: Stockholm 1787.

Marmontel, [Jean-François]: *Bélisaire* (1767).

Paris 1821.

Maupertuis, [Pierre Louis Moreau de]: *Les oeuvres de M. de Maupertuis*. G. C. Walther: Dresde 1752.

Mercure de France. Tome LXIX: juillet-décembre 1755. Slatkine Reprints: Genève 1970.

Montesquieu, [Charles-Louis Secondat de]: *Lettres persanes* (1721). Tomes I–II. Librairie de la Bibliothèque Nationale: Paris 1894–1895.

Montesquieu, [Charles-Louis Secondat de]: *De L'Esprit des loix, ou du rapport que les lois doivent avoir avec la constitution de chaque gouvernement, les moeurs, le climat, la religion, le commerce, & c. A quoi l'Auteur a ajouté des recherches nouvelles sur les loix romaines, sur les loix francoises, et sur les loix feodales*. Tomes I–II (1748). La Compagnie: Amsterdam 1749.

More, Thomas: *Utopia* (1516). Edited with Introduction and Notes by Edward Surtz, S.J. Yale University Press: New York and London 1964.

[Morelly]: *Naufrage des isles flottantes, ou Basiliade du célébre Pilpai*. Poëme héroique. Traduit de l'Indien par M. M******. Tome premier. Une Société de Libraires: Messine 1753.

Plato: *The Republic of Plato*. (First published in 1968). Translated with notes and an interpretative essay by Allan Bloom. Basic Books: New York 1991.

Pope, Alexander: *An Essay on Man* (1733). A critical edition of the major works. Ed. by Pat Rogers. Oxford University Press: Oxford & New York 1993.

Prévost, [Antoine François]: *Le Philosophe Anglois, ou Histoire de monsieur Cleveland, fils naturel de Cromwell*; ecrite par lui- même, Et traduite de l'Anglais (1731). Nouvelle édition. Tome second. Etienne Neaulme: Utrecht 1736.

Raynal, Guillaume Thomas, [Abbé]: *Histoire philosophique et politique. Des établissemens et du Commerce des Européens dans les deux Indes* (1770). Tome dixième. Jean-Leonard Pellet: Geneve 1781.

Renouvier, Charles: *Uchronie. L'Utopie dans l'histoire. Esquisse historique apocryphe du développement de la civilisation européenne tel qu'il n'a pas été, tel qu'il aurait pu être*. (Publiée pour la première fois en 1857). Fayard: Paris 1988.

Restif de la Bretonne, [Nicolas Edme]: *La Découverte australe par un Homme-Volant ou le Dédale français* (1781), 4 vol. Préface de Jacques Lacarrière. "Bibliothèque des utopies". France Adel: Paris 1977.

Restif de la Bretonne, [Nicolas Edme]: *L'An deux mille*. Heitz & Mündel: Strasbourg 1790.

Rétif de la Bretonne, [Nicolas Edme]: *Le paysan perverti, ou Les dangers de la ville,*

Histoire récente. Tome quatrième. Amsterdam 1776.

Rétif de la Bretonne, [Nicolas Edme]:
L'Andrographe, ou idées d'un honnête-
homme, sur un projet de reglement,
proposé à toutes les Nations de l'Europe,
pour opérer une Réforme générale des
moeurs, & par elle, le bonheur du Genre-
humain. Avec des Notes historiques et
justificatives. *Idées singulières.* Tome
quatrième. Gosse et Pinet: A La-Haie, et se
trouve à Paris 1782.

Rétif de la Bretonne, [Nicolas Edme]: Le
Thesmographe, ou Idées d'un honnête-
homme sur un projet de reglement, Proposé
à toutes les Nations de l'Europe, pour
operer une Réforme generale des Loix.
Avec des Notes historiques. *Idées
singuliers.* Tome cinquième. Gosse et
Pinet: A La-Haie, et se trouve à Paris 1789.

Rétif de la Bretonne, [Nicolas Edme]: *Les
Posthumes. Lettres recues après la mort du
Mari, par sa Femme, qui le croit à Floren-
ce.* Tomes I–IV. Duchêne: Paris 1802.

Rousseau, Jean-Jacques: *Discours sur les
sciences et les arts* (1750). *Discours sur
l'origine et les fondements de l'inégalité
parmi les hommes* (1754). Flammarion:
Paris 1992.

Rousseau, J.-J.: *La Nouvelle Héloïse.* Vol. IV
(1761). Hachette: Paris 1925.

Rousseau, Jean-Jacques: Du contrat social, ou
principes du droit politique (1762).
Oeuvres complettes de J.J. Rousseau. Tome
deuxième. Nouvelle édition. Bélin, Caille,
Grégoire, Volland: Paris 1793.

Rousseau, J.-J.: *Émile ou de l'éducation*
(1762). Nouvelle édition. Garnier Fréres:
Paris 1904.

[Sade, Donatien Alphonse François, Marquis
de]: *Valmor et Lydia, ou voyage autour du
monde de deux amans qui se cherchoient.* 3
vol. A Paris an VII [1804].

Saint-Pierre, Abbé de: *Abrege du projet de
paix perpetuelle,* Inventé par le Roi Henri le
Grand, Aprouvé par la Reine Elisabeth, par
le Roi Jacques son Successeur, par les
Republiques & par divers autres Potentats.
Rotterdam 1729.

Saint-Pierre, Bernardin de: *Paul et Virginie*
(1788). EDDL/ Bussiere: Saint-Amand
Montrond 1996.

Sénèque: *La vie heureuse. La brièveté de la
vie.* Traduit du latin par François Rosso.
Suivi de la correspondance entre Descartes
et la princesse Élisabeth sur la vie heureuse.
Arléa 1995.

Spinoza, [Benedictus de]: *The Collected
Works of Spinoza.* Edited and translated by
Edwin Curley. Princeton University Press:
Princeton 1985.

Turgot, [Anne Robert Jacques]: Second
discours (de Sorbonne), sur les progrès
successifs de l'esprit humain, prononcé le II
décembre 1750. *Oeuvres de Turgot.*
Nouvelle édition classée par ordre de

matières avec les notes de Dupont de
Nemours augmentée de lettres inédites, des
questions sur le commerce. Tome second.
Guillaumin: Paris 1884.

Vauvenargues, [Luc Capiers de] : Réflections
sur le caractère des différents siècles.
Moralistes français. Firmin Didot
Frères:Paris 1864.

Volney, [Constantin François de Chasseboeuf,
comte de]: Les Ruines, ou méditation sur
les révolutions des empires. *Oeuvres
choisies de Volney.* Lebigre Frères: Paris
1836.

Voltaire, [François Marie Arouet]:
Dictionnaire philosophique (1734). Ernest
Flammarion: Paris [s.a.]

Voltaire, [François Marie Arouet]: *Oeuvres
completes de Voltaire.* Tome quarante-
quatrieme. Charles Guillaume Ettinger:
Gotha 1787.

Secondary sources

Adorno, Theodor W & Horkheimer, Max:
Dialectic of Enlightenment. Trans. by John
Cumming. Verso Editions: London 1979.

Alkon, Paul K.: *Origins of Futuristic Fiction.*
The University of Georgia Press: Athens
and London 1987.

Alkon, Paul: "The Paradox of Technology in
Mercier's L'an 2440". *Utopian Vision.
Technological Innovation and Poetic
Imagination.* Ed. by Klaus L. Bergham –
Reinhold Grimm. Carl Winter
Universitätsverlag: Heidelberg 1990, 43–
62.

Alkon, Paul K.: *Science Fiction before 1900.
Imagination Discovers Technology.* Twayne
Publishers: New York 1994.

Ariès, Philippe: *L'enfant et la vie familiale
sous l'ancien régime.* (Publié pour la
première fois en 1960). Éditions du Seuil:
Paris 1973.

Ariès, Philippe: Introduction. *A History of
Private Life III: Passions of the
Renaissance.* Ed. by Roger Chartier. Trans.
by Arthur Goldhammer. The Belknap Press
of Harvard University Press: Cambridge,
Massachusetts and London 1989, 1–11.

Ariès, Philippe: *Western Attitudes toward
Death from the Middle Ages to the Present.*
Trans. by Patricia M. Ranum. Marion
Boyards: London & New York 1994.

Asplund, Johan: *Teorier om framtiden.* Andra
upplagan. LiberFörlag: Stockholm 1981.

Atkinson, Geoffroy: *The Extraordinary
Voyage in French Literature from 1700 to
1720.* Paris 1922.

Baczko, B.: "L'utopie et l'idée de l'histoire-
progrès". *Revue des sciences humaines* no
155/1974, 473–491.

Baczko, Bronislaw: *Lumières de l'utopie.*
Payot: Paris 1978.

Baczko, Bronislaw: *Job, mon ami. Promesses*

du bonheur et fatalité du mal. Éditions Gallimard: Paris 1997.

Badinter, Elisabeth & Badinter, Robert: *Condorcet (1743–1794). Un intellectual en politique.* Fayard: Paris 1988.

Baker, Keith Michael: "Politique et opinion publique sous l'Ancien Régime". *Annales* 42:1/1987, 41–71.

Becker, Carl L.: *The Declaration of Independence. A Study in the History of Political Ideas.* Vintage Books: New York 1962.

Becker, Carl L.: *The Heavenly City of the Eighteenth-century Philosophers.* (First published in 1932). Yale University Press: New Haven & London 1965.

Béclard, Léon: *Sébastien Mercier. Sa vie, son oeuvre, son temps. Avant la Révolution 1740–1789.* H. Champion: Paris 1903.

Bell, Michael: *Sentimentalism, Ethics and the Culture of Feeling.* Palgrave: Basingstoke, Hampshire and New York 2000.

Beriger, Hanno: "Mercier et ´Sturm und Drang´". *Louis-Sébastien Mercier précurseur et sa fortune.* Avec des documents inédits. Recueil d'études sur l'influence de Mercier. Sous la direction de Hermann Hofer. Vilhelm Fink Verlag: München 1977, 47–72.

Berlanstein, Leonard R.: "Women and Power in Eighteenth-Century France. Actresses at the Comédie-Française". *Visions and Revisions of Eighteenth-Century France.* Ed. by Christine Adams, Jack R. Censer, and Lisa Jane Graham. The Pennsylvania State University Press: Pennsylvania 1997, 155–190.

Berneri, Marie Louise: *Journey through Utopia.* (First published in 1950). Routledge & Kegan Paul: Boston 1951.

Berthier, Philippe: "Mercier surréaliste?". *Louis-Sébastien Mercier précurseur et sa fortune.* Avec des documents inédits. Recueil d'études sur l'influence de Mercier. Sous la direction de Hermann Hofer. Wilhelm Fink Verlag: München 1977, 301–309.

Bloch, Ernst: The Utopian Function of Art and Literature. *Selected Essays.* Trans. by Jack Zipes and Frank Mecklenburg. (First published in 1988). The MIT Press: Cambridge 1989.

Bloch, Ernst: "Ennakoitu todellisuus – mitä on utooppinen ajattelu ja mitä se saa aikaan". *Utopia, luonto, uskonto. Johdatusta Ernst Blochin ajatteluun.* Toim. Keijo Rahkonen ja Esa Sironen. Kansan Sivistystyön liitto: Helsinki 1985, 22–33.

Bluche, François: *L'Ancien Régime. Institutions et société.* Éditions de Fallois: Paris 1993.

Bollème, Geneviève: "L'ecriture, cet art inconnu". *Dictionnaire d'un polygraphe.* Textes de Louis-Sébastien Mercier, établis et présentés par Geneviève Bollème. Union générale d'éditions: Paris 1978, 7–83.

Bonnet, Jean-Claude: "La littérature et le réel". *Louis Sébastien Mercier (1740–1814). Un hérétique en littérature.* Sous la direction de Jean-Claude Bonnet. Mercure de France: Paris 1995, 9–32.

Bosher, J.F.: *The French Revolution.* W.W. Norton & Company: New York & London 1988.

Bousquet, Jacques: *Les thèmes du rêve dans la littérature romantique (France, Angleterre, Allemagne). Essai sur la naissance et l'évolution des images.* Marcel Didier: Paris 1964.

Bowman, Frank-Paul: "Religion, révolution, utopie. Étude des éléments religieux dans les projets d'utopie d'avant et d'aprés 1789". *Le préromantisme: hypothèque ou hypothèse?* Colloque organisé à Clermont-Ferrand les 29 et 30 juin 1972 par le Centre de Recherches Révolutionnaires et Romantiques de l'Université. Éditions Klincksieck: Paris 1975, 425–442.

Braudel, Fernand: *Civilization and Capitalism 15th – 18th Century. Vol.I: The Structures of Everyday Life. The Limits of the Possible.* Trans. and revised by Siâm Reynolds. Collins: London 1981.

Browne, Alice: *The Eighteenth Century Feminist Mind.* The Harvester Press: Brighton 1987.

Brumfitt, J.H.: *The French Enlightenment.* London and Basingstoke 1972.

Bruneteau, Claude et Cottret, Bernard: Introduction. *Parallèle de Paris et de Londres* (c. 1780). Un inédit de Louis-Sébastien Mercier. Didier Érudition: Paris 1982, 9–50.

Buber, Martin: *Paths in Utopia.* Trans. by R.F.C. Hull. (First published in 1950). Beacon Press: Boston 1958.

Burke, Peter: *Varieties of Cultural History.* Polity Press: Cambridge and Oxford 1997.

Burke, Peter: *Popular Culture in Early Modern Europe.* (First published in 1978). Wildwood House: Aldershot 1988.

Bury, J.B.: *The Idea of Progress. An Inquiry into its Origin and Growth.* MacMillan and Co: London 1920.

Campbell, Colin: *The Romantic Ethic and the Spirit of Modern Consumerism.* Basil Blackwell: Oxford 1987.

Camporesi, Piero: *Bread of Dreams. Food and Fantasy in Early Modern Europe.* Trans. by David Gentilcore. Polity Press: Cambridge 1989.

Cassirer, Ernst: *La philosophie des lumières.* Traduit de l'allemand et présenté par Pierre Quillet. Fayard: Paris 1966.

Castiglione, Dario: "Excess, Frugality and the Spirit of Capitalism: Readings of Mandeville on Commercial Society". *Culture in History. Production, consumption and values in historical perspective.* Ed. by Joseph Melling & Jonathan Barry. University of Exeter Press: Exeter 1992, 155–173.

Cattin, Geneviève: "Bibliographie critique". *Louis-Sébastien Mercier précurseur et sa fortune*. Avec des documents inédits. Récueil d'études sur l'influence de Mercier. Sous la direction de Hermann Hofer. Wilhelm Fink Verlag: München 1977, 341–361.

Cazes, Bernard: *Histoire des futurs. Les figures de l'avenir de saint Augustin au XXIe siècle*. Éditions Seghers: Paris 1986.

Censer, Jack R.: *The French Press in the Age of Enlightenment*. Routledge: London and New York 1994.

Chadourne, Marc: *Restif de la Bretonne où le siècle prophétique*. Hachette: Paris 1958.

Charlton, D.G.: *New Images of the Natural in France. A Study in European Cultural History 1750–1800*. Cambridge University Press: Cambridge 1984.

Chartier, Roger: *Cultural History. Between Practices and Representations*. Trans. by Lydia G. Cochrane. Cornell University Press: Ithaca and New York 1988.

Chartier, Roger: Introduction. *A History of Private Life III: Passions of the Renaissance*. Ed. by Roger Chartier. Trans. by Arthur Goldhammer. The Belknap Press of Harvard University Press: Cambridge, Massachusetts and London 1989, 163–165.

Chartier, Roger: *The Order of Books. Readers, Authors, and Libraries in Europe between the Fourteenth and Eighteenth Centuries*. Trans. by Lydia G. Cochrane. Polity Press: Cambridge 1994.

Chase, Malcolm & Shaw, Christopher: "The dimensions of nostalgia". *The imagined past. History and nostalgia*. Ed. by Christopher Shaw & Malcolm Chase. Manchester University Press: Manchester and New York 1989, 1–17.

Chaunu, Pierre: *La civilisation de l'Europe des lumières*. (Publié pour la première fois en 1971). Flammarion: Paris 1982.

Chinard, Gilbert: *L'Amérique et le rêve exotique dans la littérature française au XVIIe et au XVIII siècle*. Hachette: Paris 1913.

Choron, Jacques: *Death and Western Thought*. (First published in 1963). Collier MacMillan Publishers: New York and London 1976.

Christodoulou, Kyriaki: "Le Paris des Lumières dans L'an 2440 de Louis-Sébastien Mercier". *Travaux de littérature*. Publiés par l'Adirel IV: Paris 1991, 171–182.

Cioranescu, A: *Bibliographie de la littérature française du dix-huitième siècle*. Tome II: E–Q. Éditions du Centre National de la Recherche Scientifique: Paris 1969, 1234–1239.

Cioranescu, Alexandre: *L'Avenir du passé. Utopie et littérature*. Editions Gallimard: Paris 1972.

Cioranescu, Alexandre: "Épigone, le premier roman de l'avenir". *Revue des sciences humaines. "L'utopie"*. No 155, 3/1974, 441–448.

Cioranescu, Alexandre: "La littérature française et la recherche du bonheur". *La quête du bonheur et l'expression de la douleur dans la littérature et la pensée françaises*. Mélanges offerts à Corrado Rosso. Edités par C. Biondi, et al. Droz S.A.: Genève 1995, 23–28.

Citron, Pierre: *La poésie de Paris dans la littérature française de Rousseau à Baudelaire*, tome I. Les Éditions de Minuit: Paris 1961.

Claeys, Gregory and Sargent, Lyman Tower: "On the Frontiers of Utopia: Satires and Robinsonades". *Utopia. The Search for the Ideal Society in the Western World*. Ed. by Roland Schaer, Gregory Claeys, and Lyman Tower Sargent. The New York Public Library/Oxford University Press: New York and Oxford 2000, 180–183.

Clarke, I.F.: *The Pattern of Expectation 1644–2001*. J. Cape: London 1979.

Coates, Willson H., White, Hayden V., & Schapiro, J. Salwyn: *The Emergence of Liberal Humanism: an intellectual history of Western Europe. Vol. I: from the Italian Renaissance to the French Revolution*. McGraw-Hill Book Company: New York & London 1966.

Cobban, Alfred: *A History of Modern France. Vol. One: Old Régime and Révolution 1715–1789*. Benguin Books: Harmondsworth 1957.

Cobban, Alfred: "The Enlightenment and the French Revolution". *The Influence of the Enlightenment on the French Revolution. Problems in European Civilization*. (First published in 1964). Edited and with an introduction by William F. Church. D.C. Heath and Company: Lexington 1974, 183–194.

Cohen, I. Bernard: *Revolution in Science*. The Belknap Press of Harvard University Press: Cambridge and London 1985.

Cohn, Norman: *The Pursuit of the Millenium. Revolutionary millenarians and mystical anarchists of the Middle Ages*. (First published in 1957). PIMLICO: Chatham 1993.

Collier, Simon: "Mercier's Enlightenment utopia: progress and social ideals". *The Enlightenment and its Shadows*. Ed. by Peter Hulme and Ludmila Jordanova. Routledge: London and New York 1990.

Corbin, Alain: *The Foul and the Fragrant. Odor and the French Social Imagination*. (Originally published in 1982). Trans. by Miriam L. Kochan, Roy Porter, and Christopher Prendergast. Harvard University Press: Cambridge 1986.

Cousin d'Avalon, Charles-Yves: *Merciériana, ou Recueil d'anecdotes sur Mercier: ses paradoxes, ses bizarreries, ses sarcasmes, ses plaisanteries, etc, etc*. Krabbe: Paris

1834.

Coward, David: "Entre l'instinct et la raison: l'utopisme de Rétif". Rétif de la Bretonne et l'utopie. *Études rétiviennes 1992–1993.* Revue semestrielle publiée par la Société Rétif de la Bretonne. No 17, Décembre 1992, 9–17.

Crocker, Lester G.: Introduction. *The Age of Enlightenment. A Volume in Documentary history of Western Civilization.* Ed. by Lester G. Crocker. Harper & Row: New York, Evanston, and London 1969, 1–30.

Cuénin, Micheline: "Evolution and Revolutions in the Pursuit of Happiness in France from 1688 to 1750". *Culture and Revolution.* Ed. by Paul Dukes and John Dunkley. Pinter Publishers: London and New York 1990, 60–70.

Darnton, Robert: *The Literary Underground of the Old Regime.* Harvard University Press: Cambridge & London 1982.

Darnton, Robert: *The Great Cat Massacre and other Episodes in French Cultural History.* (First published in 1984). Penguin Books: Harmondsworth 1988.

Darnton, Robert: *The Kiss of Lamourette. Reflections in Cultural History.* W.W. Norton & Company: New York & London 1990.

Darnton, Robert: *La fin des lumières. Le mesmérisme et la révolution.* Traduit par Marie-Alyx Revellat. Editions Odile Jacob: Paris 1995.

Darnton, Robert: *The Forbidden Best-Sellers of Pre-Revolutionary France.* (First published in 1996). Fontana Press: London 1997.

Daumas, Maurice: *La Tendresse amoureuse, XVIè-XVIIIè siècles.* Hachette/Pluriel: Paris 1996.

Davis, J.C.: *Utopia and the ideal society. A study of English utopian writing 1516–1700.* Cambridge University Press: Cambridge 1981.

Davis, J.C.: "Utopia and the New World, 1500–1700". *Utopia. The Search for the Ideal Society in the Western World.* Ed. by Roland Schaer, Gregory Claeys, and Lyman Tower Sargent. The New York Public Library/Oxford University Press: New York and Oxford 2000, 95–118.

Dawson, Christopher: *Progress and Religion. An Historical Enquiry.* Sheed and Ward: London 1929.

Delaporte, André: *Bergers d'Arcadie. Poètes et philosophes de l'age d'or dans la littérature française du XVIIIe siècle.* Pardès: Puiseaux 1988.

Delon, Michel: Préface générale; Piétons de Paris. *Paris le jour, Paris la nuit.* Éditions Robert Laffont: Paris 1990, I– XXIV.

Delon, Michel, Mauzi, Robert & Menant, Sylvain: *De l'Encyclopédie aux Méditations. Histoire de la littérature française.* Nouvelle édition révisée. Flammarion: Paris 1998.

Delumeau, Jean: *La peur en Occident (XIVe–XVIIIe siècles). Une cité assiégée.* Fayard: Paris 1978.

Delumeau, Jean: *Le péché et la peur. La culpabilisation en Occident (XIIIè–XVIIIè siècles).* Fayard: Paris 1983.

Delumeau, Jean: *Une histoire du paradis. Le jardin des délices.* Fayard: Paris 1992.

Delumeau, Jean: *Mille ans de bonheur. Une histoire du paradis.* Fayard: Paris 1995.

Denoit, Nicole: *Mercier utopiste: L'an 2440.* Thèse de Doctorat de Lettres Modernes. IIIè Cycle. Paris IV, 1983.

Denoit, Nicole: "La rencontre de l'utopie et de certaines valeur- clés des Lumières: Louis Sébastien Mercier utopiste, L'An 2440". Actes du Septième congrès international des Lumières. Budapest 26 juillet – 2 août 1987. *Studies on Voltaire and the Eighteenth Century* 265, 1989a, 1625–1628.

Denoit, Nicole: "Louis-Sébastien Mercier, prophète et juge de la Révolution de L'an 2440 au Nouveau Paris". *L'Image de la Révolution française,* vol. 3. Sous la direction de Michel Vovelle. Pergamon Press: Paris, Oxford & New York 1989b, 2031–2038.

Deprun, Jean: *La philosophie de l'inquiétude en France au XVIIIè siècle.* Librairie philosophique J. Vrin: Paris 1979.

Desnoiresterres, Gustave: *Grimod de la Reynière et son groupe.* Didier: Paris 1877.

Didier, Béatrice: *Littérature française 11. Le XVIIIe siècle III, 1778–1820.* Arthaud: Paris 1976.

Dorigny, Marcel: "Du ´despotisme vertueux´ à la république". *Louis-Sébastien Mercier (1740–1814). Un hérétique en littérature.* Sous la direction de Jean-Claude Bonnet. Mercure de France: Paris 1995, 247–277.

Doyle, William: *Origins of the French Revolution.* (First published in 1980). Oxford University Press: New York 1988.

Dubos, René: *The Dreams of Reason. Science and Utopias.* Columbia University Press: New York and London 1961.

Dubos, René: *Reason Awake. Science for Man.* Columbia University Press: New York and London 1970.

Duby, G. & Mandrou, R.: *Histoire de la civilisation française. XVIIe – XXe siècle.* Armand Colin: Paris 1958.

Dupront, Alphonse: *Qu'est-ce que les Lumières?* Gallimard: Paris 1996.

Döring, Ulrich: "Images d'un monde meilleur? Louis-Sébastien Mercier: L'an 2440. Rêve s'il en fut jamais (1770)". *Ouverture et Dialogue. Mélanges offerts à Wolfgang Leiner.* Édités par Ulrich Döring, Antiopy Lyroudias, et Rainer Zaiser. Tübingen 1988, 653–668.

Eaton, Ruth: "The City as an Intellectual Exercise". *Utopia. The search for the Ideal Society in the Western World.* Ed. by Roland Schaer, Gregory Claeys, and Lyman

Tower Sargent. The New York Public Library/Oxford University Press: New York and Oxford 2000, 119–131.

Eggli, Edm.: "Une méditation de Sébastien Mercier". *Mélanges offerts par ses amis et ses éléves a M. Gustave Lanson*. Slatkine Reprints: Genève 1972, 258–267.

Ehrard, Jean: *L'idée de nature en France dans la première moitié du XVIIIe siècle*. (Première édition en 1963). Albin Michel: Paris 1994.

Eliade, Mircea: *Aspects du mythe*. Gallimard: Paris 1963.

Eliade, Mircea: "Paradise and Utopia: Mythical Geography and Eschatology". *Utopias and Utopian Thought*. Ed. by Frank E. Manuel. (First published in 1965). The Riverside Press: Boston & Cambridge 1966.

Eliade, Mircea: "The Yearning for Paradise in Primitive Tradition". *Myth and Mythmaking*. Edited and with an Introduction by Henry A. Murray. (Originally published in 1959). Beacon Press: Boston 1969a, 61–75.

Eliade, Mircea: *Le mythe de l'éternel retour. Archétypes et répétition*. Nouvelle édition revue et augmentée. Gallimard: Paris 1969b.

Elias, Norbert: *Power & Civility. The Civilizing Process: Vol. II*. Trans. by Edmund Jephcott. (Originally published in 1939). Pantheon Books: New York 1982.

Elias, Norbert: *Time: An Essay*. Translated in part from the German by Edmund Jephcott. Basil Blackwell: Oxford and Cambridge 1993.

Elliott, Robert C.: "The Costs of Utopia". *Progress and its Discontents*. Ed. by Gabriel A. Almond, Marvin Chodorow, and Roy Harvey Pearce. University of California Press: Berkeley, Los Angeles, & London 1982, 470–481.

Fabre, Jean: *Lumières et romantisme. Énergie et nostalgie de Rousseau à Mickiewicz*. Nouvelle édition revue et augmentée. Éditions Klincksieck: Paris 1980.

Farge, Arlette: *Subversive Words. Public Opinion in Eighteenth- Century France*. Trans. by Rosemary Morris. (First published in 1992). Polity Press: Cambridge 1994.

Favre, Robert: *La mort dans la littérature et la pensée françaises au siècle de lumières*. Presses universitaires de Lyon: Lyon 1978.

Finley, M.I.: *The Use and Abuse of History. From the myths of the Greeks to Lévi-Strauss, the past alive and the present illuminated*. (First published in 1975). Penguin Books: Harmondsworth 1990.

Finnis, John: *Natural law and natural rights*. Clarendon: Oxford 1980.

Forsström, Riikka: "Kaupunki utopiana. Mercierin Pariisi vuonna 2440". *Kaupunki kohtauspaikkana. Näkökulmia kulttuuriseen kaupunkitutkimukseen*. Toim. Harry Schulman & Vesa Kanninen. Yhdyskuntasuunnittelun täydennyskoulutuskeskuksen julkaisuja C 33: Espoo 1995, 21–28.

Foucault, Michel: *Les mots et les choses. Une archéologie des sciences humaines*. Éditions Gallimard: Paris 1966.

Foucault, Michel: *Surveiller et punir. Naissance de la prison*. Éditions Gallimard: Paris 1975.

Fralin, Richard: *Rousseau and Representation. A Study of the Development of His Concept of Political Institutions*. Columbia University Press: New York 1978.

Frantz, Pierre: "L'usage du peuple". *Louis-Sébastien Mercier (1740–1814). Un hérétique en littérature*. Sous la direction de Jean-Claude Bonnet. Mercure de France: Paris 1995, 55–79.

Frye, Northrop: "Varieties of Literary Utopias". *Utopias and Utopian Thought*. Ed. by Frank E. Manuel. (First published in 1965). Riverside Press: Boston & Cambridge 1966, 25–49.

Frängsmyr, Tore: *Framsteg eller forfall. Framtidsbilder och utopier i västerländsk tanketradition*. Liber Förlag: Stockholm 1981.

Frängsmyr, Tore: *Gubben som gräver. Människor och miljöer i vetenskapens värld*. Författarförlaget Fischer & Rye: Stockholm 1989.

Furet, François: *La Révolution. De Turgot à Jules Ferry 1770–1880*. Hachette: Paris 1988.

Gagliardo, John G.: *Enlightened Despotism*. Routledge & Kegan Paul: London 1968.

Gaillard, Francoise: "Le préromantisme constitue-t-il une période? Ou quelques réflections sur la notion de préromantisme". *Le préromantisme: Hypothèque ou hypothèse?* Colloque organisé à Clermont-Ferrand les 29 et 30 juin 1972 par le Centre de Recherches Révolutionnaires et Romantiques de l'Université. Éditions Klincksieck: Paris 1975, 57–72.

Gay, Peter: *The Party of Humanity. Essays in the French Enlightenment*. Alfred A. Knopf: New York 1964.

Gay, Peter: *Deism: An Anthology*. D.Van Nostrand: Princeton 1968.

Gay, Peter: *The Enlightenment. An Interpretation. Vol. II: The Science of Freedom*. Weidenfeld and Nicholson: London 1970.

Gellner, Ernest: *Reason and Culture. The historic Role of Rationality and Rationalism*. Blackwell: Oxford & Cambridge 1992.

Gillet, Jean: *Le paradis perdu dans la littérature française. De Voltaire à Chateaubriand*. Klincksieck: Paris 1975.

Gillet, Jean: "Le modèle anglais: histoire d'un revirement". *Louis Sébastien Mercier (1740–1814). Un hérétique en littérature*. Sous la direction de Jean-Claude Bonnet.

Mercure de France: Paris 1995, 375–395.

Girard, Gilles: "Inventaire des manuscrits de L.-S. Mercier à la Bibliothèque de l'Arsenal". *Dix-huitième Siècle*, no 5/1973, 311–334.

Girouard, Mark: *Cities & People. A social and architectural history* . (First published in 1985). Yale University Press: New Haven & London 1989.

Gonnard, René: *La légende du bon sauvage. Contribution à l'étude des origines du socialisme*. Éditions politiques, économiques et sociales: Paris 1946.

Goodman, Dena: "Public Sphere and Private Life: toward a Synthesis of current historiographical Approaches to the Old Regime". *History and Theory*. Vol. 31/No 1/1992, 1–20.

Gossman, Lionel: *French Society and Culture. Background for 18th Century Literature*. Prentice-Hall, Inc.: New Jersey 1972.

Goubert, Pierre & Roche, Daniel: *Les Français et l'Ancien Régime 1. La societe et l'etat*. Armand Colin: Paris 1984.

Goulemot, Jean Marie: "Literary Practises: Publicizing the Private". *A History of Private Life III: Passions of the Renaissance*. Ed. by Roger Chartier. Trans. by Arthur Goldhammer. The Belknap Press of Harvard University Press: Cambridge, Massachusetts and London 1989, 363–395.

Graham, Lisa Jane: "Crimes of Opinion: Policing the Public in Eighteenth-Century Paris". *Visions and Revisions of Eighteenth-Century France*. Ed. by Christine Adams, Jack R. Censer, and Lisa Jane Graham. The Pennsylvania State University Press: Pennsylvania 1997, 79–103.

Gurevich, Aaron: *The Origins of European Individualism*. Trans. by Katherine Judelson. Blackwell: Oxford & Cambridge 1995.

Guthke, Karl S.: *The Gender of Death. A Cultural History in Art and Literature*. Cambridge University Press: Cambridge 1999.

Haakonssen, Knud: *Natural law and moral philosophy. From Grotius to the Scottish Enlightenment*. Cambridge University Press: Cambridge 1996.

Habermas, Jürgen: *Järki ja kommunikaatio. Tekstejä 1981–1985*. Valinnut ja suomentanut Jussi Kotkavirta. Gaudeamus: Helsinki 1987.

Habermas Jürgen: *The Structural Transformation of the Public Sphere. An Inquiry into a Category of Bourgeois Society*. Trans. by Thomas Burger with the assistance of Frederick Lawrence. (First published in 1962). Cambridge Polity Press: Cambridge 1989.

Hampson, Norman: *The Enlightenment*. (First published in 1968). Penguin Books: Harmondsworth 1981.

Hampson, Norman: "What Difference did the French Revolution Make?". *History. The Journal of the Historical Association*. Vol. 74/Number 241/June 1989, 232–242.

Hankins, Thomas L.: *Science and the Enlightenment*. Cambridge University Press: Cambridge 1985.

Harvey, David: *The Condition of Postmodernity. An Enquiry into the Origins of Cultural Change*. (First published in 1989). Basil Blackwell: Oxford & Cambridge 1990.

Hautamäki, Antti: "Individualismi on humanismia". *Yksilö modernin murroksessa*. Toim. Antti Hautamäki et al. Gaudeamus: [Helsinki] 1996, 13–44.

Hawthorn, Geoffrey: *Enlightenment and Despair. A History of Sociology*. Cambridge University Press: Cambridge 1976.

Hazard, Paul: *La Crise de la conscience européenne 1680–1715*. Tomes 1–2. Gallimard: Paris 1961.

Hibbert, Christopher: *The French Revolution*. (First published in 1980). Penguin Books: Harmondsworth 1982.

Hibler, Richard: *Happiness through Tranquility. The school of Epicurus*. Lanham: New York & London 1984.

Hofer, Hermann: "Louis-Sébastien Mercier (1740–1814) et la révolution. Une documentation". *Le préromantisme: hypothèque ou hypothèse?* Colloque organisé à Clermont-Ferrand les 29 et 30 juin 1972 par le Centre de Recherches Révolutionnaires et Romantiques de l'Université. Éditions Klincksieck: Paris 1975, 246–258.

Hofer, Hermann: Introduction. Situation de Mercier. *Louis- Sébastien Mercier précurseur et sa fortune*. Avec des documents inédits. Récueil d'études sur l'influence de Mercier. Sous la direction de Hermann Hofer. Wilhelm Fink Verlag: München 1977a, 13–36.

Hofer, Hermann: "En guise de préface: en quête d'un auteur peu connu". *Louis-Sébastien Mercier précurseur et sa fortune*. Avec des documents inédits. Récueil d'études sur l'influence de Mercier. Sous la direction de Hermann Hofer. Wilhelm Fink Verlag: München 1977b, 7–12.

Hoffmann, Paul: *La femme dans la pensée des lumières*. Slatkine Reprints: Genève 1995.

Hofmann La Torre, Gabriela: "Vision et construction: Louis- Sébastien Mercier, L'an 2440 – Christoph Martin Wieland, Le Miroir d'Or". *De l'Utopie à l'Uchronie. Formes, Significations, Fonctions*. Édités par Hinrich Hudde et Peter Kuon. Actes du colloque d'Erlangen 16–18 octobre 1986. Günter Narr Verlag: Tübingen 1986, 99–108.

Holstun, James: *A rational millenium. Puritan Utopias of Seventeenth-Century England & America*. Oxford University Press: New York 1987.

d'Hondt, Jacques: "Le bonheur du cosmopolite". *La quête du bonheur et* l'expression de la douleur dans la littérature et la pensée françaises. Mélanges offerts à Corrado Rosso. Édités par C. Biondi, et al. Droz S. A.: Genève 1995, 269–278.

Hudde, Hinrich: "L'an 2440 de Louis-Sébastien Mercier". *Le discours utopique. Publications du centre culturel de Cerisy-la-Salle*. Actes du colloque tenu à Cerisy-la-Salle, du 23 juillet au 1er août 1975. Publications du centre culturel de Cerisy-la-Salle: Paris 1978, 250–256.

Hudde, Hinrich & Kuon, Peter: "Utopie – Uchronie – et après: Une réconsidération de l'utopie des Lumières". *De l'Utopie à l'Uchronie. Formes, Significations, Fonctions*. Actes du colloque d'Erlangen 16–18 octobre 1986. Édités par Hinrich Hudde et Peter Kuon. Günter Narr Verlag: Tübingen 1986, 9–17.

Häyry, Heta & Häyry, Matti: "Hume – Sympatian tunne ja sen merkitys toiminnan säätelijänä". *Tunteet*. Toim. Ilkka Niiniluoto ja Juha Räikkä. Helsinki University Press: Helsinki 1997, 55–64.

Iggers, Georg G.: "The Idea of Progress in Historiography and Social Thought Since the Enlightenment". *Progress and its Discontents*. Ed. by Gabriel A. Almond, Marvin Chodorow, & Roy Harvey Pearce. University of California Press: Berkeley, Los Angeles, & London 1982, 41–66.

James, Susan: *Passion and Action. The Emotions in Seventeenth- Century Philosophy*. (First published in 1997). Clarendon Press: Oxford 1999.

Jarrett, Derek: *Three faces of Revolution. Paris, London and New York in 1789*. George Philip: London 1989.

Jean, Georges (avec la collaboration de Nathalie Pighetti- Harrison): *Voyages en Utopie*. Gallimard: Paris 1997.

Jones, Howard: *The Epicurean Tradition*. Routledge: London 1989.

De Jouvenel, Bertrand, *The Art of Conjecture*. Trans. by Nikita Lary. Basic Books, Inc.: New York 1967.

Kartz-Matausch, Renate: "La légende des femmes révolutionnaires au XIXe siècle". *Mythe et Révolutions*. Textes réunis par Yves Chalas. Presses Universitaires de Grenoble: Grenoble 1990, 247– 267.

Kateb, George: *Utopia and its Enemies*. The Free Press of Glencoe/Collier Macmillan: London 1963.

Kennedy, Emmet: *A Cultural History of the French Revolution*. Yale University Press: New Haven and London 1989.

Kenyon, Timothy: "Utopia in reality: ´Ideal´ societies in social and political theory". *History of Political Thought*. Vol. III/1/ Spring 1982, 123–155.

Keohane, Nannerl O.: "The Enlightenment Idea of Progress Revisited". *Progress and its Discontents*. Ed. by Gabriel A. Almond, Marvin Chodorow, & Roy Harvey Pearce.

University of California Press: Berkeley, Los Angeles, & London 1982, 21–40.

Koivisto, Juha, Mäki, Markku & Uusitupa, Timo: Esipuhe. *Mitä on valistus?* Toim. Juha Koivisto et al. Vastapaino: [Tampere] 1995.

Koselleck, Reinhart: *Futures Past. On the Semantics of Historical Time*. (First published in 1979). Trans. by Keith Tribe. The MIT Press: Cambridge, Massachusetts, and London 1985.

Koselleck, Reinhart: *Critique and Crisis. Enlightenment and the Pathogenesis of Modern Society*. (Originally published in 1959). Berg: Oxford 1988.

Krauss, Werner: "Quelques remarques sur le roman utopique au XVIIIe siècle". *Roman et lumières au XVIIIe siècle*. Colloque sous la présidence de MM. Werner Krauss. Centre d'etudes et de recherches marxistes. Revue "Europe". Editions sociales: Paris 1970, 391–399.

Krieger, Murray: "The Arts and the Idea of Progress". *Progress and its Discontents*. Ed. by Gabriel A. Almond, Marvin Chodorow, & Roy Harvey Pearce. University of California Press: Berkeley, Los Angeles, & London 1982, 449–469.

Kumar, Krishan: *Utopia and Anti-Utopia in Modern Times*. Basil Blackwell: Oxford & New York 1987.

Labbé, François: "L'An 2440: une lecture maçonnique". *Lendemains*. Zeitschrift für Frankreichforschung + Französischstudium 11. August 1978, 41–53.

L'Aminot, Tanguy: "Le pédagogue: la leçon de Rousseau". *Louis Sébastien Mercier (1740–1814) un hérétique en littérature*. Sous la direction de Jean-Claude Bonnet. Mercure de France: Paris 1995, 279–294.

Landes, Joan B.: *Women and the Public Sphere in the Age of the French Revolution*. Cornell University Press: Ithaca and London 1988.

Lapouge, Gilles: *Utopie et civilisations*. Flammarion: Paris 1978.

Lapouge, Gilles: *Le singe de la montre. Utopie et histoire*. Flammarion: Paris 1982.

Lasky, Melvin J.: *Utopia and Revolution. On the Origins of a Metaphor, or Some Illustrations of the Problem of Political Temperament and Intellectual Climate and How Ideas, Ideals, and Ideologies Have Been Historically Related*. The University of Chicago Press: Chicago and London 1976.

Le Breton, André: *Le Roman Français au dix-huitième siècle*. Boivin & Cie: Paris [1898].

Le Febvre, Georges: "Le monde occidental en 1789". *La Révolution française. Peuples et civilisations XIII. Histoire générale*. Par LeFebvre, Georges, Guyot, Raymond & Sagnac, Philippe. Publiée sous la direction de Louis Halphen et Philippe Sagnac. Félix Algan: Paris 1930.

Le Flamanc, Auguste: *Les utopies Prérévolutionnaires*. J. Vrin: Paris 1934.

Le Goff, Jacques: *History and Memory*. Trans. by Steven Rendall and Elizabeth Claman. Columbia University Press: New York 1992.

Lequenne, Michel: "Rétif, Mercier, Sade et Casanova, quatre utopistes à la veille de la révolution". *Études rétiviennes*, no 17, décembre 1992, 33–39.

Le Roy Ladurie, Emmanuel: *The Ancien Régime. A History of France 1610–1774*. Trans. by Mark Greengrass. Blackwell: London 1996.

Leterrier, S.A.: "Mercier à l'Institut (1795–1814)". *Louis Sébastien Mercier (1740–1814). Un hérétique en littérature*. Sous la direction de Jean-Claude Bonnet. Mercure de France: Paris 1995, 295–326.

Levitas, Ruth: *The Concept of Utopia*. Philip Allan: London 1990.

Lichtenberger, André: *Le socialisme et la révolution française. Étude sur les idées socialistes en France de 1789 à 1796*. Félix Alcan: Paris 1899.

Lichtheim, George: *The Origins of Socialism*. Weidenfeld and Nicolson: London 1969.

Lough, John: *An Introduction to Eighteenth Century France*. (First published in 1960). Longmans: London 1961.

Lough, John: *Writer and Public in France. From the Middle Ages to the Present Day*. Clarendon Press: Oxford 1978.

Lovejoy, Arthur O.: *The Great Chain of Being: A Study of the History of an Idea*. (First published in 1933). Harvard University Press: Cambridge, Mass., 1950.

Lowe, Donald M.: *History of Bourgeois Perception*. The Harvester Press: Brighton 1982.

Lowenthal, David: *The Past is a Foreign Country*. (First published in 1985). Cambridge University Press: Cambridge 1986.

Macchia, Giovanni: *Paris en ruines*. Traduit de l'italien par Paul Bédarida avec la collaboration de Mario Fusco. Préface d'Italo Calvino. (Publié pour la première fois en 1985). Flammarion: Paris 1988.

MacIntyre, Alasdair: *After Virtue. A study in moral theory*. Second edition. (First published in 1981). Duckworth: London 1987.

Mack, Phyllis: "Women and the Enlightenment: Introduction". *Women and the Enlightenment*. Ed. by Margaret Hunt, et al. The Haworth Press: New York 1984.

Majewski, Henry F.: *The Preromantic Imagination of L.-S. Mercier*. Humanities Press: New York 1971.

Mandrou, Robert: *L'Europe "absolutiste". Raison et raison d'Etat 1649–1775*. (Publié pour la première fois en langue allemande sous le titre *Staatsräson und Vernunft*, 1649–1775 en 1976). Fayard: Paris 1977.

Mannheim, Karl: *Ideology & Utopia. An Introduction to the Sociology of Knowledge*. (First published in 1936). Routledge & Kegan Paul: London 1972.

Mantion, Jean-Rémy: "L'oeil: modes d'emploi. Les psychés de Louis-Sébastien Mercier". *Louis-Sébastien Mercier (1740–1814). Un hérétique en littérature*. Sous la direction de Jean-Claude Bonnet. Mercure de France: Paris 1995, 153–198.

Manuel, Frank E.: *The Eighteenth Century Confronts the Gods*. Harvard University Press: Cambridge, Massachusetts 1959.

Manuel, Frank E.: Introduction. *Utopias and Utopian Thought*. Ed. by Frank E. Manuel. (First published in 1965). The Riverside Press: Boston & Cambridge 1966a, vii–xxiv.

Manuel, Frank E.: "Toward a Psychological History of Utopias". *Utopias and Utopian Thought*. Ed. by Frank E. Manuel. (First published in 1965). The Riverside Press: Boston & Cambridge 1966b, 69–98.

Manuel, Frank E., Manuel, Fritzie P.: *Utopian Thought in the Western World*. (First published in 1979). Basil Blackwell: Oxford 1982.

Marin, Louis: "Toward a semiotic of utopia: Political and fictional discourse in Thomas More's *Utopia*". *Structure, Consciousness, and History*. Ed. by Richard Harvey Brown and Stanford M. Lyman. Cambridge University Press: Cambridge 1978, 261–282.

Martin, Rex: "The Ideal State in Plato's Republic". *History of political Thought* 2/1981, 1–30.

Mauzi, Robert: *L'idée du bonheur dans la littérature et la pensée françaises au XVIIIe siècle*. (Première édition en 1979). Albin Michel: Paris 1994.

Mauzi, Robert & Menant, Sylvain: *Littérature française 10. Le XVIIIe siècle II 1750–1778*. Arthaud: Paris 1977.

McMahon, Darrin M.: "The Counter-Enlightenment and the Low-Life of Literature in Pre-Revolutionary France". *Past & Present*. Number 159/May 1998, 77–112.

McManners, John: *Death and the Enlightenment. Changing attitudes to death among Christians and unbelievers in eighteenth-century France*. Oxford Clarendon Press: Oxford & New York 1981.

Merchant, Carolyn: *The Death of Nature. Women, Ecology, and the Scientific Revolution*. (First published in 1980). Harper & Row: San Francisco 1983.

Meyer, Jean: *La France moderne de 1515 à 1789*. Fayard: Paris 1985.

Minois, Georges: *History of Old Age. From Antiquity to the Renaissance*. (First published in 1987). Trans. by Sarah Hanbury Tenison. Polity Press: Southampton 1989.

Minois, Georges: *Histoire des enfers*. Fayard: Paris 1991.

Minois, Georges: *Histoire de l'avenir. Des Prophètes à la prospective*. Fayard: Paris 1996.

Minois, Georges: *History of Suicide. Voluntary Death in Western Culture*. Trans. by Lydia G. Cochrane. The Johns Hopkins University Press: Baltimore and London 1999.

Monselet, Charles: *Les Oubliés et les Dédaignés. Figures littéraires de la fin du 18e siècle*. Tome 1. Alencon: Poulet-Malassis et de Broise 1857.

Moos, Rudolf & Brownstein, Robert: *Environment and Utopia. A Synthesis*. Plenum Press: New York and London 1977.

Mornet, Daniel: *Les origines intellectuelles de la révolution francaise (1715–1787)*. Armand Colin: Paris 1933.

Mornet, Daniel: *La pensée francaise au XVIIIe siècle*. Armand Colin: Paris 1969.

Morris, David B.: *The Culture of Pain*. (First published in 1991). University of California Press: Berkeley, Los Angeles & London 1993.

Mortier, Roland: *Clartés et ombres du siècle des lumières. Etudes sur le XVIIIè siècle littéraire*. Droz: Genève 1969.

Mortier, Roland: "L'autre XVIIIe siècle". *Dix-huitième siècle européen*. En hommage a Jacques Lacant. Textes réunis par Claude De Grève. Aux Amateurs de Livres: Paris 1990, 27–31.

Mucchielli, Roger: *Le mythe de la cité idéale*. Presses Universitaires de France: Paris 1960.

Männikkö, Matti: "Historiantutkimuksen ja tulevaisuuden tutkimuksen suhteesta". *Historia ja tulevaisuus*. Toim. Kari Immonen. Turun yliopiston historian laitos: Turku 1983, 32– 44.

Männikkö, Matti: "Tulevaisuuden aspekti valistusajattelussa". *Futura* 3/1986, 30–36.

Männikkö, Matti: "Tulevaisuudentutkimus ja historiankirjoitus". *Miten tutkimme tulevaisuutta? Kommunikatiivinen tulevaisuudentutkimus Suomessa*. Toim. Matti Vapaavuori. Painatuskeskus: Helsinki 1993, 262–270.

Männikkö, Matti: "Onnen odotusta ja pahan pelkoa. Maailmanlopun idea länsimaisessa tulevaisuusajattelussa". *Lopun alku. Katastrofien historiaa ja nykypäivää*. Toim. Hannu Salmi. Turun yliopiston historian laitos: Turku 1996, 145–165.

Neyton, André: *L'âge d'or et l'âge de fer*. Les belles lettres: Paris 1984.

Niiniluoto, Ilkka: *Järki, arvot ja välineet. Kulttuurifilosofisia esseitä*. Otava: Helsinki 1994.

Nisbet, Robert: *Social Change and History. Aspects of the Western Theory of Development*. (First published in 1969). Oxford University Press: London, Oxford & New York 1970.

Nisbet, Robert: *History of the idea of Progress*. Heinemann: London 1980.

Nisbet, Robert: *The Making of Modern Society*. Wheatsheaf Books: Brighton 1986.

Nyman, Magnus: *Upplysningens spegel. Götheborgs Allehanda om Frankrike och världen 1774–1789*. Atlantis: Stockholm 1994.

Ouellet, Réal & Vachon, Hélène: "La présentation de Paris dans L'an 2440 de L.-S. Mercier où les métamorphoses du cercle radieux". *La ville au XVIIIè siècle*. Centre aixois d'études et de recherches sur le XVIIIè siècle. Colloque d'Aix-en-Provence 29 avril – 1er mai 1973, 83–90.

Outram, Dorinda: *The Body and the French Revolution. Sex, Class and Political Culture*. Yale University Press: New Haven and London 1989.

Outram, Dorinda: *The Enlightenment*. Cambridge University Press: Cambridge 1995.

Ozouf, Mona: "La Révolution française au tribunal de l'utopie". *The French Revolution and the Creation of Modern Political Culture. Vol. 3: The Transformation of Political Culture 1789–1848*. Ed. by François Furet and Mona Ozouf. Pergamon Press: Oxford 1989, 561–574.

Palmer, R.R.: *The Age of the Democratic Revolution. A political history of Europe and America, 1760–1800. The challenge*. (First published in 1959). Princeton University Press: Princeton 1962.

Passmore, John: *The Perfectibility of Man*. (First published in 1970). Duckworth: London 1972.

Patterson, Helen: *Poetic Genesis: Sébastien Mercier into Victor Hugo*. Studies on Voltaire and the Eighteenth Century, vol. XI. Voltaire Foundation: Geneve 1960.

Peyre, Henri: "The Influence of Eighteenth-Century Ideas on the French Revolution". *The Influence of the Enlightenment on the French Revolution*. Second Edition. Edited and with an introduction by William F. Church. (First published in 1964). D.C. Heath and Company: Lexington 1974, 161–182.

Pfeifer, Johan Peter: *Kaupunkimallit; Niiden synty ja kehitys*. Yhdyskuntasuunnittelun jatkokoulutuskeskus. Teknillinen korkeakoulu: Espoo 1979.

Pike, Burton: *The Image of the City in Modern Literature*. Princeton University Press: Princeton & Guilford 1981.

Pingaud, Bernard & Mantéro, Robert: *Les infortunes de la raison 1774–1815*. Hatier: Paris 1992.

Pitkänen, Pirkko: *Platonin hyvän elämän filosofia*. Helsinki University Press: Helsinki 1996.

Plum, Werner: *Les utopies anglaises, modèles de coopération sociale et technologique*. Cahiers de l'Institut de recherches de la Fondation Friedrich Ebert: Bonn 1975.

Plumb, J.H.: *The Death of the Past*. MacMillan: London 1969.

Poggi, Gionfranco: "The Modern State and the Idea of Progress". *Progress and its Discontents*. Ed. by Gabriel A. Almond, Marvin Chodorow, and Roy Harvey Pearce.

University of California Press: Berkeley, Los Angeles, & London 1982, 337–360.

Polak, Fred L.: *The Image of the Future. Enlightening the past, orientating the present, forecasting the future. Volume one: The Promised Land, Source of Living Culture.* Trans. from the Dutch by Elise Boulding. A.W. Sythoff & Oceana Publications: Leyden & New York 1961.

Polak, Fred L.: *Prognostics. A science in the making surveys and creates the future.* Elsevier Publishing Company: Amsterdam, London & New York 1971.

Pollard, Sidney: *The Idea of Progress. History and Society.* (First published in 1968). Penguin Books: Harmondsworth 1971.

Pomeau, René: *L'Europe des Lumières. Cosmopolitisme et unité européenne au XVIIIè siècle.* Nouvelle édition. Éditions Stock: Paris 1991.

Pomeau, René & Ehrard, Jean: *Histoire de la littérature française. De Fénelon à Voltaire.* Nouvelle édition révisée. (Publié pour la première fois en 1984). Flammarion: Paris 1998.

Pons, Alain: Préface. *L'An 2440. Rêve s'il en fut jamais.* "Bibliothèque des utopies". France Adel: Paris 1977.

Pratt, Mary Louise: *Imperial Eyes. Travel Writing and Transculturation.* Routledge: London and New York 1992.

Rahkonen, Keijo: *Utopiat ja anti-utopiat. Kirjoituksia vuosituhannen päättyessä.* Gaudeamus: [Helsinki] 1996.

Renan, Ernest: *L'Avenir de la science. Pensées de 1848.* Calmann- Lévy: Paris 1922.

Revel, Jacques: "The Uses of Civility". *A History of Private Life: Passions of the Renaissance.* Ed. by Roger Chartier. Trans. by Arthur Goldhammer. The Belknap Press of Harvard University Press: Cambridge, Massachusetts and London 1989, 167–205.

Ricken, Ulrich: "Louis-Sébastien Mercier et ses deux nouveaux Paris". *Dix-huitième siècle.* Revue annuelle publiée par la Société francaises d'Etude du XVIIIè siècle. Éditions Garnier Frères: Paris 1975, 301–313.

Ricoeur, Paul: *Lectures on Ideology and Utopia.* Ed. by George H. Taylor. Columbia University Press: New York 1986.

Rifkin, Jeremy: *Time Wars. The Primary Conflict in Human History.* (First published in 1987). Simon & Schuster: New York 1989.

Rihs, Charles: *Les philosophes utopistes. Le mythe de la cité communautaire en France au XVIIIè siècle.* Éditions Marcel Rivière et Cie: Paris 1970.

Roche, Daniel: *The People of Paris. An Essay in Popular Culture in the 18th Century.* Trans. by Marie Evans in association with Gwynne Lewis. Leamington Spa: Hamburg & New York 1987.

Roche, Daniel: *Les Républicains des lettres. Gens de culture et Lumières au XVIIIè siècle.* Fayard: Paris 1988.

Roche, Daniel: *The culture of clothing. Dress and fashion in the "ancien régime".* Trans. by Jean Birrell. Cambridge University Press: Cambridge 1996.

Roche, Daniel: *France in the Enlightenment.* Trans. by Arthur Goldhammer. Harvard University Press: Cambridge and London 1998.

Roche, Daniel: *A History of Everyday Things. The birth of consumption in France, 1600–1800.* Trans. by Brian Pearce. Cambridge University Press: Cambridge 2000.

Rosenau, Helen: *The Ideal City. Its architectural Evolution in Europe.* (First published with the title *The Ideal City in its Architectural Evolution* in 1959). Methuen: London and New York 1983.

Roudaut, Jean: *Les Villes imaginaires dans la littérature française.* Hatier: Paris 1990.

Rovillain, Eugène E.: "L'abbé Prévost et L'Homme sauvage de Sebastien Mercier". *PMLA.* vol. 45. Part XLV, 1930, 822–847.

Roy, Lucien: Préface. *Tableau de Paris.* Éd. abrégée. Louis-Michaud: Paris [s.a].

Rudé, George: *Paris and London in the 18th Century. Studies in Popular Protest.* (First published in 1952). Fontana/Collins: London & Suffolk 1974.

Rudé, George: *Europe in the Eighteenth Century. Aristocracy and the Bourgeois Challenge.* (First published in 1972). Weidenfeld and Nicolson: London 1985.

Rufi, Enrico: *Le Rêve laïque de Louis-Sébastien Mercier entre littérature et politique.* Studies on Voltaire and the eighteenth Century 326. Voltaire Foundation: Oxford 1995.

Rufi, Enrico: Louis-Sébastien Mercier. Bibliographie des ecrivains français. Éditions Memini: Paris-Roma 1996.

Ruyer, Raymond: *L'utopie et les utopies.* PUF: Saint- Pierre-de-Salerne/Brionne 1988.

Saastamoinen, Kari: *The Morality of the Fallen Man. Samuel Pufendorf on Natural Law.* Academic dissertation. SHS: Helsinki 1995.

Sagnac, Philippe: *La formation de la société française moderne. Tome II. La révolution des idées et des moeurs et le déclin de l'ancien régime (1715–1788).* Presses universitaires de France: Paris 1946.

Salmi, Hannu: "Lissabonin maanjäristyksestä Estonian katastrofiin: onnettomuuskritisointi ja tulevan pahan pelko". *Lopun alku. Katastrofien historiaa ja nykypäivää.* Toim. Hannu Salmi. Turun yliopiston historian laitos: Turku 1996, 21–40.

Sambrook, A.J.: "A romantic theme: the last man". *Forum for Modern Language Studies.* Vol. 2/1966, 25–33.

Schama, Simon: *Citizens. A Chronicle of the French Revolution.* Penguin Books: Harmondsworth 1989.

Servier, Jean: "Utopie et franc-maçonnerie au XVIIIe siècle". *Annales historiques de la*

Révolution française. Juillet- Septembre 1969, 409–413.

Servier, Jean: *Histoire de l'utopie.* Nouvelle édition. Gallimard: Paris 1991.

Shallis, Michael: *On Time. An Investigation into Scientific Knowledge and Human Experience.* (First publishd in 1982). Penguin Books: Harmondsworth 1983.

Sher, Richard B.: "1688 and 1788: William Robertson on Revolution in Britain and France". *Culture and Revolution.* Ed. by Paul Dukes and John Dunkley. Pinter Publishers: London and New York 1990, 98–109.

Shklar, Judith: "The Political Theory of Utopia: From Melancholy to Nostalgia". *Daedalus. Journal of the American Academy of Arts and Sciences.* Vol. 94, No. 2/1965, 367–381.

Shklar, Judith N.: *Men and Citizens. A Study of Rousseau's social theory.* Cambridge University Press: Cambridge 1969.

Simonsuuri, Kirsti: "Ut pictura poesis. Kirjallisuus ja todellisuus 1700-luvulla". *Taide aikansa kuvastajana.* Toim. Kari Immonen. Turun yliopiston historian laitos: Turku 1980, 23–46.

Singer, Irving: *The Nature of Love 2. Courtly and Romantic.* (First published in 1984). The University of Chicago Press: Chicago and London 1987.

Telfer, Elizabeth: *Happiness. An examination of a hedonistic and a eudaemonistic concept of happiness and of the relations between them, with a consideration of how far and in what sense either kind of happiness may be said to be the goal of human life.* MacMillan: London and Basingstoke 1980.

Thomas, Chantal: "La sphère mouvante des modes". *Louis-Sébastien Mercier (1740–1814). Un hérétique en littérature.* Sous la direction de Jean-Claude Bonnet. Mercure de France: Paris 1995, 33–53.

Tiainen-Anttila, Kaija: *The Problem of Humanity. The Blacks in the European Enlightenment.* Suomen Historiallinen Seura: Helsinki 1994.

Tod, Ian & Wheeler, Michael: *Utopia.* Orbis Publishing: London 1978.

Toulmin, Stephen: *Cosmopolis. The Hidden Agenda of Modernity.* The Free Press. A Division of MacMillan: New York 1990.

Toulmin, Stephen & Goodfield, June: *The Discovery of Time.* Hutchinson: London 1965

Traer, James F.: *Marriage and the Family in Eighteenth-Century France.* Cornell University Press: Ithaca and London 1980.

Trousson, Raymond: Introduction. *L'An deux mille quatre cent quarante. Rêve s'il en fut jamais.* Editions Ducros: Bordeaux 1971, 7–73.

Trousson, Raymond: *Voyages aux pays de nulle part. Histoire littéraire de la pensée utopique.* Éditions de l'université de Bruxelles: Bruxelles 1975.

Trousson, Raymond: "Du millénarisme à la théorie du progrès: L'an 2440 de L.-S. Mercier". *Bulletin de l'académie Royale et de littérature françaises.* Tome LX – No 3–4/1982, 270–281.

Trousson, Raymond: *Jean-Jacques Rousseau II. Le deuil éclatant du bonheur.* Tallandier: Paris 1989.

Trousson, Raymond: *Histoire de la libre pensée. Des origines à 1789.* Éditions du Centre d'Action laique: Bruxelles 1993.

Tuveson, Ernest Lee: *Millennium and Utopia. A Study in the Background of the Idea of Progress.* Peter Smith: Gloucester 1972.

Venturi, Franco: *Utopia and Reform in the Enlightenment.* Cambridge University Press: London 1971.

Vercelloni, Virgilio: *La Cité idéale en Occident.* Traduit de l'italien par Denis-Armand Canal. Philippe Lebaud: Paris 1996.

Versins, Pierre: *Encyclopédie de l'Utopie, des Voyages extraordinaires et de la Science-Fiction.* Editions L'Age d'Homme: Lausanne 1972.

Vidler, Anthony: "Mercier urbaniste: l'utopie du réel". *Louis- Sébastien Mercier. Un hérétique en littérature.* Sous la direction de Jean-Claude Bonnet. Mercure de France: Paris 1995, 223–243.

Viguerie, Jean de: *Histoire et dictionnaire du temps des lumières 1715–1789.* Éditions Robert Laffont: Paris 1995.

Viikari, Matti: *Historiallinen ajattelu, edistys ja yhteiskunta.* Toim. Tapani Hietaniemi, Tuomas M.S. Lehtonen ja työryhmä. Tutkijaliiton julkaisusarja 79: Helsinki 1995.

Vincent-Buffault, Anne: *Histoire des larmes XVIIIe–XIXe siècles.* Rivages: Paris & Marseille 1986.

Virtanen, Keijo: "1700- ja 1800-lukujen vaihteen "kaksoisvallankumous" ja sen vaikutus aika- ja tulevaisuuskäsityksiin". *Futura* 3/1986, 38– 44, 57.

Virtanen, Keijo: *Kulttuurihistoria – tie kokonaisvaltaiseen historiaan.* Turun yliopiston julkaisuja, sarja C, osa 60. Scripta lingua Fennica Edita: Turku 1987.

Vissière, Jean-Louis: "La culture populaire à la veille de la Révolution d'après le ´Tableau de Paris´ de Mercier". *Images du peuple au XVIIIè siècle.* Centre Aixois d'études et de recherches sur le dix-huitième siècle: Paris 1973, 123–137.

Vissière, Jean-Louis: "L'actualité de Mercier". *Louis-Sébastien Mercier précurseur et sa fortune.* Avec des documents inédits. Récueil d'études sur l'influence de Mercier. Sous la direction de Hermann Hofer. Wilhelm Fink Verlag: München 1977, 311–327.

Vovelle, Michel: *La mort et l'Occident de 1300 à nos jours.* Gallimard: Paris 1983.

Vyverberg, Henry: *Historical Pessimism in the*

French Enlightenment. Harvard University Press: Cambridge, Mass., 1958.

Wallgren, Thomas: "Moderni ja postmoderni käsitteinä ja tapoina kokea aikaa". *Aika ja sen ankaruus*. Toim. Pirkko Heiskanen. Gaudeamus: Helsinki 1989, 35–53.

Wallgren, Thomas: "Taide, politiikka ja muutoksen historia". *Synteesi. Taiteidenvälisen tutkimuksen aikakauslehti*, 3/1993, 4–18.

Weber, Max: *The Protestant Ethic and the Spirit of Capitalism*. Trans. by Talcott Parsons. With a Foreword by R. H. Tawney. (First published in 1930). Unwin University Books: London 1965.

White, Hayden: *Metahistory. The Historical Imagination in Nineteenth-Century Europe*. (First published in 1973). The Johns Hopkins University Press: Baltimore & London 1987.

Whitrow, G.J.: *Time in History. The evolution of our general awareness of time and temporal perspective*. Oxford University Press: Oxford & New York 1988.

Wilkie, Everett C.: "Mercier's L'An 2440: Its Publishing History During the Author's Lifetime". *Harvard Library Bulletin*. Volume XXXII/Number 1/Winter 1984, 5–29.

Williams, T.C., *The Concept of the Categorical Imperative. A Study of the Place of the Categorical Imperative in Kant's Ethical Theory*. Clarendon Press: Oxford 1968.

Windsor, Philip: "Reason becomes contingent in History: can History become Reason?" *Reason and History: or only a History of Reason*. Ed. by Philip Windsor. Leicester University Press: Leicester and London 1990, 21–34.

Wiseman, Dennis Michael: *The Utopian Vision of Sébastien Mercier*. Unpublished dissertation. University of North Carolina. Chapel Hill 1979.

Woloch, Isser: *Eighteenth-century Europe. Tradition and Progress 1715–1789*. W. W. Norton & Company: New York & London 1982.

Worster, Donald: *Nature's Economy. A History of Ecological Ideas*. (First published in 1977). Cambridge University Press: Cambridge 1985.

Wunenburger, Jean-Jacques: "Bonheur et vertu: phénoménologie de la conscience utopique". *La quête du bonheur et l'expression de la douleur dans la littérature et la pensée françaises*. Mélanges offerts à Corrado Rosso. Edités par C. Biondi, et al. Droz S.A.: Genève 1995, 517–526.

■ Index of Names

Abel, 63, 274
Adam, 59, 76, 299
Adorno, Theodor W. ,14, 28, 203, 299
Ahlefeld, Henricus ab, 49
Alberti, Leone Battista, 46
d´Alembert, Jean le Rond, 31
Alkon, Paul K., 27, 56, 254, 281
Andreae, Johann Valentin, 48
Ariès, Philippe, 142
Aristophanes, 41
Aristotle, 11, 49n, 122n, 162n
Babeuf, Gracchus (Francois-Noël), 110
Bacon, Francis 48, 48n, 54, 69n, 85–87, 87n, 93, 245, 248, 274, 279, 305
Baczko, Bronislaw, 27, 39, 49, 52, 54–55, 68, 189, 192n, 268
Baker, Keith Michael, 236
Balzac, Honoré de, 27, 65n
Barry, Mme du, 105
Bayle, Pierre, 15
Beccaria, Cesare Bonesana de, 101, 198, 225
Becker, Carl L., 63n, 130, 211
Béclard, Léon, 25–26, 33, 38, 137, 265
Bellamy, Edward, 61, 61n
Bentham, Jeremy, 101
Bergerac, Cyrano de, 48, 278
Berneri, Marie Louise, 28, 141
Berthier, Philippe, 60, 260
Bloch, Ernst, 11, 46, 117, 159n, 224
Bodin, Félix, 56, 141, 210, 225
Boileau, Nicolas, 217
Bonnet, Charles, 214, 217
Bougainville, Louis-Antoine de, 152, 182
Braudel, Fernand, 279
Brissot, Jacques-Pierre, 43
Bruno, Giordano, 90
Buber, Martin, 35
Buffon, Georges-Louis Leclerc, Comte de, 213, 225
Burke, Peter, 59
Bury, J.B, 17, 28, 209, 222 .
Byron, Lord, 207, 260n
Cabet, Etienne, 162, 269
Cagliostro, Giuseppe Balsamo, dit Alexandre, Comte de, 277, 278n
Cain, 63, 193–195, 200–201, 274, 300
Calvin, Jean, 76
Campanella, Tommaso, 48, 54, 141, 178, 182, 195, 202
Campbell, Colin, 167n
Carra, Jean-Louis, 43
Cassirer, Ernst, 20, 78n, 270
Castiglione, Dario, 171
Cato, 195
Cattin, Geneviève, 26
Cavendish, Margaret, 48
Censer, Jack R., 15
Charlton, D.G., 292

Chartier, Roger, 243n
Chastellux, François Jean, Marquis de, 219, 219n, 227
Chateaubriand, François-René de, 79n
Châtelet, Gabrielle-Émilie Le Tonnelier de Breteuil, Mme du, 24, 126, 160
Chinard, Gilbert, 186
Choderlos de Laclos, 151
Christ, 79, 189, 232–233, 302
Cioranescu, Alexandre, 13, 27, 56, 137, 225, 279
Citron, Pierre, 27, 259
Clarke, I.F., 56, 280
Clootz, Anacharsis, 43
Coleridge, Samuel Taylor, 95
Collier, Simon, 307
Comenius, Jan, 48, 48n
Comte, August, 222
Condillac, Etienne Bonnot de, 31, 92
Condorcet, Maria Jean Antoine Nicolas de Caritat, Marquis de, 43, 55, 55n, 57, 149, 149n, 222, 224, 228, 246, 249, 255, 255n, 308
Cooper, Anthony Ashley, Third Earl of Shaftesbury, 128, 136
Corbin, Alain, 174
Cousin d'Avalon, Charles-Yves, 25, 30–31, 42
Coward, David, 150
Crocker, Lester G., 255
Cubières-Palmezeaux, Dorat, 42
Dante, 47, 59–60
Danton, Georges Jacques, 241
Darnton, Robert, 20, 31–32, 39, 44, 68, 105n, 106n, 109, 233, 238n, 243, 277
Davis, J.C., 155, 159n, 178, 188, 188n
Delon, Michel, 258
Delumeau, Jean, 28, 189, 276
Denoit, Nicole, 241, 264, 276
Deprun, Jean, 17, 186, 209, 288
Descartes, René, 41, 77–78, 91–92, 124, 124n, 195, 229
Desmoulins, Camille, 43
Diderot, Denis, 14, 42, 50, 131n, 132, 132n, 151–152, 182, 215–217, 225–226, 255, 263, 285, 291, 307
Dom Deschamps, Léger-Marie, 50, 101, 162–163
Dorigny, Marcel, 102
Duclos, Charles Pinos, 220
Döring, Ulrich, 196–197, 201, 203
Eliade, Mircea, 200, 259, 273, 286
Elias, Norbert, 134, 283n
Elie, 76
Enoch, 76
d´Épinay, Mme, 54
Farge, Arlette, 21n, 237
Favre, Robert, 64n